Justice for a Generation

Papers presented in London, England
July 15-19, 1985
at the plenary sessions of a meeting
between

American Bar Association
The Senate of the Inns of Court and the Bar
The Law Society of England and Wales

ACKNOWLEDGMENTS

The President and the Special Committee on the 1985 London Meeting on behalf of the American Bar Association wish to express appreciation to the West Publishing Company for its cooperation in printing these plenary program papers for the joint meeting of the American Bar Association, The Senate of the Inns of Court and the Bar, and The Law Society of England and Wales.

ISBN: 0-89707-171-9
Library of Congress Catalog Card Number:
85-70533
West Publishing Company
St. Paul, Minnesota 55165

Published in 1985
Printed in the United States of America

FOREWORD

By holding a portion of our 1985 Annual Meeting in London, members of the American Bar Association are once more acknowledging that the roots of our legal tradition are buried deep in English soil. For the fourth time since 1924, lawyers from America are making this pilgrimage to meet with colleagues from throughout the United Kingdom, acknowledging a common heritage that antedates the signing of Magna Carta in the year 1215 A.D.

But our generation, like those which have gone before, not only has roots in the past; we also have a special responsibility to deal with issues unique to our time. The theme of this meeting -- and this collection -- is "Justice for a Generation," emphasizing mutual legal concerns on both sides of the Atlantic of particular interest to practitioners in 1985.

With the emergence of a global economy and the continuing spectre of conflict between nations, this generation of lawyers has an opportunity to "advance the rule of law in the world," as advocated by the Eighth Goal of the American Bar Association adopted in 1983.

Yet despite the contemporary character of the topics addressed in this volume, the impact of a shared legal tradition extending back many centuries still speaks to us. Magna Carta itself, for example, addresses the concern for fair treatment of those engaged in international trade discussed in many of the papers in this collection. That provision (in modern translation) reads:

> "All merchants may safely and securely go out of England and come into England, as well by land as by water, for the purpose of buying and selling, free from all evil taxes, subject to the ancient and right customs -- save in time of war..."

This principle and other ideals embodied in Magna Carta have guided and continue to guide the evolution of our joint legal inheritance. We are indebted to the paperwriters and panelists from the United Kingdom and the United States, for their scholarship and their commitment to the ideal of the rule of law as represented by this meeting, this publication, and our common heritage.

The dedication of this generation of lawyers, as illuminated by these papers, will help keep the tradition advanced by Magna Carta alive for future generations. "Justice for a Generation" will thus become our contribution to justice for the ages.

JOHN C. SHEPHERD
President
American Bar Association

1925u

Special Committee on the 1985 London Meeting
American Bar Association

David R. Brink, Chairman
J. David Andrews
Jane H. Barrett
Morris Harrell
Don M. Jackson
Wallace D. Riley
John C. Shepherd, President, *Ex Officio*
Prof. Norval Morris, Reporter
Kirsti Langbein, Editor

Joint Committee in London

The Bar of England and Wales	The Law Society of England and Wales

Joint Chairmen

Robert Alexander, Q.C., Vice-Chairman	John Bowron, Secretary-General
David Calcutt, Q.C., Chairman	Alan Leslie, President
The Hon. Mr. Justice Leggatt	John Wickerson, Vice-President
The Hon. Mr. Justice Otton	Harold B. Matthissen
John Toulmin, Q.C.	John Young
Jeremy Griggs	Toni Rudin

Secretaries

Marion Hollidge, Assistant Secretary	Juliet Heasman, Executive Officer

TABLE OF CONTENTS

TUESDAY

THURSDAY

FRIDAY

PRACTICING LAW ABROAD: A UNITED STATES VIEWPOINT

London Sessions
ABA Annual Meeting 1985
Old Library, The Guildhall
London, England

Tuesday, July 16, 1985
10:00 A.M. - 12:00 Noon

Harold H. Healy, Jr.
23rd Floor, 875 Third Avenue
New York, New York 10022

"Practicing law abroad" is a relatively new concept. With some notable exceptions, lawyers in the United States and in the United Kingdom did not, until the 1960's, practice abroad.

The advent of the creation of the European Community saw a dramatic increase in direct investment by American companies in Europe, accompanied by the opening of offices in Paris and Brussels by a number of New York law firms, as well as firms from Los Angeles, Chicago, Philadelphia, and Washington, D.C. The subsequent development of the Eurobond market led in turn to the establishment by American law firms of offices in the financial center of London.

The inflow of lawyers from Europe to the United States has only just begun. It was not until the end of October, 1972, that the first firm of London solicitors opened offices in New York. While a substantial number of European law offices have since been established in New York, there are very few offices located elsewhere in the United States today, a circumstance certainly attributable in part to the barriers that have existed in other states. More fundamentally, however, foreign law offices tend naturally to be concentrated in international centers of business, finance, and commerce, and New York has long been recognized as the principal such center in the United States.

The United States Legal Framework

To understand the legal framework bearing on foreign lawyers as it exists in several states (and the District of Columbia) requires an appreciation of three factors: In the United States, admission to the practice of law is through the courts, not the Bar; the monopoly of activity accorded admitted lawyers extends broadly to almost every conceivable kind of legal advice; and until 1973, when the U.S. Supreme Court declared it unconstitutional to do so, U.S. citizenship was almost universally required as a condition of admission to practice.

In most of the United States, unlike the United Kingdom and all of continental Europe, the Bar to which lawyers are admitted simply does not exist except as an abstraction. Bar associations, yes; the Bar, no. Admission to and disbarment from practice is by the courts exercising a strictly governmental role. In New York, one can become a member of the Bar by being admitted to practice by the Appellate Division of the New York Supreme Court, but the Bar one is admitted to has no office, no officers, no governing organization, and, until recently, no one even kept a list of the members. In the United States, then, the practice of law by anyone not admitted or licensed by governmental authority to do so is simply unlawful and subject to criminal sanction.

At the same time, in every U.S. jurisdiction, what constitutes the practice of law reserved exclusively to admitted or licensed lawyers is defined so broadly as to prohibit the unlicensed legal practitioner from giving almost any kind of legal advice to anyone except to admitted lawyers. Thus, subject to this exception, a foreign lawyer not admitted or licensed in the jurisdiction is in effect precluded from carrying on any aspect of the legal profession, even a consulting practice.

In 1973, the U.S. Supreme Court held, in In re Griffiths, that a state may not, under the federal Constitution, deny admission to the Bar solely on grounds of citizenship. Prior to this decision, U.S. citizenship was required in virtually all, if not all, U.S. jurisdictions, except that at least two states, New York and Illinois, permitted lawyers to be admitted from a non-U.S. jurisdiction where the jurisprudence is based on the English Common Law.

Avenues Open to Foreign Lawyers

Today, there are a number of avenues open to foreign lawyers who wish to practice in the United States:

- o The lawyer may seek full admission to the Bar in all U.S. jurisdictions by qualifying for and successfully completing the bar examination required for the admission of lawyers in that jurisdiction, and may be fully admitted without examination in at least two jurisdictions, Massachusetts and New York, in certain special circumstances;
- o The lawyer may be licensed without examination to conduct a consulting practice as a legal consultant in New York; and
- o The lawyer who is willing to confine his or her practice to providing legal advice to admitted lawyers, including corporate counsel in the legal departments of corporations, may conduct a consulting practice without being admitted or licensed at all in New York and, on principle, in other jurisdictions.

Full admission. A very large number of foreign lawyers have, in fact, gained admission to the Bar in the United States. The flow of lawyers and law students from abroad, seeking legal education and training in the United States, is by any measure impressive. Typically, a young foreign lawyer will attend a U.S. law school for a year and receive a master of laws degree. Increasingly, these lawyers then take and pass a U.S. bar examination and become full-fledged members of a U.S. Bar. Moreover, several states--Massachusetts, New York, and Pennsylvania, for example--and the District of Columbia now have in effect special rules to take into account the education acquired by foreign lawyers outside the United States and thereby to facilitate access to the bar examination for foreign-educated lawyers.

Licensed legal consultant. In 1974, the New York Court of Appeals adopted rules to permit the licensing as legal consultants of foreign lawyers at least 26 years of age who have practiced and remained in good standing for at least five of the preceding seven years in their home countries. Such legal consultants are entitled to give legal advice, provided advice involving New York or U.S. federal law is based upon the advice of an admitted lawyer; and are entitled to prepare legal documents with certain limited exceptions (instruments that affect title to U.S. real estate, or dispose on death of U.S. property owned by a U.S. resident, or are in respect of the marital relations, or custody of a child, of a U.S. resident). Legal consultants also are prohibited from appearing as attorneys in court proceedings. Over 70 foreign lawyers have been licensed as legal consultants in New York. Similar rules are being proposed in California, the District of Columbia, and Illinois.

Unlicensed consultant to the bar. Even without being admitted or licensed to do so, foreign lawyers should, on principle, be permitted to establish a consulting practice in any of the several states (or the District of Columbia), provided it is confined to furnishing advice to members of the Bar. Prior to adoption of the legal consultant licensing rules in New York, this was the route followed by at least one firm of London solicitors in establishing offices in New York, and it continues to be particularly appropriate for foreign lawyers willing to limit their role to serving other lawyers as experts on the laws of their own country, or indeed of any other jurisdiction, except that presumably of the lawyer being advised. The function served is essentially no different from the services provided by companies assisting lawyers in the organization of corporations or by banks advising lawyers on the preparation of wills. Because many corporations in the United States employ members of the Bar on their legal staffs or otherwise, the clients of such a consulting practice may in effect include corporations. Where the corporate counsel being thus advised is a member of the Bar from some jurisdiction other than that in which the advice is given, it is arguable, on the basis of a carping dictum in a New York case decided some years ago, that the advice constitutes unlawful practice, but it is hard to believe that argument would be taken seriously today.

Attitude of the Local Bar

With few, if any, exceptions, wherever in the United States it has been proposed to permit or to make it easier for foreign lawyers to practice, there has been opposition by some local lawyers. It took a less-than-unanimous U.S. Supreme Court decision to dislodge the barriers against practice by non-U.S. citizens, and in each of the jurisdictions where it has been proposed to license legal consultants to practice without examination, including New York, members of the local bar have at first vigorously objected.

Nevertheless, the local bar has in many instances taken a leadership role in seeking to ease the restrictions on practice by foreign lawyers. Bar association committees not only in New York, but also in California, the District of Columbia, and Illinois, have developed and strongly support the legal consultant licensing proposals in those jurisdictions.

Enforcement of Rules and Regulations

All admitted lawyers in the United States are subject to rules of professional conduct usually adopted initially by the state or district Bar Association and enforced by the courts, the ultimate sanction being disbarment. These rules generally follow model rules adopted by the American Bar Association, most recently in August 1983.

Legal consultants licensed in New York are subject to the same disciplinary rules as members of the New York Bar and thus, in addition to the restrictions on practice imposed by the legal consultant licensing rules, must observe the New York Code of Professional Responsibility, for example, as regards duties toward clients and the attorney-client privilege. As in the case of members of the Bar, enforcement is by the Appellate Division of the New York Supreme Court through a State Disciplinary Committee of lawyers and laymen appointed by the Appellate Division.

There is no mechanism in the United States for the enforcement of disciplinary rules against foreign lawyers not admitted or licensed to practice in a U.S. jurisdiction, although as indicated above, such lawyers are subject to criminal sanction in the event they engage in the unlawful practice of law.

Several years ago, the Special Committee of the American Bar Association on Cooperation with Foreign and International Organizations was asked informally by representatives of the Consultative Committee of the Bars and Law Societies of the European Community to provide confirmation on the part of the ABA that the codes of professional conduct in force in various U.S. jurisdictions based on the ABA model code apply to lawyers admitted (or licensed) in one of such jurisdictions but practicing in Europe. The Special Committee made inquiry of the enforcement authorities in ten states (the ten states having the greatest number of lawyers practicing abroad) and, in each instance, was told that the state authorities subject their lawyers abroad to professional discipline. Moreover, the New Model Rules of Professional Conduct adopted by the ABA House of Delegates in August 1983 leave no doubt on their application abroad, specifying as they do that "[A] lawyer admitted to practice in this jurisdiction is subject to the disciplinary authority of this jurisdiction although engaged in practice elsewhere."

Relations with Local Counsel

The nature of a foreign lawyer's relationship with local counsel is largely governed by the way in which the lawyer elects to establish a practice in the United States. If this is done through admission to the local bar, the lawyer simply becomes local counsel, although the question of relationships with local counsel in other U.S. jurisdictions remains. If, on the other hand, the lawyer is licensed (in New York) as a legal consultant or establishes a consulting practice limited to advising local lawyers, the relationship is basically determined by the restrictions on practice. A legal consultant needs to look to local lawyers to support advice on New York and U.S. federal law, and to refer to them matters falling within the restricted areas of probate, real estate, and domestic relations law. A foreign lawyer neither admitted to the Bar nor licensed as a legal consultant is limited to consulting with local counsel except for direct advice to corporate legal departments.

Because regulation of the Bar in the United States is effected through 51 separate sovereign jurisdictions, lawyers admitted or licensed in one jurisdiction routinely face the necessity of deciding whether and to what extent local counsel should be consulted in the other 50 jurisdictions. In matters litigated before a court, local counsel in the jurisdiction served by the court are invariably retained, although the "foreign" lawyer will frequently play a major role in the litigation, including examination of witnesses and argument to the court, perhaps being admitted to the court "pro haec vice." In other matters, the practice varies. Non-Delaware lawyers frequently pass on Delaware legal questions without involving Delaware counsel, but not from offices within Delaware. Municipal bond lawyers as a general rule give bond opinions on issues by entities of states in which they are not admitted to practice without reliance on local counsel or indeed without the involvement of local counsel. On the other hand, in financial transactions and other contractual matters, outside of the area of government finance, where there are important questions of law to be resolved in another jurisdiction, careful U.S. lawyers will usually call upon local counsel for advice, although this may very well be sought only after the transaction has been initially structured and drafts of the relevant documents prepared.

For a number of years, an obscure New Jersey case has been cited in support of the proposition that lawyers who give legal opinions on the laws of a jurisdiction other than their own are "insurers" against the consequences of being wrong. On close examination, the case appears to hold nothing of the kind, but the idea seems to persist. Perhaps the most sensible view of the obligations of the lawyer in these circumstances is the view embodied in the new ABA Model Rules of Professional Conduct, in the comment to the very first Rule enjoining the lawyer to "provide competent representation to a client." "A lawyer," the comment notes, "can provide adequate representation in a wholly novel field through necessary study;" but "[C]ompetent representation can also be provided through the association of a lawyer of established competence in the field in question." The ABA Rules make consultation with experts (or, in the case of foreign lawyers, local counsel) an ethical responsibility.

PRACTICING LAW ABROAD: THE ROLE OF INSIDE COUNSEL

London Sessions
ABA Annual Meeting 1985
Guildhall
London, England

Tuesday, July 16, 1985
10:00 A.M. - 12:00 Noon

John T. Subak
Independence Mall West
Rohm and Haas Building
Philadelphia, Pennsylvania 19105

The most dramatic change in the practice of law in the United States during the past decade has been the increase in the number of lawyers practicing as members of corporate law departments. A small minority some 20 years ago, inside counsel currently represent approximately 13-15 percent of the 600,000 lawyers in the United States.

The United States has long been overpopulated by lawyers.* Whereas one Englishman in a thousand is a barrister or solicitor, the United States numbers about 2.67 lawyers per thousand. West Germany and Japan are in even better balance, with West Germany having half as many lawyers per thousand as England and Japan one-tenth the number. Admittedly one reason for the fewer numbers of lawyers in most countries is the amount of "legal" work performed in those countries by legal advisors and others who are not counted as lawyers.

Increase in Inside Counsel

The legal explosion in the United States has now reached inside counsel. Thirty-five major corporations have more than 100 lawyers on their legal staff. Each of the five largest, AT&T, Exxon, General Electric, Mobil, and Standard Oil of Indiana, employs more than 200 lawyers, with AT&T continuing to lead the pack with nearly 500 employed lawyers. A recent directory of inside counsel listed 5,000 U.S. corporations with formal legal departments.

Inside counsel have also expanded the scope of their activities. Typically, inside counsel supervise major litigation, and for the larger companies actually litigate the cases. They handle acquisition and merger transactions and advise on securities, labor, tax, and general corporate matters. For most companies with a legal department, outside counsel deal primarily with their client's general counsel, who has become the de facto client.

Friction Between Inside and Outside Counsel

The increase in the number of inside counsel and expansion of the scope of their work has led to much debate and some friction in the United States. Outside law firms feel that their clients have become too cost conscious and are sacrificing quality to save dollars. Budgetary and other constraints are placed on the work

---

* A January 1984 Forbes article commented: "The number of lawyers is growing much faster than the business available to support them. This should have been predictable: Lawyering is clean work, no heavy lifting and fairly prestigious."

handled by outside counsel. There are concerns about the independence of inside counsel. A recent article in the Harvard Business Review by Professsor Joseph Auerbach asked, "Can inside counsel wear two hats?" and promptly answered "No."

Happily, the stresses evident in the United States have not yet become evident in Europe. There are two principal reasons for this temporary calm. First, the number of inside counsel continues to be quite modest in Europe. Second, the legal monopoly in Europe is far narrower than in the United States. Throughout Europe, it is customary for non-lawyers to be giving advice and to draft agreements and other documents that in the U.S. would be handled by lawyers.

Scope of Inside Counsel

In the United States, the lawyer's monopoly extends to the full representation of the client, not only in court but also in giving legal advice and in drafting documents. Thus, the American lawyer is not only more numerous but his monopoly is more far-reaching.

As explained in the paper authored by Messrs. Vaughan and Sheldon, the activities reserved to barristers or solicitors in the United Kingdom are far more limited. In effect, one can act as a legal advisor in the United Kingdom without being a member of the club so long as one does not engage in "reserved activities." These reserved activities are limited to litigation and certain probate and real estate matters. As a result, few limitations are placed on the activities of inside counsel. While inside counsel (as well as other nonadmitted lawyers) may not act as advocates in court, may not prepare court pleadings, and may not hold themselves out to the public at large as lawyers, these restrictions have little practical consequence for lawyers acting as corporate counsel.

Lawyers employed by U.S. corporations with offices in the United Kingdom are free to give legal advice to their employer on any subject. Whether or not admitted in the United Kingdom, inside counsel advise on any area of law in which they feel competent, including national law, European Economic Community Law, and the impact of such American laws on European business as the Arab boycott regulations and laws governing technology transfer. They prepare contracts and negotiate on behalf of their client.

The U.S. lawyer employed abroad continues to be governed by the Rules of Professional Conduct of the jurisdiction to which he is admitted. These typically have a requirement similar to §1.1 of the Model Rules of Professional Conduct:

> A lawyer shall provide competent representation to a client. Competent representation requires the legal knowledge, skill, thoroughness and preparation reasonably necessary for the representation.

Therefore, when questions of specific local laws arise in which counsel feels a lack of sufficient expertise to advise the corporation, he will (and is professionally required to) consult with local solicitors. But realistically, legal departments strive to develop the necessary expertise in-house by transferring American lawyers abroad for extended periods of time to allow them to develop expertise in local matters and by employing nationals as staff attorneys to advise on local laws.

American inside counsel in the United Kingdom feel that they are well received by British lawyers. Since the activities restricted to solicitors and barristers are relatively narrow, few questions have been raised about the ability of inside counsel to advise their corporate clients and handle the wide range of their client's work. By avoiding the reserved activities, inside counsel can ply their trade with no practical restriction. At least that was so until the recent AM&S decision discussed below.

Privilege

In May, 1982, the Court of Justice decided that European Community Law recognizes a legal privilege but that the privilege does not extend to a client's written communications with lawyers who are not admitted to practice within the EEC. (AM&S Europe Ltd. v. Commission (1982) ECR 1575). Thus, lawyers not admitted to practice in the EEC, and all inside counsel, are excluded from the protection of the privilege. Indeed, one of the memoranda which was not accorded the privilege by the Court of Justice was a memorandum from an inside English solicitor containing legal advice. The Court used traditional language in recognizing the importance of confidentiality, stating "that any person must be able, without constraint, to consult a lawyer whose profession entails the giving of independent legal advice to all those in need of it." The Court then limited the privilege to "independent lawyers, that is to say, lawyers who are not bound to the client by a relationship of employment." Inside counsel were seen by the Court as lacking the full independence required to justify the privilege.

Blanket exclusion from attorney-client privilege of communication between inside counsel and corporate clients creates enormous problems. Written opinions may have to be avoided. Requests for facts may have to be routed through outside counsel admitted to practice within the EEC. Investigations by knowledgeable counsel become difficult. In fact, companies are deprived of useful written legal advice on those matters where the loss of privilege has adverse consequences. Hopefully this decision will soon be modified.

Status of Inside Counsel

One intangible difference between inside counsel in the United States and their counterparts in Europe is their status within the legal profession. To some extent, an inside counsel in Europe is not considered a "real" lawyer. That view is particularly prevalent on the Continent. In certain European countries, an attorney employed by a corporation is no longer considered a member of the Bar. Typically he may not appear in court. In the United Kingdom, a practicing barrister may not be employed by a corporation. As a symbol of a different status, foreign lawyers employed in the United Kingdom as inside counsel only need a work permit; no letter of consent or undertaking is required. Though personally well received, inside counsel are considered more akin to a *conseil juridique* than a lawyer. In the United States that perception has changed. Inside counsel in the United States are moving to the front of the bus; some even have the temerity to drive the bus. In Europe they often encounter difficulty getting onto the bus. Given the long history of Americans to export our bad habits, this too shall pass.

PRACTISING LAW ABROAD: AN ENGLISH VIEWPOINT

London Sessions
ABA Annual Meeting 1985
Old Library, The Guildhall
London, England

Tuesday, July 16, 1985
10:00 A.M. - 12:00 Noon

David Vaughan, Q.C.
1 Brick Court
Temple, London EC4V 9BY

and

Mark Sheldon
Linklaters & Paines
Barrington House
59-67 Gresham Street
London EC2V 7JA

A Little History

It was in March 1942, a few short months after Pearl Harbor and weeks only after the surrender of Singapore.

Against this gloomy, and at first sight unlikely, background, the United Kingdom Home Office wrote to The Law Society, the professional body for English solicitors, enquiring as to the advisability of "properly qualified aliens" being allowed to set up in the United Kingdom as consultants on the laws of their own countries. The Society's response was that it had no objections to this proposal, provided the foreign lawyers were of good character, did not represent themselves as qualified to practice as solicitors or otherwise infringe the provisions of the Solicitors' Act, and provided they observed the code of etiquette applicable to English practitioners.

Although this wartime exchange of views was prompted by the immediate but temporary problem of an influx of European lawyer refugees, it laid a permanent basis for the liberal framework within which foreign lawyers, including American lawyers, have been able to work in the United Kingdom from that time onwards, subject only to compliance with certain immigration procedures outlined later in this paper.

The Society briefly flirted with a proposal for a system of compulsory registration of foreign lawyers practising in England, with a degree of control over conduct vested in the Society's Council. It was, however, pointed out that corresponding regimes might be imposed on English solicitors practising abroad, and the idea was quietly dropped.

Problems occasionally arose. For example, in 1949, certain foreign legal consultants started to advertise, quite unpardonable behaviour in those days, mitigated but not thought to be excused by the fact that the advertisements in question were by Polish lawyers in the Polish language and in the London Polish press.

Then in the late 1960s and early 1970s, there was some concern at the growing number of U.S. lawyers who had established themselves in England. This centered around the then perceived lack of reciprocity within the United States, although there was also a degree of disquiet that U.S. lawyers might make unwanted inroads into areas of work carried out by solicitors. However, the generally impeccable professional behaviour of the American legal community in London and the changes within the United States permitting foreign legal consultants to set up in New York and other states have combined to somewhat mute, though not entirely extinguish, this concern.

---

1 References in this paper to England and English should in general be taken to include Wales and Welsh.

The English Legal Profession--A Thumbnail Sketch

We should briefly outline the position of the legal profession in England and Wales.[2]

The profession is divided into two branches, namely barristers and solicitors. British citizenship is not required for either branch. Admission to the bar is controlled by the Senate of the Inns of Court and the Bar. The Law Society controls the admission of solicitors. There are some 5,000 barristers in private practise and about 38,000 solicitors. Solicitors can, and frequently do, practise in partnerships, some of considerable size, and employ other solicitors in a salaried capacity. Barristers, on the other hand, may not practise in partnership nor as employees of other barristers. They thus practise as sole practitioners, though they normally share premises (known as "Chambers") and clerical staff headed by an experienced Clerk of Chambers.

Barristers (who alone are referred to as "counsel" and members of "the Bar") mainly concentrate on advocacy (civil and criminal), pre-trial proceedings, and preparatory work for trial, although many barristers develop advisory practices, either as generalists or in specialist fields.

Traditionally, solicitors presented themselves as general family advisers, men of affairs, concentrating perhaps on conveyancing (the legal work involved in buying and selling houses, other buildings, and land) and probate and trust work but also acting as advocates in the lower courts. Solicitors also assemble and organise the written and oral evidence for trials in the superior courts in which a barrister will be undertaking the advocacy. Some solicitors have developed highly specialized fields of practice in conjunction with, or to the exclusion of, these general fields of practice, and others have built up substantial practices in the fields of corporate, financial, and commercial law.

The division of the profession hinges on the fact that by reason of the Bar's own Practice Rules, a barrister cannot accept instructions from the lay client except through the intermediary of a solicitor, the legal work in the case being divided between the two on a conventionally agreed basis. There are certain exceptions to this rule, including important relaxations in favour of foreign lawyers which we discuss later in this paper.

---

2 For simplicity this paper does not attempt to deal with the position in Scotland, Northern Ireland or the Republic of Ireland. For the same reason, the paper does not discuss the position of notaries public, whose main functions are to draw up and authenticate documents for use in foreign courts and in connection with international commerce.

"Reserved Activities" of the Legal Profession in England

Although use of the titles "barrister" and "solicitor" is reserved to qualified barristers and solicitors respectively, English law does not in general restrict the practise of law to qualified lawyers.[3-4] There are, however, certain "reserved activities," few but very important, which are so restricted as follows:

Litigation. As to advocacy, although a litigant may appear on his own behalf in any court, a layman may not represent a litigant as advocate in any court, rights of audience being reserved exclusively to barristers in the superior courts and to barristers and solicitors concurrently in the lower courts.

As to nonadvocacy functions, under the Solicitors Act 1974, only a solicitor may act as a solicitor in legal proceedings and the right to prepare instruments relating to litigation is reserved to solicitors and to barristers.

Nonlitigious work. By the same Act, only a solicitor or barrister may, on a paid basis, prepare either: (a) instruments relating to real or personal estate (other than wills, powers of attorney, agreements not under seal, and straightforward transfers of securities); or (b) papers to obtain a grant of probate to the estate of a deceased person.

There is no monopoly on the rendering of legal advice as such, and the preparation of almost all financial and commercial agreements (which do not normally require to be executed under seal) is, as a matter of law, open to all.

Moreover, relaxations are in the air. In response to heavy consumerist pressures in recent years, the Government has announced plans for legislation which would open up the legal work involved in buying and selling domestic houses to persons other than practising solicitors and barristers.

Employed Lawyers

There are a material number of barristers and solicitors doing legal work as employed lawyers, in central or local government service or in commerce, finance, and industry.

In broad terms, both barristers and solicitors working as employed lawyers remain answerable to discipline by their respective professional bodies, though the professional rules of conduct are somewhat modified. An employed solicitor is permitted to work in the

---

3 Save where otherwise indicated, references in this paper to "barristers" are to barristers in private practise and to "solicitors" are to solicitors holding a current annual practising certificate.

4 Although it is not in fact illegal to describe oneself as a barrister unless done for a purpose contrary to criminal law, e.g., to obtain money by deception.

same way as a solicitor in private practise but with one client rather than many. He may carry out all professional activities, including those reserved to solicitors and may thus appear as advocate for his employer in the lower courts. By contrast, an employed barrister is not in general entitled to act as a practising barrister, and in particular, is not entitled to appear as counsel in the superior courts.

Foreign Lawyers in England

Although some foreign lawyers practising in England have qualified as English barristers or solicitors, and in certain cases practise as such subject to the rules of the relevant professional bodies, this is not the route pursued by very many. The great majority have established themselves either:

- As self-employed consultants in the laws of their own countries, or other specialist areas of international or transnational law, either as sole practitioners or in partnership; or

- As employees of either: (a) such self-employed consultants or consulting firms; or (b) financial, commercial, or industrial firms for which they act as in-house legal advisers.

Self-employed consultants. Under U.K. immigration procedures, a foreign lawyer wishing to come to the United Kingdom to set up a new practise, either on his own or in partnership with others, as a consultant in foreign law (or to replace resident principals of an existing practise) will normally need to be in possession of a Letter of Consent issued by the Home Office when he arrives to take up residence. Before issuing the Letter of Consent, the Home Office will require to be satisfied as to the financial standing and means of the lawyer or his firm and as to his professional qualifications. The Home Office also requires a letter from The Law Society stating whether or not there is any objection to the lawyer's application. The Law Society in its turn will seek professional information about the lawyer, take up references, and request a more-or-less standard form written "Undertaking" from the applicant lawyer to the effect, inter alia, that if the lawyer is granted permission to practise in England as a consultant in the law of his own country, he will not hold himself out as qualified to act as an English solicitor and will observe the standards of conduct accepted by the legal profession in England. European Economic Community lawyers are not subject to these immigration controls.

Employed foreign lawyers. Foreign lawyers (other than EEC nationals) proposing to be employed in England and Wales by a foreign legal consultant, professional firm, or by a corporation, need to obtain a current work permit prior to arrival to take up residence. Application for the work permit must be made by the prospective employer.

Areas of Practice

Foreign lawyers resident in England and Wales who are engaged in legal practise are thought, for the most part, to concentrate on legal work involving their own systems of law. No precise figures are available (there still being no compulsory system of registration), but a count in 1983 revealed that lawyers from over 70 countries were known to be so practising, by far the largest number being from the United States. The 1984 edition of the United States Embassy list of American Attorneys and Law Firms with Offices in London, compiled on a voluntary basis, contained the names of 80 practises totalling over 170 lawyers.

Except to the extent permitted by legislation derived from the EEC, as explained later in this paper, or from the Commonwealth, a foreign lawyer practising in England may not undertake any of the "reserved activities" described above which the English profession alone may carry out, nor may he hold himself out to be practising as a barrister or solicitor. Otherwise there are no constraints on the fields of practise open to him.

In particular, there is no statutory prohibition on a foreign lawyer undertaking English law work (not constituting one of the "reserved activities") although, in accordance with that part of the immigration "Undertaking" which requires him to observe the standards of conduct accepted by the English profession, he would be expected not to undertake work unless he can handle it promptly and with due competence. Clearly any lawyer, English or foreign, needs to exercise considerable caution in advising on law in which he is not professionally qualified.

Whilst in the early post-war years most foreign lawyers established in England concentrated on providing for the English profession consultative advice in relation to their own, or international, law or undertaking international arbitration work, many American law firms now provide through their London offices comprehensive, full-service professional facilities for their American and European clients in the fields of American and international law.

Relations of Established Foreign Lawyers with the English Profession

It is the writers' experience that, in general, English-based foreign lawyers enjoy excellent relations with both branches of the English profession. In providing consultancy services in their own laws they constitute an invaluable on-the-spot service. In undertaking a wider range of legal work direct for clients, foreign lawyers (and we are here mainly talking about American lawyers) have in general taken a sensible approach to the English profession and worked in timely conjunction with English lawyers when questions of English law are involved.

It should be noted in this context that the Bar's Code of Conduct, which normally preclude barristers from accepting instructions save through solicitors, make special provisions for foreign lawyers, including those based in England. A barrister may thus accept instructions direct from foreign lawyers where the work involves neither litigation before an English Court nor conveyancing or other "reserved activities" normally carried out by solicitors--though he may not engage in substantial administrative work or the conduct of correspondence with third parties.

Permanent association with barristers in England. A foreign lawyer can make use of the Chambers of a barrister in the United Kingdom, provided that the foreign lawyer does not have any other professional address in the United Kingdom and provided that he complies with Bar rules of conduct except "insofar as such rules conflict with the ordinary or usual way in which the foreign lawyer properly conducts himself in his practise or with the rules of his own profession." There are a certain number of foreign lawyers (mostly EEC) who have taken advantage of this rule.

There are a number of barristers, fully qualified in the United Kingdom, who are also full members of the bar of another country, and practise in both capacities. In those cases, in the case of his English practise, such a barrister must observe the Bar's professional rules, and in the course of his foreign practise he must observe the rules for foreign lawyers in Chambers. These Dual Qualification Rules are at present under review.

A barrister is not normally able to accept employment with a foreign lawyer with an office in England. However, he may do so if he is also qualified as a lawyer of a foreign State, provided that he takes up the employment in the capacity of a lawyer of that foreign State and does not hold himself out as a barrister or advise on English law other than incidentally in his practise of foreign law.

Permanent association with solicitors in England. A solicitor cannot enter into partnership in England with a foreign lawyer unless the latter is dually qualified as a solicitor. A solicitor may, however, share his fees with a foreign lawyer provided the latter has his principal office outside England and Wales. Furthermore, a foreign lawyer may be an employee of a solicitor.

A foreign lawyer may make use of a solicitor's office provided the arrangements do not amount to a partnership or to holding out that the foreign lawyer is qualified to act as a solicitor. However, the foreign lawyer may not use or appear on the solicitor's stationery, nor may his nameplate appear on the solicitor's premises. Correspondingly a solicitor's name cannot appear on a foreign lawyer's English nameplate nor the solicitor's name and address on the foreign lawyer's stationery used for his English practice.

The solicitor's professional rules prevent a solicitor from taking employment in England with a foreign lawyer unless that lawyer is to be the solicitor's only client. Such a solicitor could not therefore act as a solicitor for his employer's clients--he would have to remain a backroom boy.

Disciplinary Procedures Applicable to Foreign Lawyers Established in England

Foreign lawyers established in England are not subject to discipline by the professional bodies of either the Bar or the Solicitors' profession, nor are they subject to professional controls by the English Courts. In theory, breach of the provisions of the immigration "Undertaking" might give rise to a revocation of the foreign lawyer's residence permit, but in practise this is never thought to have occurred--and probably would not occur short of the commission of a deportable offence.

In practise, therefore, the only sanction available in relation to a foreign lawyer's conduct in England would be for a complaint to be lodged with the appropriate disciplinary authority in the lawyer's home jurisdiction.

Disciplinary Procedures Applicable to English Lawyers Established Abroad

The Bar Abroad

It is of the nature of things that a barrister is more likely to export his services on an occasional basis rather than by setting up Chambers or offices abroad, although some have in fact set up such Chambers. The Bar has for some time recognised that the strict rules of discipline, relevant to the U.K. situation, were not wholly relevant to practise abroad. The Bar accordingly adopted modified rules in relation to overseas practise, and they are always subject to local laws and rules of local Bars. These rules apply to "foreign work," where it does not relate to proceedings in the United Kingdom. In such circumstances, the barrister can accept work from foreign lawyers and, in certain circumstances, from a lay client. He can also enter into partnerships.

With regard to discipline, the Bar has always exercised its disciplinary jurisdiction on a worldwide basis, even against barristers practising wholly abroad and in relation to their conduct abroad.

A barrister when practising in Europe under the Services Directive (see below) is subject to Bar discipline for breaches of the rules of the "host Bar" for misconduct in legal proceedings, but only if the misconduct was *prima facie* a breach of the Bar's Code of Conduct for misconduct in other activities.

Solicitors Abroad

A considerable number of solicitors have established offices abroad, notably in Paris, Brussels, Hong Kong, New York, and Singapore. The relevant jurisdiction of the English Court and of the Solicitor's Disciplinary Tribunal to uphold by disciplinary measures the basic ethical principles of professional conduct applies to every solicitor whether or not he holds a practising certificate and wherever he may practise.

However, the detailed Solicitors' Practice Rules as such do not apply to solicitors practising abroad (though proposals are under consideration for a code of Overseas Practice Rules to be drawn up). Thus a solicitor may enter into a foreign-based partnership with a foreign lawyer and, for example, allow his name to appear on a foreign lawyer's stationery used outside England.

EEC Aspects

Freedom of Movement of EEC Lawyers

One of the fundamental principles of EEC Law is the freedom of movement of persons and services. This freedom is for nationals of one Member State of the Community, established in the Community, to move to another Member State. This applies to lawyers as much as to other individuals, and gives them the right:

- To set up an establishment in another Member State and to carry out a profession as lawyer in that Member State; and
- To provide services in another Member State when retaining an establishment in the Member State of origin.

With regard to freedom to provide services, legislation has already been adopted [Directive 77/249/EEC] to provide that lawyers (although salaried or employed lawyers may be excluded) from one Member State may represent a client in legal proceedings or before public authorities in another Member State under the same conditions (other than conditions of residence or of registration with a professional organisation) as apply to lawyers of the receiving Member State. Such a lawyer must comply with the rules of professional conduct of the host State, without prejudice to his obligation to comply with those of his home State. For the United Kingdom, this means the rules for barristers where the activity in question is reserved to barristers, and the rules for solicitors where not so reserved. A Member State may require such a visiting lawyer to be introduced to the appropriate authorities (Judge and/or Bar) and to work in conjunction with a local lawyer who practises before the Court.

For matters other than Court work (e.g., advisory work) there is no restriction upon employed lawyers and the rules of conduct to be observed are those of the country of origin with the requirement for compliance with host rules, so far as such host rules can be objectively justified. Such host rules would relate to incompatibilities, conflicts, professional secrecy, advertising, and relations with other lawyers.

Conveyancing and certain probate work can be excluded by a Member State when implementing this Directive.

There have been some, but not many, cases where lawyers from other Member States have appeared in U.K. courts (and probably many more if Ireland and Northern Ireland are included), and a few U.K.

lawyers have appeared in courts of other Member States. The provisions of the Directive have been most frequently used in border areas and in countries with common languages. The provision of services in relation to advice in other Member States is obviously very much more common.

Freedom of Establishment

With regard to freedom of establishment, there are a considerable number of firms of solicitors and a few barristers who are established in other Member States. There is as yet no Community legislation governing the rules which are to apply in such a situation, although much work has been done by the CCBE (an organisation of European Bars and Law Societies) on the preparation of a draft Directive, a project presenting many difficulties yet to be solved.

Many of the main advances in the field of movement of lawyers have been made, not by legislation, but by decisions of the European Court of Justice. In particular that Court has established:

- That a Dutch national, educated, qualified and resident in Belgium, was entitled to be admitted as a Belgian lawyer, notwithstanding the fact that Belgian law required Belgian nationality [Reyners (1974) ECR 631];

- That a legal representative who moved his residence from Holland to Belgium could lose his rights of representation, in a situation where Dutch law required residence to be in Holland, provided that the requirement of residence was necessary for the application of professional rules such as ethics and for the proper administration of justice [Van Binsbergen (1974) ECR 1229];

- That a properly qualified Belgian lawyer, who subsequently passed his professional examination in France, was entitled to be admitted to the Paris Bar, notwithstanding the fact that he had not obtained a French doctorate, when he had obtained a doctorate in Belgium, which was recognised as an equivalent qualification for the purpose of sitting for the French professional examination (Thieffrey (1977) CR 765]; and

- That the Paris Bar could not refuse to admit a German where that German had all the requisite qualifications for admission to the Paris Bar, on the grounds that the Paris Bar had a rule allowing only one office, and the German lawyer retained an office in Germany [Klopp, Judgement of 12th July 1984].

Legal Privilege

One of the matters of the greatest importance, not only to lawyers themselves, but also, and probably more importantly, to their clients, is legal privilege. This was expressly referred to in the Directive on the provision of services by lawyers. In AM & S (1982) ECR 1575, that privilege was recognised by the European Court of Justice as a fundamental matter of Community law, despite the absence of any express reference to the privilege in Community legislation giving powers of search to the Commission. However, there are two restrictions of great significance in the context of the present paper to this principle:

- the privilege only extends to communications with a lawyer entitled to practise his profession in one of the Member States (i.e., not to U.S. lawyers, even if established in the EEC);[5] and

- the privilege does not extend to communications with in-house counsel.

So far as concerns non-EEC lawyers, the Commission has stated that it would seek authority from the Council to open negotiations with Countries prepared to do this on a reciprocal basis [13th Report on Competition Policy, pages 65 to 66]. This would be on a governmental basis, but it should be realised that unless and until the Council does give such authority the Commission can do nothing. Presumably an essential requirement of any such negotiations would be the need of the Commission to be satisfied that the lawyers of the foreign country are subject to strict and effective professional discipline.

So far as concerns in-house counsel, the most important development has been the Report of the House of Lords Select Committee on the Commission's Powers of Investigation and Inspection, which heard evidence from practising lawyers and from the Commission, and which concluded that there was a powerful case for extending the privilege to involve in-house lawyers, provided that they were subject to strict and effective professional discipline, which would be the case for all employed barristers and solicitors.

---

5 By contrast, English domestic law extends legal privilege to foreign lawyers when practising as such.

MOCK TRIAL

London Sessions
ABA Annual Meeting 1985
Great Room, Grosvenor House Hotel
London, England

Tuesday, July 16, 1985
10:00 A.M. - 12:00 Noon
2:00 P.M. - 4:00 P.M.

Section of Litigation
American Bar Association
750 North Lake Shore Drive
Chicago, Illinois 60611

The mock trial will consist of a two-part live presentation of comparative trial techniques, featuring a full scale murder trial before a jury. The case involves the use of an immunized witness, alibi testimony, and a video-taped recording of the testimony of an unavailable witness.

Members and guests are invited to observe the trial twice: In the morning the trial takes place in a United States court of general jurisdiction, and in the afternoon in the Old Bailey.

Adopted from State v. Burns through the courtesy of the National Institute of Trial Advocacy, the government charges John Burns with the murder of Theresa Carletti during the attempted robbery of the Carletti grocery store. The prosecutor's chief witness is Lauren Jones, an admitted participant in the attempted robbery. Mary Burns, John's wife, is prepared to testify for the defense that John was at home during the time when the crime was committed.

The juries in both the U.S. and British trials will be given the opportunity to deliberate to a verdict.

The mock trials have been organized by Judge William Young, the Superior Court, Boston, Massachusetts 02108 and the Hon. Mr. Justice Otton, Royal Courts of Justice, Strand, London WC2.

FOREIGN INVESTMENT IN UNITED STATES REAL ESTATE: THE NON-TAX ESSENTIALS

London Sessions
ABA Annual Meeting 1985
Ballroom 2, Hilton International
London, England

Tuesday, July 16, 1985
10:00 A.M. - 12:00 Noon

David Alan Richards
520 Madison Avenue
New York, New York 10022

The attractions for foreign investment in United States real estate have remained strong over the past several years, although the volume has fluctuated with the strength of the dollar and the level of political instability elsewhere. The sheer availability of property in the United States, in any quantity or location and for every kind of use; the established market and legal procedures, conducted in the world's leading business language; the variety of professional advisors for acquisition, management, and financing; and the stability of the U.S. government, with orderly transitions and capitalist prejudices; all encourage investors to follow the advice of the great American humorist, Will Rogers: "Buy land--they ain't makin' it anymore."

Ownership Interests

Reflecting its English parentage, real property law in the United States covers more than the surface of the soil. Buildings and those items of personal property attached to land (fixtures) are real property, as are the airspace above and subsurface rights below, which can be severed by lease or outright sale. Estates in land are present or future possessory interests, measured in terms of duration or potential. Freehold estates include the fee simple absolute, the qualified fee, and the life estate; nonfreehold estates, or leases, include estates for years, estates from period to period, estates at will, and estates at sufferance. Leases may be "net" (full insuring and repairing) or mere "space" leases (landlord retains structural, tax, and insurance liabilities). Like fee interests, leases may be mortgaged to finance development.

Nonpossessory interests include easements (appurtenant or in gross) and security interests, including the mortgage or deed of trust; nonconsensual security interests also arise upon the registration in the public land records of liens for nonpayment of taxes, judgments, and for work performed or materials furnished to the property (mechanic's or materialmen's liens).

Concurrent ownership, with undivided right of each to possess and enjoy the whole property, is effected through joint tenancy (which includes survivorship rights) or tenancy in common (the legal result if the granting instrument does not indicate survivorship rights). More sophisticated forms of concurrent ownership are the co-operative and the condominium. In the former, a "co-operative housing corporation" owns the land and building, and grants "proprietary leases" covering individual apartments to tenant-stockholders. In the condominium, now appearing in industrial as well as residential and recreational developments, each co-owner holds title to an individual "unit" and an undivided percentage interest in the common facilities.

Acquisition and Recording

The broker's role, which materially differs from that of the chartered surveyor, is to produce a customer ready, willing, and able to meet his principal's terms. The broker normally represents the seller and has a duty to obtain the best possible terms for him, but since the commission is usually paid only upon sale of the property, the broker's primary practical interest is to arrange the transaction.

The property acquisition itself begins with the sales contract and ends with the closing or settlement in an exchange of the property for the consideration. The essential ingredients of an enforceable contract of sale, which must be in writing but need not be notarized, are: names of the parties; description of the real estate and any personal property to be conveyed; the purchase price; and the parties' signatures. For most contracts, however, many other provisions regarding deed quality (general warranty or less), encumbrances and restrictions, apportionment of taxes (rates), rents and service contract charges, insurance liability and risk of loss, condition of property at closing, seller's representations and warranties, and penalties and remedies for default are common.

Every state has a recording act providing for the recording of deeds and establishing priorities among successive purchasers (and encumbrances) of land interests. Deeds are listed in grantor and grantee indices, where they become part of the public record, and all subsequent purchasers take title with constructive notice of the contents of all documents in their "chain of title."

Three-Government Legal System

Whatever the ownership interest, real estate is the subject of federal, state, and local (municipal) laws, and its ownership by foreign investors--"nonresident aliens"--is the subject of special restrictions and disclosure obligations which merit particular attention by the investor and his U.K. and U.S. counsel.

Before the last decade's rising tide of disclosure legislation, the federal government's impact on "friendly" foreign investment was minor, and generally reflected its "open door" policy on immigration, initiated in the nation's early days to encourage the development of a virgin continent. In drafting the Constitution, the states--which to the world declared themselves united--reserved to themselves individually the authority over their respective residents' disposition of property. To date, the federal power to conduct foreign relations has not been deemed to limit a state's individual restrictions on the ownership of realty by nonresident aliens.[1] Resident aliens, on the other hand, enjoy the protection of the Constitution's 14th Amendment, enacted after our Civil War, providing that "...[n]o state [shall] deny to any person within its jurisdiction the equal protection of the laws."

Real estate ownership law in the United States, therefore, is primarily state law, while use and occupancy regulation is largely the province of local authorities. State restrictions on alien landholding are the product of several historical sources: feudal restrictions on aliens imported with the English common law heritage; nineteenth-century initiatives to attract further immigration with land grants, and fears of foreign absentee landlords; populist mistrust of corporations (eastern as well as European); and, most recently, xenophobic reservations about foreign control of the agricultural heartland.[2]

Thus, counsel must determine for his foreign client that the investment entity chosen for the state in question can (a) hold certifiable legal title (b) to the type of land being purchased (c) in the quantity being purchased. Although (at last count) some 18 jurisdictions now have constitutional or statutory provisions expressly abolishing the distinction between aliens and citizens concerning the right to take and hold realty, the remaining 32

> show a bewildering variety of express or residual restrictions which cluster around one or more of the following factors: (a) the manner or source of acquisition (descent, purchase, from the state); (b) the nature of the holding (agricultural, or rural, or size of holding); (c) the status of the alien (nonresident of the state, nonresident of the United States, nondeclarant immigrant, ineligible for citizenship, citizen of a nation not affording reciprocal rights, enemy alien); (d) the remedy for a prohibited holding (escheat or mandatory alienation within a specified period of time); (e) special conditions attached to an otherwise permissible holding (registration or continuation of a particular use).[3]

After negotiating these shoals of acquisition, the foreign investor must then (like his domestic counterpart) contend with the straits of use and occupancy laws imposed by local government. Municipal ordinances control subdivison by regulating lot size and layout; grading and draining of streets; requirements for sidewalks, sewers, and water mains; and reservation of public space or amenities. Zoning laws divide the community into exclusive or permitted use areas, whether residential, commercial, industrial, or mixed, within which building height, bulk, and population density are restricted. Building and fire codes affect construction, materials, setback, and use, while landmark registration and "esthetic zoning" regulation may affect the right to demolish or alter.

Federal restrictions on foreign direct investment in real estate were previously few in number, with restrictions only in the categories of public lands, federal territories, and "enemy aliens."

Public lands are the subject of more than 2,600 acts of Congress, which themselves are not fully codified.[4] Exploitation of mineral deposits on public lands is controlled by the Mining Act of 1872 (30 U.S.C. §22) and the Mineral Lands Leasing Act of 1920 (30 U.S.C. §181), while geothermal steam leases are governed by the Geothermal Steam Act of 1970 (30 U.S.C.A. §§1001-1025 (Supp. 1977)). Grazing permits for federal lands are subject to certain limitations for aliens (43 U.S.C.A. §315b (Supp. 1978)).

United States territories constitute a second exception to the "open door" policy. Under the Alien Land Act of 1887, ownership of land in such territories is limited to U.S. citizens and to bona fide resident aliens (48 U.S.C.A. §§1501-1502 (Supp. 1977)), unless the right is specially secured by a treaty between the United States and the alien's country.

Restrictions on "enemy aliens" are a third exception.[5] Under the Trading with the Enemy Act (50 U.S.C.A. app. §§1-44 (1970)), as amended by the International Emergency Powers Act (50 U.S.C. §1601 _et seq._), property of enemy aliens may be seized and administered by the federal government. Implementing regulations include the Alien Property Custodian Regulations (8 C.F.R. §§501-510 (1978)), and the Foreign Assets Control Regulations (31 C.F.F. §500 (1977)), under which the assets of aliens from North Vietnam, North Korea, Cambodia and, during the hostage crisis of 1979, from the Government of Iran, have become "blocked" by administrative process. (Many Argentine investors in U.S. real estate feared the possible implementation of this legislation against them during the Falklands conflict with Great Britain.)

In the last decade, however, Congress's lack of concern with the foreign investor has been replaced by modest alarm at the national security implications of the steadily increasing volume of foreign investment, which has been aptly styled the "rising tide of reverse flow." Because local real property records are generally uninformative with respect to the identification of investing principals beyond the name of the grantee, the federal government has begun to require reporting by such investors or their intermediaries and to impose fines for noncompliance.

The first fruit of this legislative effort was the International Investment Survey Act of 1976, or "IISA" (22 U.S.C. §§3101-3108), administered by the Department of Commerce, which requires reports to be filed with respect to every business enterprise, including real estate, subject to United States jurisdiction, in which enterprise foreign persons (either as individuals or affiliates) have direct or indirect interest of 10 percent or more (or which interest is held by a U.S. intermediary, such as a trust or agent, for a foreign beneficial owner).[6]

Exemptions from filing under IISA are available for (i) acquisitions under $1 million in value and 200 acres in size; (ii) personal residence owned by a corporation whose shareholder occupies the property; and (iii) investments as a limited partner, but a claim for exemption must be filed. Otherwise, a form (BE-13) must be filed within 45 days of the acquisitions, describing inter alia the address to which follow-up quarterly survey reports may be mailed and the schedule of the "ownership chain back to the ultimate beneficial owner who is not owned more than 50 percent by another person, giving name, percentage ownership at each level, and indicating country of ownership." Reporting bearer share ownership or holding through a trust or other proxy is not deemed compliance with the law. However, the reporting forms themselves are confidential and cannot by law be transmitted to foreign governments or reached under the Freedom of Information Act.

The next-enacted national real estate reporting requirement was the Agricultural Foreign Investment Disclosure Act of 1978, "AFIDA" (7 U.S.C, §§3501-3508), administered by the Department of Agriculture, requiring any "foreign person" acquiring or transferring any interest (other than a security interest) of 10 percent or more in U.S. farming, ranch, or timberland to file a report of such ownership within 90 days of the acquisition.[7] Exemption is available if the tract is less than 10 acres and gross annual sales of produce are less than $1,000. AFIDA reporting form ASCS-153 requires 14 categories of information, and tracing of tiers of ownerships up through the third tier. Completed forms are available for public inspection in the Washington, D.C. office of the Secretary of Agriculture, in the local (county) Agricultural Stabilization and Conservation Service Office, and are also made available to a treaty partner making request under a mutual assistance treaty or a fiscal evasion provision of an income tax treaty.

Federal disclosure requirements were multiplied and made significantly more intrusive by passage of the Foreign Investment in Real Property Tax Act of 1980, or "FIRPTA" (94 Stat. 2682, as amended by the Economic Recovery Tax Act of 1981, 95 Stat. 172, and the Deficit Reduction Act of 1984, 98 Stat. 494). Designed to close several "loopholes" that foreign investors routinely used to escape capital gains taxation on disposition of U.S. real property interests, FIRPTA as originally enacted employed an elaborate reporting procedure, rather than the alternative of withholding by the purchaser at time of sale. At least partially in response to vigorous criticism of these reporting requirements by legal and accounting professionals, FIRPTA was amended in July, 1984, in two respects: reporting obligations were repealed in their entirety (except for foreign persons having "direct" substantial investments in U.S. realty), and a withholding tax obligation (generally in the amount of 10 percent of the gross sales price) was placed on the transference of a U.S. real property interest ("USRPI") whenever acquired from a foreign transferor.[8]

Now, although the Internal Revenue Service may not impose look-through or similar rules in connection with reporting, under which "deemed" or "constructive" holders of USRPI are required to report, a foreign person (including not only nonresident alien individuals, but foreign corporations, partnerships, trusts, and estates) who did not engage in a U.S. trade or business during the reporting calendar year in question, and whose USRPI held directly at any time during such year had a fair market value of $50,000 or more, may in the Treasury's discretion be required to file an annual information return.

If required, such returns will presumably demand declaration of the name and address of the foreign person, a description of all USRPI held thereby (including location, date acquired, and fair market value), and a schedule of all USRPI disposed of in the applicable calendar year. Civil and criminal penalties may be imposed for failure to file or for filing an incomplete return.

The fourth and latest federal statute affecting the foreign investor, but sweeping beyond real estate, is the Tax Equity and Fiscal Responsibility Act of 1982, or "TEFRA" (Internal Revenue Code §6038A), which requires every domestic and every foreign corporation engaged in trade or business in the United States to file an annual information return with the Treasury if such corporation is "controlled by a foreign person," including any nonresident alien or foreign corporation. The return requires naming the companies, the relationship between them, and all transactions between the reporting corporation and each foreign corporation that is a member of the same controlled group.[9] The law aims to curb tax avoidance through international transactions between related companies which, via pricing maneuvers, manipulate their U.S. taxable income.

State Regulatory and Disclosure Laws

As noted above, individual state laws are a patchwork (and perhaps a minefield) for the foreign investor in American realty, but with careful planning, rarely a serious impediment. As detailed surveys of state law restrictions are available elsewhere,[10] suffice it to note here that there are 14 states that either bar such investment or require the foreign corporation, as the price of market entry, to "qualify to do business," i.e., to obtain a certificate of authority to do business outside of the jurisdiction in which it is organized and to appoint a resident agent for service of legal process. These states are Florida, Kentucky, Nebraska, New Mexico, Oklahoma, and Wisconsin, with various prohibitions against foreign corporate domicile, ownership or control; Iowa, Missouri, and Minnesota, with restrictions on foreign ownership of farmland; and Arkansas, Maryland, New Hampshire, Ohio and Virginia, which grant no express rights to foreign corporations to hold real property.

Furthermore, although the investor will recognize his need to receive title that is marketable (free from defects that may prevent later alienation or development), counsel should be aware that American methods for assuring marketability are substantially different from those used in almost every other nation. In the United States, an attorney, abstractor, or title insurance company reviews documents recorded in the public land records and produces an opinion, abstract, or title insurance policy commitment based on this review, in a process occurring each time a property is conveyed. In virtually all other countries, a finding of marketability, once made, is not re-examined but merely updated to the date of conveyance. Hence, the function of title insurance, the risks covered by the policy form in use in the situs state (against title defects, unmarketability liens, and encumbrances existing at the date coverage begins, unless excepted), the cost of the title policy (in addition to recording, land survey, and building law violation searches), and the nonalienability of the policy to the next purchaser of the investment site, must all be explained in detail to the foreign investor. Furthermore, it is imperative that the investor's foreign character be disclosed to the title insurer, as failure to do so constitutes an "act of the insured" voiding the policy in the event restriction on foreign investment has been violated.[11]

Investment Entities

In order to limit personal liability and avoid the impact of U.S. estate taxes at his death, the nonresident alien investor will customarily avoid taking title to U.S. real property in his own name. Corporate ownership (whatever the country of incorporation) provides limited liability, while utilizing a domestic corporation ensures the jurisdiction of the United States over the asset and avoids the possible need to create "nationalization failsafe devices."[12]

Normally, the use of a foreign or domestic partnership as the investment entity, if engaged in a U.S. trade or business for tax purposes, will increase the overall U.S. tax burden. The decision to utilize a U.S. partnership as the investment vehicle must also be made with the realization that investor anonymity cannot be assured due to individual state requirements for filing "doing business as" ("d/b/a/") or other certificates for general partnerships, or certificates of limited partnerships required under the Uniform Limited Partnership Act in force in most states. Finally, if an unincorporated business organization created under foreign law is to be utilized for foreign tax advantages or to preserve (pre-FIRPTA) anonymity, it must be noted that the classification of such an organization as a partnership, trust, or association under U.S. tax laws is determined by U.S. tax regulations, although the local law of the foreign jurisdiction in question determines the legal relationships among the parties against which the criteria of the regulations are tested.

Means and End

Unlike his domestic counterpart, the foreign investor does not arrive in his lawyer's office equipped with a team of nonlegal professional advisors, and he may even be ignorant of his need for certain of them. The task of choosing or vetting and then coordinating nonlegal real estate and corporate professional services (broker, investment advisor, accountant, banker, local and overseas counsel, domestic corporate service agent, and property manager) often falls by default to the investor's attorney, who himself is often called upon for quasi-business advice.

Several years after coming to the United States because he has heard that "the streets were paved with gold," an Irish immigrant remarked that this was a threefold lie: first, because the streets mostly weren't paved; second, when they were, it wasn't with gold; and third and worst, _he_ had to do the paving. So too does the conveyancing attorney on the golden street of foreign investment in American real estate, and he will best serve the client by knowing his tools, and the many turns on the road ahead.

FOOTNOTES

1. See, e.g., _Lehndorff Geneva, Inc._ v. _Warren_, 74 Wisc. 2d 369, 246 N.W.2d 815 (1976); Weber, _Foreign Direct Investment in United States Real Estate: Xenophobic or Principled Reaction?_, 28 U. FLA. L. REV. 491 (1976), at 510-514.

2. Morrison, _Limitations on Alien Investment in American Real Estate_, 60 MINN. L.R. 621 (1976).

3. Fisch, _State Regulation of Alien Land Ownership_, 43 MO. L. REV. 407 (1978), at 409-410, citations omitted.

4. See, generally, Morrison, _Legal Regulation of Alien Land Ownership in the United States_, 8 REPORT TO CONGRESS ON FOREIGN DIRECT INVESTMENT IN THE U.S. at M-24 app. (1976).

5. See, generally, Goodman, _United States Government Foreign Property Controls_, 52 GEORGETOWN L.J. 769 (1974); Papernik, _Risks of Private Foreign Investment in U.S._, NEW YORK LAW JOURNAL, December 6, 1979, p. 1, col. 2.

6. See, generally, Packman, U.S. Department of Commerce Reporting Requirements, 6 TAXES INTERNATIONAL 7 (March 1980); Wilson, Foreign Investment: Investment Disclosure Requirements, 22 HARV. INT'L L.J. 694 (1981). IISA regulations were published in 15 C.F.R., Part 806, as revised and supplemented in 43 Fed. Reg., No. 226, pp. 54624 et seq., Nov. 22, 1978; 44 Fed. Reg., No. 110, pp. 32586 et seq., June 6, 1979; 46 Fed. Reg., No. 14, pp. 7214 et seq., Jan. 22, 1981; 46 Fed Reg., No. 46, pp. 23225 et seq., April 24, 1981; 47 Fed. Reg., No. 21, pp. 4530 et seq., Feb. 1, 1982; 47 Fed. Reg., No. 60, pp. 13138 et seq., March 29, 1982; and 47 Fed. Reg., No. 105, 23705, June 1, 1982.

7. See, generally, Zedalis, Disclosure of Foreign Investment in U.S. Agricultural Land, 31 MERCER L. REV. 711 (1980); Reiner, The Agricultural Foreign Investment Disclosure Act and Its Regulations, 2 AGRICULTURAL L. J. 528 (Spring, 1981). AFIDA regulations were published in 44 Fed. Reg., No. 98, pp. 29029 et seq., May 18, 1979; 44 Fed. Reg., No. 156, p. 47526, Aug. 14, 1979; 44 Fed. Reg., No. 209, pp. 61601 et seq., Oct. 26, 1979; 45 Fed. Reg., No. 18, pp. 6115 et seq., Jan. 25, 1980; 45 Fed. Reg., No. 125, pp. 7775 et seq., Feb. 5, 1980; and 48 Fed. Reg., No. 197, pp .46065 et seq., Oct. 11, 1983; and 49 Fed. Reg., No. 174, pp. 35073 et seq., Sept. 6, 1984.

8. See, generally, Feder & Parker, The Foreign Investment in Real Property Tax Act of 1980, 34 THE TAX LAWYER 545 (Spring, 1981); Kaplan, Creeping Xenophobia and the Taxation of Foreign-Owned Real Estate, 71 GEORGETOWN L. J. 1091 (1983); Richareds, FIRPTA-The-Second: Disclosure and Withholding, 58 TAXES INTERNATIONAL 15 (August, 1984). FIRPTA regulations were published in 47 Fed. Reg., No. 183, pp. 41532 et seq., Sept. 21, 1982; 48 Fed. Reg., No. 4, pp. 647 et seq.; 48 Fed. Reg., No. 183, pp. 19163 et seq., April 28, 1983; and 49 Fed. Reg., No. 23, p. 4074, Feb. 2, 1984.

9. TEFRA regulations were published in 48 Fed. Reg., No. 224, pp. 56076 et seq., December, 1983. Control is generally defined to mean ownership of stock possessing 50 percent or more of the total combined voting power of all classes of stock entitled to vote or ownership of 50 percent or more of the total value of shares of all classes of stock. Thus, the reporting requirement is triggered for any wholly-owned subsidiary of a foreign corporate parent, even if the foreign parent is publicly held.

10. Committee on Foreign Investment in U.S. Real Estate, Real Property Division, Foreign Investment in U.S. Real Estate: An Update on Federal and State Laws (forthcoming, 18 REAL PROP., PROB. & TRUST J.).

11. On title insurance and the foreign investor, see, generally, Richards, Real Estate Counsel, Contract and Closing for the Foreign Investor, 14 REAL PROP., PROB. & TRUST J. 757, at 792-795.

12. Knight, "Failsafe" Legal Structures to Protect U.S. Assets of Foreign Investors, 4 INVESTMENT/USA No. 8, Special Supplement (August, 1983).

FOREIGN INVESTMENT IN UNITED STATES REAL ESTATE: THE NON-TAX ESSENTIALS

London Sessions
ABA Annual Meeting 1985
Ballroom 1, Hilton International
London, England

Tuesday, July 16, 1985
10:00 A.M. - 12:00 Noon

Robert Finch
Linklaters & Paines
Barrington House
59-67 Gresham Street
London EC2V 7JA

'Tis the Star-Spangled banner; O long may it wave,
O'er the land of the free, and the home of the brave.

The British political upheaval of 1979 opened the way for British Investing Institutions--insurance companies, pension funds, and property unit trusts--to invest in property in foreign jurisdictions without the intervention of U.K. Exchange Control. Available statistics suggest that while overall property investment by the Institutions declined in the period between 1979 and 1984, investment in the U.S. property market, and particularly in the office sector of the U.S. property market, increased. This paper asks the questions "Why the United States?" and "What do they seek?" without crossing the Rubicon of tax considerations, which almost entirely dominate activity today.

The U.K. Investing Institutions traditionally have invested capital--whether it be in government stock, real property, or equities--over a long term in return for a guaranteed yield which can be returned to the policy holders, pensioners, or other annuitants who are the beneficiaries of their funds. In the past, the Institutions' role in property investment schemes was to provide financing for acquisition of a site (although this was by no means universal) and for construction together with its associated costs such as professional fees and the cost of short-term bank borrowings while the actual work of building was under way. In return for that financing, the Institutions expected to receive a guaranteed rate of return which would compare with the rate of return they were receiving from other types of investment in their portfolio.

The collapse of the U.K. property market in the mid-1970s caused the Investment Institutions to take another look at the earnings they were making from property investment. Developers were no longer prepared to risk much of their own capital; many of those who did so had to be rescued by the Institutions and finance houses. As developers retreated from the risk-taking aspects of property ownership and confined themselves more and more to the role of project managers, the Institutions became increasingly interested in gaining a share in the actual earnings from property, the size of which might bear no relation to a traditional rate of return on the amounts they had actually invested.

Today, U.K. property investment is based almost entirely on the outright acquisition of the fee simple, whether before or after a development is erected on it, or on the purchase of one of many varying leasehold interests. Each is used to produce income from what we now know as the fully repairing and insuring lease.

Unless an investment purchase is of an existing let and developed property, the purchase will typically originate in one of two investment techniques: the forward purchase and the sale and leaseback, both usually hand in hand with construction financing.

The technique of forward purchase--either of the fee simple or a relevant long leasehold interest--allows a developer to create and sell an investment taking with him trading profits. The transaction normally involves acquisition of a development site on a predetermined price formula, the development and letting of the site, and a final payment to the developer determined by reference to the success of the scheme. In the past, the forward purchase quite often embodied (and still does sometimes) an obligation on the part of the developer to guarantee a required return to the Institution from and after a date certain and to take a lease of the development where successful letting is not achieved within a given period. In practically every case the Institution expected the developer to top up development funds if cost overruns or other unexpected contingencies arose.

In the light of their experiences in the 1970s, developers became increasingly reluctant to provide guaranteed returns or commitments to take on leasing obligations; they wanted to be up and out. The Institution was asked to receive, and now generally expects to hold, the baby even if the bath water runs out.

In the 1970s there was a full swing towards the cult of the equity, and use of the sale-and-leaseback investment technique. The sale-and-leaseback technique was developed during the credit squeeze of 1956-58 when links were forged between developers and long-term institutions--mostly the insurance companies. The Institutions provided a line of funds secured by mortgage debenture accompanied by a large equity holding at below applicable market prices with options or conversion rights. At that time, sale-and-leaseback transactions provided Institutions with an acceptable return on capital, required tenants to accept a full repairing and insuring liability, and made provision for the periodic review of rent, usually to a percentage of open market rent.

These leases, under which the equity in property or income from property was shared, were the prototype for the leasing scheme used today when both Institutions and developers wish to maintain an interest in the same property. This type of lease makes a development possible and provides a flexible means of distributing the resulting revenue. Frequently there are two or more equity or income-sharing leases granted in sequence in respect of the same development: a headlease granted by the freeholder, who provides the land, to an Institution, which provides the financing, and an underlease to the developer who provides the expertise in organizing the development, letting it off, and managing it after completion, when revenue is produced by the tenants.

The leasehold system has provided financial partners in a development scheme with a remarkably flexible instrument with which to establish their long-term contractual relationships. The leasehold system allows each party to have a separate identity; to own an interest in a scheme which can be separately sold; and yet to retain a sufficient degree of control over, and community of interest with, the other participants to ensure that the venture remains a going concern. Other techniques available for achieving the same result, such as the partnership, the deadlock company, the trust-for-sale or co-ownership schemes are rarely used because of taxation problems or the simple fact that Institutions have always tried to own outright their own relevant interests.

The early leases were wedded to the idea of a guaranteed return either on the land or on the funds invested, irrespective of the income actually arising from the development. It is not surprising that those leases gave way to leases of a hybrid nature where the rent reserved would be a percentage share in the head tenant's net income from the development scheme but with, almost certainly, a minimum or guaranteed return. We have already seen that by the early 1980s developers had become reluctant to accept the principle of unlimited liability in the technique of the forward purchase. Likewise the prospect of being liable under privity of contract for the duration of a long lease became increasingly less attractive to the tenant developer. If the parties were to share income, why should they not share the disadvantages as well as the benefits of fluctuations in the letting market and so put both landlord and tenant in the position of risk taker? This natural evolution of the spreading of risk takes us to the early 1980s.

In the 30 years following the Second World War, the larger Institutions--the big insurance companies and the pension funds--became deeply involved in property investment and development. Through periods of credit squeeze, development control, economic stimulation, and inflation, they became knowledgeable and sophisticated equity investors, and they demanded, and succeeded in obtaining, the dominant position in the industry. The Institutions learned that money is made from equity investment and not mortgage or debt financing, and this lesson will not be lightly relinquished.

By the late 1970s, property formed a substantial part of the institutions' total portfolio of assets. The long-term funds--the insurance companies--had had a flying start, and by 1979 they had some 24 percent of their total assets in property. Public sector pension funds had a similar proportion of their assets in property while private sector funds had some 14 percent of their assets so invested.

The property portfolios of the Institutions were diversified, containing, in different ratios, investments in the office, retail, industrial, and farming sectors. Investment was in relatively small amounts (the ideal for the majors being not less than £5m nor more than £25m), preferably freehold and in the single ownership of the Institution. Institutions rarely invested in hotel or leisure developments, where rental levels are difficult to ascertain, and they disregarded any entry into the politically volatile and short-term housing market.

During the early 1980s, the U.K. property market was materially affected by a decline in economic activity. The recession produced a contraction in business operations and closure of factories and offices. The fall in the demand for accommodation produced a tenants' market for most types of property. Available factory and office space reached record levels during 1982-83. The weakness in the letting market not only led to very low rental growth but also exposed the undesirability of certain locations and buildings. Sectors particularly affected were large old factories and mills and office buildings constructed during the 1950s and 1960s.

In the last year, there has been some evidence of a resurgence of the market as the total workforce has expanded and corporate profitability has risen. In theory this should increase demand, encourage growth in rental levels, and justify further investment in property. The effect that an upturn in the economy could have on property returns is illustrated by the performance of the shops sector where prime yields have fallen to 3.65-3.5 percent in response to the strong growth in retail sales since 1982. However, few transactions are actually undertaken at this level, and because of the overall sluggish performance of the U.K. economy, property investment in the United Kingdom by the Institutions has continued to decline.

By contrast, investment in overseas property has jumped since exchange controls were lifted in 1979. For example, in 1981, the Institutions had some £3.77 billion, or 22% of their investment programme in overseas property. This was mostly concentrated in equity shares. Naturally, much of the overseas investment was in U.S. real estate. Statistics are difficult to come by, but certainly by the end of 1983 some £1,294m had been invested in U.S. real estate by the pension funds. The public sector funds were the largest contributor with holdings valued at £761m.

Why did the Institutions move so dramatically into foreign real estate? Perhaps a view could be expressed, with the benefit of some hindsight, that they took an increasingly gloomy view of the economic prospects then, and perhaps still, apparent in the United Kingdom. Sterling, then as now, was under pressure. What were the prospects for the upcoming decades when the liabilities of the Institutions would have to be paid out in pensions, sums assured, and returns to unit holders? It appeared essential to the portfolio managers to maintain a well-balanced investment programme including a substantial interest in property--but invested, at least in part, outside the United Kingdom.

The Institutions had dipped their toe into the European real estate market during the 1960s and early 1970s as a means of diversifying their property portfolios with mixed success. They were faced with differing laws and customs, differing languages, difficulties of the exchange controls then still relevant, and the need to accept a wholly different attitude toward leasing, which in the main was maintained by reference to a price index rather than to open market forces. More importantly, they had invested in economies which to a great extent were declining like the U.K. economy. They also believed that they could apply a U.K. approach to investment disregarding, in some cases, the very rules of the locality to which they should have been more aware. But in 1979, when exchange controls were lifted, new attitudes could be adopted towards North America.

The U.K. Institutions' growing awareness of their need to acquire interests in the U.S. property market was prompted by six separate factors:

1. The U.S. domestic economy had for several decades out-performed the U.K. economy, with particular areas of the United States enjoying rapid increases in population growth and business activity. This performance had been further enhanced in the property sector by fiscal and tax regimes which encouraged, rather than discouraged, commercial development and ownership of property interests by private enterprise.

2. The U.S. property market provided investing Institutions with properties at prices which offered yields substantially higher than those generally obtainable on comparable property investments in the United Kingdom.

3. Diversification of portfolios with investments in the U.S. property market would answer the need for investors to seek out stable economic and political conditions in which their investments should show good capital and rental growth.

4. It was generally considered that the acquisition of dollar assets would prove to be beneficial in the long term for investing Institutions. Furthermore, by reason of the U.S.-U.K. double tax treaty and the absence of U.S. exchange controls, the repatriation of revenue and proceeds of sale of properties would be readily achieveable.

5. Various practices in the U.S. property market made real estate investment particularly attractive. Although long-term mortgage financing has seemingly changed in the last few years, many low-interest rate mortgages entered into during previous periods still permit the transfer of properties to purchasers with the existing mortgages remaining in place. This would enable a foreign investor, even the U.K. Institutions which typically did not borrow in the United Kingdom on their property acquisitions, to limit the amount of cash investment in any given property, making possible a more substantially diverse portfolio whilst benefitting from low interest rates prevailing on the older mortgages. In addition, unlike in the United Kingdom, long-term mortgage financing in the United States was found to be generally on a nonrecourse basis.

6. Above all, the law appeared similar, the language could be understood, and the same professional routine towards making investment decisions applied.

The Institutions were, of course, not alone in investing in U.S. real estate. The Property Companies, applying as far as local custom allowed skills they had learned in the U.K. market, made many acquisitions, concentrating their activity in the major northern cities where investment opportunities could be pursued in conditions not dissimilar to those at home. The Institutions, however, found a property industry which was particularly responsive to development and investment without the apparent inhibitions largely caused by land scarcity in the United Kingdom. They were able to invest in a whole range of property interests, including particularly the limited partnership, which was not available in the United Kingdom. Prima facie the Institutions accept, as a matter of fact, the ground rules set out in David Alan Richards' paper, and the taxation consequences of U.S. investment.

It is not necessary to discuss the U.K. rules and regulations concerning real estate investment; the U.K. investor enjoys a surprising degree of freedom from alien land laws, reporting requirements, and such like. Furthermore, it is as easy to create a corporate identity and liability protection for those investing in the United Kingdom as it appears to be in the State of Delaware. Concern must be expressed as to whether freedom to invest in the United States is available, as a matter of law, to every U.K. investor; it may not be so.

Property investment activity in the United Kingdom is dominated by the Institutions. Investment by individuals, apart from a number of old family estates such as the Westminster, Portman, and Cadogan families, is rarely seen on a significant scale, but in theory the individual investor, in the absence of exchange control formalities and apart from any fiscal restraints or concerns, is able to invest where and how he wishes. The Institutions themselves must be organized in accordance with English or Scottish law, under which the principle criteria for investment abroad will be the Institution's ability under its constitutional documents, or where relevant under applicable legislation, to invest in property assets abroad. Furthermore, for reasons of limiting liability in the United States, but more importantly for reasons of creating an efficient tax structure in the United States, the investment entities may well wish to create U.S. or other offshore corporate structures centrally managed and controlled in the United States, or offshore from the United Kingdom, or to purchase either directly or indirectly other property interests. Care must be exercised in considering each trust deed, other constitutional documents or, where appropriate, relevant legislation for the purpose of ensuring that such indirect property investment is in fact permissible.

Use of the property unit trust as a vehicle by which investment in the U.S. property market is achieved, has been particularly popular in the United Kingdom. These entities were first created in 1965 and were used by the tax exempt or partially exempt pension funds and charities as cooperative investment ventures enabling unit holders to pool their resources with a view to engaging in the acquisition and management of property. They are attractive to unit holders since they are treated by the U.K. Revenue as exempt from U.K. capital gains tax and corporation tax, and although income will be assessable to U.K. income tax at the present rate of 30 percent, participants are able to reclaim the appropriate proportion of U.K. income tax suffered by the trust. Quite typically, the unit trust is formed under a trust deed, executed by a trustee, under which provision is made for the appointment of a Committee of Management made up of the unit holders. The trust funds are "unitised," that is divided into units, which will increase or decrease in value and which, subject to the terms of the trust deed, can either be marketed or redeemed. However, the vehicle is usually open-ended and must, through realisation of assets, be able to sell investments relatively quickly. The vehicle is an ideal instrument through which the smaller pension funds can invest in the United States on a cooperative basis, achieving a spread of investment and yet avoiding the problems of direct acquisition and management.

Investment in the U.S. real estate market should, for the future, be seen as a means of achieving portfolio diversification and economic protection. From the U.K. standpoint there are few legal, and then largely fiscal, ground rules which require observance; they certainly do not inhibit portfolio diversification. But the view of the U.K. Institutions is seemingly shared by many other highly sophisticated foreign Institutions who do not invest in the U.K. property market.

POSITIVE PLANNING LAW IN THE UNITED STATES

London Sessions
ABA Annual Meeting 1985
Ballroom, Dorchester Hotel
London, England

Tuesday, July 16, 1985
10:00 A.M. - 12:00 Noon

Prof. David L. Callies
University of Hawaii at Manoa
The William S. Richardson School of Law
2515 Dole Street
Honolulu, Hawaii 96822

The Place of the Plan in the U.S. Land Regulatory Process

Local Zoning "In Accordance With A Comprehensive Plan"

While the power to regulate land has always theoretically rested with the state (rather than federal) government in the United States, it is the local government which affects most land use through local zoning. That zoning should be enacted in accordance with a comprehensive plan was an early presupposition which later was virtually eliminated by the "finding" of comprehensive plans in the zoning process itself.[1-2] Thus, the comprehensive planning requirement was moribund for much of zoning's middle life.

The Plan As Law In the 1970s and 1980s

The rise of state and regional land use controls in the 1960s and 1970s also heralded the return of the comprehensive plan to a measure of importance arguably greater than that originally envisioned by the early proponents of zoning. While traditional zoning and other local land regulatory ordinances continue to be the primary method of controlling the use of urban land, a "quiet revolution" in land use controls in the 1960s and 1970s moved much of the broad policy decision-making power previously delegated to local governments back to state governments primarily because of:

- A perception that local governments were unwilling or incapable of making decisions of supra-local impact except on narrow, parochial grounds;
- A crisis of sorts regarding particularly large developments or particularly critical natural features or resources threatened by actual or pending land developments; and
- The threatened imposition of federal land use controls.[3]

Four states are particularly noteworthy for their unique land law systems, which have a considerable impact on growing populations and are frequently challenged. All four rely upon a statewide plan as a basis for exercising land use controls, which in part supercede local land use regulations.

Hawaii and statewide zoning. In 1961, Hawaii's legislature passed the nation's first statewide land use controls, and established a Land Use Commission to divide the state into four land use zones: Agricultural, Urban, Rural, and Conservation. In reclassifying land, the Commission must now conform to a later-enacted state plan.[4] Hawaii is unique among the 50 states in having converted that state plan into a statute. Its major areas of concentration include: population, the economy, the physical environment, facility systems, and sociocultural advancement. All state land use control agencies conform to the aforesaid themes, goals, policies, objectives, and priority guidelines. Only in the urban zone--less than 10 percent of the state--do local land use regulations apply.[5]

Florida and the ALI Model Land Development Code. Virtually no state besides Hawaii has passed a statewide land use classification system. Instead, a number of states have attempted to regulate the permitting process applicable to large development projects and to protect critical natural areas. This is the focus of Article 7 of the American Law Institute's annotated Model Land Development Code, which is the basis for Florida's Environmental Land and Water Management Act of 1973. The Act provides for state review of development in designated areas of critical state concern and developments deemed to have regional impact, wherever they occur (e.g., marinas), all relating to the Government Comprehensive Planning Act (LGCPA) in 1975.[6]

Vermont and the regulation of development in sensitive areas. Vermont's Act 250 was passed almost entirely in response to a ski tourism boom which led to intense and relatively large-scale development pressure in relatively fragile environmental areas: the sides of mountains and the shores of lakes and streams. Act 250 provides for a series of land use plans to be drawn up, broadly defines development, forbids development without a permit, and requires compliance with certain environmental and other impact criteria, together with certain of the plans, once adopted. To hear and pass on permit applications, the Act creates regional District Land Use Commissions, together with an Environmental Board to hear and decide appeals from Commission decisions. The Act further requires the Commissions to find that a proposed development is "in conformance with" any duly adopted local or regional plan or "capital program."[7]

Oregon, state plans, and conformance. Arguably the most plan-oriented of those states which have adopted state land use controls, Oregon is also one of the only states which requires--rather than merely permits--local zoning. (Ch. 324 Oregon Laws 1969.) Essentially, Oregon's system relies on a series of 19 statewide land use management goals adopted by a statutorily created Land Conservation and Development Commission (LCDC). All state, city, and county comprehensive plans, ordinances, and regulations must conform to the LCDC-adopted goals. Compliance is accomplished through an "acknowledgement" procedure whereby the LCDC receives the plans and ordinances and confirms that they have been adopted in accordance with the statewide goals. The courts in Oregon have been supportive of the goals and strict in their conformance requirements.[8]

Federal Planning "Requirements"

Coastal Zone Management Act. Many states and local governments failed to address coastal management problems, raising concerns that balkanized coastal protection efforts would have dire consequences for the nation's fragile coastal resources. The Federal Coastal Zone Management Act of 1972 provides some national continuity. As with many federal programs, the Act depends entirely on state and local land use regulation, but in accordance with federal standards and criteria. The federal government offered a combination of federal money for plan development and program implementation, and limited control over otherwise exempt (from state/local control) federal actions affecting the coastal zone, in exchange for local and/or state regulation of the coastal zone.[9]

Clean air. The Clean Air Act imposes the most direct federal land use controls on states and local governments, by requiring states to formulate and promulgate state implementation plans (SIP's) to reach EPA-promulgated primary and secondary ambient standards for certain named pollutants. SIP's must contain methods to bring air quality control regions which fail to meet national ambient air quality standards into compliance by regulating the operation of existing, and reviewing the construction of new, stationary sources of pollution (factories, commercial centers, and so forth). Thus, the location of major commercial and industrial development in either developed or undeveloped areas will be increasingly difficult to achieve.[10]

Clean water. To eliminate pollutant discharges into the nation's waters by 1985, the Clean Water Act reduces pollutants through structural (wastewater treatment plants) and nonstructural (planning and land use controls) techniques.[11] Through massive federal grants for the construction of publicly owned wastewater treatment works, the structural technique was tried first. Regional planning under Title II of the Act, which was supposed to precede such plant construction, followed. This is unfortunate from a land use management and control perspective because wastewater treatment works construction tended to generate urban development beyond what would otherwise have occurred. The regional land use plans to control water pollution now include techniques for controlling pollution from nonplant sources such as runoff from agricultural, silvicultural, and construction activities.

Planning for Aesthetics

The use of the police power through zoning to regulate for aesthetics raises some difficult philosophical and legal problems. While many agree that, say, the billboard is so generally offensive and its small minority of supporters so uniformly economically interested that its regulation on aesthetic grounds is a reasonable exercise of the police power, one can usually concoct other grounds--health, safety--for their regulation. But what about housing color and design? What standards should govern? Or are there special situations, special jurisdictions which, for economic reasons, have a peculiar interest in remaining "attractive"?

In Berman v. Parker, 318 U.S. 26 (1954), the U.S. Supreme Court delivered a widely quoted dictum concerning aesthetics and regulation:

> The concept of the public welfare is broad and inclusive. The values it represents are spiritual as well as physical, aesthetic as well as monetary. It is within the power of the legislature to determine that the community should be beautiful as well as healthy, spacious as well as clean, well-balanced as well as carefully patrolled.

Critical to the Court's decision was the need for a detailed redevelopment plan required before redevelopment could begin. However, the issue before the Court was whether nonblighted property could be compulsorily acquired, not whether it could be regulated for aesthetic purposes. Nevertheless, it is for the latter that it is most often cited.[12]

One of the subjects of "aesthetic" regulation has always proved easy to justify is that of billboards. Although in the early years that police power justification was often somewhat strained, this is not so today. Hawaii's State of Hawaii v. Diamond Motors, Inc. 50 Hawaii 33, 429 P.2d 825 (1967) case is a recognized classic in the field:

> We accept beauty as a proper community objective, attainable through the use of the police power. We are mindful of the reasoning of most courts that have upheld the validity of ordinances regulating outdoor advertising and of the need felt by them to find some basis in economics, health, safety, or even morality.... We do not feel so constrained.

The effort to keep highways free of billboards has been much aided by the Federal Highway Beautification Act of 1975, which requires stringent control of billboard location on all federal aid highways.

The U.S. Supreme Court in Metromedia, Inc. v. San Diego, 453 U.S. 490 (1981) recently dealt with the continued tension under our Constitutional system between freedom of expression (through political signs) and the state and local police power to regulate billboards. The City of San Diego's ordinance essentially prohibited "off-site" billboard advertising, whether or not commercial, but permitted "on-site" commercial billboards.

The Court struck down the ordinances, in part, on the ground that part of the scheme constituted an unreasonable burden on free speech, offering greater protection for commercial speech than noncommercial.

The use of the police power--whether or not through a local zoning ordinance--to require a private property owner to maintain a historic building (whether a landmark or as part of a historic district) is a fairly strong measure to accomplish what is a welfare (hardly health and safety) goal. Yet the cases are legion in support of such police power regulation, provided the owner is left with some economic use, and provided the designation process is done equitably. The activities of the National Trust for Historic Preservation have assumed greater significance over the past decade, both as a resource for preservation litigators and as a benchmark for "listing" what is to be preserved. Finally, the private development sector has become increasingly involved in preservation for profit due to changes in the tax laws making rehabilitation and commercial use of historic structures profitable.[13]

Federal Planning: Registers, Federal Grants and Planning Requirements

The National Historic Preservation Act (NHPA) is the latest in a series of federal laws directed toward the survey and preservation of historic sites. While it continues the survey and site acquisition aspects of previous legislation, its most salient preservation feature is the requirement that federal agencies "take into account" the effects of their actions on historic sites which are either listed or eligible for listing on the National Register. An Advisory Council on Historic Preservation must be permitted to comment on the proposed action. The National Register of Historic Places is maintained by the Secretary of the Department of the Interior, from sites nominated by various groups. It contains those historic resources, districts, sites, buildings, structures, and objects significant in American history, architecture, archaeology, or culture. NHPA buys time for a site. While there is no legal requirement that the federal agency involved abandon its undertaking even if the Council strenuously objects, Register listing makes it difficult for federal action to proceed.

States Laws: Registry and Preservation Through Incentives

With few exceptions, state historic protection schemes were and are responsive to, or mirror, the federal technique of listing and requiring some sort of notification to state agencies when a "listed structure" is to be altered or demolished, often through linkage to state environmental impact assessment laws. States have also enacted enabling legislation permitting (but not requiring) local government to regulate historic structures and districts under the police power, and often through local zoning and ordinances.

Local Government Plans and Historic Building

While early cases tended to support designation of historic sites by qualified public bodies, accompanied by limited restriction on alteration of visible facades, the extent to which the police power could be used to prevent the owner of such a site or structure from altering or demolishing it was not altogether clear until the recent U.S. Supreme Court decision in Penn Central Transportation Co. v. City of N.Y. 438 U.S. 104 (1978). There, the Court upheld a New York City ordinance which severely restricted the development potential of Grand Central Station solely on its historic significance. The Court recounted those aspects of the regulatory scheme which made it defensible: expertise and due process in both the selection of historic sites and the grant (or refusal) of the "certificate of appropriateness" for exterior modifications of demolition; economic viability of the site in its present condition; availability of tax relief for designated properties; and ability of the private owner to transfer air development rights to nearby properties which it also owned.

While this scheme may not be the only constitutionally permissible method of regulating historic sites, it has the imprimatur of the nation's highest Court. The process for designation includes a general survey and identification of those sites to be preserved--a historic "plan". Moreover, once designated, the owner must submit plans for any demolition or exterior (facade) modification to an expert commission. The commission may then decide that the proposed plans, if executed, would have no effect, that the effect would nevertheless be "appropriate," or that the plans are such that no approval will be forthcoming.

Planning for Infrastructure and Amenities: Promotion and Provision for Planning Gain-Type Improvements Through Planning Law Devices

New Development, the Subdivision Plan, and Subdivision Exactions

The regulation of land and the requiring of public improvements via the subdivision process is a relatively modern land use control technique.[14] The modern subdivision ordinance developed from local responses to so-called "plat acts," whereby it was declared to be legislative policy that no parcels should be divided and sold without the filing of a "plat"--a scaled drawing of the parcel showing the division or divisions into which it had been carved. The purpose of such plat acts was to aid "conveyancing," or the process of buying and selling land. As a conveyancing tool, the subdivision plats were a huge success. As a land development tool, they were often an unmitigated disaster. Larger subdivisions with many lots often were poorly planned both internally and externally in relation to adjacent parcels. Major streets in one subdivision could--and did--often lead directly into minor streets in another, and some streets simply failed to link with other parallel streets altogether.

This and other design and public facility shortcomings led to the enactment of state subdivision enabling legislation permitting local communities to adopt subdivision codes to deal with these problems. At first, the subdivision ordinances dealt primarily with an increasing volume of so-called design standards: width and composition of streets and sidewalks, perimeter linkage, uniformity of building setback, and the like. From the design and location of new public facilities it was an easy step to require their construction as a condition of subdivision approval. Next followed the mandatory showing of open space and public building sites on subdivision plats. The next step was more problematic: the required "dedication" of such park, public building, and school sites to the public, without compensation. The theory was much the same as that supporting public improvement dedication/requirements: if an owner sought to develop property so as to add to the local population, he should provide a share of the park, school, and public building needs thereby generated. If the subdivision were too small to generate the need for a "whole" site, then cash would do, to be paid to a fund for the purchase of such a site. Recent cases have upheld such mandatory dedication schemes, whether or not the dedication of land is required to fill a need attributable to the developer being asked to make the dedication or contribution.

Old Development in Urban Areas

Tax increment financing. Tax Increment Financing (TIF), often called tax "allocation" financing, has emerged as one of the more popular devices for financing parts of urban renewal and redevelopment schemes. One municipal agency or corporation pledges all or a portion of the incremental tax revenue generated by a public improvement to finance the cost of a project that has been created and initially paid for by a second agency. The amount pledged is generally derived from the *ad valorem* property taxes (rates) within the improvement district, and the incremental value thus accrued and reflected in the *ad valorem* property tax pays off bonds issued by the developing agency. This device is particularly popular among local and federally funded development agencies that must undertake major redevelopment projects. No new taxes are levied or collected. The burden is spread over an extended period of time and falls upon whichever general purpose government is pledging the increments (or a portion thereof) created by the redevelopment.[15]

Enterprise Zones. The recently introduced Enterprise Zone Tax is modeled roughly on England's enterprise zone legislation. It provides for a series of tax reductions for businesses and their employees who locate or relocate in certain economically and physically deteriorated areas. These areas, called enterprise zones, would be designated by the Secretary of the Department of Housing and Urban Development (HUD) upon application of a local government. HUD contemplates a "competition" among local government applicants for a limited number of available designations: 25 per year for 3 years. Potential enterprise zones must meet the same eligibility requirements as those receiving Urban Development Action Grants.[16] Upon designation, employers would be allowed tax credits equal to 5 to 50 percent of wages paid to eligible zone employees. Enterprise zone firms would be eligible for elimination of capital gains tax, an increase in tax credits for investments in the zone, and an extended loss carryover. Zone employees would be eligible for an income tax credit equal to 5 percent of their qualified wages. Provisions are also included for regulatory relief and the establishment of foreign trade zones.

From the perspective of land use policy, the most critical provision of the bills is that part contemplating a local government "contract" to do its share of reducing local government barriers to business investment. Among other suggested "incentives" (real property tax holiday, foreign trade zones, etc.) is the suggestion that local governments virtually do away with land use controls within the zone.

Urban Fringe/Rural Areas

Land banks. A few areas in the United States have begun to experiment with "land banks." Essentially a method of holding land or interests in land for indefinite--though presumably public--reasons, land banks have long been used in Scandinavia and elsewhere to implement land planning. Principally utilized for land reform purposes in the United States, the principal problem associated with the concept is the use of eminent domain (compulsory purchase) to acquire the land by a governmental agency. Since the recent U.S. Supreme Court decision in HHA v. Midkiff, 104 S. Ct. 2321 (1984) has virtually done away with judicial evaluation of the U.S. Constitution's Fifth Amendment requirement that private property only be taken for a public purpose, the legal obstacles to land banking have virtually disappeared.[17]

Refusal to extend city services. The dual role of many local governments as provider of utility, road, and other "infrastructure" services necessary for urban development has logically led to the attempt to control fringe and rural development (especially outside present local government boundaries) by controlling the extension of service to these areas. Refusal to extend utility (water) service to an area planned for no-growth outside Boulder, Colorado, was struck down by a state Supreme Court in 1976, in part on the ground that the City could not use its utility power (it was the sole water source in the region) to implement its land development plan. However, it is possible that if the service is merely delayed according to a reasonable development plan, a "temporary" refusal--even if potentially decades long--might work.[18] Increasingly, services and other development matters such as applicable zoning are dealt with by Development or Preannexation Agreements between developers and local government, usually under the auspices of state statutes (California, Illinois), similar to the United Kingdom's Section 52 Agreements.[19]

FOOTNOTES

1. See Haar, "In Accordance With a Comprehensive Plan", 68 Harv. L. Rev. 1154 (1955); The Standard State Zoning Enabling Act, U.S. Dept. of Commerce (1922).

2. Kozesnik v. Twp. of Montgomery 131 A.2d 1, (1957).

3. See, F. Bosselman and D. Callies, The Quiet Revolution in Land Use Controls, 1972. D. Mandelker, "The Role of the Comprehensive Plan in Land Use Regulation", 74 Mich. L. Rev. 900 (1976).

4. See, D. Callies, Regulating Paradise: Land Use Controls in Hawaii, 1984; D. Mandelker, Environmental and Land Use Controls Legislation, 1979, Ch. VII, P. Myers, Zoning Hawaii, 1976.

5. Hawaii Rev. Stat. Sec. 226-1 to -105 (Supp. 1980).

6. See, for more detailed treatment of the ELMS Act, R. Healy and J. Rosenberg, Land Use and the States, 1979, Ch. 5.

7. See, for a more thorough discussion of the Vermont legislation, R. Healy and J. Rosenberg, Land Use and the States, 1976, at Ch. 3.

8. See, for detailed analyses of the Oregon system, J. Leonard, Managing Oregon's Growth: The Politics of Development Planning, 1983.

9. See, Finell, "Coastal Zone Management: An Introduction" and "The Federal Regulatory Role in Coastal Zone Management" 1978 Am. Bar Foundation Research J. 153 and 169.

10. See, R. Liroff, Air Pollution Offsets, 1980.

11. Federal Water Pollution Control Act, 33 USC Sec. 1251 et seq. See, Goldfar, "Water Quality Management Planning: The Fate of 208," 8 Toledo L. Rev. 105 (1976).

12. E.g., State of Missouri ex rel. Stoyanoff v. Berkeley, 458 S.W.2d 305 (1970).

13. See, C. Duerksen, A Handbook on Historic Preservation Law, 1983, Ch. 7.

14. Freilich and Levi, Model Subdivision Regulations, Text and Commentary, 1975.

15. Burnside, "Tax Increment Financing: 'Rational Basis' or 'Revenue Shell Game'?" 22 Urb. L. Ann. 28 (1981); Molinaro, "Tax Increment Financing" 30 De Paul L. Rev. 459 (1981).

16. a. Unemployment at 1.5 times the national average.
    b. Twenty percent of the potential residential population "in poverty."
    c. Seventy percent of the potential residents with incomes below eighty percent of the median income of the area as a whole.
    d. Ten percent population loss.
    e. Abandonment and blight.

17. Callies, "A Requiem for Public Purpose: HHA v. Midkiff" Proceedings of the Institute on Planning, Zoning and Eminent Domain, Southwestern Legal Foundation, 1985.

18. See, Golden v. Planning Board of Town of Ramapo, 30 N.Y.2d 359, 205 N.E.2d 291 (1972).

19. See, Holliman, "Development Agreements and Vested Rights in California," 13 The Urban Lawyer 44 (1981).

POSITIVE PLANNING IN THE UNITED KINGDOM

London Sessions
ABA Annual Meeting 1985
Orchid Room, Dorchester Hotel
London, England

Tuesday, July 16, 1985
10:00 A.M. - 12:00 Noon

Prof. Jeffrey Jowell
2 Hare Court
Temple, London EC4Y 7BH

and

Peter J. Purton
Norton, Rose, Botterell & Roche
Kempson House
Camomile Street
London EC3A 7AN

The twin instruments of development plans and development control were instituted in 1947 as the principal tools of British Town and Country planning.[1] While successful as techniques of negative control for inhibiting undesirable development, they have had mixed success as instruments of positive planning to encourage and facilitate desired development. This paper will begin by looking at development plans and development control and then go on to look at the more recent techniques of positive planning.

Development Plans

Development planning is the central policy document in the British planning system. It contains the policies and proposals for the future, guiding development and coordinating investment activity in the public and private sector.

From 1947-1968, the development plan was--or became--a relatively detailed and precise document "indicating the manner" in which the local planning authority proposed that land in their area be used. The development plan had to be scrutinised by central government and then approved. These "old style" plans, based on fairly precise site allocation and designations, became too rigid, and in 1968 a new, more flexible two-tier system was introduced, consisting of _structure plans_ and _local plans_.[2]

Structure Plans

These plans are written statements containing issues of strategic policy for county authorities.[3] To avoid rigidity and to keep their broad perspective, they are not based on ordnance survey maps but on diagrams. An explanatory memorandum (formerly a "written justification") summarises the reasons for the policies and general proposals contained in the statement. After a survey of the area and the formulation of policy alternatives, the draft (having been submitted to public participation) is studied (in whole or in part) by the central government minister known as the Secretary of State for the Environment at an "examination in public" and then modified, approved, or rejected by him.

Does the structure plan form the basis of positive planning? The Plans Regulations require an authority to include in the explanatory memorandum such indications as it may think appropriate of the "regard" they have had to "social consideration," but structure plans have never quite been able to escape a preoccupation with physical planning, location, containment of growth, and arrangement of buildings. The 1968 inquiry into the old-style development plans by the Planning Advisory Group encouraged authorities to take into account social as well as physical policies, and to examine the impact of their policies on different groups in the population. In practice, however, the Secretary of State has greatly limited the extent to which structure plans themselves should attempt to influence or dictate broader social policy.

Nevertheless, some structure plans have sought to achieve some coordination of public sector policy, but most have fallen foul of the different planning timescales of different public sector activities and the uncertainty in recent years of long-term investment planning at a time of low growth.

Local Plans

These plans (known in London as district plans) are intended to develop and refine the policies of structure plans (to which they must conform) and to elaborate in detail how they relate to individual areas and sites. Drafted mostly by the lower-tier authority, they provide a detailed basis for development control and the coordination of development and other land use. While resembling the old-style development plans in that the main document is a proposals map as well as a written statement, a local plan is not a zoning system as such but more a mix of general policies for the whole area and specific proposals confined to identified areas of land, including allocations of land for future development. Local plans may be general ("district plans"), or may relate to areas selected for a development programme ("action area plans"), or deal with selected issues such as recreation, mineral extraction, or green belt (known as "subject plans").

Like structure plans, local plans have tended to be restricted to traditional land use considerations, including conservation. A recent district plan of the Westminster Council in London contained a policy that encouraged applications for planning permissions for new industrial floor space and the creation of new industrial employment. This plan went on to protect "specific industrial activities" of long-established firms such as the leather, fur, paper, and printing firms, the loss of which it was felt would threaten the viability of other important London activities. This policy was challenged on the grounds that its scope was wider than traditional land-use, that it verged on social engineering, and was based upon the irrelevant consideration of concern not with the use of land but with the protection of particular occupiers. The House of Lords, however, upheld the plan, Lord Scarman refusing to concede that questions such as the character of a community could be ignored in planning control. As he put it: "It would be inhuman pedantry to exclude from the control of our environment the human factor."[4]

The statutory plans outlined above are often supplemented by informal, nonstatutory guidelines, known in the trade as "bottom-drawer plans." These are frequently wider-ranging than the scope of structure and local plans has traditionally allowed. However, the Westminster case held invalid that section of the district plan that postponed consideration of exceptional circumstances under which office permission might be given to later nonstatutory guidance. This case restricts the scope of informal plans, but to what extent is not yet clear.

Planning permission must, in Britain, be sought from a local authority which has a choice whether to grant it and the power to name the terms on which it will grant it. In dealing with the application, the authority "shall have regard to the provisions of the development plan," (to which they need not "slavishly adhere") and to "any other material considerations." Where permission is granted, the authority may impose "such conditions as they think fit."[5] An applicant may appeal a refusal or condition to the Secretary of State through written procedures or a public inquiry.

Local authorities, and the Secretary of State on appeal, thus have wide discretion to grant or refuse planning permission, and as to the conditions that they may attach. To what extent is this discretion exercised so as to use development control as an instrument of positive planning, rather than a negative, policing exercise? To what extent is it a means of facilitating or providing needed development, rather than simply preventing the undesirable?

It is here that the courts enter the picture, as an aggrieved person may appeal for judicial determination as to what may be a "material" consideration, or what constrains the imposition of conditions. The courts have laid down three tests: (1) that the decision must not be "unreasonable" (in the sense of being arbitrary); (2) that any condition must "fairly and reasonably relate" to the application; and (3) that the decision furthers a "planning" purpose.[6]

The first test supports a general principle of administrative law that only permits judicial interference with official decisions that are somewhat capricious. It has been used, for example, to strike down a condition attached to a grant of permission that required the applicant to provide infrastructure (an access road) at his own expense,[7] and to nullify a grant of permission for private housing that required the developer to offer tenancies to people on the Council's own waiting list.[8]

The requirement that the condition "fairly and reasonably relate" to the application prevents an authority from using the occasion of the developer's application for permission on one site to control his operations--through a condition--on another site. In a leading case, an application for change of use did not allow the authority to require the building's demolition after a period, as a way of ridding the area of unsightly buildings.[9]

The third test, that the decision furthers "planning" goals, throws into relief the problem of positive planning. If courts are to strike down as "nonmaterial" criteria that serve to pursue purposes broader than the traditional land-use, then the facilitating powers of authorities would be greatly limited. In the past, the courts have indeed not permitted planning powers to be used (to provide access roads, or public housing) where other powers (involving also the payment of compensation to the owner for land actually acquired for the purpose) existed to achieve these ends.[10] Recently, however, the courts have permitted refusals of permission in order to protect existing uses or local jobs.[11] In addition, Ministerial circulars have suggested that planning be somewhat more helpful to industrial and commercial development.

A Circular, which is in effect a nonstatutory guideline, does not compel a planning authority to follow a particular course of action. It is supervisory rather than interventionist, seeking consistency in the application of the policy or practices from those to whom it is directed.

Each Circular is unique in tone, style, and content. Guidance may be vague and general or direct and precise. Because a Circular is an extra-statutory device, its contents while generally persuasive remain subject to the planning authority's discretion, although the Minister may have the last word on an appeal to him.

Circulars which have reflected a positive approach include:

- Circular No. 22/80 - Development Control - Policy and Practice. This Circular makes it clear that the "planning system should play a helpful part in rebuilding the economy." Local authorities are asked "to facilitate development." Outside of conserved areas, the presumption should be in favour of development, and aesthetic control abandoned. Under the heading of "Planning and business activity" the Circular states that "the Government wants to make sure that the planning system is as positive and as helpful as it can be to investment in industry and commerce and to the development industry." Priority with regard to development applications received by local authorities is to be given to those proposals which "will contribute most to national and local economic activity." Housing and small business development is singled out for especially favourable treatment.

- Circular No. 9/81. This Circular details the effect of the General Development (Amendment) Order 1981, which removes from detailed planning control much minor development which does not affect public amenity. "Planning authorities should not, when granting planning permission for new development, seek to remove permitted development rights other than in exceptional cases where sound planning reasons necessitate tighter than normal controls."

- Circular No. 15/84 - Land for Housing. This Circular emphasises the need for adequate supply of housing land to satisfy demand. "The planning system must continue to identify, bring forward and permit the development of sufficient new land for housing, taking account of market demand and other housing requirements. Sites must not only be free, or easily freed, from planning, physical and ownership constraints but also be capable of being developed economically."

Planning by Agreement

In the early 1970s, a time of huge increases in land values, it became clear that local authorities were by-passing the development control procedure described above and instead negotiating with applicants for planning permission for a "planning gain"--namely, a benefit not financially rewarding to the applicant and which would have been unlawful as a "material consideration" or condition in the normal way. Thus, agreements were struck to provide access roads, walkways, to build community centres, to cease nonconforming uses on other sites, and even to dedicate land for public housing.[12] Because they were agreements, and not imposed by the normal regulatory process, they could not be challenged by the applicant or successor in title.

Planning agreements thus became a favoured way of achieving positive results out of a planning application. The high increase in land value occasioned by the grant of planning permission usually gave the developer some margin of profit to dispose back to the "community." After the property bubble burst, however, the developer had less to give away, and some took exception to the pressures to "buy" their permission. An advisory group suggested a prescription against planning gain except where the agreement provided for infrastructure without which the development could not proceed, or when the application contained "mixed" elements, where losses could be offset against gains.[13]

Planning agreements are still pursued, often to the benefit of the developer, authority, and public, but a recent Circular--Circular 22/83-Planning Gain--attempts to advise on their scope providing that "a wholly unacceptable development should not be permitted just because of extraneous benefits offered by the developer." Nor should an applicant's need for permission be treated as an opportunity to enact an "extraneous benefit" or a "payment for the ratepayers at large."

Enterprise Zones

Special areas known as Enterprise Zones have been created in order to reverse urban decline, to attract commercial activity to depressed areas, and to produce a climate which can attract private enterprise and a return of prosperity to such areas. Although a limited amount of public investment is required to create an Enterprise Zone, the underlying objective is to generate private investment. £157 million has been invested in the existing 23 designated zones (£120 million from private sources).

There are four major incentives provided in Enterprise Zones:

- Exemption from local taxation (rates;
- Full capital allowance against Corporation and Income Tax for capital spending on industrial and commercial buildings S.74 Finance Act 1980);

- A simplified planning system incorporating automatic planning permission for development which conforms with the defined terms of the scheme; and

- Exemption from Development Land Tax (S.110 Finance Act 1980) within 10 years of designation.

An Enterprise Zone is created by invitation from the Secretary of State to a planning authority to prepare a draft scheme specifying the suggested area which may be designated as an Enterprise Zone for a period of up to 10 years. An Enterprise Zone allows private capital to be invested in the community within broad objectives that have been framed by the planning authority. Another positive aspect of the Enterprise Zone is certainty for developers that if a proposed development is within the defined scope of the Enterprise Zone, planning permission will be forthcoming. Against the positive aspects of an Enterprise Zone is set the criticism that they have the potential to blight development in adjoining areas.

A recent example illustrates the effectiveness of the Enterprise Zone. A private developer in partnership with the London Docklands Development Corporation has produced Lanterns' Court--the first development of small industrial units completed in the London Enterprise Zone. Already more than half of the units have been reserved on a 24-year lease at £3.75 per square foot.

Urban Development Corporations

Urban Development Corporations (whose objective is to regenerate urban areas) arise following designation by the Secretary of State--a decision made without consultation with the planning authority. The Urban Development Corporation consists of nominated members appointed by the Secretary of State as opposed to elected members who make up a planning authority--a cause for criticism by some.

Land which is already vested in public ownership is transferred to the Corporation. Privately owned land may be subject to compulsory purchase. The objective is to attract industry and commerce and to provide a balanced community with housing and social facilities. An Urban Development Corporation has wide powers for the acquisition and disposal of land, buildings and other operations and may generally do anything necessary or expedient in order to accomplish this objective.

Proposals for the development of land within an Urban Development Area are submitted to the Secretary of State, who after consultation only with the planning authority may approve the proposals incorporating any appropriate modification. The Secretary of State may make a Special Development Order (see below) granting automatic planning permission for development which complies with such proposals.

Unless the Secretary of State stipulates to the contrary, the planning authority is unable to influence the type of permitted development, although development not permitted by such Special Development Order still requires an application to be submitted to the planning authority in the usual way. The power for the Secretary of State to make an order under which the Urban Development Corporation overrides the powers of local government and undertakes the role of development control authority for the area has attracted opposition from local government.

The success of the first two Urban Development Corporations (London's Dockland and Merseyside) has been undermined by the resistance of the planning authorities affected. The aim of improving the economic and social conditions in a depressed community appears attractive on paper but such demarcation disputes may produce negative results in other areas of planning policy and decision.

Simplified Planning Zones

This is prospective initiative which has yet to be implemented. It seems to be a "natural extension" to the Enterprise Zone. Again the underlying principle is to encourage development in depressed areas.

A Simplified Planning Zone would arise from a plan published by the planning authority showing the boundaries of the Zone and specifying development for which planning permission would be granted and any conditions or limitations which would be attached (confined to those satisfying health and safety requirements and the protection of the surrounding environment). Public participation would be an integral part of the process. One objective would be to remove the adversarial treatment of development proposals which are in conflict with local policies. But Simplified Planning Zones are not designed to undermine development control in areas where restraint and intervention are necessary. Also by relieving the existing congested system more time will be available for considering controversial applications.

Simplified Planning Zones would also allow local authorities to encourage development where ownership of the land is vested in the private sector, hence avoiding the expenditure and delay incurred through the acquisition of land and the preparation of sites for development. The Government believes Simplified Planning Zones will provide "a means for local authorities to make more positive use of the planning system."

Special Development Order

Under Section 24 of the Town and Country Planning Act 1971, the Secretary of State has power to create such orders. These provide for the automatic grant of planning permission for specified development without need for the normal application, e.g., development in new towns, national parks, and areas of outstanding natural beauty. Following submission of a proposal by the planning authority, the Government (through the negative resolution procedure in Parliament) authorises the order.

An example is the New Town Special Development Order, which grants permission for any development carried out by a development corporation pursuant to proposals approved by the Secretary of State under S. 31(1) of the New Towns Act (1965).

A special Development Order allows for construction which will not conflict with conservation or other restraints on development but will "stimulate development by providing the developer with the prospect of speed and certainty of decision with the minimum of red tape."

Architectural Competitions

As part of a Government initiative to achieve improved standards of architectural design, Government Development Agencies, new towns, and regional development corporations are required to organise at least one architectural competition each year. Recent examples have included the EFFRA site at Vauxhall Bridge on the South Bank of the River Thames and the proposed extension to the National Gallery in Trafalgar Square.

With the EFFRA site, the planning authority compiled a planning brief indicating the acceptable range and style of development. But the Secretary of State offered the developers an opportunity to bypass the planning authority's intervention by suggesting that if the scheme was submitted as a contender in the architectural competition he would "call-in" the resulting planning application and grant the required consent. To ensure that his enticement became a reality for the developers, the Secretary of State made a Special Development Order for the site. As a consequence of the delay and controversy, the developer withdrew and eventually collapsed financially. For the National Gallery site, the scheme was awarded in principle but the conditions of compliance laid down by the Secretary of State are such that the proposal seems to have ground to a halt.

In theory, architectural competitions may encourage a positive attitude by developers to submit proposals which are ambitious and progressive. But each competition requires substantial financial resources, and architectural talent does not always go hand in hand with such resources. Architectural competitions are no guarantee of excellence in the urban environment. There is also no guarantee of consent.

Development Boards

Development Boards (alternatively known as Enterprise Boards) are public sector development bodies providing equity and loan finance to firms situated within a local authority's area for a stated period of time--usually 10 years. The aim is to ensure that selected companies can survive and expand.

One example is the West Midlands Enterprise Board funded by a grant authorised under Section 137 of the Local Government Act 1972. Its policy is to assist companies independent of large groups. A company wishing to take advantage of the scheme provides the Board with a business plan which (if acceptable to the Board) results in investment by the Board under the terms of a planning and investment agreement.

Action Areas

Action Areas arise under a local action area plan prepared by the planning authority. Classification as an action area confers a programme of comprehensive treatment by development, redevelopment, or improvement within a prescribed period. In addition to the objective of producing a positive improvement in areas where planning action is required there is the additional factor of achieving the stated results by a specified date. This intention has recently been emphasised by the Secretary of State when he declared that action areas "are envisaged for early treatment, early development, redevelopment and improvement."

An illustration of the progressive mood that an action area plan should reflect is the Woolwich Action Area Plan. The three main policies that form the basis of the plan are: (1) to increase office and industrial development; (2) to increase shopping floorspace; and (3) to improve the environment.

FOOTNOTES

1. Town & Country Planning Act, 1947.

2. By the Town & Country Planning Act, 1968, now consolidated as the Town & Country Planning Act, 1971, as amended.

3. Since 1974, England has been divided into two-tier authorities, the upper tier being the County and the lower tier the District. Metropolitan Counties are, at the time of writing, threatened with extinction.

4. Great Portland Estates plc v. Westminster City Council [1984] 3 All E.R. 744 at 750.

5. Town & Country Planning Act, 1971, S.29(1).

6. These tests were spelled out in Newbury D.C. v. Secretary of State for the Environment [1981] A.C. 578.

7. Hall v. Shoreham-by-Sea U.D.C. [1964] 1 All E.R. 1.

8. R. v. London Borough of Hillingdon ex p Royco Homes Ltd [1974] 2 W.L.R. 805.

9. Newbury case, above, note 6.

10. Hall case, above, note 7.

11. Clyde & Co v. Secretary of State for the Environment [1977] 1 W.L.R. 926.

12. Under the powers of S.52 of the Town & Country Planning Act, 1971 and S.33 of the Local Government (Miscellaneous Provisions) Act, 1982, as well as local acts. See J. Jowell "Bargaining in Development Control" (1977) Journal of Planning Law, 414.

13. The Property Advisory Group, PLANNING GAIN (1981).

FOREIGN INVESTMENT IN THE UNITED STATES:
WILL AND TRUST PLANNING FOR FOREIGNERS' INVESTMENTS

London Sessions
ABA Annual Meeting 1985
Ballroom 2, Hilton International
London, England

Tuesday, July 16, 1985
2:00 P.M. - 4:00 P.M.

Robert A. Hendrickson
200 Park Avenue
New York, New York 10166

Anyone who tries to navigate this topic--or half of it--in 3,000 words or less, as suggested by the Chairman, is forever poised between the tip of an iceberg and a cliche. As Harold Macmillan wrote in Winds of Change, he must write "as a banker writes, touching only the needful"--and then make big cuts in the needful.

This paper is written from the point of view of the foreign investor's U.S. adviser. It is intended to be complementary to, and fit together with, the advice the foreign investor receives from his adviser abroad, personified here today by Mr. George M. H. McLoughlin.

In general, these comments apply not only to a foreigner's investment in U.S. real estate, but to his other kinds of U.S. investment as well--an asset or business in corporate form, a partnership venture, works of art, passive portfolio investments in stocks and other securities, bank accounts, certificates of deposit, mutual funds, insurance policies, and so on.

This morning's paper, "Foreign Investment in U.S. Real Estate: The Non-Tax Essentials" concluded that the foreign investor should customarily not take title to U.S. real property in his own name.

In whatever legal structure his U.S. investment is packaged when he acquires it, the nonresident alien of the United States--hereafter a "foreigner"--should consider how it is to be managed currently, what happens to it in the event of his own disability or death, and the U.S. income, gift, estate and generation skipping tax consequences, and other costs. The context of U.S. nontax and tax law is superimposed on his own domiciliary nontax and tax law, and the law imposed by treaties, and of reciprocity, conflict of laws and comity, so lifetime estate planning is much more essential--and complicated--for him than his U.S. counterpart.

Legal structures for management of a U.S. investment familiar to the common law and recognized in all states of the United States include a power of attorney, a will, and one or another of the several kinds of inter vivos personal trusts. In the United States, it is state law, not U.S. federal law, that governs such structures and property rights generally. One state's law may or may not be significantly different from that of any other. In every case, the foreign investor's representative should check the state law of each state in which, for both nontax and tax purposes, the foreigner's U.S. investment might be claimed to be situated.

Situs of Property

The situs of the foreigner's U.S. investment depends on the legal classification of the property for conflict of laws or tax purposes. For purposes of lifetime and probate administration, situs may differ from situs for purposes of U.S. federal income, gift and estate, and foreign taxation. As everywhere, real property owned outright is deemed to be located where it is physically situated. Tangibles such as automobiles, works of art, and personal effects, and intangibles, such as stocks, bonds, and other securities, bank accounts, etc., are for some purposes (such as taxation) deemed to be situated where the owner is domiciled at the time of his death, for other purposes (such as probate administration), where the physical evidence--the certificate or the bank--is situated. The Uniform Probate Code, in effect in some states, sets forth still other situs rules for administration of property: commercial and investment paper and other such instruments are deemed located where the instrument is situated, while other debts are situated where the debtor resides, or maintains its principal office.

The Durable Power of Attorney

The simplest management structure is a power of attorney from the foreigner to a local attorney-in-fact, giving the latter authority to deal with the U.S. investment property. It is often accompanied by a "side letter" setting forth the circumstances in which it is to become effective. It may operate on securities or other assets left in a bank or stock broker's custodian account, in an anonymous nominee's name. In most states it may be "durable" and remain in effect even when the foreign principal becomes incompetent or disabled, but the attorney's power to act under it terminates upon the principal's death. A "power coupled with an interest" is recognized, but rarely practicable. Third parties, such as custodians, banks, or stock transfer agents with whom any attorney-in-fact must deal, sometimes refuse to recognize his authority when the date is stale, or without formal proof that the foreign principal is still alive at the moment action is to be taken.

Without some such arrangement, upon an allegation by a creditor or next of kin that the foreign owner is disabled, incapacitated, incompetent, too long absent, or simply showing poor judgment handling his U.S. investment, a court may appoint a conservator, committee, guardian or guardian ad litem with respect to the U.S. investment. The proceeding is upon notice, but the appointment may be made without the foreigner's consent, or even over his objection. Court procedures with respect to the foreigner's investment property can result in unwanted loss of control, uncertainty, complexity, publicity, delay, and expense. They vary widely from state to state.

Wills and Probate Administration

When a foreign investor dies, leaving property in the U.S. in his own name, the principal estate administration proceeding would be at his domicile, say in England. An ancillary proceeding may have to be instituted to probate his will in the county of the state of the United States where his investment property is deemed to be situated. One difficulty with an ancillary proceeding is that ancillary assets are required to be remitted to the place of domiciliary administration, a result the foreigner would often prefer to avoid. An alternative to such conventional linkage of domiciliary and ancillary probate and administration under a single domiciliary will is a domiciliary will to operate only upon non-U.S. property, and one or more separate wills for original nondomiciliary probate in one or another of the states where the U.S. investment is situated. Such a U.S. will would dispose of the U.S. investment asset directly to beneficiaries, without remission to the U.K. domiciliary administration. Whether or not there is an organized domiciliary administration, his U.S. nondomiciliary will can stand alone.

If the foreigner's spouse or other relative is a nonresident noncitizen of the state where the property is situated, such person is usually ineligible to qualify as executor under his local will, or as an administrator, ancillary fiduciary, committee, conservator, or guardian. Where there is no effective will disposing of the foreigner's U.S. investment, a local probate court may appoint a stranger, or the local public administrator, to administer the foreigner's U.S. assets.

Inter Vivos Trusts

The American investor in the United States is confronted by no such context of complexity as confronts the foreign investor, but to avoid probate and for other reasons, Americans often place substantial investment assets in the name of an inter vivos trust. Such a trust provides effective management of the investment during the owner's life. It serves as a power of attorney substitute in the event of his disability, incapacity, or absence. It also serves as a will substitute for noncourt disposition of his investment after his death. As a substitute for both a power of attorney and a will, an inter vivos trust is likely to be more effective, confidential, and flexible than either.

Any type of trust may have its situs in the state of the United States where the investment is situated, or in another state, or in a foreign country, provided such country's legal system recognizes the validity of common law trusts. It may be a "mobile trust," changing its situs at any time, or from time to time, from one jurisdiction to another, for example to escape a local threat, or simply for the convenience of the parties. It may have as its trustee or successors the grantor alone, or a disinterested individual, or both, or a bank, or any combination. It may provide for an unlimited number of future changes and contingencies. If it is revocable, or ultimately for charitable purposes, its existence may be perpetual. If, or after it becomes irrevocable, it may continue for 100 years or more--lives in being at the time it becomes irrevocable plus 21 years--or plus 30 years, if South Dakota law governs.

Protective Features of Trust Ownership of Foreigner's Investment

A will must be publicly probated in court, the very existence of a corporation depends on an official filing in a public office, and publicly filed business certificates are required of limited and general partnerships and proprietorships. But in the case of a trust, no evidence of the trust's existence may ever need to be filed in a U.S. court or other public office. The trust must file for a U.S. tax identification number for trust tax returns. The trust's filing may or may not include a copy of the trust instrument. Filing is routine, and kept strictly confidential by U.S. law. There are already so many trusts in the United States that their very commonplaceness provides a measure of anonymity for the law-abiding foreigner that may serve him better, as a practical matter, than any bank secrecy laws of an exotic foreign tax haven. Such foreign tax haven contacts may only create unwelcome suspicions on the part of U.S. authorities.

Even a fully revocable trust provides some lifetime protection and insulation of the foreigner's asset, and the foreigner himself, from claims of creditors, spouses, heirs at law, and even tort and contract claimants. More is provided by a conditionally revocable trust. The trustee can properly seek protective court adjudication of any claims against the trust. Any recovery is usually limited to the value of the trusteed property. Trustee ownership can protect the foreigner's investment during his life and after his death against claims that it has become community property through commingling, or is subject to equitable distribution, or to a spousal elective share or usufruct, or forced shares in issue or parents, or certain foreign claims, such as foreign tax judgments, or for support arising out of foreign matrimonial disputes, or foreign exchange control claims. The trust's administrative provisions may include authorizations that give the trustee complete flexibility to deal with all tax and other planning options--income/principal allocations, reserve funds for contingencies, tax cost basis distributions, etc. Trust ownership (even by a "revocable" trust) may cause foreign tax authorities to regard distributions of principal from it as not taxable under foreign tax laws, even though it has income. Placing the foreigner's U.S. investment in a trust involves a moderate amount of immediate and ongoing inconvenience, expense, and "red tape" but the advantages often outweigh the disadvantages.

Foreign Situs or U.S. Situs Trust?

Many a foreigner wishes to have as little formal legal involvement with the United States as possible, other than ownership of the U.S. investment itself. For U.S. income tax purposes, a trust will be considered a foreign trust if it is administered outside the United States, its trustee is foreign and, if corporate, has no branches in the United States; the trust's assets are kept outside the United States; the trust is formed in and governed by the law of a foreign jurisdiction; and it has no U.S. investment adviser with unfettered investment discretion.

In a typical arrangement, the foreign situs trust holds and votes the shares of a non-U.S. or U.S. domestic corporation. The corporation in turn carries out the foreigner's investment activities in the United States. The foreign trust may also hold title to the foreigner's U.S. investment directly. Bermuda, Barbados, the Bahamas, the Cayman Islands, and Panama impose little or no income or transfer taxes, have sophisticated banking and legal facilities, and are currently favored by foreigners for siting foreign trusts to hold U.S. investments.

For U.S. tax purposes, a foreign situs trust is treated as if it were itself a nonresident alien individual. Like such individuals, it receives more favorable U.S. tax treatment than a U.S. individual. The trust's periodical gains, profits, and income (e.g., passive investment income) not effectively connected with the conduct of a U.S. trade or business is subject only to the U.S. 30-percent (or lower treaty) rate of withholding tax on remittances to it from the United States. On interest-bearing obligations payable outside the United States, received after July 18, 1984, even the U.S. 30-percent withholding requirement has been eliminated. By contrast, for U.S. persons, U.S. income tax rates reach 50 percent, and state and local income taxes may add on more percentage points.

In general, U.S.-source capital gains realized by the foreign trust, as a nonresident alien, are not subject to U.S. capital gains tax so long as the trust is not engaged in a U.S. trade or business and is not resident in the United States except to the extent that tax is imposed by the U.S. Foreign Investment in Real Property Tax Act. (U.S. rates on capital gains reach 20 percent for individuals, 28 percent for corporations). Non-U.S.-source income derived by the trust is not subject to U.S. taxes, although there may be tax withholding at source on remittances to the trust from foreign countries whose tax laws, like the United States's, requires such withholding.

A foreigner's gift of intangible personal property (not situated in the United States) to a trust is not subject to U.S. gift tax. His shares in a foreign (non-U.S.) corporation, which in turn holds U.S. investment assets, is not regarded as situated in the United States either for U.S. gift or estate tax purposes. Assuming that any U.S. tax liability of the trust is fully satisfied by withholding, the trustee of such a trust is not required to file U.S. tax or information returns. The 35-percent U.S. excise tax (Internal Revenue Code Section 1491) on unrealized gains on assets transferred to foreign entities, including foreign trusts and corporations, covers only U.S. citizens or residents, not foreigners. Thus, where all interests--grantor, trustee, and beneficiaries--are non-U.S. persons, a foreign trust for the foreigner's U.S. assets will minimize required U.S. disclosures and preserve secrecy for all parties. But where any one of the parties involved--grantor, trustee, or beneficiaries--is or becomes a U.S. person, the U.S. tax treatment of the foreign situs trust does not merely equate it with a domestic trust; the treatment is much less favorable. In such event, good tax reasons would exist to domesticate the foreign situs trust to the United States. The terms of the trust instrument can look ahead, or be amended, to cover the situation.

All foreigners, foreign trusts, and beneficiaries should obtain comprehensive tax advice before making any change from nonresident alien to resident or immigrant status, or vice versa. Any person staying in the United States for 183 days or more, over a period of three years, and any holder of a "green card," is considered a U.S. resident. There is no step up in cost basis for appreciation of a foreigner's assets before he becomes a U.S. resident.

There are practical complications and expenses involved in actually setting up and operating a foreign situs trust in one of the traditional island tax haven jurisdictions. American trust or foreign situs trust? If the foreigner's motivation to invest in the United States in the first place was its presumed safety for his capital, his motivation to place title to his investment in a foreign situs trust--a jurisdiction exposed to Grenada-like takeovers--may seem rather paradoxical.

The "Revocable" U.S. Situs Trust

A foreigner's creation and funding of a U.S. situs "revocable" trust to hold U.S. investments--or non-U.S. assets for that matter--need not necessarily have any U.S. tax consequences, though it is legally effective as a trust for nontax purposes. Such a trust provides many U.S. and state tax advantages, a lack of disadvantages, and practical economies in the handling of his investment, that may outweigh those offered by a foreign situs trust.

If the foreigner's U.S. investment generates income which, if received by a nonresident alien of the U.S., would be deemed income from sources outside the United States, or not effectively connected with the conduct of a U.S. trade or business, no U.S., state, or city income, capital gain, or personal property taxes are necessarily payable. Upon his death, no U.S. estate tax is payable on its assets not deemed U.S. situs assets. Many excellent U.S. investments are defined as non-U.S. situs assets for U.S. tax purposes, including interest bearing U.S. bank accounts, securities of foreign (non-U.S.) corporations, and shares of offshore mutual funds. On such property not deemed situated within the United States, there is, of course no U.S. withholding at source. No fiduciary income tax would normally be payable by the revocable trust itself, at least as to ordinary income. The trustee's fiduciary income tax return filings would simply refer details concerning income to the foreign grantor for him to report. The foreign grantor (if not himself a trustee) would not necessarily have any U.S. tax reporting obligation. A trust's investment "mix" of both non-U.S. and U.S. situs assets, and available deductions, credits, exemptions, and exclusions can keep the level of the foreigner's U.S. income, estate, gift, and generation skipping tax exposure, and his and the trust's actual U.S. tax liability, to any desired minimum.

The Irrevocable U.S. Situs Trust

United States and state tax laws generally treat an irrevocable, "nongrantor" trust, in the person of the trustee, as a separate taxpayer entity, required to account for and be taxed on gross income, and entitled to appropriate deductions, including a deduction for distributable net income (DNI) distributed to beneficiaries. If the trust accumulates ordinary income or realizes capital gains, to the extent that it does not distribute them, it is required to pay income tax on the accumulation. Transfer by a foreign grantor of property deemed "situated within the United States" to the irrevocable trust is subject to a U.S. gift tax, but gifts of intangibles deemed situated elsewhere, including even securities of U.S. domestic issuers, even when the certificates are physically within the U.S., are not subject to U.S. gift tax. Property held in the trust may escape U.S. estate tax in the foreigner's estate if he has retained no proscribed interests or powers. In general, a foreign grantor's trust sited in a state like New York, which is constitutionally prohibited from taxing trusts of nonresidents of New York, would not be subject to any state or local taxes.

As a separate taxpaying entity, an irrevocable trust might be effectively used to accumulate income or realize capital gains at lower (U.S., state, and local if applicable) tax rates than if the same were paid out to the grantor, or to a beneficiary who had other taxable U.S. gross income. The irrevocable trust also permits the grantor to pass trust assets when he dies from one generation to another, avoid their taxation in his own estate, and postpone or avoid some future generational or generation-skipping death taxes.

What is sometimes overlooked is that the foreigner may, if he finds it to his advantage, permit or cause his irrevocable trust to be subject to U.S. and state income, gift, and estate tax treatment in the same manner as if it were a revocable or "grantor" trust. All he need do is retain or obtain one or more rather limited or unimportant powers, while keeping the trust legally irrevocable for other, nontax purposes.

A leading civil law commentator, in the foreword of his dissertation on trusts observed:

> Rome has made a synthesis of the law of contracts; France a synthesis of the law of torts; England a synthesis of the law of fiduciary relationships. It must be believed that a fundamental synthesis requires such an amount of cleverness and tenacity that one civilization can hardly realize more than one at the same time.[1]

The most comprehensive definitions fall short of describing all of the useful functions that a common law trust may serve in a foreigner's international estate plan for his U.S. investments.

A fully orchestrated estate plan for a foreigner's U.S. investments may make use of some or all of the legal structures mentioned above in concert: a durable power of attorney with a "side letter," a custodian account, a revocable or irrevocable trust (either "standby" or fully funded), and a will for U.S. nondomiciliary probate. Ask your American lawyer for further details. A paper this short--with but a single footnote--can touch only the needful tip of the iceberg of international estate planning which is encompassed by the annexed Bibliography.

FOOTNOTES

1. J. Limpens, in the foreword to C. De Wulf, The Trust and Corresponding Institutions in Civil Law (Brussels, 1965) p. 10.

BIBLIOGRAPHY

Committee on Pre-Death Planning--General, "Legal Problems in Controlling Devolution of Property under Multi-State Trusts and Relevant Varying Situs Rules of Multiple Jurisdictions," ABA Real Property Probate and Trust Journal, 18, No. 2 Summer 1983, pp 331-406.

Dyer and Van Loon, Report on Trusts and Analogous Institutions, Document No. 1, The Hague Conference on Private International Law, May 1982.

Hendrickson, American Trusts for Non-Resident Aliens, Trusts & Estates, Vol. 123, No. 2, February 1984, pages 40-48.

Hendrickson, Choice of Law Directions for Disposing of Assets Situated Elsewhere than the Domicile of Their Owner--The Refractions of Renard, ABA Real Property, Probate and Trust Journal, Vol. 18, No. 2, Summer 1983, pp. 407-425.

Hendrickson and Silverman, Changing the Situs of a Trust, Law Journal Seminars-Press, New York, N.Y., 1982, with Supplements, 1983 and 1984.

Hendrickson and Stevens, editors, Current Legal Aspects of International Estate Planning, American Bar Association, Sections of International Law and Real Property, Probate and Trust Law, Chicago, Illinois, 1981, 472 pages.

Newton, International Estate Planning, Shepard's/McGraw-Hill, 1983, with Supplements, Appendices, and Index.

Schoenblum, Multistate and Multinational Estate Planning, 2 Volumes, Little Brown & Company, 1982, Vol. 1, 809 pages; Vol. 2 721 pages.

FOREIGN INVESTMENT IN THE UNITED STATES: WILL AND TRUST PLANNING FOR FOREIGNERS' INVESTMENTS

London Sessions
ABA Annual Meeting 1985
Ballroom 2, Hilton International
London, England

Tuesday, July 16, 1985
2:00 P.M. - 4:00 P.M.

G. Mark McLoughlin
Herbert Smith & Co.
Watling House, 35-37 Cannon Street
London EC4M 5SD

As I am of Irish descent, I am not inhibited in recalling the old story of a visitor to Ireland who asked a local the way to another town, and received the reply "To be sure, if I was going there, I wouldn't start from here." It is usually inevitable that the approach of a lawyer to the fiscal and other laws of another jurisdiction is, to some extent, influenced by his knowledge and experience of the laws and regulations of his own country. It may therefore be helpful to commence this paper by indicating what appear to be some of the factors that the American lawyer may find are relevant to the starting point of his English counterpart.

The U.K. Background

U.K. Exchange Control

The Second World War resulted in a comprehensive system of exchange controls being imposed on U.K. residents, and these controls were in force for approximately 40 years until they were suspended on the 24th of October, 1979. During most of this period, the authority for the exchange controls came from the Exchange Control Act 1947 (which largely replaced the emergency wartime Regulations) and the countless administrative notices made under the 1947 Act by the Bank of England on behalf of the Treasury.

Apart from certain types of business investment, which a commercial enterprise might be authorised to make in order to either protect its existing business or further the potential for export business, a U.K. resident only had the expectation of being authorised to acquire foreign currency to purchase either portfolio investments in foreign currency securities or a holiday home for his personal use. If an investment was authorised for such securities or a holiday home, it was necessary for it to be made with currency acquired through the investment currency pool, the premium for which constantly varied but did at times stand at 40 percent or more.

Even if a proposed inter vivos settlement of foreign currency assets was intended to be in favour of one or more U.K. residents, Bank of England consent could not have been expected unless the proposed trustees were resident within the United Kingdom or certain other Scheduled Territories. The Scheduled Territories, which were originally based on the Commonwealth countries and colonies, were restricted in 1972 to the United Kingdom, the Channel Islands, the Isle of Man, Eire, and Gibraltar. Thus the creation of a trust of land or other investments in the United States of America would rarely have been contemplated by a U.K. resident when our exchange controls were in force.

Nationality, Domicile and Residence

In relation to non-U.K. taxes, it may be important to ascertain the nationality of any person who is contemplating making an investment in the United States or creating an inter vivos settement to hold such an investment. There are many cases of people with U.S. nationality, particularly wives of U.K. nationals, who have been resident in the United Kingdom for many years, and have largely forgotten, or have never fully appreciated, the fiscal implications arising from their U.S. nationality.

However, in the United Kingdom, nationality is normally of no direct consequence to fiscal matters: although it may of course have a bearing on the question of domicile. The important factors for U.K. Revenue purposes are domicile and residence.

Generally, a person who is resident within the United Kingdom but who is domiciled outside the United Kingdom will only be liable to pay U.K. taxes on income and capital gains arising within or remitted to, the United Kingdom. Obviously, therefore, there is much scope for any nondomiciled person of wealth to gain substantial tax advantages by so organising his affairs that all his U.K. living expenses are met through remittances from original sources of capital. A person who is not domiciled (or deemed to be domiciled) within the United Kingdom may also be able to avoid any capital transfer tax liability by vesting the ownership of any assets which he wishes to acquire in an off-shore company.

It follows that it may not always be correct to assume that any U.S. tax liabilities are likely to be relieved under the U.S./U.K. double taxation treaties in relation to similar liabilities in the United Kingdom, because in the case of some U.K. residents there may be an almost complete freedom from U.K. taxes. The United Kingdom can arguably be said to be one of the greatest tax havens in the world for a person who is not domiciled within its territories, and what other tax haven has a theatre of Broadway standards?

The Usual Form of U.K. Trusts

Traditionally settlements were largely used to secure the devolution, on the basis of primogeniture, of the large landed estates, so that, in the case of a titled family, the wealth and title went hand in hand. In Victorian times, "Trader's Settlements" came into fashion so that the generator of newly acquired wealth could at least attempt to control its destination during his lifetime and/or from his grave. Of course there always were, and still are, cases where the principal motivation for trusts is a real or imagined need for the financial protection of the intended beneficiary from the consequences of the acquisition of wealth.

However, in the last half century, most trusts were created with some intention of tax avoidance. In order to obtain any income tax advantages, it normally was, and still is, necessary for the settlor and any spouse of the settlor to be excluded from actual or potential benefit, although in certain limited circumstances, the possibility of a future reversion to the settlor or a spouse has been unobjectionable. Until capital transfer tax was introduced to replace estate duty in 1975, it was essential, if a gift was to be effective for the purposes of death duties, that the settlor should thereafter be excluded from actual or potential benefit from the gifted property. The period of seven years by which the settlor had to survive the gift if it was to fall out of account for death duties would not run if the settlor was not so excluded. Thus, almost all tax avoidance trusts were irrevocable.

Provided that the settlor does not have an immediate right to continue to enjoy income, a gift in trust can now be immediately effective for capital transfer tax purposes even if the settlor is a potential beneficiary and he may therefore, in some circumstances, be able to "have his cake and eat it too" in this respect. A settlor who wants to do something about capital transfer tax mitigation may in some circumstances be advised to create either a discretionary trust or a trust which gives a person other than himself or his spouse an interest in possession in the income but confers on the trustees a power to benefit the settlor or his spouse. This may be a particularly attractive arrangement if the income of the settled fund is in practice likely to be low or nonexistent. For this and other reasons, revocable trusts have become somewhat more common in the United Kingdom since 1975, although it is probably fair to say that many professional advisers still view them with suspicion. In any event, the creation of such a trust is likely to involve payment of some capital transfer tax if the aggregate of the gifts made by the settlor over a period of 10 years (which do not qualify for some exemption) exceeds a statutory maximum (presently £64,000) and, if the trust is a sprinkler or discretionary trust, other periodic charges, at modest rates, are likely to be involved.

A Lack of Fashion in Trusts

After many years of governmental attack on the fiscal advantages to be gained from the use of trusts, their popularity in the United Kingdom has undoubtedly declined. Latterly, legislative changes have resulted in a positive balance of tax advantages to be gained in many cases from the use of trusts; but memories are liable to die hard.

It is not uncommon to find people who have reservations about the idea of trusts: trustees may have been perceived to have been uncooperative or inefficient; beneficiaries may have suffered frustration from an inability to get their hands on capital, which they have regarded as being their moral entitlement; administration costs and fees may have seemed inadequate to the persons charging them, and exorbitant to the beneficiaries; and tax liabilities may have arisen unexpectedly from laws introduced with retroactive effect. Against a general tendency during most of the period from the last World War for the tax advantages of trusts to decline, real or imagined grievances of this sort have been more inclined to give trusts a bad name. Certainly they do not seem to be so readily accepted as they are in the United States; but then many of the best English inventions seem to have been exploited to the greatest effect by other countries!

Direct Investment in the United States

The Appeal of Simplicity

For the reasons just explained, the apparent simplicity of the idea of direct investment in the United States may initially be much more appealing to some people than the use of a trust. Almost certainly, individual investors and their financial advisers do not always fully appreciate the complications and additional expense which can arise, in particular on the death of the owner of foreign property but those potentially adverse factors are comprehensively indicated in the other papers on this topic.

However, it will be clear that if the establishment of a trust is likely to give rise to immediate tax liabilities in the United Kingdom, this may give rise to a convincing argument against its creation. Any capital gain arising for capital gains tax purposes on a disposal to foreign trustees, cannot be "held over" (i.e., deferred) at the election of the settlor as it can in the case of a U.K. resident trust. If, therefore, assets are pregnant with gain, there may be a very positive tax disadvantage in putting them into a foreign trust, even if the settlor himself retains an immediate entitlement to income in order to avoid any potential charge to capital transfer tax on the creation of the settlement. If a settlement is set up in circumstances that give rise to an appreciable liability for capital gains tax, and the settlor should die within a relatively short period, a capital gains tax liability will have been incurred when no such liability would have arisen on the settlor's death; indeed, if the assets had remained in his ownership, they could have acquired a new and advantageous base cost for capital gains tax purposes based on values at the settlor's death.

Possible Advantages of the Retention of Ownership

There are also certain circumstances in which the creation of a trust may result in the loss of potential fiscal advantages in the United Kingdom. First, for example, there is now a wide scope for what is commonly called "post mortem tax planning." It is possible, under our 1978 Finance Act, for the dispositions of a deceased person (whether effected by will or as a result of the intestacy laws, or the laws relating to joint ownership) to be varied within two years of the death and for an election to be made so that, for the purposes of capital transfer tax and capital gains tax, the varied dispositions shall be treated as the effective dispositions in computing the tax consequences on the death. The variation itself will give rise to no tax charge, other than perhaps to stamp duty, if the appropriate elections are made. However, the relevant provisions do not apply in relation to any property settled before a death, and therefore there can sometimes be less flexibility if a person is at death entitled to an interest in possession in the income of a trust made by a U.K. domiciled settlor (so that for capital transfer tax purposes the settled property is liable to be treated as part of the deceased's estate) than if the property had actually been comprised in the estate of the deceased.

Secondly, if a person is contemplating emigration from the United Kingdom, it may be much better that the creation of any settlement is deferred until he is no longer domiciled or deemed to be domiciled (by reason of at least 17 years' residence) in the United Kingdom. If a settlement of property outside the United Kingdom is created by a settlor who is not domiciled within the United Kingdom, the trust funds will be excluded property for the purposes of capital transfer tax, and provided they remain outside the United Kingdom, they will stay outside the capital transfer tax net for the whole of the duration of the trust. This can clearly be particularly beneficial if some of the beneficiaries are likely to remain in the United Kingdom. In contrast, a trust created by a person domiciled in the United Kingdom will remain subject to the provisions of our capital transfer tax for the whole of its duration, even if it has ceased to have any real connection with the United Kingdom by reason of there being no resident beneficiaries, no property in the United Kingdom, and no resident trustees.

Separate Wills

As the lex situs will apply in relation to any holding of land, it is almost always more satisfactory to arrange for there to be a separate will in the jurisdiction where the land is situated if it is different than that of the owner's domicile.

First, it is to be expected that it will be simpler and less costly to ask an American lawyer to prepare a will dealing with land situated in his state than to consider the possible effects of the trusts and administrative provisions of an English will in relation to the devolution of that land. Secondly, one gains the great advantage of being able to commence an ancillary administration at the earliest possible opportunity after the owner's death.

Very often it will be found that a U.K.-domiciled testator will wish to leave a surviving spouse an absolute interest or an immediate income interest in the foreign property because there will then be no liability to U.K. capital transfer tax as long as the testator's spouse is also domiciled in the United Kingdom.

The Trust Route

Exchange Control Protection

Although currently there are no U.K. exchange controls, they may well be brought back in the future. The Labour Party have for some time made it clear that they would reintroduce exchange controls and at the Labour Party Conference in October 1984, Mr. Roy Hattersley,

Labour's Deputy Leader and Shadow Chancellor, indicated that a Socialist Chancellor would take whatever fiscal and monetary steps he could to ensure that penalties would be imposed on persons who did not bring their money back to the United Kingdom.

The best way to attempt to avoid future exchange controls does seem to be the use of a trust with foreign trustees, the terms of which ensure that it cannot, at least in theory, be in any way controlled by any person within the United Kingdom. Although in the United Kingdom, only limited use is made of what are sometimes known as "flee" clauses, which provide for the automatic transfer of a trust to another jurisdiction if certain eventualities happen, it is increasingly common in the case of off-shore trusts to vest a power of appointment and removal of trustees in a Committee of Protectors, the members of which are resident outside the United Kingdom. If the settlor does not have any adviser or friend living outside the United Kingdom whom he feels is suitable for such a role, it is sometimes necessary to confer those powers on persons in the United Kingdom with the proviso that they shall not be exercised in such a way as to cause U.K. residents to be appointed as trustees or to cause the administration of the trust to be conducted within the United Kingdom.

It has to be recognised that however watertight any foreign trust arrangements may be, it would nonetheless be possible, as Mr. Hattersley has indicated, to bring pressure to bear on any connected person who continued to live in the United Kingdom. Sanctions might be imposed against any U.K. resident settlor or beneficiaries of a foreign trust. There is, in fact, some precedent for this in our capital transfer tax legislation. Section 25 of the Finance Act 1975 imposed in certain circumstances an accountability for tax on the settlor of a trust, the trustees of which were not for the time being resident in the United Kingdom. The relevant provisions of Section 25 applied to trusts in existence before the introduction of capital transfer tax, as well as trusts created thereafter.

It will be clear that any powers which the settlor may retain in order to ensure that the settlement is regarded as a grantor trust for U.S. tax purposes, or for other reasons, may give rise to potential difficulties if exchange controls are reintroduced in the United Kingdom. On the other hand, a prospective settlor faced with the possibility that legislation in years to come might impose on him a liability for tax or other penalities designed to encourage the repatriation of funds to the United Kingdom, may in some cases feel that the retention of a degree of control is in fact a desirable safeguard from his personal point of view.

Deferral of Capital Gains Tax

There is often a prospective capital gains tax advantage in having a foreign trust. In the case of a trust with at least a majority of nonresident trustees, the general administration of which is conducted outside the United Kingdom, it is possible to defer the payment of any capital gains tax which might otherwise be assessed on U.K. resident beneficiaries by reference to the trustees' capital gains. Under Section 80 of our Finance Act 1981, any such liability to capital gains tax can be postponed until a U.K. resident and domiciled beneficiary receives a capital payment from the trustees. It is not at present entirely clear what may amount to the receipt of a capital payment and whether, for example, the beneficiary's free use of a holiday home in the United States owned by the trust, could trigger a liability under Section 80. However, with care, it may in many cases be possible to postpone any U.K. capital gains tax liability for many years, and if a beneficiary is or becomes nonresident, to effectively expunge it by an advance of capital to that nonresident beneficiary. It is also to be noted that the anti-avoidance provisions of Section 80 do not operate in any circumstances if the settlor has never been domiciled in the United Kingdom.

The Situs of the Trust

Although tax and possible future exchange control considerations in the United Kingdom may be liable to complicate arrangements for a U.S. trust which will qualify for grantor status, it should nonetheless normally be possible to devise an acceptable solution that will give the settlor sufficient actual or nominal control over income and capital to secure grantor status during his lifetime. For example, a life interest trust where the settlor is to retain (a) the right to income, (b) the possibility of receiving principal, and (c) the power to agree to any amendment or revocation of the trust by the trustees, should give rise to no U.K. tax problems while the settlor is entitled to his income interest.

A sprinkler or discretionary trust is liable to give rise to U.K. tax liabilities on its creation in the case of a U.K. domiciled settlor and, unless it complies with the U.K. requirements necessary to qualify it as an accumulation and maintenance trust for persons under the age of 25 years, there will likely be a periodic charge for U.K. capital transfer tax at least once every 10 years. Any requirement for the trustees to obtain the settlor's consent in connection with the distribution of income should not give rise to any problem while the beneficiaries are under the age of 18 years, but thereafter may be inconsistent with gaining the favourable treatment available for certain accumulation and maintenance trusts from a U.K. capital transfer tax point of view. Any attempt to secure grantor status for a trust after the settlor's death may result in the arrangements being vulnerable to any U.K. exchange controls which are introduced in the future.

Any investor who contemplates that he may some day wish to live in the United States will doubtless wish to ensure that he has from the outset a U.S. trust set up in the most advantageous way. Persons, however, who do not intend to establish any greater connection with the United States than making an investment in its land or economy may well prefer the off-shore solution, with the land or investments being owned by a tax haven corporation which is, in turn, owned by a tax haven trust in a tax haven (other than the great U.K. tax haven!).

In the context of international tax planning, it often seems a sound principle to arrange matters so that trust assets are situated in a different jurisdiction to that in which the trustees are residents and the trust is administered. In a case where there are to be protectors of the settlement, they should ideally be resident in yet another jurisdiction. If this philosophy is followed a tax haven settlement would in any event be the preferred solution rather than a trust of U.S. assets established in the United States.

Conclusion

Although the topic for discussion relates principally to investment in land in the United States, scant reference has been made to that type of investment in this paper because from a U.K. tax point of view it is largely immaterial whether any U.S. investment is in land or securities.

To quote, a great American, namely, Benjamin Franklin, "In this world nothing can be said to be certain, except death and taxes." It is however, almost certain that unless the persons advising an English resident, who proposes to make an investment in the United States, examine in depth the implications arising from the tax laws of both countries, there will be a great risk that the best arrangements will not be implemented.

MARKETING OF LEGAL SERVICES

London Sessions
ABA Annual Meeting 1985
Audley Suite, Grosvenor House Hotel
London, England

Tuesday, July 16, 1985
2:00 P.M. - 4:00 P.M.

"Preparation and Utilization of the Law Firm Brochure"

Samuel S. Smith
8th Floor
1111 Lincoln Road Mall
Miami Beach, Florida 33139

"Marketing the Law Business: Expanding the Scope of Legal Services"

Luther J. Avery
Suite 900, 601 Montgomery Street
San Francisco, California 94111

"The Development of Practice Development in England and Wales"

Graham Lee
5 Thamesgate Close
Ham, Richmond, Surrey

PREPARATION AND UTILIZATION OF THE LAW FIRM BROCHURE

Samuel S. Smith

Identification of Purposes and Goal

Recruiting

1. Real.
2. Imagined.

Education

1. Existing clients.
2. Forwarding attorneys.

Advertising

Distribution

1. Mailing.
2. Programs.
3. Point of purchase.

Letter Size Considerations

Standard Letter (8-1/2 x 11)

Letterfold

Booklet

Printing Guidelines

Paper

1. Glossy.
2. Pulp textured.

Color Utilization

Type Styles

Copy Content

History

Fee Discussions

Areas of Practice

Community Involvement

Photographs

Working

Rogue's Gallery

Graphics

Biographical Information

Undergraduate

Law School

Year Indications

Honors

Areas of Practice

Community

Personal

Professional

Amendment Capability

Reprinting

Insert

Standard

Conclusion

Expense

Goals vs. Reality

Client Reaction

Proof of Worthiness

MARKETING THE LAW BUSINESS:
EXPANDING THE SCOPE OF LEGAL SERVICES

Luther J. Avery

Introduction

Building a Successful Law Practice: Quality of Life versus Economics

History of Restraints on Lawyer Marketing Activities

1. Laissez-faire.
2. Regulation/restriction.
3. Law practice is a business.

Planning as the Most Important Aspect of Marketing

1. Preparing a situation analysis.
2. The importance of market research.
3. The importance of knowing what business you are in.
4. Engaging in the planning process.
5. Positioning your practice.
6. Developing a budget.

The Use of Marketing Experts

Creating the Marketing Plan as a Part of Creating the Production Unit

Recapturing the Business: Offering Nontraditional Services

Analysis of Offering Nontraditional Services

Management Policy Issues

1. Quality control procedures.
2. Creating new markets.
3. Competing with nonlawyers.
4. Analysis of objectives.
5. Cost-benefit analysis.

"Legal Services" Defined: What Lawyers Think They Do

"Nontraditional Services" Defined: Unmet Legal Needs

Should Lawyers Fight Unlawful Practice Battles?

Should Lawyers Create New Legal Products?

Should Lawyers Be a Protected Class?

Should Lawyers Be Less of a Profession and More of a Business?

Lawyers Need Comparative Pricing to Compete Effectively

Lawyers Need a Basis For Comparison of Legal Services With Nonlawyer Services--A Relative Value Scale

The Public Needs To Compare the Value of Services Among Lawyers and Between Lawyers and Nonlawyers

1. The need for better commmunications.
2. The need for product comparison.
3. The need for price comparison.
4. The need for quality control standards.
5. The need to utilize "malpractice liability" as a means of assigning responsibility for faulty services.

Comparison of Costs of Lawyers With Costs of Nonlawyers Rendering Comparable Legal Services

Comparative Pricing of Legal Services Involves Projection of Probable Outcome From Alternative Courses of Action

The Case For Published Fee Schedules

The Need For Improvement of Lawyers' Performance

Quality Control Standards

1. The need for standard terminology.
2. The need for generally accepted procedures.
3. The need for ability to compare: time, price, utility.
4. The need for implementation of quality control programs: Self-appraisal, peer review, client-implemented, government or court-implemented.

Improved Lawyer-Client Relationship

1. The client's Bill of Rights.
2. The lawyer's Bill of Rights.

How Lawyers Can Compete By Delivery of Services Related To "Legal Services"

The Field of Real Estate

The Field of Estate Planning, Fiduciary Administration, and Financial Planning

The Field of Domestic Relations

How Lawyers Can Compete By Re-entry of Fields "Lost" By Lawyers

Taxation

Business Organizations and Finance

Litigation and Litigation Support

How Lawyers Can Compete By Entry Into "New" Fields

Legal Health Maintenance Organization ("LHMO")

Liability Insurance Defenses Services

Private Courts and Dispute Resolution Systems

Community Education About the Law

Financial Planning

"Private" Criminal Punishment

Private Protection Services

Computerized Information Management Services

Conflicts of Interest Problems Arising Out of "Full Service" Activities of Lawyers Delivering Nontraditional Legal Services

ABA Model Rules of Professional Conduct

Conflicts of Interest Arise When the Lawyer Fulfills More than One "Function" Because the Lawyer Can No Longer Serve As Independent Counsel Evaluating the Performance of Others

Conclusion

Lawyers Need to Develop Greater Facilities to Render Effective Legal Services: As the Competition With Lawyers Expands in Financial Strength and in Size So Must Legal Delivery Service Units

Lawyers Need to Reexamine What Are Legal Services and What is Their Exclusive Responsibility With a View to Expansion

Lawyers Should Consider Taking Back Fields of Activity Now Dominated By Government Legal Service Corporation, Public Defender Services, A.C.L.U., and Charities, and Putting the Activity on a Profitable Basis

Lawyers Should Sue Nonlawyers for "Legal Malpractice" to Improve Quality of Legal Problem-Solving Services Rendered by Nonlawyers

Lawyers Should Facilitate Consumer Self-Help as a Way of Allowing Lawyers To Function Profitably

Lawyers Should Analyze What Functions They Can Perform That Will Benefit the Client and Lawyers Should Charge Clients the Fees or Costs Necessary to Render Those Services

THE DEVELOPMENT OF PRACTICE DEVELOPMENT IN ENGLAND AND WALES

Graham Lee

"Practice Development" is the term that was used in the days when few people believed that professionals could, or indeed, should market their services. Of course, this objection took no account of the fact that lawyers had always marketed their services and that law firms would not exist if this were not so. But there were strict limitations on what could and could not be done to build up a practice--no touting, no advertising, no "unfair competition," and so on.

In England and Wales, change in attitudes toward marketing of legal services first manifested itself in the early 1970s. At that time the growth of competition from non-solicitor conveyancing companies began. For some time, disquiet had been expressed, mainly by politicians, about the so-called conveyancing monopoly of solicitors. Under the Solicitors Acts (the latest is that of 1974), only solicitors are able to draw the essential transfer document in a conveyancing (i.e., real estate) transaction. In the 1970s, a growing number of people were prepared to risk prosecution under these Acts, by undertaking conveyancing work for the public in competition with solicitors.

At the same time, in the United Kingdom as in the United States, the concept of consumerism was growing in influence. This concept led people more and more to question the authority of "experts," whether lawyers or others. People also became more inclined, as a result, to consider employing those who offered what seemed to be similar services at a price lower than that of the expert, and they also became more willing to do things themselves, whether it was their own house repair or their own legal action. Some of these "do-it-yourselfers" acquired a measure of experience, which persuaded them to set up in business selling the services they had originally performed for themselves.

Whilst many solicitors probably see nonlawyer competition still in terms of conveyancing, it has in fact developed to encompass a wide range of lawyer activity and still is developing. Examples of nonsolicitor competition can be seen in employment law, accidents, wills and probate, matrimonial and family law, and other areas of practice. There is no doubt that this trend will continue.

Despite this growing competition, it was not until the end of the 1970s and the beginning of the 1980s that the solid and, it has to be said, almost natural complacency of the profession was shaken. In 1978, The Law Society undertook a corporate advertising campaign on behalf of the profession in an effort to improve the general image of solicitors. This was followed by two further campaigns in 1980 and 1981.

At the same time, I and some others began to investigate whether marketing deserved the calumny that had been heaped on it by some and whether it should be ignored as it largely had been by the legal and many other professions, or whether there were aspects of it that could be adapted for the benefit of legal practice. In the autumn of 1981, I wrote an article, which was published in The Law Society's Gazette, entitled "Future Shock--A Midsummer Nights Dream." This article presented a scenario of 1991 where, it was suggested, much of the work that solicitors had believed was exclusively theirs had vanished to nonsolicitor competitors. The message was that this could happen, but need not, if the profession became competition minded. Since the early 1980s, the idea of practice development as an essential activity of a law firm began to grow and to be more and more widely accepted by the profession.

From the start, of course, solicitors divided themselves into two camps. The first camp consisted of those who resisted--and some still resist--all change, believing that none but solicitors are capable of doing solicitor work or should be allowed to do it. The second camp was comprised of those solicitors who recognised change to be inevitable. Whether or not they liked the fact was beside the point. They decided they had to do something to meet the challenge of nonsolicitor competition, and many saw practice development and the use of marketing techniques as an important means of meeting it.

I helped these developments along with invaluable assistance from a leading marketing consultant Aubrey Wilson and from industrial psychologist Lynda King Taylor. We were aided very substantially by the ABA's Section of Economics of Law Practice, of which I am proud to be an honorary member, and by many friends within that section. The Section has had a great influence on the growth of practice development in England and Wales, and it is right that this should be acknowledged. Whilst we do some things differently from our U.S. friends and colleagues, practice development runs on substantially the same lines in both countries.

Over a period of 18 months, from late-1981 to mid-1983, a series of workshops and seminars on practice development were organised for solicitors. At the start, these meetings were attended by small audiences, but enthusiasm and the demand for information about practice development increased to a point where several of the later sessions designed to explain practice development were substantially oversubscribed and had to be rerun to meet audience demand.

In June 1983, came the first of two epochal events in the recent history of the solicitors' profession: the introduction in Parliament of a private bill by Austin Mitchell, M.P., intended to abolish the solicitors' conveyancing monopoly. The bill received substantial support in Parliament, despite a spirited campaign against it by The Law Society. However, the Government, in February 1984, effectively took over the bill. At the time I write this (August 1984), the government appears intent on legislating to open up conveyancing to nonsolicitor "licensed conveyancers" and possibly also to Banks and Building Societies.

The fears of the profession, which had existed for many years, thus have finally materialised. It has been said the Austin Mitchell Bill is a catalyst for change, and this may well be right. Certainly it has led to a substantial rethinking by the profession of its attitudes toward competition, marketing, practice development, and communication in general. Before the autumn of 1983, the solicitors' profession was solid in its resistance to individual advertising. Since the reality of impending change became apparent, the profession has become strong, if not solid, in its demands to be permitted to advertise and promote its services. In this, if nothing else, the Austin Mitchell Bill has indeed been a catalyst.

The Austin Mitchell Bill and solicitors' reaction to it led to the second epochal event for the solicitors' profession in recent years: the loosening of restrictions on profession advertising. In June 1984, the Council of The Law Society decided to relax its rules on advertising and issued guidelines which were published in The Law Society's Gazette of 1 August 1984. They are as follows:

"As from 1 October 1984, solicitors may advertise in England and Wales:

(A) in the press or on radio;

(B) by direct mailing, including sending a copy of the solicitors' brochure to:

   (1) present or former clients (except any former clients whom the solicitor should know are not likely to return to them as clients);

   (2) prospective clients who ask for information about the firm;

   (3) the solicitors' professional connections;

(C) on the solicitors' premises; and

(D) in directories which are open to the whole profession or, in the case of local directories, in directories open to all local solicitors.

"Solicitors may not advertise by any other means unless specifically so permitted by a Council ruling or direction.

"The permitted advertising, which includes brochures, must be subject to the following:

(1) The advertising must be in good taste and not of such a character as may reasonably be regarded as likely to bring the profession into disrepute.

(2) The advertising must not contain any inaccurate or misleading statements and any factual information must be verifiable.

(3) (a) The advertising may refer to the quality of service provided by solicitors in general but not that provided by the firm. Advertisements must not suggest that the firm is superior in its practice to other solicitors nor directly or indirectly criticise or compare its services or charges with those of other solicitors.

(b) No statement may be made as to quantity of work, names of clients, names of staff other than partners (but as to brochures see (6) below), fee income, past cases, or success rate.

(4) Categories of work that may be advertised are limited to those in which the firm has experience. No special expertise or specialism may be claimed.

(5) (a) If charges are advertised, it must be stated what services will be provided for those charges and in what circumstance they may be increased.

(b) A fee stated to be from or upwards of a certain figure is prohibited, as is the advertising of a discount or reduction of a specified percentage or amount.

(c) A total fee for a specific service must state whether that includes disbursements and value-added tax.

(d) If the basis of charges is advertised it must be clearly explained.

(e) If residential conveyancing is advertised but not a charge therefor the advertisement must include a statement to the effect that if required a written estimate of costs in respect of such work will be given. This estimate must be comprehensive and accord with the Notes for Guidance for the time being in force, published with The Society's Domestic Conveyancing Charges Form.

(6) If direct mailing is used, multiple copies must not be sent to any addressee.

(7) (a) In brochures, fee-earners may be named, but if they are not partners, their status must be indicated.

(b) If residential conveyancing (but not a charge therefor) is advertised in brochures, it is not obligatory to include a statement to the effect that if required a written estimate of costs in respect of such work will be given, but a statement offering a written estimate is considered to be good practice. Estimates that are given in respect of residential conveyancing must be comprehensive and should preferably be on The Society's Domestic Conveyancing Charges Form and have regard to the Notes for Guidance therewith."

This, then is the basis on which practice development currently rests. It is now, perhaps, appropriate to look briefly and, having regard to restriction of space, sketchily, at where practice development stands at this time in England and Wales.

As in the case of marketing of U.S. law firms, so clearly outlined by Luther Avery in his paper, the essential basis of practice development in England and Wales is planning. The planning process, as I conceive it, is, again, similar to that outlined by Luther Avery. It is based on the need for high-level communication between everyone involved in the practice--partners, assistants (associates), staff, and even major clients. This communication must ensure that all involved are committed to a generally agreed strategy for the future of the firm and that those, such as staff, who have to assist in the implementation of such strategy, understand it and, ideally, accept it.

Once commitment to the concept of achieving a corporate strategy is obtained, the planning process can commence. This, in essence, consists of the following elements:

- An assessment of the present position of the firm, its strengths and weaknesses, the strengths and weaknesses of competitors, the areas of work it undertakes, its clientele, and an attempt to answer the vital question: "What business are we in?" As Luther Avery has pointed out, an answer to this question is crucial. It is simplistic, and indeed potentially self-deceiving, to answer "the legal advice business," or at least it is in all but the very smallest firms. Kathryn Marshall, one of the Section's leading members, and a person who has been of unbounded assistance to the English and Welsh legal profession, has suggested that some firms might consider themselves to be in the "stress reduction" business. This, at the least, has the merit of demonstrating that the definition should be much wider than a purely legalistic identification of what the firm is aiming to do;

- The setting of goals that the firm aims to achieve through a workable plan;

- The establishment of a strategy to achieve these goals. This is the core of the plan. The assessment shows the firm where it is now, the goals show the firm where it wants to be in (say) two years, and the strategy shows how to go about reaching those goals in that time scale. The strategy must include an outline of what resources are needed to ensure success. The goals must be examined in human, material, and monetary terms to determine the availability of, and need for, staff, premises and equipment, and financial support to implement the strategy; and

- o The monitoring of what is happening and adjustments where necessary to improve, alter, sometimes abandon, and above all make the firm capable of handling effectively the result of the successful implementation of the plan.

Our approach, following the emphasis on basic planning, is to ensure that the profession is aware that practice development is essentially a communication process. This process falls under two heads, each of which complements the other:

- o External action--establishment of a firm "image"; building up of public awareness of the firm and the services it offers, and use of marketing techniques to obtain and keep clients; and

- o Internal action--personal motivation of all partners and staff, development of client communication and interview skills, setting measurable standards of service, and design of premises to attract and keep clients.

The process of finding and gaining clients, and of keeping them, are closely interrelated, and it is vital that a balance be carefully established between them. Few firms can exist in the hope of keeping old clients and ignoring the need to attract new ones. Conversely, even fewer firms can survive long with a stream of new clients who never return a second time. The stream will dry up sometime.

The object of establishing an image is to enable the public, or that portion of it the firm hopes to convert into clientele, to know the firm exists, what services it offers, and what its approach to practice is--i.e., it is a caring firm, a socially committed firm, an aggressive, growth orientated firm, or whatever. Public knowledge of the services a firm offers is critically important. Too many clients, when asked, are not aware that the firm that represented them in (say) a personal injuries claim also offers help with (say) matrimonial problems, or house purchase. Such ignorance is a recipe not only for a failure of clients to materialise but for existing clients not to come back when they have a different legal problem.

Many of the techniques of marketing are available to solicitors but remarkably few are aware of this. Part of an effective practice development plan consists of a careful and informed choice of those marketing tools that are appropriate for the firm in question. Those right for one may be quite inappropriate for another.

The "external" communication methods are those which spearhead a firm's practice development programme. But unless the firm has equipped itself to consolidate the image it is seeking to promote within the office, the external promotion of that image will at best be ineffective and, at worst, is likely to be counter-productive. The firm must show itself to be "client centred," with a staff trained and premises designed to ensure the best and most effective service for, and the clearest and most open communication with, the client. Otherwise there is a serious risk of client dissatisfaction, which can lead to any number of results, including misconduct complaints, professional negligence (malpractice) suits, or at least, a failure to retain the client.

Thus there is need for staff training schemes, the maximisation of job satisfaction of all staff, of whatever grade, and the motivation of all to recognise that the client is the life-blood of the practice. Leading directly from this is the need to ensure that identifiable standards are set for the provision of the services the firm offers. These can then be monitored by the use of quality control techniques which ensure that standards are maintained. Use of the ABA Section of Economics of Law Practice's excellent handbook on "How to Create a System" can help substantially in this. Through an arrangement between the Section and the Law Society, this and other Section books are available for purchase by solicitors in England and Wales.

Part of this internal communication process is the careful and scientific planning of the law firm's premises to be efficient, functional, and yet to provide an ambience that puts clients at ease and ensures they give of their best and recognise that their solicitor is doing so too. This is augmented by the lawyer's use of good interviewing and communications technique. Too many lawyers believe that interviewing and client communication is an instinctive skill. Too many professional misconduct and malpractice complaints prove them wholly wrong. Interviewing is a skill that requires study and involves the analysis of the process, the formalisation and systemisation of parts of it and, above all, a recognition that the decisive element in any communication is not what is said or written, but what is heard, read, and understood.

So, let us assume all these guidelines have been observed, the firm has its practice development plan set out on paper, and is ready to put it into effect. What, in England and Wales, can it do to give the public--its potential and existing clients--the message it wishes to transmit? This is where the tools and techniques of marketing have to be studied to determine which ones are appropriate both for the firm in question and the plan it wishes to put into effect.

Many solicitors, at the time of writing at least, seem to think that advertising is the only marketing technique available. This is untrue, and in many cases, advertising will be less helpful and less cost and time-efficient to a firm than one or more of the other available techniques.

These other techniques include public relations, where the promotion of a firm's name by permissible publicity, articles, etc. may be appropriate. Also suitable in some areas of practice may be the establishment of client training schemes, including seminars and conferences, exhibitions, sponsorships, and client entertainment. The Law Firm brochure is one of the most powerful aids to marketing although, as will be seen from The Law Society Guidelines, solicitors are not allowed to go quite so far in their brochure as U.S. lawyers can, as Sam Smith has so ably demonstrated in his paper.

Newsletters also have an important place. A quarterly bulletin to clients, informing them of changes in the law that may affect them and of the firm's ability to advise them, ensures constant contact, even when the firm is not currently acting on behalf of the client.

Add-on services are an interesting field for development. Some solicitors now give a free will with every conveyancing transaction. Packaging is also an underrated tool. Some firms today hand to clients an attractively printed file containing copies of vital documents for the client's personal records.

Whilst pricing in England and Wales is often controlled by the courts or by government regulation, it is possible to use it as a marketing tool in some areas of legal work. It is anticipated that competitive pricing will increase as solicitors become more experienced in practice development.

And last, but neither least, nor in exhaustion of the range of available tools, there are techniques for encouraging and developing the vital production of referrals. It is estimated that up to 80 percent of solicitors' work comes from referrals from friends or relatives of clients, or other professionals such as bank managers, accountants, etc. There are clear and increasingly sophisticated techniques for ensuring that such people are motivated to refer potential clients to a particular firm in preference to others.

In conclusion, it ought to be necessary to draw distinctions between practice development in England and Wales and in the United States. In fact, I find few distinctions to draw. Thinking in the United States on the subject is, perhaps, more developed than in the United Kingdom. U.S. lawyers have been at it longer. Regulation of the U.S. legal profession allows more freedom in some respects than regulation in England and Wales; but I would not like to speculate how long that slight distinction will continue. We are intent on developing new areas of practice which will widen and round out the services offered. One of my favourite new practice areas is that of the legal audit--the review of the client's legal affairs, with the object of preventing problems from arising rather than treating them when they've arisen.

In short, practice development in the United States and United Kingdom are running on substantially parallel lines. This is why a session such as the one for which this paper is written is so important. It is also why I seize again the opportunity to thank the ABA Section of Economics of Law Practice for its leadership in the area of practice development, and to acknowledge the help it has given to me, The Law Society, and the legal profession in England and Wales.

A BILL OF RIGHTS: SHIELD OR SHACKLE OR SHAM?

London Sessions
ABA Annual Meeting 1985
Ballroom, Park Lane Hotel
London, England

Tuesday, July 16, 1985
2:00 P.M. - 4:00 P.M.

The Hon. J. Skelly Wright
U.S. Court of Appeals for
the D.C. Circuit
Washington, D.C. 20001-2867

When people agree, either directly or through their chosen representatives, to create a government to rule themselves, they of course also agree to surrender some portion of their personal sovereignty to that government. So that the dimension as well as the detail of that surrender is clear, the final agreement is usually reflected in a written constitution. So that the new government will not unwittingly or deliberately trench on their most precious human rights and freedoms, the people usually insist that protection of those rights and freedoms be spelled out in writing, in a bill of rights, in the basic constitutional agreement. As James Madison, the author of the American Constitution, put it:

> If men were angels no government would be necessary. If angels were to govern men, neither external nor internal controls on government would be necessary. In framing a government which is to be administered by men over men, the great difficulty lies in this: you must first enable the government to control the governed; and in the next place oblige it to control itself.[1]

Thus a bill of rights forces the government to control itself with respect to the human rights and freedoms of its people--or suffer the consequences.

For 200 years the written Constitution of the United States has contained a bill of rights which, I submit, has worked well. For that submission I offer as my witness the distinguished scholar, jurist, and statesman, Lord Scarman. The occasion for his testimony was the Joint Conference in 1980 of the British Institute of Human Rights and the United Kingdom Association for European Law. After the speaker preceding him at the conference had been ventilating on the difficulties of drafting a charter of human rights "which takes account of present day situations," Lord Scarman interposed: "May I just say that the Americans still do very well with a bill of rights drafted in 1791."[2]

Of course Lord Scarman's riposte was overgenerous to the United States. It is not self-evident that Australian or British subjects, without a written bill of rights, are less free or equal than their American counterparts with one. Despite the Bill of Rights the United States has, over time, made grievous mistakes that have inflicted untold injustice and suffering, primarily upon the poor, the underprivileged, and the minorities. Under our Constitution, as adopted and for half a century thereafter, Negroes were slaves who were denied all rights of citizens. As late as 1857, our Supreme Court in the *Dred Scott* case could decide consistently with our Constitution that "Negroes had *no* rights which the white man was bound to respect."[3] This decision brought on our Civil War, a fratricidal blood bath in which thousands of our people, black and white, died. And the United States today is far from free of the racial discrimination resulting from our human rights mistakes of the past and some of our current ones. Certainly our Bill of Rights has not been a panacea--indeed it has only come into its own in the last half century--but I am reluctant even to speculate as to what our country would be like today without.

Having made my mea culpas, let me advance to the subject at hand, drawing on my experience as a United States judge enforcing the American Bill of Rights in our Southland where I was born and raised--New Orleans, Louisiana, to be precise. From this perspective, I will suggest why I think our Bill of Rights has worked for us and then raise questions as to whether that experience might be exportable.

The American Bill of Rights

A Bill of Rights? "Nonsense on stilts" was the reaction of Britain's great constitutional theorist Jeremy Bentham to the suggestion that fundamental human rights be protected from Parliament's encroachments. Thomas Jefferson, author of our Declaration of Independence, differed; "A Bill of Rights," he wrote James Madison, is "what the people are entitled to against every government on earth, general or particular, and what no government should refuse or rest on inference."[4] I do not propose to take up either Bentham's or Jefferson's gauntlet, at least insofar as each makes some claim for the universality of his view. History and experience, far more than theory, settle such things for a nation. And besides, my task is to raise questions, not to answer them.

In the United States, the Bill of Rights has of course been a fixture of our historical experience for two centuries. Though, as our recent debate over organized prayer in the public schools points up, there are those who seek to alter some of our constitutional protections, the Bill of Rights is generally secure. More interesting is the current British debate over whether to adopt a bill of rights. Although the debate has waxed and waned for some two decades, this is no ground for pronouncing the issue dead. Hasty change, after all, is not a hallmark of modern English law or politics. Others know better than I the prospects for a British bill of rights. I assume only that those prospects are neither so dim nor so bright that they moot a discussion of whether or not a bill of rights is necessary or desirable in Great Britain.

The obvious first question to be asked by any nation considering a bill of rights is: what good is it? Or, put another way, does a bill of rights really work as a means of securing the rights described in the document? On the whole, history does not yield up much of an affirmative answer. Written international and national constraints on government--such as the Universal Declaration of Human Rights that theoretically binds all United Nationas members--have in practice been largely ignored. In my own country the record is far from unblemished. "Riding a man out of town on a rail is as much a part of the American tradition as declaring inalienable rights," it has been said.[5] And our legacy of shame, Jim Crow, snuggled comfortably beside the guarantees of rights in our Constitution for almost a century after we had theoretically secured the blessings of liberty in equal measure for all persons, black and white.

Nonetheless, I daresay the American experience does have something hopeful to say about the prospects for an efficacious bill of rights. To make my point, I want to begin the discussion, not with the Bill of Rights itself, but with our Constitution's Preamble, which tells us what the early Americans thought they were up to in their exercise of constitution-making. It reads:

> WE THE PEOPLE of the United States, in Order to form a more perfect Union, establish Justice, ensure domestic Tranquility, provide for the common defence, promote the general Welfare, and secure the Blessings of Liberty to ourselves and our Posterity, do ordain and establish this Constitution for the United States of America.

The first three words, "WE THE PEOPLE," doubtless strike the modern ear as a hackneyed reaffirmation of the Anglo-American tenet that all sovereignty rests in the people. But to the first American citizens few words could have been more vital. As the citizens of one Connecticut town put it in 1783: "There is an original, underived and incommunicable authority and supremacy in the collective body of the people, to whom all delegated power must submit, and from whom there is no appeal."[6] In that first decade of the new nation, before the Constitution was adopted, the people's acute awareness of their sovereignty precipitated a good bit of tumult; rampant public distrust of all who exercised delegated political authority crippled the first state legislatures and brought on the political crisis out of which the Constitution was born.

As the Preamble instructs us, the Constitution is the exercise of this "underived authority and supremacy" of the "WE THE PEOPLE...to form a more perfect Union...to secure the Blessings of Liberty to ourselves and our Posterity." The early Americans saw in these goals a dilemma: how could they create a new national power to bring them out of the "critical period" of political disintegration under the Articles of Confederation, while doubting the ability of any political form to represent the people adequately and fearing in government a menace to the very liberty they sought to secure? Their resolution is as ingenious to their time as it is familiar to ours: a national government of enumerated powers, a complex governmental structure, and a specific guarantee of fundamental liberties in the Bill of Rights.

Before turning to the Bill of Rights itself, I want to pause for a moment on the implications of our Constitution's representational structure; an understandng of the premises of this structure will inform our appreciation of the Bill of Rights and will be of paramount importance when we discuss possible adoption of a bill of rights in Britain. It is crucial that one grasps that the American constitutional scheme flows from a rejection of the notion that a body of elected representatives in a legislature could always be depended upon to represent adequately the will of the people. Madison warned in Federalist 48 that the legislature was a seedbed of tyranny; "It is," he said "against the enterprising ambition of this department that the people ought to indulge all their jealousy and exhaust all their precautions."[7] Primarily out of this abiding distrust of accretions of legislative power our tripartite governmental structure was born: Congress as the law-maker, the President and the executive branch as the law-enforcer, and the Supreme Court and the judiciary as the law-interpreter. Tyranny, especially of the legislative variety, is checked through dispersal of power and the pull and haul, branch against branch, that this dispersal engenders--a system of checks and balances.

Structure, however, was thought by many to be an insufficient bulwark against tyranny. Some provisions of the Articles of the Constitution--e.g., the guarantee of habeas corpus and the prohibition against ex post facto laws--reflect this perception. But these protections did not satisfy the citizens of several states crucial to ratification of the Constitution. And so only after the Bill of Rights incorporated into the fundamental law a specific enumeration of those aspects of liberty most deeply cherished did the People lend their collective assent to the Constitution. And so only after the Bill of Rights incorporated into the fundamental law a specific enumeration of those aspects of liberty most deeply cherished did the People lend their collective assent to the Constitution. Thus, in the words of Thomas Paine, the Constitution and Bill of Rights serve "not only as an authority, but as a law of control to the government[,]...the political bible of the state."[8] Paine's metaphor of holy scripture was apt. The precise point of the Constitution and Bill of Rights is to serve as higher authority, to place fundamental liberties beyond the reach of normal politics. Because the Constitution expresses the complete collective authority of "WE THE PEOPLE" and the day-to-day acts of government at most flow from the exercise of a partial and incomplete authority, the acts of government must conform to the Constitution.

In my judgment, our constitutional guarantees have worked well for us, indeed have proven decisive at a critical juncture in our nation's history. In the American Southland, in the troubled middle decades of this century, the Constitution ultimately broke the back of Jim Crow and unrelentingly brought home to our people the chasm of contradiction between our cherished principles and our contemptible customs. And it was upon the Constitution that we United States judges stood when the dark torrents of misdirected passion raged about us. Finally, I take comfort from the thought that some of the ablest British thinkers, including Lord Scarman, would seem from their advocacy of a bill of rights for Britain to have drawn the same lessons from America's experience as I have.

That the Bill of Rights can work--even in the face of strong political hostility--is perhaps illustrated best by the confrontation in Little Rock, Arkansas in 1957. In the fall of that year, President Eisenhower dispatched the United States 102nd Airborne Division to Little Rock to enforce the constitutional rights of nine black children to attend Central High School. These nine, seeking to attend Central High pursuant to a local desegregation plan for public schools implemented in the wake of Brown v. Board of Education, had earlier been driven away by a phalanx of Arkansas national guardsmen placed there by a race-baiting governor. The United States troops remained the entire year to safeguard the nine children from the incited mob that the state officials' obstructionism had brought into being. The importance of this decisive federal action to protect constitutional rights in the face of intense political hostility should not be underestimated.

I relate this Little Rock episode to bolster my claim that a written constitutional guarantee can hold fast even in a maelstrom of aroused political passions. The crucial question for us in the present context is why? This question brings me back to the notion that these constitutional guarantees embody the fundamental collective will of "WE THE PEOPLE." To suggest that we take constitutional guarantees seriously because they are fundamental law verges, of course, on the tautological. Yet the source of the guarantees is crucial to their authority. We recognize the Bill of Rights not as law imposed from above but as a collective expression of fundamental principle from the people. Thus the original Americans were quite comfortable with the idea of a constitution's supremacy over the subsequent majority will of a legislature, state or national.

That does not satisfactorily explain, however, why generations of Americans have likewise accepted this original expression of collective sovereignty over and above modern legislative will. The fact that the Constitution is in written form has something to do with its ability to command the assent of generations of Americans, as does the fact that the document itself demands that we take it seriously. Article VI of the Constitution is crucial in this respect. The Supremacy Clause makes clear that "This Constitution shall be the supreme law of the land." And the oft-overlooked Oath Clause demands that all federal and state government officials "shall be bound by oath or affirmation to support this Constitution." When the Supreme Court evaluated the actions of the state of Arkansas in the Little Rock incident, in Cooper v. Aaron, the Court found great force in Article VI. Said the Court: "[T]he interpretation of the Fourteenth Amendment enunciated by this Court in the Brown case is the supreme law of the land, and Art. VI of the Constitution makes it of binding effect on the states... Every state legislator and executive and judicial officer is solemnly committed by oath taken pursuant to Art. VI, cl. 3, 'to support this Constitution.'...No state legislator or executive or judicial officer can war against the Constitution without violating his undertaking to support it."[9]

In the end, though, fiat from the dead hand of the past does not compel us to accept the Bill of Rights. The Constitution and the Bill of Rights challenge every generation to affirm its belief in our most fundamental principles. The fact that the Bill of Rights exists in written form and self-consciously claims to be higher law, and that Americans have for generations accepted this claim, make the guarantees in the Bill of Rights impossible to ignore, even when amnesia might be the better part of valor. Yet we are never without a choice. If present circumstances compel us to conclude that a principle once thought fundamental no longer makes sense, Article V of the Constitution provides a clear path to the people to change the Bill of Rights. So we must put up or shut up--apply our fundamental principles or decide that we no longer believe in them and act upon this decision.

The one option the Bill of Rights doe not leave open--at least in theory--is expediency. However deafening the roars of the lynch mob might become, the Bill of Rights--with a judicial forum to give voice to the claim--will not allow us to ignore the solitary voice of the oppressed. It is this function, forcing us to choose, that in my judgment has been crucial to the American experience. Perhaps Learned Hand was correct when he said, "Liberty lies in the hearts of men and women; when it dies there no...constitution can save it."[10] But a Bill of Rights most assuredly can keep liberty alive in the hearts of men and women by challenging them again and again to choose liberty over expediency.

With this appreciation of the decisive importance of the written fundamental law in United States history, I turn now to the issue at hand: should an enlightened, humane nation like the United Kingdom likewise adopt a fundamental written law to protect basic human rights?

Is a Bill of Rights Compatible with British Political Theory?

It is axiomatic that, in great Britain, Parliament is sovereign, its power "illimitable, perpetual, and indivisible."[11] Britain, in other words, grounds the legitimacy of its parliamentary system on precisely the premise that the American Constitution rejects. In place of the American premise of distrust, reflected in our Constitution's limits on government, the British operate from a premise that Parliament can and does represent the will of the people and thus cannot, and need not, be limited. Indeed traditionally Parliament was the guardian of liberty against the oppressions of the Crown and it remains difficult for many an Englishman to think of Parliament itself as capable of infringing liberty.

This theoretical incompatibility is perhaps the greatest impediment in the path of those who favor a British bill of rights and has led crusaders to search for other routes. Rather than demanding any absolute entrenchment of fundamental rights as against

Parliament, advocates have instead proposed several less-protective measures. These primarily include techniques of statutory interpretation such as: construing subsequent legislation to avoid overriding a provision of the bill of rights, or requiring that parliamentary enactments never be read as abrogating a provision of the bill of rights unless such abrogation is <u>expressly</u> required in the enactment. Some have gone so far as to suggest that Parliament could itself pass a permanent self-restricting law and confer enforcement power on the courts, and others have suggested that a bill of rights might be established subject to override only by a two-thirds vote of Parliament.

Such measures merit--and have received--serious consideration. Perhaps what matters for Britain is not the degree of entrenchment but the basic decision to reduce guarantees of liberty to unambiguous words. As I see it, though, the core purpose of a bill of rights is to place basic liberties wholly beyond the politics of the day. Thus I propose to push a little further. I first raise the possibility that the guarantee in Britain of at least some rights found in America's Bill of Rights is essential to the fair and accurate functioning of the representational processon which Parliament's legitimacy is staked. I also suggest, albeit tentatively, that to the extent that a bill of rights is incompatible with the premise of parliamentary sovereignty, perhaps some conditions conducive to a rethinking are emergent.

No one can doubt that the right to speak freely, to associate for common purposes, to assemble, to petition government for redress of grievances, to vote, and to have that vote count for as much as the vote of any other citizen, are at the core of self-government. The process of representation requires clear channels of communication between the people and their representatives. The electorate must have the means to inform itself and to make its views known to its representatives. Constitutional guarantees of free expression and association and of political equality ensure that the process of democratic decision-making works. If the legitimacy of parliamentary supremacy rests on the belief that Parliament's actions do accurately reflect the will of the people, then the argument is, it seems to me, compelling that Parliament's power should not reach so far as to permit infringement of rights essential to self-government.

This argument, of course, embraces only some guarantees commonly associated with a bill of rights. Any attempt to entrench other rights--fair trial rights, privacy and autonomy rights, and the like--requires a different justification. I see some signs that the theory and practice of British government today might be hospitable to the idea of entrenching such rights. Recent scholarship has demonstrated that the idea of absolute parliamentary supremacy was in some measure a superimposition of the nineteenth century thinkers Bentham, Dicey, and Austin, and that a certain tradition of common-law limits on Parliament has existed at least since the time of Sir Edward Coke.[12] Also, to my mind British decisions to accede, at least somewhat, to authorities higher than Parliament by recognizing the European Convention on Human Rights and joining the European Economic Community signal that the authority of Parliament is now viewed as less than "illimitable."

Other developments similarly suggest that the time may be ripe for rethinking on the question of a bill of rights for Britain. One is the much-discussed devolution of authority to Scotland and Wales. Devolution does not, of course, compel adoption of a bill of rights but it does suggest some erosion of the principle of one sovereign parliament. Moreover, the move to a federal scheme may require a written charter outlining the respective powers of local and national parliaments and may require as well a court to adjudicate the boundary disputes that will inevitably arise in a system of dual sovereignty. Such problems may well--as Anthony Lester suggested in his Owen Roberts lecture at the University of Pennsylvania several years ago--bring about a "new constitutional settlement."[13] If so, conditions may be ripe for considering a bill of rights.

A second development is the recent explosive growth of minority populations in Great Britain. Treatment of the large populations of black, Asian, and Indian subjects may compromise the claims of legitimacy of parliamentary sovereignty. My sensitivity to such questions may, in light of my own nation's long and shameful racial experience, be overly acute. But perhaps nothing so rends the soul of a nation as race hatred. For nations committed as ours are to liberty and equality, the spread of the bitter weed of bigotry calls our very legitimacy into question. When bigotry takes root the normal processes of representational politics are, as America's experience teaches, often powerless to arrest its spread. Not only will its victims likely be political minorities but the political process itself may well become the engine of oppression; representatives may well curry favor with the majority precisely by oppressing the minority. Of course the Constitution did not prevent race hatred in America. But, political methods proving inadequate, the Constitution was eventually the tool with which we began to uproot bigotry from our soil. I do not mean to suggest that Britain will likely duplicate our shameful racial practices. If, however, minority groups in Great Britain fail systematically to secure basic rights through the political process, one may question whether racism has so polluted the process that the theory of parliamentary supremacy translates into the reality of racial supremacy.

In a broad sense, the themes of devolution and fairness to minority populations raise the same point. Both involve recognition of the increasingly pluralistic nature of British society--a political recognition of regional and ethnic diversity. The American experience illustrates the link between pluralism and the need for a bill of rights in a democratic society. When a society is relatively homogeneous, the notion that a government will treat all people fairly, and that a legislature will represent all constituents adequately, is far more plausible. Consensus emerges more readily, and government officials are less likely to oppress people whose interest they can identify closely with. When, however, those in power are less readily able to empathize with certain groups in society, government becomes less reluctant to trench on the freedoms of those groups. The paramount example in my nation is, of course, the government's refusal to recognize blacks as citizens. But other examples abound. Constitutional protection of expression became increasingly important as the government sought to squelch political views it found dangerous, and these views often spread in the first decades of the twentieth century among newly arrived immigrant populations. Anthony Lester has made this point most perceptively in the British context:

> The best conditions for the working of the system were those of Victorian society: a society self-conscious in its homogeneity and insularity, that overshadowed its professed ideals of tolerance and fair play; a society rejoicing in its abundant wealth, the fruits of early industrialization and exploitation of a vast empire; a society of _laissez-faire_ in which there was minimal legislative intervention...[14]

The basic point, I think, is that Benthamite political theory premised on homogeneity of individual interests--however valid it might once have been--may no longer serve as society becomes increasingly diverse.

A third development is the growth in recent decades of the bureaucratic state. This brings up two points. First, the modern state's capabilities for intrusion into personal privacy far exceed any that could have been imagined even a century ago when the premise of trust in government was in full flower. I do not mean to conjure up an Orwellian spectre, but I think it fair to say that the limits of technology that de facto protected privacy in the past no longer constrain government's ability to peek, to probe, to monitor. Second, as government takes on the role of provider, a firm due process guarantee against administrative caprice may be essential.

I have tried to sketch why some rethinking might be in order on the question of a bill of rights for Britain. To all of this any loyal British subject could, I suppose, enter a demurrer. British citizens have long enjoyed the blessings of liberty in full measure without a written constitution, and I may not have stated a sufficient reason for altering the status quo. I cannot with great confidence rebut this point. Perhaps America needs a bill of rights because it has always had one, while Great Britain does not need a bill of rights because it has never had one. In other words, the existence of a bill of rights and concomitant judicial review to ensure fidelity to those rights, has left the people free from the responsibility of daily individual vigilance to ensure that government respects those rights. In Great Britain, the absence of a bill of rights and judicial review may have led to the evolution of a deeply and widely held cultural sense of the importance of basic rights that sufficiently checks Parliament.

In answer, I can only say that a bill of rights is of utmost import in the worst of times, when the passions of the day threaten basic values. My nation's history amply shows that such passions can overwhelm even those who love liberty. In such times the existence of a fundamental law beyond the reach of politics may provide the only bulwark sufficient to secure the blessings of liberty. As I have stressed, the written constitutional guarantee of a right--combined with a judicial forum for calling attention to government efforts to trench on it--make the existence of the fundamental right impossible to ignore even when for political reasons it would be most convenient to do so.

Are Conditions Ripe for the Birth of a British Bill of Rights?

How would a British bill of rights be brought into being? I am drawn again to those first words of the Preamble "WE THE PEOPLE," and to the wisdom of Tom Paine: "A constitution is not the act of a government but of a people constituting a government."[15] A bill of rights is not something that a government can successfully impose from above. What can awaken the collective popular will sufficiently to bring about the birth of a bill of rights? Looking to the American experience, the ineluctable fact is that the Bill of Rights and the later guarantees of liberty and equality in the Civil War amendments were born of crisis and conflict. The rights enshrined as fundamental were the rights being fought about. Perhaps an atmosphere of conflict and crisis is essential to the birth of a bill of rights.

Arguably, crisis engenders three conditions that lead to a durable and efficacious bill of rights. First, conflict clarifies what rights are deemed important; a crisis is a crucible in which fundamental rights are forged. Second, crisis produces consensus. Third, in a time of crisis, the guarantee of fundamental rights is unlikely to proceed from government. Indeed the illegitimacy or weakness of established authority may often precipitate the crisis that generates a constitutional settlement. Thus the bill of rights will be produced outside the channels of normal politics. This last condition is, as I have suggested, of particular importance. A bill of rights works when it is believed to be fundamental law beyond the reach of the politics of the day.

I cannot claim that crisis is necessary, but I see some risks in attempting to adopt a bill of rights absent such an atmosphere. The primary risk is that a bill of rights will not be a statement of fundamental law but a product of normal politics. Traces of this problem were evident in the debates over a bill of rights among members of Parliament several years ago. Labourites sought to incorporate socialist programs into the proposed charter while the Conservatives stressed protection of property against an encroaching state.

Though this absence of consensus perhaps means that the current climate cannot nurture a bill of rights, I do not think such dire evaluations are in order. A lack of consensus on such issues as whether a bill of rights should enshrine affirmative rights to employment or housing does not preclude consensus on at least some procedural or political rights of due process and free expression. And the problem of defining the content of these rights in the absence of a crisis can perhaps be sidestepped by resort to the ready-made bill of rights in the European Convention on Human Rights.

Conclusion

I have not tried in this discussion to range comprehensively through all the issues that a proposed British bill of rights raises. Many of those issues are of great importance: should judicial review accompany a bill of rights and if so, in what form; should special courts be created to adjudicate constitutional claims; should basic interpretive guidelines be established to guide the courts. Perhaps the most intriguing question is whether a bill of rights would define only the relationship between citizen and government or would apply as well to the relationship between citizen and other "powers that be" such as corporations and trade unions. This is the age of collective action. Both the American and British economies are dominated by huge corporate combines not even remotely in the contemplation of those who wrote the Constitution and the Bill of Rights. Likewise, unions wield great power both in the political arena and in the daily lives of union members. Corporate decisions on such matters as investment, pricing, and plant location directly affect the lives of all citizens in ways at least as profound and wide-ranging as those of government. It may be that a modern constitutional settlement might set about to define some aspects of a citizen's relationship to such powerful entities.

Despite these crucial questions and a wealth of others, I have confined my discussion primarily to issues of the compatibility of a bill of rights with British political theory and of the possibility of an effective bill of rights arising in the current climate because these are the primary questions that must be grappled with before a people can go on to decide exactly what should be enshrined as fundamental law.

Of course the primary purpose of these discussion papers is to suggest reasons why a civilized country like the United Kingdom might find a bill of rights desirable or undesirable. Instead of providing only reasons of my own in this paper, I have drawn extensively from British sources far more familiar with the question whether Britain needs a bill of rights than I could ever hope to be. Moreover, this approach involves far less presumption on my part. To the extent that my discussion has been presumptuous in favoring the notion of a British bill of rights I hope you will forgive me.

SOURCES

1. THE FEDERALIST, No. 51, at 349 (J. Madison) (J. Cooke ed. 1961).

2. The statement is contained in a report of the Joint Conference in 1980 of the British Institute of Human Rights and the United Kingdom Association for European Law entitled "Two New Directions," at pages 24-25 n.115.

3. Dred Scott v. Sandford, 60 U.S. 393, 407 (1856) (emphasis added).

4. Letter to James Madison, December 20, 1787, quoted in H. ARENDT, ON REVOLUTION 143 (Penguin ed. 1977).

5. G. WILLS, INVENTING AMERICA xiii (1978).

6. Hartford Courant, August 12, 1783, quoted in G. WOOD, THE CREATION OF THE AMERICAN REPUBLIC 1776-1787 382 (Norton ed. 1972).

7. THE FEDERALIST, No. 48, at 334 (J. Madison) (J. Cooke ed. 1961).

8. T. PAINE, THE RIGHTS OF MAN 422 (Anchor Press ed. 1973).

9. Cooper v. Aaron, 358 U.S. 1, 18 (1958).

10. L. HAND, THE SPIRIT OF LIBERTY 144 (1958).

11. G. MARSHALL, CONSTITUTIONAL THEORY 35 (1980).

12. Id. at 35-53.

13. Lester, Fundamental Rights in the United Kingdom: The Law and the British Constitution, 125 U. PA. L. REV. 337, 348 (1977).

14. Id. at 343.

15. T. PAINE, THE RIGHTS OF MAN 420 (Anchor Press ed. 1973).

A BILL OF RIGHTS

London Sessions
ABA Annual Meeting 1985
Ballroom, Park Lane Hotel
London, England

Tuesday, July 16, 1985
2:00 P.M. - 4:00 P.M.

Robert Alexander, Q.C.
1 Brick Court
Temple, London EC4Y 9BY

What contribution can the English make to discussion on the value of a Bill of Rights? For nearly 200 years the structure of your nation has rested on a constitution which contains such a Bill. The separation of powers which this constitution contains, and the prescribed duty under which your judges act as interpreters, is ingrained in your legal process and your political fabric. You may understandably feel that there is little to be learned from a country which possesses no comparable charter.[1]

The issue is whether, as my distinguished co-panellist Judge Skelly Wright has written, we should place "fundamental liberties beyond the reach of normal politics."[2] To do so would be a major development in a country whose history has established the supremacy of Parliament. It is true that the idea of a solemn declaration of fundamental rights, the idea which inspired your Founding Fathers, has its origins deep in English history. Our constitution, often described as unwritten, in fact contains great instruments: Magna Carta (1215), the Petition of Right (1628), the Bill of Rights (1689), and the Act of Settlement (1701). The 1689 Bill of Rights included the provision which subsequently became your Eighth Amendment. Yet these instruments were, as Tom Paine wrote, "essentially treaties between the Monarch on the one hand and some other power, the feudal lords, or Parliament, on the other."[3] Their primary object was not a direct guarantee of individual rights. The Courts took sporadic part in the struggle against the power of the Crown in the seventeenth century, but the principal combatant was Parliament, whose aim was to establish its own supremacy. There was no impetus towards a sophisticated constitutional balance between executive, legislature, and judges.

The defeat of the Crown in this struggle left Parliament triumphant. In 1765, Blackstone pronounced that Parliament "hath sovereign and uncontrollable authority in the making, confirming, enlarging, restraining, abrogating, repealing, reviving and expounding of laws concerning matters of all possible denominations ...."[4] He precluded the possibility of an English Marbury v. Madison.[5] To permit the Courts to review unreasonable legislation, Blackstone believed, "were to set the judicial power above that of the legislature, which would be subversive of all Government."[6] In 1784, the French commentator De Lolme observed: "It is a fundamental principle with the English Lawyers that Parliament can do everything except making a woman a man, or a man a woman."[7] It was the Victorian scholar, Professor A.V. Dicey, however, who gave classic expression to the doctrine of absolute parliamentary sovereignty. According to Dicey, the English constitution countenances no fundamental rights which are anterior to, or set limits on, the authority of Parliament. Such notions are best left to less fortunate people. "Now most foreign constitution-makers" he condoled, "have begun with declarations of rights. For this they have often been in no wise to blame."[8] Understandably, so the same thinking goes, your new country no doubt needed an entrenched, written constitution in which the courts had a potentially powerful role.

The supremacy of Parliament remains official orthodoxy in England to the present day. Meanwhile, your Bill of Rights has grown in significance, and, particularly in the last 30 years, your constitution has come to be perceived as a potent instrument of social change. Especially in the fields of criminal procedure, race, and freedom of expression, the Supreme Court has brought about a transformation which only now shows signs of slowing. In 1973, the Court established at a single judicial blow a right to abortion which it took eight parliamentary struggles spread over 50 years to achieve in this country.[9] Recent history tends to vindicate de Tocqueville's comment that "There is hardly a political question in the United States which does not sooner or later turn into a judicial one."[10]

Not only in the United States, however, has the emphasis on individual rights gained momentum. On March 8th, 1951, the United Kingdom became the first nation to ratify the European Convention on Human Rights. Since then it has been joined by 21 other countries. The Convention comprises an international Bill of Rights, which reflects the Universal Declaration of Human Rights (1948) of the United Nations and guarantees rights which include life; freedom from torture, inhuman or degrading punishment; liberty and security of person; a fair trial; respect for private and family life; and freedom of thought, expression, and association. Under English law, an international treaty does not become part of the internal law of the land, enforceable in the ordinary courts, except by specific legislative enactment.[11] The guarantees of the European Convention have been incorporated by Westminster legislation into the constitutions of some 24 former colonies upon their gaining independence.[12] In such new countries they have been regarded as essential. Moreover, since 1966, the United Kingdom has accepted a right of individual petition to the European Commission of Human Rights at Strasbourg. Under this procedure, if the Commission upholds a complaint against a signatory state, the case may be referred to the European Court of Human Rights for adjudication. The Convention has not, however, yet been enacted into English law. Our domestic courts cannot give it direct application. Decisions of the European Court are not binding, though it is embarrassing for governments to ignore them and their persuasive effect is considerable.

In addition to these external influences--which Judge J. Skelly Wright described as the "pull" across the Atlantic and the "push from across the channel"--changes have taken place in the structure of British domestic politics which have called into question the traditional conception of Parliament as the custodian of individual liberties.[13] The growing involvement of government in many areas of people's lives and the tremendous upsurge in regulations have both heightened the need for Parliament to scrutinise legislation and reduced its ability to do so. Another trend has been the increasing dominance of the legislature by the executive, exemplified by the greater use of the "whip" and the "guillotine"--devices, respectively, to compel voting along party lines and to prevent filibustering. At the same time as the potential for the misuse of power by government has grown in these ways, the composition of British society has become more heterogeneous. With the expansion of immigrant populations and with rising demands for regional automomy, the need is greater than ever to protect "discrete and insular minorities" against the "tyranny of the majority."[14-15]

It is these experiences which have prompted the call that Britain should have a new Bill of Rights. The proposal first became a prominent issue in 1974 when Sir Leslie (now Lord) Scarman gave the Hamlyn Lecture.[16] Lord Scarman identified the challenges by which he saw English law to be confronted and stressed the need for a curb to be placed on the sovereignty of the legislature. He called for "entrenched or fundamental laws protected by a Bill of Rights, a constitutional law which it would be the duty of the courts to protect even against the power of Parliament.[17]

The theme was taken up from amongst the ranks of all the political parties. A leading proponent of a Bill of Rights has been Lord Hailsham, the Lord Chancellor. In his book The Dilemma of Democracy, Lord Hailsham diagnosed the dangers of absolute legislative power and testified to his experience that Parliament has become an "elective dictatorship."[18] He prescribed a new constitution to protect individual rights and to limit the presently untrammelled powers of the legislature. Many leading politicians and lawyers have from time to time given their support. A fellow English barrister, Anthony Lester, who presciently opened the discussion in 1968, has been an articulate and thoughtful advocate.[19]

Yet, despite such influential backing, no modern British Bill of Rights has so far been adopted. No steps have been taken towards designing a new Constitution. Even Bills seeking to incorporate the European Convention into domestic law have failed to pass, although they have been debated on a number of occasions by both Houses of Parliament. Twice--in 1979 and again in 1981--such a Bill, pioneered by the Liberal Peer, Lord Wade, was approved by the House of Lords, only to founder in the Commons.[20] It appears that both Labour and Conservative parties, however willing they may be to entertain the idea of a Bill of Rights whilst in opposition, are unwilling to support it when in office. Governments have a reluctance to legislate for restraints on their power and there are urgent demands upon their resources and parliamentary time which make a charter of individual rights--a cause carrying few votes, and long-term rather than short-term benefits--a low priority. There are also concerns about the wisdom of a Bill of Rights which mean that the impetus has never become irresistible. For you who take such a charter for granted, it may be interesting briefly to deploy the dissenting arguments. For many of us they lack conviction, and with the confidence bred of the workings of your own constitution you may find them illusory. They are more fully summarised than the scope of this paper permits by Professor Michael Zander, of the London School of Economics, in an available pamphlet.[21]

One of the arguments against a Bill is the view that our liberties are already adequately protected. True it is that in many cases our record is good. There would be few who would say with confidence that it is incapable of improvement. A stream of complaints against the United Kingdom before the European Human Rights Commission, now numbering some 800 a year, and more importantly the number held to be admissible for consideration--over 80 since 1966--eloquently illustrates the scope for both vigilant scrutiny and steady improvement.[22] Moreover, a Bill of Rights is not to be seen in a short term-scale: it is a check against abuses of power in a future which extends beyond the next few years and decades.

There is an argument that a Bill of Rights would be ineffective. This gloomy prognostication echoes the contention advanced by the Federalists in your own constitutional debates--liberty cannot really be secured by "a Bill of Rights, or any characters drawn upon paper or parchment, those frail remembrances."[23] The riposte is surely that of Madison: that even "paper barriers" can have a salutary effect against the abuse of power.[24] The political tradition and the will of a country are of the most importance in the preservation of liberties, but the support of the law can be valuable. Our recent experience with legislation against race and sex discrimination is a cogent illustration; they have not achieved all their objects, but they have advanced the position considerably.

There are also arguments against a Bill which reflect our long tradition of parliamentary supremacy. Thus it is said to be better to leave our constitution flexible, and for Parliament to legislate in specific situations. These objections miss the mark as well: it is against the abuse which a flexible system permits, and either the nonintervention or oppressive intervention of the legislature, that a Bill of Rights is largely needed. It is also said that no charter could be entrenched against repeal by a subsequent Act of Parliament. For entrenchment, as it is cogently urged, is inconsistent with the doctrine that Parliament cannot bind its successors.[25] Assuming this to be right, the argument ignores the political and public effect of an attempt to repeal a well-regarded written constitution. As Lord Denning said, in the context of the contemplated enactment of the Treaty of Rome into English law: "But legal theory does not always march alongside political reality .... Freedom once given cannot be taken away."[26]

It is when we consider the practical consequences of a Bill of Rights that we penetrate the fundamental issue of political principle. For the effect of such a Bill on the constitutional balance of power is clear; it erodes the supremacy of Parliament and puts a separate responsibility in the hands of the judges. It gives judges a potential political and social role of the kind to which you are accustomed and we are not. The difficulty lies not in the suggestion that our judges may by training and techniques be unfitted for such a role. This claim is belied by the record of the Judicial Committee of the Privy Council in handling appeals concerning constitutional guarantees in new Commonwealth countries.[27] Judges would adapt to their task and perform it with similar distinction to your own. A more substantial fear is that judges who adjudicate on controversial questions involving fundamental rights would be drawn into the political arena. The result, it is predicted, would be to undermine their reputation for impartiality and eventually to politicise the appointment process. The example of the United States is said to be one to be avoided. Appointments to the bench might be affected by ideological loyalties. Many would consider that this would sacrifice the political neutrality of judges, and potentially compromise their independence. Such concerns have led Lord Devlin, the former Law Lord, to conclude that "The Supreme Court, like the vines of France, is not for transplantation. The soil and climate in which it flourishes are not those of Britain."[28]

This is a legitimate area of sensitivity. Already some figures on the political left contend that the British judiciary is not only involved in politically sensitive issues, but reveals a fundamentally Conservative bias.[29] They express the fear that the judges, equipped with a Bill of Rights and the power of review, would use their position to strike down the programmes of a future socialist government. In recent years, our courts have asserted powers of control over the decision-making process and a limited power to quash administrative decisions, which is a reaction to the growth of executive power. Some of these decisions--affecting the powers of local government and the rights of trade unions--have been criticised as reflecting precisely such a political bias. Even if such claims are ill-founded, they can erode the confidence which our society has in a politically neutral, utterly independent judiciary. Furthermore, with a Bill of Rights, the judiciary would have a greater power to frustrate the wishes of a democratically elected Parliament. It is this objection--that the power to administer a Bill of Rights is undemocratic--which lies at the heart of the opposing argument. We must acknowledge that decisions determining basic human rights are frequently controversial. The debate which they occasion often reflects deep-seated differences of moral, political and even social principle. In a democracy, the argument runs, the responsibility for such decision-making should not lie with the judges, who are unelected, nonrepresentative, and accountable to no constituency. It should rather rest, and rest only, with the elected representatives of the people.

From your jurisprudence you will readily recognize much of this argument. It is true that for you the issue is not whether you should have a judicially enforceable Bill of Rights, because that is a "given," but rather as to its scope and meaning. Your debate, broadly stated, is whether the Bill of Rights should be regarded as a general mandate for the protection of the individual, or as a narrowly circumscribed list of exceptions to the principle of democratic rule. The more restrictive view has been favoured by such proponents of judicial restraint as Justice Frankfurter, as well as some of the present members of the Supreme Court, one of whom at least has spoken out extrajudicially against those petitioners who seek to use the Constitution as "a formula for an end run around popular government."[30-31] To my mind the classic statement of this position is that of Judge Learned Hand in his celebrated Holmes Lectures, where he described how it "would be most irksome to be ruled by a bevy of Platonic Guardians, even if I knew how to choose them, which I assuredly do not."[32]

What then are the prospects of Britain adopting a new Bill of Rights in the foreseeable future? It would be wholly unrealistic to suppose that we seriously contemplate a new, written constitution after your own model. Not only are there no signs at the moment of any such development, but history teaches that radical constitutional change is only likely to occur at a time of political discontinuity. The Magna Carta and the 1689 Bill of Rights were, no less than the Declaration of Independence and the United States Constitution, forged out of revolution and the unanimity born of common struggle. No such conditions now obtain. In the United Kingdom today there is neither the consensus to create a new constitutional settlement, nor the crisis to compel one.

There is much more hope, and to my mind an ultimate inevitability, about the enactment of the European Convention into our domestic law. The Government is committed to the Convention by treaty. Individuals regard a petition to the Commission as a means of seeking redress for breach. The decisions of the European Court are generally influential and respected domestically. The Convention already has been regularly interpreted in case law in the judgments of the European Court. It has become a familiar feature of our legal life. It has been invoked on numerous occasions in English cases--not, of course, as binding authority--but as an aid to interpretation, under the principle that our municipal law should be presumed as far as possible to accord with our international obligations.[33] Moreover, in other areas, the English legal system is slowly becoming assimilated, and used, to Europe. In joining the European Economic Community, Britain has already acceded to a supra-national legal order, presided over by the European Court of Justice at Luxembourg, whose decrees are directly applicable in our Courts.

Most significantly of all, since the right of petition to Strasbourg has been recognised, a series of suits involving the United Kingdom has come before the European Court of Human Rights. These cases have concerned such matters as alleged restrictions on the correspondence of prisoners and on their access to legal advice, inhuman treatment of suspected terrorists in Northern Ireland, judicial birching in the Isle of Man, interference with freedom of expression caused by a House of Lords decision on the doctrine of contempt, the oppressive operation of the "closed shop," criminal laws in Northern Ireland against homosexual acts between consenting adult males, inadequate review procedures for the detention of mental patients, corporal punishment in the Scottish school system, and insufficient protection of personal privacy against telephone tapping by the police.[34-42] Most of these cases have brought about changes in the United Kingdom law and practice. Even without direct enforceability, the European Convention has had an undeniable impact.

It can be said, not altogether whimsically, that there is something in favour of the status quo. To deny the European Convention direct application may help preserve the political neutrality of our own judiciary. At the same time, permitting recourse to Strasbourg allows the Convention to exert an indirect influence and exposes the United Kingdom to the valuable stimulus and sometimes corrective of European juridical thought. Constructive criticism of existing practice may be more likely to originate from an outside body than from our own domestic tribunals. It is also easier to accept judgments with resignation, blaming it all on the continental Europeans who fail to understand the value of our admirable practices.

Against this, for many of us decisively, the present position is wholly anomalous. Our country acknowledges by treaty the importance of individual rights. We acknowledge the entitlement of an aggrieved individual to petition to protect those rights, but we do not allow his claim to be adjudicated upon in our own country. To obtain a remedy, claimants are not entitled to invoke their own laws but are obliged to undertake costly and protracted proceedings abroad, and then rely on the persuasive effect of a favourable decision. We deny our own judiciary the custody of the most substantial bill of rights to which we are party, while entrusting it to a tribunal that, in Dr. F. A. Mann's words, "is predominantly foreign in nationality, training and standards, that includes Judges from...countries as diverse as Malta and Iceland, Turkey and Portugal, Cyprus and Luxembourg and that displays little inclination to seek guidance from comparative material, or, in particular, from the wealth of American learning and its British ideological base.[43] Illogically and unworthily, we shy off the ultimate recognition of a charter, with whose merit no one valuing liberties can even begin to quarrel. It is the very untenable nature of this position which at present offers the greatest hope that the Convention will in due course become, perhaps in the end uncontroversially, part of our own law.

FOOTNOTES

1. This English author has been greatly assisted by George Leggatt, Barrister at Law (Middle Temple).

2. J. Skelly Wright, A Bill of Rights: Shield or Shackle or Sham? (A.B.A. Discussion Paper, 1985).

3. Thomas Paine, Rights of Man (Penguin Ed. 1969) (1791).

4. Sir William Blackstone, Commentaries on the Law of England Vol. I 128 (4th Ed. 1876) (1765).

5. 5 U.S. (1 Cranch) 137 (1803).

6. Blackstone, supra n. 4, at 66.

7. J. L. De Lolme, The Constitution of England 117 (1834 Ed.) (1784).

8. A. V. Dicey, Introduction to the Study and Law of the Constitution 198 (10th Ed. 1959).

9. Cf. Roe v. Wade, 419 U.S. 113 (1973).

10. Alexis de Tocqueville, Democracy in America 270 (Mayer Ed. 1969).

11. See, e.g., Cheney v. Conn [1968] 1 W.L.R. 242; compare The Paquete Habana 175 U.S. 677, 700 (1900).

12. Listed in A. Lester, Fundamental Rights: The United Kingdom Isolated (1984) Pub. L. Rev. 46 n. 51.

13. J. Skelly Wright, The Bill of Rights in Britain and America--A Not Quite Full Circle, 55 Tul. L. Rev. 291, 325 (1981).

14. United States v. Carolene Products Co., 304 U.S. 144, 152 n.4 (1938).

15. De Tocqueville, supra n. 10, at 250.

16. Sir Leslie Scarman, English Law--The New Dimension (1974).

17. Id. at 20.

18. Lord Hailsham, The Dilemma of Democracy (1978).

19. See, e.g., A. Lester, supra n. 12; Democracy and Individual Rights (1968) Faber Tract No. 390; and Fundamental Rights in the United Kingdom: The Law and the British Constitution 125 U. Pa. L. Rev.337 (1976).

20. See A. Lester, supra n. 12, at 62.

21. M. Zander, A Bill of Rights (3rd Ed. 1985).

22. See A. Lester, supra n. 12, at 65.

23. John Dickinson, Letters of Fabius (1788), quoted in B. Schwartz, The Great Rights of Mankind 112 (1977).

24. J. Madison, Speech to Congress (June 8th, 1789), quoted in B. Schwartz, supra n. 23 at 168.

25. See, e.g., Dicey, supra n. 8, at 145.

26. Blackburn v. Attorney-General [1971] 1 W.L.R. 1037, at 1040.

27. See S. A. de Smith, Constitutional and Administrative Law (3rd Ed. 1977) 442 n. 25 and cases cited therein.

28. P. Devlin, The Judge 7 (1979).

29. See, e.g., J.A.G. Griffith, The Politics of the Judiciary (1977).

30. See, e.g., A.F. of L. v. American Sash Co., 335 U.S. 538, 555 (1948).

31. W.J. Rehnquist, The Notion of a Living Constitution, 54 Tex. L. Rev. 693, 706 (1976).

32. L. Hand, The Bill of Rights 73 (1958).

33. See, e.g., A-G v. BBC [1981] A.C. 303, 354, per Lord Scarman, and see generally A.Z. Drzemczewski, European Human Rights Convention in Domestic Law 178-186, 314-322 (1983).

34. Golder v. U.K. 1 EHRR 524 (1975); Silver v. U.K. 5 EHRR 347 (1983).

35. Ireland v. U.K. 2 EHRR 25 (1978).

36. Tyrer vs. U.K. 2 EHRR 1 (1978).

37. The Sunday Times v. U.K. 2 EHRR 245 (1979).

38. Young, James & Webster v. U.K. 4 EHRR 38 (1981).

39. Dudgeon v. U.K. 4 EHRR 149 (1981).

40. X v. U.K. 4 EHRR 188 (1981).

41. Campbell & Cosans v. U.K. 4 EHRR 293 (1982).

42. Malone v. U.K. (as yet unreported).

43. F.A. Mann, Britain's Bill of Rights 94 L.Q.R. 512, 530 (1978).

JURISDICTIONAL CONFLICTS ARISING FROM ANTITRUST ENFORCEMENT

London Sessions
ABA Annual Meeting 1985
Ballroom, Dorchester Hotel
London, England

Wednesday, July 17, 1985
10:00 A.M. - 12:00 Noon

John H. Shenefield
Suite 900, 1825 I Street, N.W.
Washington, D.C. 20006

Speakers are fond of remarking to Anglo-American audiences that our two great nations are separated only by the temperature of our beer, our driving habits, and our common language. In recent years, another item might have crept onto that short list--our different views concerning antitrust jurisdiction over transnational commerce.

In the last ten years, the relations between our governments have occasionally included an element of irritation over the assertion of U.S. antitrust jurisdiction over foreign conduct and parties. It is a tribute to our joint determination to maintain close ties that the problem has been the subject of continual study and consultation. And it is a vindication of that determination that we can see today, with only a few reservations, the potential for progress toward harmony on this troublesome issue.

The first step was to recognize that the issues raised by the application of national antitrust laws to international commerce were important. The limited world of antitrust is a useful microcosm to examine for clues as to ways in which the larger issues of concurrent jurisdiction, including sovereignty and conflicting economic regimes, might be resolved. Most importantly, antitrust provides recent concrete examples of how the problems arise in the real world and therefore offers lessons, both as to the potential of these differences for resisting resolution, and the most likely avenues for progress.

The Background

The controversy about antitrust jurisdiction over transnational commerce was slow in developing. Although the U.S. antitrust statutes speak explicitly of "foreign commerce," the earliest effort to apply the laws to conduct beyond the borders of the United States elicited from Justice Holmes, who had no great enthusiasm for antitrust, a flat rejection of the theory.[1] But that first test was misleading. Over the course of the next 36 years, courts struggled to circumvent Justice Holmes's holding. They were usually able to find enough activity within the United States to proceed on the basis of strict territorial jurisdiction, even when the result was to reach predominantly foreign activity. The result was that <u>American Banana</u> was steadily eroded, but never flatly overruled.[2]

American antitrust jurisprudence took a turn toward the controversial with Judge Hand's decision in the <u>Alcoa</u> case, which involved a cartel of Canadian and European aluminum producers, formed overseas, with a quota on production including imports into the United States market. The decision held that the antitrust laws could apply to conduct by foreigners in foreign countries, "if [these agreements] were intended to affect imports and did affect them."[3]

The "effects" test was unpopular from the start. Foreign commentators saw the standard as "extraterritorial," and thus inconsistent with international law. They reasoned that expansive application of laws reflecting principles of economic organization would occasionally lead to conflicts among nations, without apparently enough doctrinal flexibility to adjust those conflicts. Whatever the merits of their assessment of international law, these predictions of trouble ahead were on the mark.

When the "effects" test proved resilient even in the face of substantial criticism, foreign governments increasingly complained. Subscribing to the "nationality" principle and strict "territorial" principles of jurisdiction, many foreign governments disapproved of pegging jurisdiction to the effects of conduct, regardless of its situs. In several recent cases, the unhappiness of foreign governments with what they regarded as the intrusive reach of U.S. jurisdiction into their sovereign affairs boiled over.

In 1976, the United States initiated a grand jury investigation of the worldwide uranium cartel. Although the government eventually declined to seek indictments of any foreign companies or individuals, the wide-ranging scope of the investigation triggered hostile reaction in several foreign capitals. When that was followed by the Westinghouse suit for treble damages, concerned governments made their disapproval crystal-clear. Another grand jury was empanelled, this time to investigate the North Atlantic shipping industry, again involving foreign as well as U.S. firms. Despite elaborate consultations, involving explanations of the unique circumstances of the investigation, the reaction to the grand jury's indictment of foreign firms and individuals was one of shock. Then, too, private suits followed, and it was clear from diplomatic notes that the reaction to American antitrust jurisdiction was heating up. Nothing summed up the fever of reaction more pointedly than the rush by many foreign governments to enact protective legislation designed to defeat the enforcement of U.S. antitrust laws against their citizens. Such laws generally blocked U.S. antitrust investigation of foreign conduct or individuals, and in extreme cases, created a retaliatory right of action against successful antitrust plaintiffs for the amount of the awards.

Dissatisfaction with the state of the law had already prompted a few U.S. courts to search for ways to temper the "effects" standard. The gist of these efforts was the development of a "balancing" approach, weighing factors for and against the exercise of jurisdiction.[4] Cases such as <u>Timberlane</u> and <u>Mannington Mills</u> offered a reformulation of the jurisdictional test reconciling antitrust enforcement with legitimate foreign concerns regarding intrusions on sovereignty through the flexible medium of a jurisdictional rule of reason. Several circuits have now endorsed this approach, and indeed, one appellate court has used it to dismiss a case.[5]

Congress has also recently altered the jurisdictional language of the Sherman Act to make it clear that wholly foreign commerce, without any effects in the United States, does not provide a basis for Sherman Act jurisdiction. Although no major change can be expected in government prosecutions, which have all along been guided by the kind of standard now made explicit in Title IV of the Export Trading Company Act, Title IV will bar suits that some judges and commentators had previously allowed.[6]

Recent years have thus seen controversies and efforts to resolve them. Progress remains to be made. The elements of continuing disagreement persist in the conflicting views that the United States and other nations retain on the issue of antitrust enforcement.

The Non-U.S. Perspective

Many nations object in principle to one country's extension of its jurisdiction, on the basis of an effect in its own territory, to regulate conduct that takes place outside those boundaries. They view any such assertion of jurisdiction as unsanctioned by international law. Moreover, they are resolved not to acquiesce in the unacceptable political inference that they have yielded control over conduct within their own borders. Their objection is all the more intense when the conduct at issue is supported by official government policy.

At another level, the dispute concerns a conflict in economic regimes. Many nations as a matter of national policy do not choose to rely on competition as the sole regulator of markets. While the contrasts between nations are less sharp now than is sometimes claimed, the application of U.S. antitrust law to international commerce can appear to subject foreign industries to a competitive regime that is inconsistent with their country's own policy.

Next, other nations object to antitrust enforcement procedure. Criminal penalties for antitrust violations, wide-ranging pre-trial discovery, frequently labeled "fishing expeditions" by foreign authorities, treble damages, and the award of reasonable attorneys' fees to the plaintiff--all of these are familiar to the American system of jurisprudence. Foreign nations object to each of them as inappropriate in a sensitive area of concurrent jurisdiction. They further object to the vast expense and the uncertainty involved in litigating antitrust cases. Even if the principled objections to the "effects" doctrine were to be resolved, the irritation at the mode of enforcement would remain.

U.S. Perspective

The United States in turn believes that the assertion of jurisdiction based on effects within the United States is appropriate, and fully consistent with international law and the practice of other nations, including the antitrust enforcement of the Federal Republic of Germany and the European Community. The United States believes that exercise of that jurisdiction must nevertheless take into account the policies, laws, and practices of other countries. As an official matter, it is willing to consider methods of resolving not only individual controversies but the underlying jurisdictional dispute, but it has not abandoned the central tenet that there are situations in which conduct abroad that creates effects within the United States can be regulated by U.S. law.

The United States remains generally committed to competition as the central organizing principle of its economy. Although there have been some relevant changes in law or policy, such as the new legislation with respect to ocean shipping and the new policy on international aviation, there remain clear differences between the United States and other nations as to the extent of reliance on competition.

Finally, the United States acknowledges that its procedures are unique. Some changes are possible, but a complete overhaul is neither likely nor desirable.

Trends and Dangers

There have been efforts to bridge these differing views, and now there does seem to be the potential for substantial improvement. Lest anyone assume that the entire problem is behind us, however, we should be warned by the _Laker_ litigation.[7]

Laker Airways filed an antitrust suit in a U.S. court against domestic, British, and other foreign airlines. A scant three months after the filing of the antitrust case, the foreign airlines filed suits in the High Court Of Justice of the United Kingdom seeking an injunction forbidding Laker from prosecuting its suit in the United States. That Court and the Court of Appeal issued injunctions ordering Laker to dismiss its suit against the British airlines. Laker countered by requesting injunctive relief in the U.S. court to prevent the remaining defendants from seeking a British injunction with respect to them. The U.S. court issued the injunction, which was affirmed on appeal. Although the court's opinion acknowledged the limitation on the judiciary's ability to resolve the underlying conflicts of policy, it decided that the principles of comity and concurrent jurisdiction were not inconsistent with the use of an injunction to protect jurisdiction, thus permitting the United States claim to go forward free of foreign interference.

The _Laker_ case proves two things. First, while there has been some progress toward resolution of these disputes, there have also been setbacks, chief among them the tendency to utilize blocking legislation that neutralizes the process of accommodation by creating instant confrontation. Second, the need for determined efforts by all concerned nations to solve these problems is therefore greater than ever.

The United States has been sensitized to the problem by the experience of the last few years. As a result it is in the process of making important changes in its procedures and its substantive law. Many other countries, including particularly Australia, have also had innovative and useful ideas to propose. Thus there does seem to be a general willingness to grapple with underlying issues and to ensure that they are resolved as amicably and harmoniously as possible.

The U.S. government has taken a variety of steps to ease the tension. First, the invariable practice in an antitrust investigation or case that might concern a foreign government is to give an advance notification through the State Department. Second, the advance notice permits consultation between U.S. enforcement authorities and appropriate officials of a foreign government, a process that has been extensively utilized in the last several years to avoid misunderstanding or surprise. Putting the notification and consultation procedures into regulation form may offer some additional reassurance to concerned foreign governments.

Third, U.S. antitrust enforcement authorities proceed where possible by way of voluntary requests for information, as opposed to compulsory discovery demands. That voluntary procedure, usually equally effective, may be less of an affront to sovereignty, particularly when it is in a foreign company's own interest to supply proof of its innocence.

Fourth, the U.S. government has made clear in recent years that questions of conflicts in jurisdiction are considered explicitly in the exercise of prosecutorial discretion. Fifth, U.S. courts have followed this lead in moving from the simpler "effects" doctrine of *Alcoa* to the more flexible and accommodating approach outlined in *Timberlane* and *Mannington Mills*. While the precise nature of the analysis remains to be worked out, the courts now seem more willing to take into consideration the fact of concurrent jurisdiction and the extent to which foreign individuals or firms are likely to be adversely affected by a particular enforcement action.

Sixth, there have been significant changes in U.S. legislation and policy. The enactment of Title IV of the Export Trading Company Act has eliminated Sherman and Federal Trade Commission Act jurisdiction for conduct that occurs wholly abroad and is without any substantial effect in the United States. Moreover, the United States has enacted an entirely new regulatory scheme for ocean shipping, which will bring the United States into closer conformity with the regulatory pattern in the rest of the world. Similarly, a new executive branch policy toward international aviation has for now, eliminated much of the potential for disagreement with other countries.

There have also been several encouraging multilateral or bilateral developments involving the United States. These include the 1979 OECD Recommendation on Cooperation and the antitrust enforcement agreements with Australia, Canada, and West Germany. These agreements are predicated on the assumption that not all substantive disagreements can be eliminated, but that a procedure enabling countries to exchange information and views is likely to reduce the level of tension and enhance the chances for amicable resolution of the disputes.

Proposals To Resolve Conflict

While there has thus been some progress, further effort is needed, not just by the United States but by all countries interested in resolving this ongoing dispute. The following suggestions might be the heart of an agenda for action.

The U.S. government can be more helpful in the context of the private treble damage suit, especially where the perspective of the government on the appropriateness of a court's taking jurisdiction in particular circumstances is relevant. Accordingly, the government should, by way of amicus participation or otherwise, routinely advise the court on those aspects of the jurisdictional decision as to which it has special competence.

Further, with respect to private treble damage suits, a more thoroughgoing reform is in order. By their nature, such suits are especially disruptive of harmonious international relationships. The solution is a revision of the authorizing statute. First, the jurisdictional rule of reason concept, derived from the balancing of interests approach of _Timberlane_ and _Mannington Mills_, should be codified. It should no longer be open to courts to decide whether they are willing or able to weigh competing interests to determine the existence of jurisdiction, as difficult as that task may be. Second, private suits premised on rule of reason violations or following federal criminal convictions should be confined to single damages. In the former case, given the complexity of a rule of reason analysis, it would seem unfair to subject defendants, whether domestic or foreign, to the highly punitive treble damage remedy if they happen to guess wrong or be poorly advised by counsel. In the latter case, the investigative work has largely been done, whether or not a plaintiff will have access to it, and the fact of a grand jury indictment and conviction is of substantial significance to private plaintiffs. In such circumstances it would scarcely seem necessary to subsidize their litigation further by treble damages.

These two categories would address the majority of private suits against foreign defendants in recent years. There would remain the category of private litigation involving per se offenses, such as price-fixing or division of markets, in which the U.S. government had no prior grand jury investigation, and for these actions treble damages would seem entirely appropriate.

An alternative proposal would be to eliminate treble damages in cases involving conduct that took place predominantly outside the United States, with exceptions in the court's discretion to avoid unfairness or, when necessary, in the interests of justice. This provision would apply to domestic as well as foreign defendants.

Any new statute should also take two additional steps. First, it should require notification of the Department of Justice about cases in which there are foreign defendants. This would have the effect of triggering executive branch consideration of amicus participation and it would provide an an early warning system for foreign governments. Second, any such statute should explicitly preempt state antitrust laws. The situation is complicated enough without having 50 separate state jurisdictions in which foreign antitrust defendants may be sued.

In addition to this statutory change, it continues to be important for the U.S. government to negotiate antitrust agreements with other governments. These have been successful in alleviating tension and enhancing understanding, and they would seem an obvious way of continuing to make progress. In addition, multilateral agreements that seek more fully to harmonize the substantive antitrust regimes of all nations remain an important objective and the efforts to build on the United Nations Principles and Rules on Restrictive Business Practices should be accelerated.

Finally, it would be a constructive step to consider avoiding the application of blocking statutes, and, if possible, to repeal them completely. As long as they exist and are utilized frequently, no broad progress in achieving harmonious relations in this area is likely to be made.

Were all of these efforts successful, the prospects for solving the problem of the conflict of antitrust jurisdictions would seem excellent. But such efforts need to be undertaken immediately, on both governmental and unofficial levels.

There is, therefore, a role in that effort for the private practitioners of the affected nations. Let us here in London in 1985 resolve to do our part to assist in reaching a mutually acceptable solution.

FOOTNOTES

1. American Banana Co. v. United Fruit Co., 213 U.S. 347 (1909).

2. See, e.g., United States v. Sisal Sales Corp., 274 U.S. 268 (1927); United States v. American Tobacco Co., 221 U.S. 106 (1911).

3. United States v. Aluminum Co. of America, 148 F.2d 416 (2d Cir. 1945).

4. Timberland Lumber Co. v. Bank of America, N.T. & S.A., 549 F.2d 597 (9th Cir. 1976) (Choy, J.); Mannington Mills, Inc. v. Congoleum Corp., 595 F.2d 1287 (3d Cir. 1979).

5. Montreal Trading Ltd. v. Amax, Inc., 661 F.2d 864 (10th Cir. 1981), cert. denied, 455 U.S. 1001 (1982).

6. Pub. L. No. 97-290, §402, 96 Stat. 1233, 1246 (1982) (codified at 15 U.S.C. §§6a, 45(a) (1982)).

7. See Laker Airways, Ltd. v. Pan. Am. World Airways, 559 F. Supp. 1124 (D.D.C. 1983), aff'd, 731 F.2d 909 (D.C. Cir. 1984).

JURISDICTIONAL CONFLICTS ARISING FROM ANTITRUST ENFORCEMENT

London Sessions
ABA Annual Meeting 1985
Ballroom, Dorchester Hotel
London, England

Wednesday, July 17, 1985
10:00 A.M. - 12:00 Noon

Sir Alan Neale
95 Swains Lane
London N6 6PJ

It has become the received wisdom that in a world where multinational companies conduct much transnational business across instant electronic links, territorial limits to jurisdiction are outdated and impracticable. It is believed, with particular reference to antitrust enforcement, that international law entitles us to apply our own laws to actions of foreigners abroad which adversely affect us. It is recognized that this may create conflicts and disagreements but these can be resolved by applying a soothing balm of "comity" which will lead us to exercise our jurisdiction with discretion and restraint after balancing all the interests involved.

I aim to persuade you that this doctrine is mostly misguided. To us in Britain, "comity," far from eroding sovereignty in a spirit of "you scratch my back and I'll scratch yours," is a strict injunction not to trespass on another sovereign's domain. To ask the courts in any of our countries to weigh in the balance the interests and value judgments which underlie our differing laws and practices is to face them with issues that are not in principle justiciable. All signs indicate that in the United States judges are unwilling in practice to accept the charge.

For these reasons it seems to me necessary to look elsewhere for solutions, and the search cannot exclude looking again at the justification for extending jurisdiction on the basis of effects. But we are commonly enjoined on this subject to avoid issues of principle and adopt a problem-solving approach. Accordingly, I shall start by reviewing the cases to see how far, and in what classes of case, it is really true that effective antitrust enforcement depends on claiming jurisdiction over the actions of non-Americans outside the United States. For reasons of space I shall have to confine myself mainly to what the Draft Reinstatement calls <u>jurisdiction to prescribe</u>, and deal only in passing, or by way of footnotes, with <u>jurisdiction to enforce</u> and the extraterritorial aspects of problems of discovery.[1-2]

Is Your "Effects Doctrine" Really Necessary?

First, then, no problem for antitrust enforcement arises when foreign companies operate actively in the United States. A Beecham or Unilever, making and distributing products through branches or subsidiaries in the United States, must conform to the antitrust laws in the same way that other visitors must obey traffic regulations or liquor laws. This principle extends to the activities of foreign interests which clearly control and direct the trading practices of associates in the United States. Thus, in the <u>Swiss Watchmakers</u> case, the Swiss defendants sought to control closely the use by their American associates of watchmaking machines and components from Switzerland, and their arrangements involved blacklisting and other sanctions against numerous U.S. companies. The justifiable criticism of the case was not that jurisdiction to prescribe was wrongly invoked against these activities in the United States, but that in his initial decree, the trial judge claimed undue jurisdiction to enforce by purporting to lay down rules governing what the Swiss industry and the Swiss authorities might enact in Switzerland.

Secondly, as with activity on the part of foreigners within the United States, so too illegal conduct by American companies outside can be reached without serious difficulty. Nobody would suppose that a price-fixing conspiracy intended to operate in the United States could be safely set up by U.S. companies just by holding meetings in Acapulco rather than Atlanta. As was stated in the Lotus case: "No one disputes the right of a State to subject its citizens abroad to the operation of its own penal laws, if it sees fit to do so."[3] In any event, such a conspiracy could hardly be implemented without giving rise to evidence of activity in the United States.

This "nationality" basis for jurisdiction can properly reach to predatory or monopolistic conduct of large American corporations towards smaller rivals where foreign institutions and even governments are cajoled or suborned into aiding and abetting the rough play. It is a curious paradox that so much of the discussion of the legitimate extent of U.S. jurisdiction over foreign cartel activity comes from cases (from American Banana through Sisel Sales to Timberlane and beyond) in which the alleged antitrust offenders have been American, not foreign, and it is hard to see why it has been thought necessary to invoke the "effects doctrine." In Sisal Sales, the Supreme Court held that the basic conspiracy to monopolize was "entered into by the parties within the United States and made effective by acts done therein," even though it was also aided by discriminatory legislation procured in Mexico in favour of the associated Mexican company. The rule that predatory conduct in securing such advantages abroad may be adduced as evidence of conspiracy to monopolize in the United States is of interest to aspiring monopolists and with hindsight might perhaps have been applied in American Banana[4] But what does it have to do with us?

Thirdly, there has been no difficulty about effective antitrust enforcement against illegal business activity in which Americans and non-Americans conspire or combine together. In the classic cases of carving up world markets, such as ICI/du Pont or GE/Philips, there was always important activity on the part of the foreign companies in the United States, in particular the exclusive licensing or assignment of their American patents as a means of giving effect to illegal restrictive schemes.

Jurisdiction over American participants is usually enough for effective enforcement against international cartels, for where U.S. firms have a major stake in world markets, it is highly unlikely that a cartel will be effective when their participation is withdrawn. Indeed it has been common in the past for the Department of Justice to refrain from proceeding against foreign parties in a cartel. Thus in National Lead Justice Burton noted that the complaint did not attempt to make any foreign companies parties defendant and added (two years after ALCOA) "the District Court recognised that it did not have jurisdiction over such co-conspirators." Similarly, in an action against a wire nails cartel, the Japanese producers were not indicted, and jurisdiction was confined to the restrictive activities of the U.S. importers within the United States.[5]

There is thus a vast area of commerce over which antitrust can be effectively enforced through the jurisdiction which you properly exert, and the rest of us do not dispute over activity within the United States or over U.S. nationals. All that is left for which the "effects doctrine" is indispensable as the basis for jurisdiction to prescribe is the offshore cartel consisting solely of foreign parties acting abroad or with only insignificant U.S. participation.[6] The number of cases of this kind has always been very small; in terms of recent controversies, the uranium litigation is the outstanding example, though the complaint against OPEC would no doubt have been even more troublesome but for the saving grace of the Act of State defence.

The Search for Solutions

The amount of attention given to the search for solutions is in itself an acknowledgment that the exercise of jurisdiction in this small remaining area arouses troublesome international reactions. As noted in relation to OPEC, the various Act of State and sovereign immunity defences still further limit the scope for successful enforcement action. This is of only limited comfort, however, to those abroad, as it seems anomalous that the law should discriminate between actions of similar economic purpose and effect according to their outward form. Thus a developing country which, wisely or not, seeks to maximise its revenue from some commodity in strong demand may achieve its purpose by levying some form of tax on its producers or by requiring them to sell only through a State export company and these methods will not be open to antitrust action. It seems of little practical sense or value to insist that if the price-fixing is left to its merchanting companies (in your terms a Webb-Pomerene association) it will be actionable under the Sherman Act.

The chief reassurance we are offered, however, is the "principle of reasonableness." Thus the Draft Restatement has it that a state may not apply its law "when the exercise of such jurisdiction is unreasonable;" and whether it is unreasonable is "judged by evaluating all the relevant factors.[7] It is hard to take too much comfort from this when one recalls the strong tradition in antitrust case-law against admitting economic and commercial grounds for justifying restraints of trade. All the way from Addyston Pipe through Trenton Potteries to Professional Engineers, the courts have avoided what Judge Taft called "setting sail on a sea of doubt" and have held, in the words of Justice Stevens, that "the rule does not open the field of antitrust inquiry to any argument ... that may fall within the realm of reason." A rule of reason requiring an even broader evaluation of the political and social factors relevant to applying antitrust standards to foreign business activity abroad would surely sail beyond the limit of the justiciable. As Kingman Brewster once put it: "the essence of the judicial message is that if you give this job to the courts in the form of criminal or public tort adjudication, you must expect the courts to act like courts."

It is already clear that many judges do not take kindly to the type of judicial balancing process proposed by Judge Choy in *Timberlane*. Thus Judge Marshall in the uranium litigation declared *it totally* impossible to set the interests of Canada against the policy underlying antitrust, and Judge Wilkey in his opinion on the recent *Laker* appeal said: "We are in no position to adjudicate the relative importance of antitrust regulation or nonregulation to the United States and the United Kingdom." The fact is that in any country the judiciary, with its obligation to uphold the law, has no suitable standards of reference by which to modify the application of law in deference to other interests. Hence, as Joseph Griffin has pointed out: "there has not been a case in which a U.S. court clearly had prescriptive jurisdiction under U.S. standards but declined to exercise it after conducting a *Timberlane/Mannington Mills* analysis."[8]

These considerations also run against putting too much trust in executive intervention. Consultation may well be of value in relation to legal action which is at the discretion of government agencies. But the main anxiety of foreign companies is likely to be private treble-damage actions. The suggestion that U.S. government agencies should intervene in such litigation with *amicus curiae* briefs or Suggestions of Interest may well meet resistance from the judges. So long as the courts believe that they are properly vested with jurisdiction over foreign parties on the basis of effects, it is not to be expected that they will trim the rights of litigants to the behests of the executive arm.[9] As believers in the separation of powers, we may properly decide that some disputes should be settled by diplomatic means and others by judicial process but it is hard to justify a mixture of the two.

From a foreign standpoint, a more promising way forward might be found in the standard adopted for proving *intent* in antitrust cases against foreigners acting abroad. Judge Hand himself, it will be recalled, assumed in *ALCOA* that Congress could not have meant the Sherman Act to cover agreements made abroad unless they were both intended to have, and shown actually to have, effects on United States commerce. It is not wholly clear whether Hand meant more than *mens rea* in the sense that a man is deemed to intend the natural consequences of his acts. The jurisdictional "rule of reason" proposed by Atwood and Brewster, however, requires that a foreign defendant should not be held liable unless shown to have "explicitly aimed at and actually restrained" American commerce.[10] With such a requirement it would be hard to prove that an offshore cartel which simply announced abroad a schedule of prices to all comers was specifically intended to affect American commerce; harmful effects might be foreseeable but they would not be the primary or specific purpose of the cartel.

A stricter test of intent, however, while it would help the defence, would not necessarily persuade the courts not to exercise jurisdiction. For this reason and because other solutions, as explained above, make unacceptable demands on the judiciary, foreign opinion would prefer a solution setting agreed limits to jurisdiction and cannot avoid therefore looking again at the validity of the "effects doctrine."

The "Effects Doctrine" Re-examined

I acknowledge, of course, that in this area there is no appeal to indisputable authority in international law. Submission to the jurisdiction of the International Court of Justice is by consent. We can all cite the majority opinion from _Lotus_, which holds that international law leaves States a wide measure of discretion as regards extending the application of their laws to persons and acts outside their territory. And anyway the Germans do it! On grounds like these the wise money will no doubt back the conclusion of Rosenthal and Knighton that "there seems to be no possibility that the United States will spontaneously modify" its position on the "effects doctrine."[11]

Lotus also held, however, that "international law forbids a state to exercise _jurisdiction to prescribe_ other than on an accepted basis of jurisdiction." I am unwilling to accept without a trial that a representative body of American lawyers is not open to argument on the question whether effects are an accepted or sufficient basis for jurisdiction.

First, then, I ask you to recall the three cases cited by Judge Hand as authority for describing the effects doctrine as "settled law." One--_Ford v. United States_--involved British defendants running liquor into San Francisco Bay during Prohibition; this was a combined operation with other defendants inside the United States where, as the evidence showed, most of the illegal acts took place; and the United Kingdom had accepted a treaty obligation specifically providing for U.S. jurisdiction in such circumstances. The other two cases dealt with schemes to defraud initiated respectively in Illinois and Washington, D.C. to take effect in Michigan and New York City, and it was held that the states in which the schemes took effect had valid claims to jurisdiction.[12] Can a rule to deal with interstate fraud really be good authority for making non-Americans liable under your law for conduct abroad which is within their own law?

Next, as it is sometimes implied that Justice Holmes's statement of the territorial principle in _American Banana_ was an outdated and idiosyncratic view even before _ALCOA_, I remind you that, on the contrary, it has been upheld in your courts on many occasions up to very recent times. I have already noted that Justice Burton, after ALCOA, endorsed the view that National Lead's foreign co-conspirators were outside the jurisdiction. If space permitted, I could cite several more examples (with Supreme Court Justices Taft, Lamar, McKenna, Minton, and Reed among them) of the view that the Sherman Act has no extraterritorial application and cannot control foreign citizens or corporations operating abroad.[13]

Passing from precedent to principle, if the "effects doctrine" is to come within an accepted basis for jurisdiction, this must be the "objective territorial principle" under which a State has jurisdiction to prosecute for crimes started outside but completed within its territory. The leading American authority, John Bassett Moore, defined it as "the principle that a man who outside of a country wilfully puts in motion a force to take effect in it is answerable at the place where the evil is done."[14] It has been applied by both English and American courts for two centuries, and it clearly requires a closer nexus than that of a course of conduct in one country simply having effects in another. Thus Jennings holds that the principle is "limited to those 'effects' which form part of the *actus reus*"[15] and Moore himself requires either "immediate effect or ... direct and continuous causal relationship."

These tests are met by the classic example of the bullet fired across a frontier or, for example, where oil spilled from a negligent tanker out to sea can be traced all the way to the beach it pollutes. Similarly, a blackmail note or a fraudulent prospectus will take effect in the country where it is delivered, even though mailed from elsewhere. The same prospectus, or a libel, circulated in Country A may have damaging effects on citizens of Country B but will only be actionable in Country A. This key distinction between "taking effect" and "having effects" was not recognised by Hand, even though it is well illustrated by the smuggling and fraud cases which he cited.[16] Applying it to antitrust, when the sales office of a wholly foreign cartel offers goods to all comers at a fixed price, it is unplausible to hold that it is setting in motion forces to take effect against the U.S. economy or that effects on U.S. trade are somehow a "constituent element" of the operation. The nexus with the U.S. economy is not indeed formed at all unless and until Americans choose to trade on the terms offered. Nobody forced Westinghouse to buy uranium from RTZ *et al*.

The argument may be clarified by considering the case where non-American parties refuse to supply U.S. buyers at all. Suppose the world supply of some substance with impressive cosmetic or curative properties is in the hands of foreign companies which, for good reason or bad, agree not to supply U.S. importers. There will clearly be restrictive effects on U.S. commerce but it is equally clear that it cannot conceivably be within the ambit of U.S. domestic law to require those concerned to meet American demand. Even assuming no problem of *in personam* jurisdiction, it is unrealistic to suppose that a U.S. court could order them to supply U.S. customers. How much and on what terms?

In my belief, the only conclusion consonant with international law, and indeed with common sense, is that foreigners outside the United States, whether acting individually or in concert, are fully entitled, subject to the law of their own States, to offer or not offer their goods or services to U.S. or any other buyers and to offer them on any terms that they choose.

Let me briefly restate the argument. Jurisdiction based on effects is not an accurate application of the "objective territorial" principle. It is rarely needed in practice for effective antitrust enforcement. To insist on retaining it for the rare offshore cartel which is not protected by the "Act of State" defence loses more in damage to international relations than it can possibly gain in advantage to your consumers. Solutions offered in terms of balancing interests as an exercise of comity and reasonableness take courts beyond their proper role. More broadly, the idea that our interdependence in the modern world justifies us in encroaching on one another's sovereignty creates more problems than it solves. In the most hard-headed of profit-and-loss terms, the game is not worth the candle.

FOOTNOTES

1. Restatement of the Foreign Relations Law of the United States (Revised) (Tent. Draft No.2, 1981) at 88 (Introductory Note to Section 401).

2. Nor can I deal here with the special problem of carriers in international sea and air transport whose business is to ply between States. Several States may have valid claims to jurisdiction to prescribe for them but should acknowledge a need to avoid facing them with conflicting requirements.

3. Case of the S.S. Lotus, 1927 P.C.I.J., ser. A, No. 10: Problems may, of course, arise for U.S. managers of companies incorporated under other jurisdictions who may be held liable under U.S. law for actions on the part of such companies that are required by the law of the foreign sovereign. For this reason the Draft Restatement (supra note 1, at Section 418) proposes that the United States should not "require conduct that is prohibited or ... prohibit conduct that is required" in a host state.

4. American Banana might properly have been distinguished, however, by the fact that the injury done to the plaintiff was by acts of the Costa Rican government, not of the defendant. It is noteworthy that courts have continued to refuse relief where a plaintiff's allegations have impugned the conduct or motives of foreign governments. See, e.g., Hunt v. Mobil Oil Corp., 550 F.2d 68 (2d Cir.), cert. denied, 434 U.S. 984 (1977).

5. United States v. R. P. Oldham Co., 152 F.Supp. 818 (N.D. Cal. 1957). Judge Murphy said "there is no attempt here to regulate Japanese commerce...or to indict Japanese firms... Only American corporations and American nationals are named as defendants."

6. It is important to distinguish cases for which the "effects doctrine" is indispensable as the basis for jurisdiction from cases in which the language of effects is used loosely and sometimes without justification. Thus in Laker Airways Ltd. v. Sabena, 731 F.2d 909 (D.C. Cir. 1984) Judge Wilkey referred more than once to the effects on American commerce of the conspiracy alleged by Laker. Whatever the other issues in this litigation, it is hardly in question that the various airlines involved were doing business in the United States and that the matters complained of involved activity there.

7. Draft Restatement, supra note 1, at Section 403.

8. Griffin, Possible Resolutions of International Disputes Over Enforcement of U.S. Antitrust Laws, 18 Stan.J. Int'l L. 279, 295 (1982). Subsequently the trial court to which the Timberlane case was remitted by the Ninth Circuit has dismissed the case for lack of jurisdiction. Timberlane Lumber Co. v. Bank of America, 574 F.Supp. 1453 (N.D. Cal. 1983), and this has been seen as an example of the balancing process in action. But as the case was a dispute between two groups of Americans over the assets of a failing Honduran lumber mill, and as the court found little or no cause of antitrust action but that there were issues of tort and contract for which Honduran jurisdiction was appropriate, it is unlikely to be seen outside the United States as relevant to foreign concerns about antitrust.

9. Still less to those of foreign governments. When the governments of the United Kingdom, Canada, Australia, and South Africa appeared as amici (with the encouragement of the U.S. State Department) before the Seventh Circuit in the uranium litigation, the court declared itself shocked by their "intermeddling." In re Uranium Antitrust Litigation, 617 F.2d at 1255-56.

10. 2 J. Atwood & K. Brewster, Antitrust and American Business Abroad 349-51 (2d ed. 1981). It is noteworthy that the most recent resolution on the subject by the International Law Association also requires that the "effects" in the country claiming jurisdiction should be both substantial and "a direct and primarily intended result" of conduct outside the territory. International Law Association, 1972 New York Conference Report 138. This is clearly a more stringent test than that in Section 403 of the Draft Restatement.

11. Rosenthal and Knighton, National Laws and International Commerce (Chatham House Paper 17, Royal Institute of International Affairs 1983) at 85.

12. Strassheim v. Daily, 221 U.S. 280 (1911); Lamar v. United States, 240 U.S. 60 (1916). It should be observed that the judgments in each case were written by Justice Holmes who clearly did not regard them as inconsistent with his statement of the territorial principle in American Banana.

13. Consider in particular Justice Lamar in United States v. Nord Deutscher Lloyd: "what was done lawfully in Germany cannot be punished as a crime in New York. The statute, of course, has no extraterritorial operation." 223 U.S. 512, 517 (1912).

14. 2. J.B. Moore, A Digest of International Law 244 (1906).

15. Jennings, Extra-territorial Jurisdiction and the United States Antitrust Laws, 46 British Yearbook of International Law 159 (1957). Jennings added: "If indeed it were permissible to found objective territorial jurisdiction upon the territoriality of more or less remote repercussions of an act wholly performed in another territory, then there were virtually no limit to a state's territorial jurisdiction."

16. F. A. Mann in The Doctrine of Jurisdiction in International Law, 111 Recueil des Cours 1, 104 (1964) observed that "the type of 'effect' which the ALCOA ruling has in mind has nothing in common with the effect which by virtue of established principles of international jurisdiction confers the right of regulation."

PROFESSIONALISM, LEGAL SERVICES AND LAWYER COMPETENCY

London Sessions
ABA Annual Meeting 1985
Audley Suite, Grosvenor House Hotel
London, England

Wednesday, July 17, 1985
10:00 A.M. - 12:00 Noon

Prof. Roger C. Cramton
Cornell University School of Law
Ithaca, New York 14853

Oceans of ink have been spilled in recent years on the subject of lawyer competence. My own exertions have contributed a barrel or two to this outpouring. Lawyer competence has been described, analyzed, and assessed. Empirical inquiries have attempted to pinpoint the extent of the problem and its sources. Numerous reforms have been proposed. There has been much preaching to the converted and a great deal of professional "viewing with alarm."[1]

I will not repeat here what I have said before on this subject. In a thumbnail, I have conceded that Chief Justice Burger has raised important questions, although doubting whether the extent of incompetence at the trial bar or elsewhere is either as large or as curable as his remarks have occasionally suggested. As an academic lawyer, I have bridled at implicit or explicit arguments that American law schools were the source of the problem--which presumably would go away if only we academics would shape up and do a better job. More constructively, I have argued that law schools have an obligation to introduce law students to the theory and practice of basic lawyer skills, such as interviewing, counseling, fact investigation, negotiation, drafting, and advocacy. And I have praised law schools for steady advances in these areas--finding the resources, people, teaching materials, and underlying theory to illuminate the lawyering process in a manner deserving of a university department. This arduous task, undertaken at many schools by many teachers and researchers, is now bearing modest fruits; and more will come in the years ahead if we persevere.

Today I want to suggest that our lawyer competency talk has some negative aspects deserving consideration. The man in the street (whether a consumer of legal services or not) should beware: lawyer competency may be hazardous to your health!

How is this possible? How can a good thing like more competent lawyers not be in the public interest? My answer explores three propositions: First, unless "lawyer competence" is viewed in a broad humanistic sense, it neglects the intangible qualities that characterize the good lawyer. Second, what the public needs <u>most</u> is not more technically expert lawyers, but morally better <u>lawyers</u>. Third, enhanced technical expertise is not a free lunch but something the consumer of legal services must pay for, and the price tag includes reduced access to higher-cost legal services.

I

The relationship between legal education and a highly competent legal profession is an important and complex one. Yet it is impossible to talk intelligently about "skills training" in a law school setting without having a working definition of what it means to be a good lawyer. Until one has in mind the attributes of the "competent lawyer," it is difficult to identify those areas in which the law school experience, as distinct from apprenticeship or other experiences, can make a distinctive or necessary contribution. And one cannot talk intelligently about lawyer competency without reference to the social environment in which a lawyer's activities take place.

What do we mean by "lawyer competence"?[2] One's ability to perform a task at an acceptable level must first be distinguished from the reality of doing so in a given situation. Clients are interested in lawyer performance--the routine delivery of high-quality legal services--not the capacity of a lawyer to do a good job.

Repeated studies have shown that most deficiencies in lawyer behavior are due, not to lack of competence, viewed as one's basic ability to do a satisfactory job, but to other factors: inattention, laziness, the press of other work, limited financial rewards, or just plain mistakes.[3] Any comprehensive approach to lawyer competence must begin with the practitioner's knowledge of legal theory, doctrine, and practice, and the ability to understand, communicate, and apply that knowledge. It must also, however, include an evaluation of other values--integrity, industry, and professional reliability.

Preparing individuals for the legal profession is a complicated task because the profession is so diverse and changeable. Law school graduates travel many different paths after graduation. Although there are elements that unify them, legal careers are highly varied. About 15 percent of law graduates do not practice law, but use their legal education in business, politics, government service, or some other endeavor. But there is also considerable diversity among those who practice law: a trial lawyer specializing in product liability cases; a public defender working in a metropolitan criminal court system; a general practice lawyer engaged in routine wills and real estate transactions; a patent lawyer on the legal staff of a large chemical company; a lobbyist representing timber interests in Washington; and a large firm corporate lawyer engaged in fighting off takeover bids--all are lawyers, but there are vast differences in the knowledge, skills, and personal qualities required in their daily work. Lawyers, it is clear, do a great many different things.

Moreover, our society changes very quickly, and lawyers are always on the cutting edge of those developments. During a single 40-year career, dramatic transformations in law and legal institutions will occur. This mutability is one reason why it is a mistake to rigidify the law curriculum by mandating particular courses for admission to the bar. This regimentation not only turns an intellectual experience into a boot camp, but the prescription itself soon becomes obsolete. As Whitehead said, "information doesn't keep any better than fish."

This diversity and change has implications for legal education. Either different law schools must prepare graduates for specific roles in the profession or all must concentrate on the lowest common denominator--basic knowledge and skills that cut across all law careers. In the United States, we do some of both: each law school has a somewhat different market for its graduates; and all law schools concentrate on the common denominator--knowledge and skills. That is, legal education is in some respects differentiated in an effort to prepare graduates for somewhat varying professional roles; but the common elements are stressed everywhere.

The most important skills law school can teach are those that will help law graduates adapt to a changing society and continue to grow as professionals. This ability depends more on intellectual curiosity, skills of self-learning, integrity, and professional responsibility than it does on the information content of law school courses.

Legal education cannot be focused on the nuts and bolts of law practice. The speculative and theoretical must be given a central place in the law school curriculum because they stimulate the intellect, provide a general framework that makes specific information useful, and establish the foundation for any effective application of law. A lawyer cannot deal effectively with any problem unless he has a sound command of the moral and theoretical foundations of applicable doctrine. Problems of individual responsibility in criminal law are one example. Only the lawyer who understands the moral and theoretical foundations of individual responsibility for crime can operate effectively in cases in which persuasion of a jury, framing an instruction for the judge, or seeking a new departure from an appellate court is the task at hand. On the other hand, a strong emphasis on applicational skills and on professional realities can enrich legal education and produce better lawyers.

These implications are borne out by a study of professional competence undertaken in North Carolina some years ago.[4] Medical experts evaluated the quality of the daily work of a large sample of general practice physicians. They found that a substantial minority of the physicians routinely met the highest standards of medical care in dealing with their patients. Most of the rest usually did, but there were some significant lapses. A small percentage were guilty of much more frequent and serious lapses. Researchers then correlated this performance information with everything they could discover about the physicians: age, sex, race, schools attended, years of practice, clinical experience, courses taken, and the like. Computer analysis revealed that performance did not relate significantly to any of these variables. It did, however, correlate with an odd assortment of things, such as class standing in medical school (a modest correlation with good performance), number of professional journals subscribed to (a more substantial correlation), and attendance at continuing education courses held out of town (a strong correlation--although attending courses given at home was not significant!).

The report discusses these and other factors at great length but never states the obvious: what differentiated the physicians who consistently did good work--whether or not they had a cold, or a family problem, or the patient could not pay--was a set of intangible qualities. They cared about medicine in the sense that they had a strong intellectual interest in it; they cared about the well-being of their patients; and they cared about their own image as professionals. In short, they had a sense of craftsmanship--a self-esteem that led them to internalize and update good professional standards of behavior, that reinforced pride in their work, that pushed them to provide a high quality of service routinely. When similar studies of lawyers are carried out, I am confident they will reveal similar patterns.

The difficult task of legal education and of the organized bar as a supporting institution is this: how can we best nurture these delicate and intangible qualities in young men and women who are drawn to the law? How can we feed their intellectual curiosity so that they will continue to keep abreast of changes in the law through the indefinite future? How can we develop their ability to learn independently and to be sensitive to the limits of their competence? For they cannot be truly competent lawyers unless they understand what tasks they are able to do themselves and what they should refer to others. And how can we give them a positive image of themselves as professionals, as craftsmen who take pride in their work, as lawyers who always give good measure because that is the only way they can look themselves in the mirror when they get up in the morning?

II

Any consideration of "lawyer competence" poses a teleological question: what do we mean by "the competent lawyer"? If we are to arrive at our goal, we must have a clear idea of what we seek.

Definitions of "lawyer competence" speak solely of technical expertise instrumentally applied for a client's benefit. The only moral dimension in these definitions is that the lawyer be "professionally responsible." Here the reference is not to rules of ordinary morality, but to the special rules of lawyer conduct the profession has promulgated since 1969 to govern its own affairs.[5] There is a vast difference, however, between the "good lawyer"--the morally upright lawyer--and the "competent lawyer" who conforms to the dominant contemporary notion of "anything for the client, provided it doesn't involve the lawyer actually breaking the law."

When Chief Justice Burger speaks about incompetent trial lawyers, the examples he gives involve inexperience, lack of knowledge or lack of skill: a trial lawyer does not know how to lay a foundation for the admission of a particular document; or he is unable to phrase a question on cross-examination in a manner that, against objection, will elicit the desired information.[6] The implicit assumption is that the profession's concern for the public interest will be met if lawyers are technically competent. Lawyers' ethics and behavior being what they are, greater technical expertise on the part of lawyers may contribute to societal problems rather than to their solution.

The dominant model of professional behavior today is aptly described as the total commitment model--the lawyer should do everything for the client that the client would do for himself if he had the lawyer's skill and knowledge. Professional rules add some discretion to depart from total commitment to the client's cause, but the basic constraints are references to general law--the lawyer should not become a law-breaker on behalf of a client. But much that is immoral or undesirable is not illegal, so the total commitment model pushes lawyers toward amoral, if not immoral, behavior in advancing the client's interest. Yet, the profession asserts, the lawyer is not morally accountable either for the client's goals or for his own actions on the client's behalf.

How can this be so? The traditional answer is that the lawyer is "only doing his job"--the adversary system requires him to be a zealous advocate on behalf of his client, and justice in the long run is best served if the lawyer is a dutiful functionary performing this assigned role. This excuse--"I was only doing my job"--is rejected when it comes from the likes of Eichmann, Calley, Erlichman, and other actors. Does it stand on any better footing when it comes from lawyers?[7]

An initial problem is that the justification based on the lawyer's role in the adversary system only extends as far as the merits of that system. If other methods of ascertaining the truth in contested matters, involving less harm to participants and the public, would do the job just as well, the lawyer's reliance on the adversary system to justify immoral behavior disappears. For argument's sake--or for the sake of values of individual freedom and dignity served by our current criminal justice system--I will assume the adversary system is at least as good a way to serve justice as any other. Even so, protecting the freedom and dignity of an individual against the power of the state is one thing; maximizing the gains of a private individual or corporation is another. The paradigm of total commitment is that of a Clarence Darrow defending at trial an innocent person charged with a crime; the reality of most civil litigation is that only money is involved, many of the participants are corporations or other artificial entities, and the resolution of disputes primarily involves negotiated settlements that involve cooperative as well as adversary behavior.

A second problem with the adversary system excuse is that most of what lawyers do does not involve adversary adjudication, civil or criminal. The total commitment model presumably serves justice when the interests of opposing parties and the public are protected by an equally aggressive and competent lawyer adversary and by an impartial tribunal (often including a jury as well as a judge); the impartial tribunal divines a just result out of adversary presentation of proofs and argument. With most lawyer behavior--the lawyer sitting in his office advising clients or drafting documents for them--there is no impartial tribunal to sort out adversary proofs and arguments. In many of these planning and counseling situations, there is even no adversary: if anyone is to look after the interest of those affected and of the general public, it must be the lawyer because there is no one else to do the job. Yet professional rules largely fail to reflect this distinction, and the prevailing zeitgeist is that of total commitment. For these and other reasons the lawyer cannot escape moral accountability for acts done on behalf of a client, merely by reciting that the profession's rules require him to be zealous, and he was "only doing his job."

Modern American lawyers--accustomed to reading justifications of zealous but immoral competence in their professional journals--are unaware of how novel and extreme many current conceptions of lawyering are.[8] They were not the views of Abraham Lincoln and other lawyers of his generation. Nor were they those of the first lawyers to address professional responsibility in a systematic fashion. David Hoffman, for example, writing 150 years ago, even espoused a model of diminished representation of the guilty and clearly took moral responsibility for everything done for a client. Pleading the statute of limitations against a just debt, he believed, was immoral conduct in which he would never participate.[9] These older ideas began to fade only when a new breed of lawyers sought after the Civil War to rationalize their activities on behalf of emerging corporate interests.[10] But the views of that generation of American lawyers concerning how far it was appropriate to go for a client were moderate compared to the hired-gun expressions of the contemporary bar.

The disarray of the system of justice is all too apparent. The problem is not one of a lack of competence on the part of its lawyer participants, but of a lack of civilizing and moderating qualities that include accommodation, trust, compassion, and similar qualities. More competent technicians, lacking in these qualities and adhering to the total commitment model of today's codes, will multiply litigation, abuse every possible procedural device, and employ any stratagem or tactic that will help win for a client. The result is not justice but social disaster. Increasingly, many lawyers have lost a sense of obligation to courts, opponents, and the general public. Only the client--and the lawyer's self-interest--count. "The vision of modern America," Robert Stevens has warned, "is psychiatrists telling their patients that they should have no guilt and lawyers telling their clients they have no responsibilities and accepting none for themselves.[11]

I do not contend that the narrowness of the technical expert is the universal pattern to which today's lawyers are cut. But it is the dominant pattern, increasing in prevalance and in official ideology. Many lawyers continue to take a broader view of their function--they engage in moral discourse with their clients, and a sense of moral vision informs what they say and what they do. They understand--and so do some of their clients--that technical expertness is too narrowly focused and that the very best lawyering rests on a broad comprehension of the social and cultural environment in which the legal system operates, and on an imagination that is creative because it is enriched by literature, religion, and history, which provide the symbolic and theoretical resources for envisioning new possibilities. Although it need not be so, the lawyer competency movement tends to be allied with the narrowly instrumental focus that concentrates on the nuts and bolts of helping the client win, pushing legal education toward preparing students, not for a learned profession, but for initial partisan endeavors. Lawyer competency, so viewed, may provide lawyers who are technically more proficient but morally indifferent or worse.

III

My third theme is that increased competency has important implications for access to legal services and their cost.[12] Lawyer competence clearly involves thorough fact investigation, comprehensive legal research, and a prudent choice among alternative courses of action. Current definitions of lawyer competence suggest the practice of a first-class corporate law firm. Limitations of time and resources are mentioned in connection with the execution of relevant strategies, but not in connection with fact investigation or legal research. One recent statement emphasizes that economic pressures cannot excuse less than competent action: "The need to earn a living is no justification for performance below an adequate level of competence."[13]

The competent lawyer, under this attractive ideal, has the responsibility to learn all the facts and legal options before advising the client and picking a strategy. But the realities of the market place cannot be banished by fiat. Lawyers in the sector of the profession dealing with private individuals must provide the degree of service that these clients can and will pay for. The small claim and the client with limited resources cannot expect the amount of lawyer's time devoted to larger matters in the large-firm setting--with the hourly meter ticking away. Lawyers who are making a living dealing with ordinary people must handle many clients and the time spent on individual matters must be limited. Problems of lack of preparation or follow-through stemming from excessive case loads and limited time for preparation are facts of life that cannot be disregarded. The realistic choice in many situations is between lower levels of service than envisioned by the lawyer competency movement or no service at all. Because it is probably more important that some service be available, the choice must often be made in favor of broad access rather than a uniform minimum level of competency.

The irony is that, at the same time that market forces are reshaping the legal profession, the profession is attempting to define standards that pretend that these forces do not exist. One suspects there is a subtle relationship between the two developments. The growing commercialization of law practice, increased competition for legal business, development of new forms of legal practice, and the like are profoundly disturbing developments that threaten the familiar and secure contours of the lawyer's world. The increased anxiety leads to a desire to restate professional standards in a way that abolishes the sources of discontent. Professionals gather to discuss ethical codes not when a shared ethical consensus is operating effectively, but only when it has broken down.

We are schizophrenic about the values to be served: at one moment we have before us the image of the independent professional who always operates at a uniformly high level of performance.[14] At other times we are more concerned with access to legal services--ensuring that both those who can and who cannot pay have their basic legal needs met. The recent emphasis on client autonomy and informed consent provides a third set of values emphasizing the consumer's interest and choice.[15] Recognition of these values of access and client autonomy threatens the image of the independent professional because they involve increased bureaucratization of the profession, reduced lawyer autonomy, and a more commercial environment.

The remorseless direction of change in the profession renders much of our lawyer competence talk ineffective. Market forces have been unleashed; to a substantial extent the legal profession has been deregulated. Minimum fee schedules have been eliminated; restraints on group legal services and prepaid plans have been abandoned; lawyer advertising is here to stay; and further changes are bound to come. The large number of lawyers, their aggressive and competitive posture, and the growing commercialization of law practice at every level all point in the direction of legal services as a commodity offered under very flexible terms in a variety of forms and quantities, with consumer choice as the basic determinant. How can these overwhelming currents be displaced by any attempts to define lawyer competence as if all legal services were provided in corporate law firms for deep-pocket clients?

Although frequently discussed remedies for lawyer incompetence include reforms in legal education, performance testing on bar examinations, improved or mandatory continuing legal education, peer review, improved lawyer discipline, and bridge-the-gap training, there is very little discussion of a remedy that is likely to be more effective--giving aggrieved consumers of legal services an effective damage remedy against negligent lawyers.[16] The profession's distaste for the malpractice remedy (at least as applied to itself) is seen in the struggles over the wording used in various provisions of the Model Rules--with the choice being made for the formulation that is likely to have the least effect on creation of civil liability. Yet if the profession is really serious about achieving a uniform minimum standard of lawyer performance, a broadening of the malpractice remedy may be one place to start that will not unfairly discriminate against legal clinics, prepaid plans, and other new modes of providing legal services to individual Americans.

Our future is partly determined and partly free. Real choices are presented but circumstances and fate impose many constraints. In dealing with its future, the profession needs a modest optimism based on ideals and values--a moral framework--and a better notion of what is the good lawyer, not merely the proficient technician. Our idealism--our aspiration to create and to become a truly "good lawyer"--must be moderated by a prudent skepticism that takes account of trends in America and in the profession that are not going to go away by themselves, including:

- The narcissistic and self-indulgent individualism that emphasizes rights, downplays responsibilities, and constantly whines "what's in it for me?"

- The decay of the sense of community--either in the neighborhood, the region, or the nation--that nurtures altruism, trust, compassion, sharing, caring, and most of the other things that really matter.

- The tendency to view "law" solely in instrumental and market terms as the outcome of aggressive assertion by adversary interests in courts, legislatures, and other institutions, and to consider "justice" as largely subsumed by what the pluralistic system comes up with.

Our concepts of the profession and its obligations, and our ideas of law and justice, must grapple with and not ignore these basic realities. Fortunately, a time of swift change is one of great challenge and opportunity.

FOOTNOTES

1. See, e.g., Warren E. Burger, The Specialized Skills of Advocacy: Are Specialized Training and Certification of Advocates Essential to Our System of Justice?, 42 Fordham L. Rev. 227 (1973); Roger C. Cramton, Lawyer Competence and the Law Schools, 4 U. Ark.-Little Rock L.J. 1 (1981); Cramton, Rising Expectations in Law Practice and Legal Education, 7 No. Ky. L. Rev. 159 (1980); ABA Section of Legal Education and Admissions to the Bar, Report and Recommendations of the Task Force on

Lawyer Competency: The Role of Law Schools (1979) [Cramton Report]; ALI-ABA Committee on Continuing Professional Education, Enhancing the Competence of Lawyers: The Report of the Houston Conference (1981) [Houston Conference Report]; Judicial Conference of the United States, Final Report of the Committee to Consider Standards for Admission to Practice in the Federal Courts, 83 F.R.D. 215 (1979) [Devitt report]; Anthony Partridge and G. Bermant, The Quality of Advocacy in the Federal Courts (Washington, D.C., 1978); Roger C. Cramton and Erik M. Jensen, The State of Trial Advocacy and Legal Education: Three New Studies, 30 J. Legal Educ. 253 (1979); Dorothy Maddi, Trial Advocacy Competence: The Judicial Perspective, 1978 Am. B. Found. Research J. 105.

2. At a sufficient level of generality, there is a great deal of agreement concerning the basic elements of lawyer competence. The most recent and comprehensive statement, that of the ALI-ABA Committee on Continuing Professional Education, a Model Peer Review System, at 11 (Philadelphia, 1980), is as good as any:

   Legal competence is measured by the extent to which an attorney (1) is specifically knowledgeable about the fields of law in which he or she practices, (2) performs the techniques of such practice with skill, (3) manages such practice efficiently, (4) identifies issues beyond his or her competence relevant to the matter undertaken, bringing these to the client's attention, (5) properly prepares and carries through the matter undertaken, and (6) is intellectually, emotionally, and physically capable. Lawyer incompetence is measured by the extent to which an attorney fails to maintain these qualities.

3. See, e.g., F. Raymond Marks and Darlene Cathcart, Discipline Within the Legal Profession, Is It Self Regulation?, 1974 U. Ill. L. F. 193; Susan Martyn, Lawyer Competence and Lawyer Discipline: Beyond the Bar?, 69 Geo. L.J. 705 (1981).

4. The study is summarized in Douglas Rosenthal, Evaluating the Competence of Lawyers, 11 Law & Soc'y Rev. 257, n. 18, 261, discussing Peterson, Andrews, Spain & Greenberg, An Analytical Study of North Carolina General Practice, 1953-54, 31(2) J. Med. Educ. 1, 82, 86 (1956).

5. The earlier formulations of professional ethics were aspirational in tone and moralistic in content. The ABA Model Code of Professional Responsibility, promulgated in 1969, separated the modern version of these aspirational statements ("ethical considerations") from the "disciplinary rules" that alone (in theory) would be the basis for lawyer discipline The new ABA Model Code of Professional Conduct (1983) eliminates moral and hortatory provisions, confining itself to minimum prescriptions to govern a regulated sphere of activity.

6. These examples give a false impression of what are the real problems of lawyer failure (see note 3, supra), and hence suggest solutions that fail to address the major problems. Measures designed to enhance lawyer skill, for example, may be totally unavailing with respect to personal failure (e.g., carelessness, laziness, alcoholism, etc.) or structural factors (e.g., economic pressures).

7. See articles by Richard Wasserstrom, David Luban, Alan Donagon, and Murray L. Schwartz in David Luban (ed.), The Good Lawyer (Totowa, N.J., 1983).

8. See Thomas L. Shaffer, American Legal Ethics: Text, Readings, and Discussion (mimeographed, 1983) cc. 2-3.

9. David Hoffman, A Course of Legal Study (2d ed., Baltimore, 1836), discussed in Shaffer, supra note 8.

10. See Michael Schudson, Public, Private, and Professional Lives: The Correspondence of David Dudley Field and Samuel Bowles, 21 Am. J. Legal Hist. 191 (1977).

11. Address of Robert B. Stevens, The Nature of a Learned Profession, 34 J. Legal Ed. p. 580 (Dec. 84).

12. See discussion by Bryant Garth, Rethinking the Legal Profession's Approach to Collective Self-Improvement: Competence and the Consumer Perspective, Wis. L. Rev. 639 (1983).

13. A Model Peer Review System, supra note 8, at 15 (comment 2 to §5).

14. See ABA Section of Tort and Insurance Practice, The Lawyer's Professional Independence: Present Threats/Future Challenges (Chicago, 1984) (containing articles by Robert S. Alexander, Peter Megargee Brown, Archibald Cox, and Robert B. McKay).

15. See David Rosenthal, Lawyer and Client: Who's in Charge?, (New York, 1974); Robert A. Burt, Conflict and Trust Between Attorney and Client, 69 Geo. L.J. 1015 (1981).

16. See the papers in the Houston Conference Report, supra note 1; Joel C. Henning, Lawyer Competence in the 80's: Lots of Smoke but Where's the Fire? (mimeographed address, Feb. 4, 1984).

LAWYER COMPETENCY AND BAR ADMISSIONS: THE ROLE OF THE LAW SCHOOL AND THE ROLE OF THE PROFESSION

London Sessions
ABA Annual Meeting 1985
Audley Suite, Grosvenor House Hotel
London, England

Wednesday, July 17, 1985
10:00 A.M. - 12:00 Noon

Prof. Aubrey L. Diamond
Institute of Advanced Legal Studies
University of London
17 Russell Square
London WC1B 5DR

Educ: during the holidays from Eton.

Who's Who entry for
Sir Osbert Sitwell, 1892-1969

A comparison of the literature addressing lawyer competency shows an astonishing discrepancy between preoccupations in the United States and in England and Wales.[1] When one looks at the flood of reports and articles in the former country dealing with the problem of incompetent lawyers one might feel that there they "speak of little else." The dearth of literature on this topic in England may, on the other hand, lead one to think that here there is no problem worth talking about. Whatever the American position may be, that would not be a true conclusion as to the English situation. In recent years a lot of attention has been paid to two questions: how to ensure that English lawyers are competent and how to minimise the damage if they are not.

Educating the Profession

The English scene is complex. The two branches of the legal profession maintain their own exclusive routes to qualification, with their own courses and examinations.[2] The normal, though not the invariable, path to entry is to start by obtaining a law degree, which may be taken at a university or at a polytechnic or college of higher education. There are 39 university law schools in the United Kingdom and 23 law schools at polytechnics or other institutions of higher education.[3] The distinction between universities and polytechnics is not one that would be easy to explain in a few words. The law degree, normally a B.A. or LL.B., is of course a first degree in Britain.

If a person with a degree in a subject other than law wishes to enter the legal profession it is necesssry to take an intensive one-year course covering six basic legal subjects, usually referred to as the "core subjects." At one time it was thought that this one-year course for "nonlaw" graduates would be common to both branches of the legal profession; hence the Law Society's name for it is the Common Professional Examination (C.P.E.). The Council of Legal Education, however, calls for the aspiring barrister to obtain a Diploma in Law.[4]

A law degree, C.P.E., or Bar Diploma completes the academic stage of legal education. Each branch then requires a further one-year course of a vocational rather than academic nature (for the Law Society's final examination this is taken at the Society's own College of Law or at one of a select group of polytechnics; for the Bar Finals it is taken at the Council of Legal Education's own Inns of Court School of Law). On completion of the final examination, the prospective solicitor must serve two years as an "articled clerk," a form of apprenticeship, while the barrister who wishes to practise in this country must become a pupil to an established barrister for one year.

The Academic Stage

The law degree (or the non-law degree coupled with the C.P.E. or Diploma in Law) is known as the academic stage. It is generally accepted that the function of the academic stage is not to attempt to teach the aspiring lawyer all the law he or she needs to know.

Reporting in March 1971, the Committee on Legal Education said that the academic stage should provide the student with three of the essential requirements of the practitioner: "a basic knowledge of the law and where to find it; an understanding of the relationship of law to the social and economic environment in which it operates; and the ability to handle facts and to apply abstract concepts to those facts."[5] The committee spoke of the need to develop the intellectual processes "which are usually referred to as 'thinking like a lawyer.'" The curriculum, it was said, must be "prototypical in character" so that the student can apply the modes of thinking he has learned in the study of a limited number of legal subjects to other fields as and when the occasion arises.

Competence

The arrangements that have been briefly described are relatively recent in their present form. Over the past ten or fifteen years, the proportion of graduates (law or other) entering the two branches of the profession has greatly increased. The vocational nature of the finals courses was deliberately introduced to improve the quality of the education and training received by new entrants to the profession.

The system of articles or pupillage enables the practising profession to monitor the quality of the education received at the various law schools. It is said that solicitors are, in the main, more satisfied with the usefulness of articled clerks who have undergone the vocationally oriented solicitors' final course than they were with those in the past who had come straight from university (when it was usual to take the final examination after service under articles had been completed).

Interviews

At one time everyone seeking to become a solicitor, whether or not possessing a degree, was interviewed personally. It was open to the interviewing panel to refuse to permit the applicant to enroll as a student with the Law Society. The rationale of this procedure was said to be that it enabled the profession to exclude unsuitable persons. With a growing number of entrants the procedure made heavy demands on the time of those willing to serve on interviewing panels, and it was far from clear that it did in fact serve any useful purpose. The interview of all was therefore replaced by the interview of those about whose suitability some doubt had arisen, mainly because of conviction for a criminal offence. Since most offences are minor transgressions, the majority of those now interviewed are eventually permitted to register as students.

Limited Practice

The newly qualified barrister is called to the bar after passing the Bar Finals, and then serves his pupillage after he is qualified.[6] For the first six months of pupillage, he is not permitted to accept work on his own account. Thereafter he may. His work does not come direct from lay clients but from solicitors.

Solicitors are not admitted to the roll until they have both passed the Solicitors' Final examination and completed their service under articles. For the first three years after qualification they are not permitted, without permission of the Law Society, to set up in practice on their own account or to enter into partnership. Of this requirement, introduced in 1970, the Royal Commission on Legal Services says that it "was intended to provide a further period of in-training and to avoid risks to the public which the Law Society had found by experience might arise if a newly qualified solicitor was permitted to set up in practice prematurely."[7]

Incompetence in Practice

High educational standards, such as both branches of the profession would claim to apply, may exclude those without the intellectual capacity to practise law, though no study has ever demonstrated a correlation between the standard of examination results and success in legal practice (even assuming it is possible to define success in practice). The law schools, whether independent (universities and polytechnics) or controlled by the profession (the College of Law and the Inns of Court School of Law), cannot, however, guarantee professional competence, which depends on so many more things than mere intellectual ability.

Incompetence in practice may be noticed by other practitioners and may inconvenience the client. But it is when the client's interests are harmed that it becomes necessary to consider how to minimise the damage or to compensate the client. Most of what follows will deal with the solicitors' branch of the profession since it is they who are in direct touch with clients.

In order to practise as a solicitor on one's own account, or as a partner, it is necessary to take out an annual practising certificate. There are two requirements for the annual certificate that are relevant to this paper. Each solicitor must produce a certificate from an accountant to state that the rules relating to solicitors' accounts have been complied with, and in particular that clients' money has been kept separate from the solicitor's own money at all times. This is a check more on honesty than on competence, but it does check competence in some aspects of money management.

The second requirement is compulsory insurance. The Law Society takes out a master policy on behalf of all practising solicitors and each solicitor or firm must pay the appropriate premium to secure cover under the policy. This professional negligence policy is an attempt to ensure that clients do not suffer financially because of their solicitor's negligence. The amount of cover is related to the number of partners in the firm.

The master policy does not cover the client against the solicitor's dishonesty. For this the Law Society maintains its own Compensation Fund to which every solicitor must contribute the prescribed amount in order to obtain the practising certificate.

Discipline

The Law Society and the Inns of Court exercise disciplinary control over the members of their respective branches. This disciplinary control is based on the commission of acts which can be classed as professional misconduct. Negligence is not itself professional misconduct--at any rate, not a single act of negligence--and no disciplinary powers can at present be exercised on that ground. The remedy lies in the hands of the individual harmed by the negligence who can claim under the general law and who can, if successful, be sure that money is available at least up to the extent of compulsory insurance cover.

The advice to a client who has suffered at the hands of a negligent solicitor is therefore that he should consult another solicitor. The Law Society maintains panels of solicitors in all parts of the country who are willing to advise clients on negligence claims against solicitors. It is often said that "you can't find a lawyer who is willing to sue another lawyer," but this is simply not true. However, the need to seek fresh legal advice is far from popular, the inability of the Law Society to act on its own initiative causes resentment, and an action for negligence does nothing to stop the defendant from continuing to practise negligently. As a result, there has been discussion over the years whether the Law Society should take powers to treat professional negligence as professional misconduct with the possibility of disciplinary proceedings that might lead to suspension from practice or even to the name of the offender being struck off the roll of solicitors. There seems to be no similar call for disciplinary action against incompetent barristers, if there are any. The Law Society is also discussing the possibility of an arbitration scheme to deal with complaints about bad professional work.

Standards and Specialisation

In its report in 1979 the Royal Commission on Legal Services wrote that "The law and the work of lawyers become more complex. The profession has grown rapidly in the last ten years. Public expectations become higher. It therefore becomes more difficult to maintain a uniformly high quality of service by traditional methods alone."[8] The recommendation that followed was that both branches of the profession should devise written Professional Standards that would be published. A serious or repeated failure to comply with them should be treated as a breach of professional discipline. As far as is known no such standards have yet been published.

Lively discussion is proceeding in the solicitors' branch of the profession on the question of specialisation. Many solicitors, perhaps the majority, specialise in particular categories of work. The questions are whether they should be permitted to advertise their specialities and whether there should be any certification by the Law Society of their special competence in the area or areas of specialisation.

Many lectures, conferences, and courses are held which are open to practising lawyers. The Law Society has now approved a scheme whereby continuing education will be compulsory for all solicitors in the first three years after qualification. The barristers' branch of the profession believes that continuing education should not be compulsory, though the Royal Commission disagreed with this view.[9]

Conclusion

It is apparent from this discussion that the concerns that have been voiced in recent years in the United States have their counterparts in the United Kingdom even if we are less vocal about them. Much thought has been given to the problems even though less ink has been spilled. In neither country can we claim to have solved the problems. Perhaps they are insoluble.

FOOTNOTES

1. I apologise for concentrating on England and Wales (one of the three jurisdictions in the United Kingdom). I hope I will not seem too unusual if I say that it seemed better to talk of something I know about.

2. The two branches are of course barristers and solicitors. In England the words "the bar" are normally reserved for the barristers' branch of the profession.

3. This refers only to law schools where a law degree can be obtained.

4. The Law Society is the governing body for solicitors. The Council of Legal Education is responsible for the education of prospective barristers. The C.P.E. can be taken at a number of polytechnics, but not at a university. The Diploma in Law can be taken at one (different) polytechnic, or at one university which does not have a law school teaching for a law degree.

5. This committee was set up by the Lord Chancellor. Its report was published by Her Majesty's Stationery Office under reference number Cmnd. 4595. The quotations that follow are from paragraphs 101 and 102.

6. It must be left for others to explain the purpose of the requirement that a bar student must eat a minimum number of dinners at his or her Inn of Court before being called to the bar.

7. The Royal Commission on Legal Services reported in 1979. Its report was published by Her Majesty's Stationery Office under reference number Cmnd. 7648. The quotation that follows is taken from the chapter on Legal Education, paragraph 38.33.

8. _Ibid._ paragraph 22.57.

9. _Ibid._ paragraphs 39.85 and 39.86.

PIRACY AND THE NEW TECHNOLOGIES

London Sessions
ABA Annual Meeting 1985
Ballroom 2, Hilton International
London, England

Wednesday, July 17, 1985
10:00 A.M. - 12:00 Noon

Arthur J. Levine
1111 - 19th Street, N.W.
Washington, D.C. 20036

> Copyright is the Cinderella of the law. Her rich older sisters, Franchises and Patents, long crowded her into the chimney-corner. Suddenly the fairy godmother, invention, endowed her with mechanical and electrical devices as magical as the pumpkin coach and the mice footmen. Now she whirls through the mad mazes of the glamorous ball. (Chafee, Reflections on the Law of Copyright, 45 Col. L. Rev. 503 (1945)).

The new technologies that have been developed since the Second World War have produced staggering changes for both creators and users of intellectual property. For example, Professor Chafee's whimsical statement concerning the "magical" mechanical and electrical devices preceded by several years the first functional, commercial computer. Even a scholar as prescient as Professor Chafee could not have imagined that the computer would transform society in the last half of the twentieth century much as the invention of movable type and the steam engine had transformed the world in earlier centuries. The magic of the pumpkin and the mice footmen is less astonishing to a generation now able to accomplish once-Herculean tasks by merely pushing a few buttons on a keyboard.

Although the last two decades have seen the emergence of new technologies of wondrous scope, each age has produced its own new technologies which allow the gifted to express themselves in unique and creative ways. The burst in technologies today, however, also facilitate the easy, quick, cheap reproduction and piracy of these original expressions.

Perhaps the most creative products of the computer age are the software programs which permit the computer to perform such wondrous acts. In the early generations of computers, programs were created for and capable of performing only on single-purpose machines. The physical restrictions imposed upon copying such single-purpose programs apart from the computer, and the limited use of such programs, provided sufficient protection against widespread illegal copying. Today the format and use of programs is radically different. Most programs are stored in chips, disks, and tapes, and are compatible with numerous computers. Just as computers have become consumer items, so too have the programs used on those computers. Programs which may have been months and years in development can now be reproduced quickly, cheaply, and in large quantities. As stated by the National Commission on New Technological Uses of Copyrighted Works ("CONTU"):

> [I]f the cost of duplicating information is small, then it is simple for a less than scrupulous person to duplicate it. This means that legal as well as physical protection for the information is necessary incentive if such information is to be created and disseminated.

Legal protection for computer software has been the subject of discussion in the United States for more than twenty years and, apart from contractual rights, has developed along three paths: trade secrecy, patents, and copyrights.

Trade Secret Protection for Computer Programs

Trade secret protection has been effectively employed by the owners of software to prevent the unauthorized disclosure of the confidential material in programs. A trade secret is defined as "any formula, pattern, device, or compilation of information which is used in one's business and which gives him an opportunity to obtain advantage over competitors who do not know or use it."

Trade secrecy is a creature of state law and, therefore, differs somewhat from state to state. In all cases, however, in order to obtain and maintain trade secret protection, a substantial element of secrecy must be kept. Among the factors that must be considered in determining whether the information is "secret" and can therefore be protected are:

- The extent to which the information is known to persons other than the proprietor;
- The measures taken by the proprietor to guard the secret;
- The efforts expended in developing the information; and
- The ease or difficulty with which the information can properly be acquired or duplicated by others.

The courts have consistently held that like other industrial processes, computer programs are processes for processing information and eligible for trade secret protection. In addition to imposing civil penalties, courts have held defendants who copied computer programs guilty under state theft-of-trade-secret laws.

Trade secret protection is not available or effective for all forms of programs. Secrecy is essential to maintaining protection, and therefore it is of questionable utility for programs sold over the counter or otherwise widely disseminated. Likewise, the proprietor of a trade secret has no protection against third parties who have obtained the secret in good faith.

Patent Protection for Computer Programs

In theory, it can be argued that the most effective method of protection for computer programs is under the patent laws. A patent could protect the invention disclosed in the program without the necessity of maintaining secrecy. The patent holder has exclusive rights in the patented process against a second inventor who may have independently written a similar program. Patent laws are national in scope and provide effective remedies against infringements. To date, however, it has been very difficult for patent applicants to secure a patent in a program, since novel and useful mathematical formulas are not patentable. The decision of the Supreme Court in Diamond v. Diehr suggests that a process which includes a mathematical formula "when considered as a whole" may be protected by a patent. Thus if the processes underlying computer programs are more than mere algorithms, patent protection may be available.[1] Notwithstanding the possible availability of patent protection for programs, realistically only a very few programs can qualify as patentable subject matter, and even those that do may not satisfy the patent law requirements of nonobviousness and novelty.

Copyright Protection for Computer Programs

In the mid-1960s, the United States Copyright Office announced that it would register claims to copyright in computer programs under the 1909 Copyright Act as "books" if "the elements of assembling, selecting, arranging, editing, and literary expression...are sufficient to constitute original authorship." From 1964 through the end of 1977, fewer than two thousand programs were registered.

The 1976 Copyright Act, which became effective on January 1, 1978, did not specifically provide for protection for computer programs.[2] The legislative history of the Act makes clear, however, that Congress believed computer programs to be copyrightable from the outset as "literary works," under Section 102(a) of the Act "to the extent that they incorporate authorship in the programmer's expression of original ideas, as distinguished from the ideas themselves."[3] This "idea-expression" distinction was made explicit in the 1976 Act in Section 102(b):

> In no case does copyright protection for an original work of authorship extend to any idea, procedure, process, system, method or operation, concept, principle, or discovery, regardless of the form in which it is described, explained, illustrated, or embodied in such work.

Section 102(b) was specifically included in the 1976 Act to make as clear as possible the scope of copyright protection in computer programs. The report of the House of Representatives Judiciary Committee accompanying the 1976 Act states:

> Section 102(b) is intended, among other things, to make clear that the expression adopted by the programmer is the copyrightable element in a computer program, and that the actual processes or methods embodied in the program are not within the scope of copyright law.[4]

On December 31, 1974, before the 1976 Act was passed, Congress established a commission, the National Commission on New Technological Uses of Copyrighted Works ("CONTU"), to study and compile data on computer uses of copyrighted works.[5] In its Final Report, delivered to the president and Congress on July 31, 1978, CONTU recommended, inter alia, that the copyright law be amended "to make it explicit that computer programs, to the extent that they embody an author's original creation, are proper subject matter of copyright." CONTU proposed that a definition be added to Section 101 stating that a computer program is "a set of statements or instructions to be used directly or indirectly in a computer in order to bring about a certain result."

The Commission further recommended that the law be amended to enable the owner of a copy of a copyrighted program to adapt or make a copy of a program for archival and other limited purposes. The recommended changes were adopted by Congress and signed into law on December 12, 1980.[6] These amendments represented the first explicit mention of computer programs in the copyright law.

The CONTU Report on computer programs contained a strong dissent by one of the Commissioners, John Hersey, who argued that computer programs in their machine-control phase should not be entitled to copyright protection. He argued that such programs communicate only with a machine and not with any human audience and were not "writings" within the meaning of Article 8, Clause 8, of the U.S. Constitution. Many of Mr. Hersey's arguments were reiterated by defendants accused of infringing copyrights in computer programs.

The first case involving computer programs under the 1976 Act raised issues which echoed in several cases thereafter. In Data Cash Systems, Inc. v. JS&A Group, Inc., the court decided that a read-only-memory chip (ROM) was not a copy of the program embodied in it.[7] The court held that ROMs are utilitarian devices which are incapable of being perceived by humans. On appeal, the lower court's decision of non-infringment was upheld but the appellate court did not deal with the issue of copyrightability, deciding the case in favor of the defendant because the plaintiff failed to affix a copyright notice on the ROMs.[8]

The Data Cash case was the first case to deal with the copyrightability of computer programs but the unsettled questions soon were being litigated in a number of courts: Is object code protectible even though it does not communicate with humans? Is object code embodied in ROMs and other memory devices subject to protection? Should operating system programs, as well as application programs, be protected? Notwithstanding the district court's decision in Data Cash, subsequent cases have, for the most part, answered all of those questions in the affirmative. In GCA Corporation v. Chance, the court found a program in object code copyrightable since the object code was merely the "encryption" of the source code version of the program.[9] In Williams Electronics, Inc. v. Artic International, Inc., the Third Circuit Court of Appeals found that a program for an electronic video game in object code embodied in a ROM chip was entitled to copyright protection.[10] The court recognized that if the rule were otherwise, an infringer would need only wait until a program is fixed in a machine-readable form for use with a computer before safely copying the valuable work of the programmer.

> We cannot accept...an unlimited loophole by which infringement of a computer program is limited to the copying of the computer program text but not to duplication of a computer program fixed on a silicon chip.

Just three days prior to the Williams decision, the trial court in the now-famous case of Apple Computer, Inc. v. Franklin Computer Corp. refused to grant plaintiff a preliminary injunction, notwithstanding clear evidence of blatant copying of Apple's program by Franklin.[11] In denying the injunction, the court questioned whether programs in ROMs and object code are copyrightable and whether operating system programs are entitled to protection. The court based its opinion, in part, on the lower court's decision in Data Cash. On appeal, the Third Circuit Court of Appeals reversed the lower court, finding that programs in object code are copyrightable, even though such programs do not communicate to humans. The court was unable to find any basis in the statute or in the CONTU report that a work must be intelligible to humans in order to qualify for copyright protection. The court relied on its decision in Williams in finding that the Apple programs embodied in ROMs were copyrightable.

The court rejected the defendant's argument that an operating system is a utilitarian device because it directs the activities of a computer, analogizing such programs to written rules that instruct people on how to play a game.

The court also was satisfied that the definition of a computer program in the Copyright Act makes no distinction between application programs and operating system programs. The defendant argued that protecting operating system programs would restrict the use of the ideas in the programs so that others would be prohibited from creating programs that make the Apple computer performs its tasks. The court stated, "if other programs can be written which perform the same function as an Apple's operating system program, then that program is an expression of the idea and hence copyrightable." The court remanded to the trial court the question of whether the operating system program was capable of being expressed in more than a limited number of ways, but the lawsuit was settled before the trial court had an opportunity to hear evidence on that issue.

Illegal copying of computer programs also takes place outside the borders of the United States, and preventing the importation of such programs is becoming a primary focus of some copyright owners. Section 602 of the Copyright Act makes unauthorized importation an infringement. Copyright owners, in conjunction with the United

States Customs Service, were able to exclude the importation of computers containing infringing programs. Enterprising copyists, however, in order to avoid the detention and confiscation of their computers, imported computers absent the ROMs. After the computers were safely in the United States, the ROMs were placed back into the computers. The Customs Service ruled that it was outside its authority to ban the importation of ROM-less computers, since only piratical copies of copyrighted works could be excluded under its regulations, and the ROM-less computers were not copyrightable subject matter.[12]

Apple Computer, Inc., however, pursued its remedies under Section 337 of the Tariff Act of 1930. Under that Section, the International Trade Commission (ITC) has the authority to exclude "unfair methods of competition and unfair acts in the importation of articles into the United States." In the case of In re Certain Personal Computers and Components Thereof, the ITC excluded the importation of ROM-less computers which were to be fitted with copies of Apple programs, finding the importation of such computers to be a step in the direct infringement of Apple's rights of reproduction and distribution and a contributory infringement, since only Apple programs could cause the computer to function.[13]

The Semiconductor Chip Protection Act of 1984

The decision in Williams v. Artic and Apple v. Franklin would appear to have settled any remaining questions concerning copyright protection for computer programs embodied in ROMs. Legislation was needed, however, to protect the semiconductor chip or integrated circuits, apart from the programs embedded in them. It has been estimated that the cost of developing a new chip could reach $100 million, while the cost of copying it by photographing the chip and its layers, can be less than $50,000. The U.S. Congress believed that the ease and cost of copying would necessarily produce an industry of piratical copyists, resulting in a "devastating disincentive to innovative research and development." Consequently, in October, 1984, Congress passed, and shortly thereafter President Reagan signed into law, the Semiconductor Chip Protection Act of 1984.

The new Act protects semiconductor chip products under a SUI-generic form of intellectual property which is similar to copyright protection but which differs from existing copyright law in several ways. The Act protects mask works and defines them in terms of the two- and three-dimensional features of the topography of the chip to which the mask work relates. Unauthorized reproduction and distribution and illegal importation would all be infringing acts, but "reverse engineering" of the mask work is permissible under the terms of the Act. The Act contains provisions for notice, remedies, ownership, and transfer similar to those found in Title 17, the copyright law.

Audio and Video Piracy

Motion pictures and sound recordings have long been subject to piratical copying. With the advent of video and audio tape, the ease with which cassettes may be reproduced has resulted, at times, in infringements of massive proportions. Prior to the 1971 Sound Recording Amendment to the Copyright Act (effective as to sound recordings fixed on or after February 15, 1972), the audio tapes were protected from piracy under the laws of the individual states.[14] Under the provisions of the 1976 Copyright Act, states are now precluded from affording copyright-like protection to sound recordings or any other type of works of authorship.

The Copyright Act contains provisions for criminal copyright infringement and the motion picture and recording industries have enlisted the assistance of the Federal Bureau of Investigation and the Justice Department in their efforts to bring the piracy problem under control. Under Section 506(a) of Title 17, "any person who infringes a copyright willfully and for purposes of commercial advantage or private financial gain" has committed a federal criminal offense. The penalties for criminal infringement of the reproduction and distribution rights in sound recordings and motion pictures were increased by amendment to the statute in 1982 making the penalties for infringing those rights significantly greater, both as to monetary fine and jail term, than the penalties for criminally infringing any other type of copyrighted work.

In addition to the possibility of criminal prosecution, a person who pirates copyrighted sound recordings and motion pictures may be subject to civil remedies under the copyright statute. Both preliminary and final injunctions may be obtained. Generally, in copyright cases it is considerably easier to obtain a preliminary injunction than in most other cases. Additionally, infringing copies and all means by which such copies are made may be impounded during the pendency of the action. If the plaintiff is successful, the infringing articles may be destroyed or otherwise disposed of. Monetary relief in the form of actual damages such as lost sales, or the profits of the infringer attributable to the infringement, less properly deductible costs, may be awarded to the successful plaintiff. Alternatively, at the copyright owner's election, he may obtain statutory damages ranging from between $250 and $10,000 (or $250 and $50,000 if the infringment is willful). Full costs and reasonable attorney fees may also be awarded by the court.

Conclusion

The U.S. Congress and courts have thus far been responsive in reacting to the pirating of works of the new technologies. The enactment of the CONTU recommendations, the Semiconductor Chip Protection Act, and the increased criminal penalties all indicate an attempt by Congress to protect the authors and owners of new technology products. Likewise, the courts and administrative agencies in the United States have given an expansive treatment to the protection of computer software. It is certain that "mechanical devices and electrical devices as magical as the pumpkin coach and mice footmen" will continue to be developed. Whether the law will continue to grow to protect the intellectual property rights of creators remains to be seen.

FOOTNOTES

1. 450 U.S. 175, 67 L.Ed. 2d 155, 101 S. Ct. 1048 (1981)
2. P.L. 94-553 (1976) codified as 17 U.S.C. 101 et seq.
3. U.S. Congress, House Judiciary Committee, 94th Cong., 2d Sess., 1976, H. Rept. 1476 p.54 (hereinafter cited as House Report)
4. House Report, p.57
5. P.L. 93-573 (1974)
6. P.L. 96-517 (1980)
7. 480 F. Supp. 1063 (N.D. Ill. 1979)
8. 628 F. 2d. 1038 (7th Cir. 1980)
9. 217 U.S.P.Q. 718 (N.D. Cal. 1982)
10. 865 F. 2d 870 (3d Cir. 1982)
11. 714 F. 2d. 240 (3d Cir. 1983)
12. _In re Apple Computer, Inc._, 28 PTCJ 75 (U.S. Customs Service March 20, 1984)
13. CCH Copyright Law Decisions 25, 651 (Int'l Trade Comm. 337-TA-140, March 9, 1984)
14. P.L. 92-140 (1971)

PIRACY AND THE NEW TECHNOLOGIES, PART I: THE PROTECTION OF COMPUTER SOFTWARE AGAINST PIRACY

London Sessions
ABA Annual Meeting 1985
Ballroom 2, Hilton International
London, England

Wednesday, July 17, 1985
10:00 A.M. - 12:00 Noon

Robert J. Anderson
Lovell, White & King
21 Holborn Viaduct
London EC1A 2DY

The U.K. courts currently face the problem, in dealing with cases involving computer technology, of applying law that has been left behind by developments. The 1956 Copyright Act never envisaged the protection of computer software, while the 1977 Patents Act has only created new uncertainties.

The explosion in sales of micro computers, and the ease and cheapness of producing copies of software, has led to a boom in piracy. Concern is growing in the computer industry that new legislation is needed.

Computer programs can be written in:

- o <u>High-level languages</u> such as BASIC, COBOL, FORTRAN, etc. These resemble human language and use ordinary or modified English words, but have to be "translated" into machine code to be understood by the computer;

- o <u>Machine code</u>. This is written in binary form (a series of ones and zeroes) understandable directly by the computer. It is difficult for humans to use because of the notation; and

- o <u>Assembly language</u>. This is a compromise between high-level languages and machine code, uses a combination of mnemonics and figures, and because instructions can be written more concisely than with a high-level language, it is more efficient in terms of processing speed. Again, it must be translated into machine code for the computer.

Assembly and high-level languages are referred to as "source codes." Programs written in a form directly intelligible to the computer are "object codes."

English law offers three types of protection for computer software.

Contract/Confidentiality

Contractual provisions between licensor and licensee may prohibit disclosure or copying, but difficulties arise if the program becomes available to persons not party to the contract.

In complex commercial software, where the number of users may be limited, reasonably effective confidentiality restrictions can be imposed. However, secrecy is of little value where programs are sold by their thousands.

Patent Protection

Courts in many jurisdictions have considered whether software can ever be patentable, bearing in mind the principle that products of the intellect are not patentable unless applied in some "industrial" process.

The U. K. Patent Office tended to disallow claims to methods of operating computers whilst accepting some claims to programs embodied in some material form. Gever's Application [1970] RPC 91 held a program on a punched card was no different from a special design of cam for a machine (which can be patentable). Both are followed by some sensing device. Logically, there should be no difference between programs on punched cards, discs, or even paper in a form which can be read by an optical character reader.

Burroughs Application [1973] FSR 147 held that the distinction between a method of operating and a computer programmed to operate in a certain way was not justifiable. A mere idea or method was not patentable. However, if the use of the method resulted in improved apparatus operating in a novel way, with consequent industrial advantages, then it may be patentable.

The 1977 Patents Act now declares expressly that computer programs as such are not patentable. The courts have so far expressed no view as to whether the 1977 Act has changed the law. This wording closely follows that of the European Patent Convention. The guidelines for examination in the European Patent Office indicate that if the only novelty of a claim resides in the program it will be rejected, however the claim is actually framed. Whether the U.K. courts will adopt a similar approach or follow the pre-1977 Act case law remains to be seen.

Copyright

There is no conclusive U.K. decision that copyright exists in computer programs.

In 1977, the Whitford Committee when considering copyright reform concluded that computer programs produced "in writing" were probably protected as literary works, but thought the law should be clarified.

Sega v. Alca [1982] FSR 516 and Sega v. Richards [1983] FSR 73 concerned applications for temporary injunctions to restrain copying of a video game called "Frogger" in which the player manipulated representations of frogs to avoid various hazards. The overall screen display was generated by the program but the positioning of some of the images was dictated by the players' "input." In the first case, the plaintiffs claimed literary copyright, in the program resident in the EPROM (Electrically Programmable Read Only Memory--a semi-permanent memory which can be erased electrically). They also claimed the screen display was a cinematograph film (expressly protected under the 1956 Copyright Act). Both allegations were held to be arguable.

In the second case, the plaintiffs expanded their claim to cover not only the program and the sequence of moving images, but also the drawings from which the screen display was derived. The judge held that copyright subsisted in the source code but expressed no view as to whether the machine (object) code program from which the defendant had admittedly derived his game was a separate copyright work.

In subsequent interlocutory decisions judges have accepted similar arguments.

In the Australian "Wombat" case (Apple Computer v. Computer Edge 1983), the ROMs in the Taiwanese "Wombat" computer contained operating programs written in machine code. These were virtually identical to, and had evidently been copied from, machine code programs stored on ROMs in the Apple II computer. The Apple machine code programs had been translated (by computer) from programs written in assembly language upon paper and then "typed" into the machine.

One of the appeal judges would not accept that copyright existed in the machine code programs or the assembly language, because programs were not literary works within the meaning of the Copyright Act. Referring to an old English decision, Hollinrake v. Truswell [1894] 3 Ch 420, he said that literary works were intended to provide "information, instruction or pleasure in the form of literary enjoyment." Computer programs provided none of these.

The other judges, considered that the assembly language programs were protected as literary works because they expressed "meaning as to the arrangement and ordering of instructions for the storage and reproduction of knowledge." This must be right. The Hollinrake case is old and it has since been made abundantly clear in legislation that "literary merit" is wholly irrelevant to the question.

It was also held that the storage of the program in the computer memory was (as is required to constitute infringement) a reproduction in a material form. A ROM chip can store a program, for example, as a specific arrangement of electrically charged electrodes. The storing and reproduction of information in this matter is surely no less "material" than an arrangement of graphite particles on a piece of paper.

Are Programs Not Written on Paper Protected by Copyright?

The Copyright Act defines literary works to include "any written table or compilation" and writing to be "any form of notation whether by hand or by printing, typewriting or any similar process."

It is assumed that the notation must be in material form, but what if a program written on the computer has never been reduced to writing on paper? The program appears on the screen as luminescent dots. These dots are generated by the computer's operating system in response to input information stored in the random access memory (RAM), either electronically or magnetically. As mentioned in the previous section, an arrangement of electrical charges is probably as "material" as anything else. It is also argued that such information is not in any form of "notation" but this seems illogical. Why disallow protection simply because the work is recorded in a new form? Shorthand was at one time wholly new but was nevertheless afforded copyright protection. Perhaps the only real necessity is that the program should be recorded in some form which will enable it to be read and understood.

Can Machine Produced Works be Protected?

Programs produced by computers are usually just translations into machine code of a program written in a high-level language by a human.

In the future, however, one can imagine that computers will be writing programs which are more arguably original. However, the Act limits copyright protection to the author's lifetime--clearly inappropriate for a computer! It seems that a change in the law may be needed to provide proper protection for programs with nonhuman authors.

There is already a problem in relation to computer-produced data such as statistical tables, drawings, etc. Who should be the copyright owner? In the case of computer aided design (CAD), it is arguable that the computer acts merely as a tool, and the copyright owner is the draughtsman using the computer.

In other cases, where the only creativity consists in the typing of the input data, the operator may be no more the copyright owner than a typist typing to dictation. Moreover the operator may press only one key to select the input data which may be stored on disc. Arguably then there is no copyright protection for the computer output since the skill and labour (which is always necessary to generate copyright protection) resides either in the computer (at least as far as the labour is concerned), or in the person who devised the program for processing the data.

The Whitford Committee suggested that the originator of the input data and the programmer should own copyright jointly. A government proposal is to make the programmed computer "the tool" and the operator the owner. Neither is wholly satisfactory.

Conclusion

The widespread view that computer software is not protected by the law is almost certainly not correct. English judges are prepared to protect computer software from piracy. However clarification is needed, and specific legislation should be called for to deal with copyright in computer output.

PIRACY AND THE NEW TECHNOLOGIES, PART II:
THE ENTERTAINMENT INDUSTRY, PIRACY AND REMEDIES

London Sessions
ABA Annual Meeting 1985
Ballroom 2, Hilton International
London, England

Wednesday, July 17, 1985
10:00 A.M. - 12:00 Noon

David Calcutt, Q.C.
Lamb Building
Temple, London EC4Y 7AS

Piracy: The Nature of the Problem

In the United Kingdom, as in the United States, the entertainment industry has the benefit of copyright protection against the unauthorised duplication of its sound recordings, its music, and its cinematograph films. Piracy of records since the 1970s, and video in the 1980s, has been a serious problem for the entertainment industry, and the object of this part of the paper is to explain some of the remedies available to copyright owners against the pirates. The same remedies are, of course, open to the owner of any copyright which may subsist in a computer programme.

The piracy problem is recognised as falling into two distinct categories, domestic and commercial.

Domestic piracy is also known as in-home taping. It applies, now, equally to video as to audio products and in each case has mushroomed.

Commercial piracy takes several forms. "Counterfeiting" a record or film is to reproduce the real owner's product in such a way as to enable the counterfeiter to pass his product off as the real thing. "Bootlegging" is the unauthorised recording of a live performance, which is then produced in the form of records or tapes, and which does not purport to be a lawful operation. The problem has, until now, been largely confined to audio records and tapes. Finally, there is a market for video tapes which are unauthorised copies of the original cinematograph film and as to which the maker of that copy makes no pretence that it is an unauthorised recording.

Who are the Victims?

The victims of piracy include the "makers" of the sound recordings and the films, that is the record companies and the film companies; the authors or publishers of any musical, literary, or dramatic work which is embodied in the sound recording or film; and artists or performers whose royalties are calculated by reference to the number of sales.

Remedies to Combat and Compensate for Commercial Piracy

There are four remedies available to a copyright owner, assignee, or licensee for the infringement of copyright.

Financial

Damages. The plaintiff is entitled to compensation for loss which he has actually suffered or he may be deemed to have suffered. Accordingly, he is entitled to recover the loss of profit he would have made upon sales made by the defendant of the pirated copies. There is also jurisdiction under the Copyright Act to award "additional damages" where the infringement is flagrant, the defendant has benefited from it, and effective relief would not otherwise be available to the plaintiff.[1]

Account of profits. The plaintiff may claim, as an alternative to damages, the profit made by the defendant from the piracy. The remedy, which is discretionary in any event, is rarely used because of its expense and the complexity of the quantification of the profit payable.

Conversion damages. A "pirate" may be liable not only for infringement damages or any account of profits but, additionally, to deliver up to plaintiff all pirated films or records made or held by him or, if he is no longer in a position to deliver up, he may be ordered to pay to the plaintiff a sum equal to the value of the films or records. It has been recommended, and it is the government's declared intention (as at July 1981), that the remedy in conversion be abolished.[2-3]

Injunctions

Once the pirate has been detected, the court may grant an injunction restraining the further duplication, distribution, or sale of any infringing records or films. This remedy at trial, perhaps 18 months after the action is commenced, would be of little or no use if the pirated article is, for example, a "pop" record and has, by then, lost much or all of its commercial value.

Injunctive relief is, therefore, normally sought immediately upon discovery of the infringing act. Whether the court, having heard evidence on affidavit only, will grant an interlocutory injunction, a discretionary remedy, will depend upon the following analysis:[4]

- Whether there is a serious issue to be tried. If there is no serious issue, but this is rarely the case, no injunction will be granted; and
- If the plaintiff can be adequately compensated in damages at trial no injunction will be issued. If the defendant, on the other hand, can be adequately compensated in damages at trial if an injunction were ordered, and the plaintiff would be able to pay those damages, then an injunction should be ordered.

Provided, therefore, the plaintiff has adequate affidavit evidence of infringement, because he could rarely be compensated in damages for his loss of market, the injunction will normally be ordered.

Anton Piller Orders

The most important development in piracy case law is probably the decision in Anton Piller v. Manufacturing Process Ltd (1976) RPC 719. It is always a copyright owner's concern that the pirate, if served with or threatened with proceedings will dispose of plates, the pirated goods, and documentary evidence of the size of his operation and distribution network. In the Anton Piller case, the plaintiff therefore applied for, and was granted, an order requiring the defendants to permit them to enter the defendant's premises in order to inspect, remove, or make copies of documents belonging to the plaintiff. The application for such an order is made ex parte, that is, without notice to the defendants, and in camera.

Because of the exceptional nature of the relief, the order will be made only in serious cases. The nature of the order is not effectively to give the plaintiff a search warrant; the order is that the defendant permit the plaintiff access. If he refuses, he may be in contempt, but the plaintiff is not allowed to force an entry onto the defendant's premises. If the defendant permits execution of the order, his remedy is not to seek to discharge the order, but to proceed against the plaintiff after the trial upon the plaintiff's cross-undertaking as to damages.

The remedy has been further extended as a result of the Court of Appeal decision in CBS v. Lambert (1982) 3 AMER 237. The defendant had put the proceeds of his piracy into chattels, such as motor cars, which were readily saleable or which he could easily hide from creditors. The evidence of piracy was very strong, and the court ordered delivery up into the plaintiff's solicitor's hands of those chattels, pending trial of the action.

There has been one particular restraint upon the making of an Anton Piller Order which deserves mention. In Rank Films v. Video Information Centre, the House of Lords held that the defendant was entitled to rely upon the privilege against self-incrimination (that is exposure to criminal charges) in order to resist an order for disclosure of, for example, the addresses of suppliers.[5] This rule has for the most part been abrogated by the Supreme Court Act 1981. Because there are circumstances where the rule does still apply, any plaintiff or defendant must consider its application to his particular case.

The Anton Piller Order may be used in respect of any copyright protected material; provided computer software is so protected, there is no reason why this form of relief should not be available against computer pirates.

The Criminal Law

Although rarely employed, the criminal law may be brought to bear upon the pirates. In relation to any record or film it is, under the Performers Protection Acts, an offence to make, sell, or use for a public performance any record or film without the performer's written consent to the making of the record or film.

The Copyright Act 1956, S 21, does create an offence of commercial dealing (the definition is drawn more precisely) with infringing copies of literary, dramatic, or musical works.

Remedies to Combat Private Copying

Private copying presents a considerable threat to the profitability of both the record and video industries. Any private recording of copyright material, whether of sound recordings, videos, or computer software (where protectable), and whether from another recording or from a broadcast, is an infringement of that copyright. The difficulty in relation to private copying is not only detection but also enforceability: it is simply not cost effective to sue private copiers. The criminal sanctions effectively only apply to commercial pirates. The industry's proposed solution is a levy on hardware and/or on software, but in the Green Paper the government has rejected the proposal.

Protection of United States Copyright Materials in the United Kingdom

United States sound recordings, films, and computer software (where capable of attracting copyright protection if a British product) are generally protectable against unauthorised duplication in the United Kingdom. By virtue of both countries membership of the Universal Copyright Convention, the United Kingdom law gives protection against copying if the maker is a national of or a company incorporated in the United States or if the record, film, or programme is first published in the United States or first published elsewhere "simultaneously," that is no more than 30 days prior to first publication in the United States.

FOOTNOTES

1. S 17 (3).

2. Report of the Committee to consider the Law on Copyright and Designs, Cmnd. 6732, March 1977, known as the Whitford Report.

3. Green Paper, Cmnd. 8302.

4. American Cyanamid v. Ethicon [1975] A.C. 396.

5. [1982] A.C. 380.

THE AMERICAN JURY

London Sessions
ABA Annual Meeting 1985
Westminster Room, Inter-Continental Hotel
London, England

Wednesday, July 17, 1985
10:00 A.M. - 12:00 Noon

The Hon. Marvin E. Frankel
919 Third Avenue
New York, New York 10022

Still exhibiting the zeal of converts, Americans profess and exhibit a more unalloyed devotion to the jury than do their counterparts in Britain, from whence this and so many other parts of the American legal system have come. The institution is enshrined for the federal courts in the Sixth (criminal) and Seventh (civil) Amendments to the U.S. Constitution, and is similarly preserved in many of the states. While in both countries the jury is the classic model for the felony trial, in the United States it also has a wide role in civil cases, a role that has largely disappeared from the British scene.

It is true, of course, that in the United States, as in Britain, some of the lyricism regularly inspired by juries must be appreciated with restraint. For all the adoration, litigants display marked reservations about placing their fate in jurors' hands. Not one felony trial in 20 is tried to a jury; the rest go off mostly on guilty pleas, commonly the result of a plea bargain, or bench trials. Civil litigants settle their disputes or waive juries on a far larger scale. Still, the jury verdict, or the prospect of one, remains the chancy measure of what justice may be expected to entail.

In an effort to reflect the continued importance of the jury in the American legal systems, but without pretending to exhaust the subject, this essay will touch upon some currently live issues in the areas of jury selection, composition, competence, and authority.

Selection

The American views Englishmen's high regard for randomness as the touchstone for jury selection as variously enviable for amusing, depending upon his own state of contentment or misery with the American jury system. While the American legal community shares the view that jurors should be summoned on the basis of chance rather than culled purposefully, American lawyers are a long way from thinking randomness is enough. The random selection of a potential jury panel for the particular case is, for the American lawyer, a step close to the beginning of the process rather than its probable end. As a second cut, advocates and their clients alike want to explore both general issues, like the clear preconceptions of a venireman or his relationship to a political party, and also subtler indicators, like ideological, social, and economic affiliation and attitudes. The actual breadth and form of inquiry permitted by the court varies with the case and the place, and may consume hours, days, or weeks.

The Voir Dire

The interrogation of panel members preliminary to challenges, either peremptory or for cause, may be conducted either by the judge or by counsel. Not surprisingly, counsel prefer to conduct the interrogation themselves. They argue that they know better than the judge the facts and the qualities that must be discovered for the intelligent exercise of challenges. Opponents of voir dire by counsel object that lawyers conducting it tend to pervert and unduly prolong the process, using the voir dire as an occasion to preliminarily persuade ("soften up") prospective jurors or to woo them with counsel's real or imagined charms. As is true of most perennial divisions in the law, there is something on both sides of this one.

By contrast, both laymen and professionals are widely dissatisfied with the prolonged process of jury selection. The burden and expense are not confined to the litigants; members of the venire called upon to endure the process find it onerous as well. There is no imminent prospect, however, of a "cure," or even substantial amelioration.

Peremptory Challenges Based on Race

Both sides normally have allotments of peremptory challenges. In serious noncapital federal criminal cases, the prosecution has six, the defense ten peremptory challenges, with discretionary increases for multi-defendant cases. State provisions are comparable. Among currently unsettled questions is the constitutionality of employing peremptory challenges to eliminate members of a particular racial or ethnic group.

The doctrinal story begins suitably for present purposes with *Swain v. Alabama*, 380 U.S. 202 (1965). *Swain* held, as a matter of the equal protection clause of the Fourteenth Amendment, that a prosecutor (a public official with us) may use the government's peremptory challenges to remove minority jurors, creating a rebuttable presumption that the state's challenges have been used to obtain a fair and impartial jury. The burden of proof imposed upon the defendant seeking to prove bias in the voir dire has often been insurmountable.

Later decisions of the Supreme Court have cast doubt on the continuing vitality of *Swain*, but so far the Court has appeared disinclined to overrule the 1965 case. At least two states however, Massachusetts and California, have not felt so constrained, finding *Swain* no longer to be good law. And recently, the federal Second Circuit held that a mistrial must be declared as a matter of Sixth Amendment law if peremptory challenges have been used in a racially discriminatory way.

The balance between the objective of an impartial jury and the deep constitutional animus against racial discrimination is by no means an easy one to strike. It is an unblinkable fact that America's history of racial and ethnic prejudice is not ended, just as comparable histories elsewhere have not yet drawn to a close. If people of Race A tend noticeably to favor others of their race or to nurse an animus against Race B, a responsible lawyer can scarcely be expected to ignore that as a factor in jury selection. However, if the prosecutor is barred from racially grounded peremptory challenges, it appears as a matter of fairness and constitutionality that the defense must be similarly constrained. The jury to be empanelled is, after all, an agency of the state, at least *pro tem*, and its infection by racially motivated standards of selection would seem to generate similar fundamental objections no matter who injected the illicit criterion. Clarification from the Supreme Court, if not a totally final resolution, is awaited with widespread interest.

"Scientific" Jury Selection

There is a small store of lawyers' wisdom about attributes thought to be relevant to jury selection and, particularly, the exercise of peremptory challenges. Young people, especially males with long hair or females thought to look markedly "liberated," are suspected to sympathize more with criminal defendants than are "establishment" types and older people. There is also a short list of supposedly useful ethnic and religious clues. Protestants, Roman Catholics, and Jews are supposed to rank in that order in their degree of establishmentarian, pro-prosecution tendency.

Other characteristics--such as level of education, occupation, employment, recreational habits, views about sex and a host of other qualities--may effect attitudes toward particular litigants. The possibility of making use of such factors in jury selection has created the foundation for a small but growing industry often known as "scientific" jury selection.

Sociologists and opinion samplers in related fields of study have been employed in recent years to take surveys in the area from which a venire will be drawn. Some studies of this nature have served as grounds for a change of venue because of an allegedly prejudiced population in the designated forum. Others are used in order to draw profiles of desirable (i.e., favorable) or undesirable jurors as aids in the exercise of challenges. Another technique is the use of mock juries to prepare for trial. Such simulations are used to test preliminary theories about jury selection criteria. They also allow the attorney to decide which evidence and arguments to stress. There are credible reports that enterprises of this nature have made a significant difference in outcomes of both civil and criminal jury trials.

Use of these behavioral science techniques raises questions of morality and equity. The techniques, if effective, skew the ideal of the impartial jury; further, they are expensive, and therefore accessible chiefly to wealthy litigants. While these considerations produce a certain uneasiness, there has been no suggestion that the techniques should or may be outlawed or seriously regulated, and their use appears to be growing.

Numbers and Unanimity

The Declining Magic of "12"

The origin and necessity of the requirement of 12 members on the English and, until lately, the American jury, has been the source of much speculation. Supreme Court cases of the last decade have significantly diminished the requirements of size of the American jury and unanimity of its verdicts. Verdicts of as few as six unanimous jurors have been approved in both civil and criminal trials, and majority verdicts have been approved in criminal cases. In about one-quarter of the states, juries of six to eight members have been adopted for both civil and criminal cases.

The changes have not happened without controversy, and they remain subject to rearguard attack. Opponents argue inter alia that a jury of, say, six members is likely to move with relative haste and undue unanimity toward its verdict. While proponents of the diminished jury have called the number 12 a historical accident rather than a constitutional requirement, critics have argued that the diminished jury does violence both to legal history and to empirical evidence.

While it has sanctioned smaller juries, the Supreme Court has acknowledged that a decline in jury size may lead to less accurate factfinding and a greater risk of convicting an innocent person. In addition, statistical and empirical data establish that because it decreases the number of hung juries, a reduction in the size of the jury in criminal cases works primarily to the disadvantage of the defense. Finally, with diminution of the panel, the opportunity for minority representation also diminishes.

Powers and Capacities

The American jury has sometimes been hailed as the embodiment of all juridical wisdom, and sometimes regretted as a historical affliction that keeps our courts from approximating justice. Jurors are thought to be so stupid that many judges still forbid them to take notes, explaining (a) that this will distract them unduly (though it is thought not to have that affect on the note-taking judges who say this), and/or (b) that note-taking jurors will overbear those who merely remember, a danger not believed to be avoidable by instructions to citizens of normal wit. Conversely, judges cheerfully read 100 typed pages of instructions to juries deliberating multiple interlocking conspiracies, imagining that the jurors will sort everything out sensibly and justly.

The contradictory postures reflect a complex reality. Because of the accidental leadership of one or two members, some juries are brilliant beyond all expectations. Other juries are individually and collectively stupid. Fallible or not, the jury has until lately been presumed conclusively to be capable of comprehending and deciding any questions, however complex, served up to it for decision. The jury has also been thought by many jurists and scholars to function worthily when it rules in purposeful contravention of the law. These issues--the role of juries in complex cases, and the question of jury nullification--occupy our remaining pages.

Complex Cases

Judges on courts of general jurisdiction sometimes encounter litigation of agonizingly complex matters, such as elaborate patents, engineering issues, or vast historical events. When subjects of this nature are tendered to a jury, the argument is heard with increasing frequency that this _ad hoc_ lay group cannot plausibly be expected to get the facts straight enough for intelligent decision-making. A small but growing body of case law has developed as a result.

The federal courts are split on whether a jury can be denied in a complex case. Critics of jury trial in complex cases argue that where issues of law and fact are so complex that the average jury could not arrive at a rational decision, trial by jury violates the right of due process. A major case supporting this argument is our Third Circuit's decision in _In re Japanese Electronic Products Antitrust Litigation_ (_Matsushita_) 478 F.Supp 889 (1979), _rev'd._ 631 F.2d 1069 (3d Cir. 1980). There the trial judge _denied_ the defendants' motion to strike the plaintiffs' demand for trial by jury. The Court of Appeals reversed, holding that in a complex case, the defendants' right to due process outbalances the right to jury trial.

There is strikingly little empirical evidence in the Court of Appeals opinion in _Matsushita_. Commentators have suggested that simplifying the mechanics of the jury trial to cope with the complexity, rather than eliminating use of the jury altogether, would avoid throwing out the baby with the bath water. At the same time, one may wonder how, in a matter of weeks, a lay jury is expected to understand a highly technical case that both attorneys and experts in the field have spent years preparing.

Nullification

Some of the dramatic moments in the jury's history have been occasioned when ordinary folk in the jury box resisted, in some cause now deemed noble, the heavy hand of authority represented by the judge. The English thrill to the defiant triumphs in the trials of John Lilburne. Americans, the blood coursing the way it does for the majority over revolutions long since won, have similar feelings about Peter Zenger and other cases we could name.

Again, the complexities of the subject of jury nullification outrun easy generalities. At a few points in American history, southern juries have announced bland and expected acquittals of white defendants for the lynch murders of blacks or their white civil rights supporters. People who regretted those cases have felt otherwise about the acquittal of anti-war activists who engaged in civil disobedience. Transcending specific cases, serious scholars have argued that the price is worth paying in cases we may hate because the "lawless" jury is exercising a power needful for its (and our) liberties. Distinguished judges have argued that the jury's instructions should include reference to the group's power to disregard the law.

Critics of jury nullification argue variously that it encourages anarchy, that it is unnecessary, that it is unwise, or that the power is necessary, but better left unstated. Even proponents of jury nullification do not appear to sanction the exercise of a comparable power by the judge--i.e., the power in "conscience" secretly to ignore or override the law.

Conclusion

While the role of the American jury is certainly in a state of flux, it continues to function as the main embodiment of the legal system's aspiration to discover the truth as the route to justice. It stands to the jurisprudential scholar as a model of participatory democracy, to the judge as a cherished if troublesome adjunct, and to the trial lawyer as the audience for a lifetime of performances--or a tough nut to crack.

JURIES

London Sessions
ABA Annual Meeting 1985
Westminster Room, Inter-Continental Hotel
London, England

Wednesday, July 17, 1985
10:00 A.M. - 12:00 Noon

John Mathew, Q.C.
5 Paper Buildings
Temple, London EC4Y 7HB

and

Sir David Napley
Kingsley Napley & Co.
107-115 Long Acre
London WC2E 9PT

In the earliest methods of trial, the burden of proof rested on the defendant, who could prove his innocence in one of three ways, namely by oath, ordeal, or battle. It was not until the year 1166 that the Assize of Clarendon introduced into the English criminal process the jury system. Trial by ordeal was the most popular method of settling disputes until it ceased, due to the intervention of Pope Innocent III in 1215, and trial by battle fell into disuse and was finally abolished in England in 1819.

It must be remembered that in those early days the number of citizens residing in England were few by comparison with the present population. Moreover, the police force had not yet been conceived, and the maintenance of law and order coupled with the detection and punishment of crime was secured by the citizens within the cities, townships, and villages spread around the country generally at places distant from one another. The jury, in its origins, was formed from the same persons who made the accusation against the defendant, and the vital decision between guilt and innocence was based upon the jurors' knowledge of the defendant, his character, and an assessment of the probability that he committed the offence of which they were accusing him. It is perhaps not surprising that the jury system was not very popular in criminal trials as opposed to trial by jury on civil issues.

Over the next 500 years of English history, various improvements were made, and, such was the nature of trial by jury at its inception, room for improvement was easy to find. For instance, the number of jurors was reduced to 12, and the accused was given a general right to protest against particular persons sitting on the panel. The jury's function of giving evidence and acting on its own knowledge was abolished, and in its place it became the duty of the jury to evaluate the evidence given by others in court. Another principle reform was the development of the rules governing the evidence adduced, although it should be remembered that it was not until 1701 that witnesses for the defence were permitted to give evidence on oath, and it was even later, in 1898, that the accused was allowed to give evidence on oath in his own defence.

By the middle of the twentieth century, trial by jury had established itself as the fulcrum upon which justice was balanced in the United Kingdom and the Unites States of America. It is perhaps trite to observe that whilst those things which come easily are the least appreciated, those which are achieved through a struggle against adversity, hardship, and injustice are regarded as having the greatest value and are subjected to the most jealous protection. Just as the conflict and struggle which preceded the American Declaration of Independence and the founding of the American Constitution have become acts of faith in the eyes of the American people, so trial by one's peers has been similarly regarded over generations, not only by the citizens of the United States but by those in this country as well. Indeed, anyone today studying the history of the jury system finds it difficult to understand how the injustices perpetrated in its name were endured for so long. Juries who had returned verdicts that were not acceptable to the judge or to the King were sometimes subjected to punishment. Indeed, the Court of Star Chamber, before it was abolished, was apt to treat as corrupt any acquittal which it considered to be against the weight of evidence. Unanimity was always regarded as essential, and to achieve it intense pressures were often placed upon the jury. The most favoured method was to keep the jury together without food, drink, fire, or candle until they agreed. Lord Devlin in his admirable work "Trial by Jury" quotes a case in the eighteenth century where the jury, having been absent for some while, were searched and found that some had figs and others had pippins. Those who confessed to having eaten some of them before they had reached their verdict were fined, and for good measure those who had not eaten any were fined as well.

Another undoubted virtue of the jury, which is still well noted and remembered by those who currently oppose any changes in the system, is the part juries have historically played in ameliorating and sometimes stultifying harsh laws. At the time when sheep stealing was a capital offence, some juries, despite the peril in which they placed themselves by so doing, refused to return verdicts of guilt with the consequence that in order to obtain convictions, the penalty of capital punishment for such offences had to be abolished.

The right to trial by jury has come to be regarded in this country as the major bastion of liberty, and although there have been criticisms of some aspects of the system it has rarely if ever been suggested that it should not be retained as part of the criminal process. As an institution it developed alongside the right to have one's civil disputes tried by jury. However, the growing complexity of a civil trial at law, the time which it occupied, and the expense which it involved resulted in the curtailment of that right in 1933, with the result that today trial by jury in the civil courts is quite exceptional, requires a special Order of the Court before it is afforded, and is largely limited to actions for defamation or causes for which the court must be convinced a jury is appropriate.

There is no doubt that the virtual abolition of juries in civil trials has played some part in developing a school of thought amongst informed persons that since no dire consequences seem to have flowed from the unthinkable abolition of juries in civil causes, perhaps no serious consequences would flow from their curtailment in criminal trials. In recent years, until 1974, all persons of either sex between the ages of 21 and 60 were eligible for jury service, provided they were the owners of property, and thus ratepayers. The disqualifications were of a limited nature, and included aliens who had not lived in the United Kingdom for ten years, persons convicted of buggery, lawyers, and persons who were not on the electoral role. The number of jurors in each case was 12, and the verdict had to be unanimous. A verdict which was not unanimous did not result in an acquittal, but in re-trial, which was an example more of pragmatism than of logic. In modern times the onus of proof is upon the prosecution to satisfy the jury of guilt beyond a reasonable doubt. If a number of jurors remain unconvinced, it could be argued that the prosecution had failed to discharge the onus upon it and should thus be denied a further bite at the cherry. Indeed, the only logical basis to justify a further trial is to make the assumption that those who refused to agree with the majority of the jury must have been acting from perversity, which is generally unlikely to be the case. It is only if disagreement still results at the second trial that the practice has developed to abandon the prosecution.

In 1974, the Juries Act made certain changes in regard to qualifications and procedure. The property qualification was abolished, and any person on the electoral role between the ages of 18 and 65 became eligible for service on a jury. Those disqualified included a person who had been sentenced to imprisonment for five years or more and those who within the last ten years had served any part of a three month or longer sentence. The Act also introduced for the first time majority verdicts whereby the verdict of at least 10 out of the 12 jurors, or 9 out of 10 jurors, was acceptable. However, it is necessary for them to be allowed a reasonable time to consider their verdict, which must be at least two hours, before the judge can direct that a majority verdict will be accepted. Some lawyers believe that the introduction of majority verdicts has been an improvement in the system, whilst others remain unconvinced. In fact, it is not possible to obtain clear statistical evidence of the consequences of the change and, largely because the deliberations in the jury room are secret, little or no research has been conducted over the years into the efficacy of the jury system. The philosophy underlining the introduction of majority verdicts was that it would reduce the risk of one or two perverse jurors preventing the conviction of the guilty. In the absence of statistical and other information, however, one cannot speculate as to whether there are cases in which perverse jurors frustrate the acquittal of those who are innocent.

Another question that remains wholly unsettled is the extent to which jurors are perverse in the sense that they return or refuse to return verdicts from motives inconsistent with their sworn undertaking to return true verdicts according to the evidence. In the 1950s, research was undertaken at the University of Chicago into the jury system, and the results were published in 1966, in a book called "The American Jury." The inquiry sampled 3,576 jury trials, and some 600 judges participated in the study. Little or no evidence was found of perversion on the part of juries, who appeared in the vast majority of cases to have reached the same sort of decision as the judge would have reached sitting alone. In the course of the study, those conducting it sought the assistance of the then Lord Chief Justice, Lord Parker, who consulted the British judges as to their experience with juries. Their conclusions were much the same as was revealed in America, namely that it was very rare (and, in the experience of some judges, unknown) for juries to have reached decisions which were obviously perverse.

One of the major differences between the British system and that obtaining in America is the right to challenge. Hitherto in this country the defence had seven challenges without cause, but are now permitted only three. There is no procedure whereby the defence can cross-examine jurors unless they are challenging for cause. The voir dire procedure in empanelling jurors is a long and, in the view of many, tedious process. Jurors are often seen to be excluded on what in this country would be regarded as inadequate and inexcusable grounds, for example that the juror was distantly related to a police officer. In 1963, a judicial exchange occurred between judges and lawyers in the respective countries, when the British team was able to witness the voir dire in operation. The unanimous conclusion of the team was that from all appearances the American system tended to produce, by use of the voir dire, much the same sort of jury as the British system produced without it. In Britain, any challenge for cause is tried by the trial judge, but a prima facie case must be shown before a juror can be cross-examined. Probably the last occasion when this was done was at the Central Criminal Court in 1969 at what became known as the Kray Trial, when jurors were allowed to be cross-examined as to whether they had read and been influenced by certain prejudicial newspaper reports. In the trial of Jeremy Thorpe, as an alternative to permitting jurors to be questioned, the judge himself, at the invitation of the defence, enquired of the jurors whether they had read a book by two journalists which had been an initiating factor in the launching of the prosecution.

Whatever criticisms are made in this country of the jury system, there has been no serious suggestion that it would be improved by permitting a greater number of challenges to the jury, and certainly there is no demand for the introduction into our system of the American procedure.

Recently there has been, in some quarters, some criticism of trial by jury. This has largely been generated by the quality of jurors rather than by any evidence that the system has produced any significant number of wrong decisions. There are those who believe that the changes which were made in the eligibility of jurors by the 1974 Act were retrogressive. Whilst a most rough-and-ready test, the ownership of property tended to be some evidence of the possession of a greater responsibility and played a part in eliminating those who had little experience of life, and it is suggested that the extensive widening of the catchment area has meant that it increases the likelihood of including the illiterate and the innumerate, as well as those of inadequate education or intelligence. Some find it an inadequate answer that those categories of persons are cushioned by the presence of the remainder of the jury. This, it has been said, is a matter of special concern in long and complicated cases, particularly those involving highly technical and sophisticated evidence relating to commercial frauds. Indeed, a committee under the chairmanship of Lord Roskill is currently considering this aspect of the matter in the context of whether alternative methods of trial for such offences is a practical and desirable possibility. It is understood that in the United States, and in particular in New York, there is a system under which suitable cases can be tried by judge alone, but whether public opinion is currently prepared to accept such a system in this country is certainly open to doubt.

One of the great defects of jury trials from the point of view of the purist lawyer is that the jury gives no reasons for its decisions, which renders it exceedingly difficult for appellate courts properly to review the verdict. A virtue of trial by judge would be that he gives a reasoned judgment, which has the advantage of enabling the public to observe the ratio by which he reached his decision.

One of the suggested changes being canvassed by the Roskill Committee is trial by judge and assessors, the assessors being specialists in the particular field of commerce with which a case is concerned. Providing the assessors are parties to the decision, and their duties are not confined to advising the judge, this might be acceptable. Certainly we take the view that it would be a worthwhile experiment, in the first instance at the option of the defendant. A further possibility which merits consideration is for the trial to be by "special jury" of up to seven, drawn from panels comprised of persons with such qualifications of intelligence, experience, and responsibility as to form a fair tribunal to try complicated issues.

Trial by jury has been the basis of the criminal process for centuries and is regarded, as previously indicated, as being a fundamental part of the national heritage. A system in which the ordinary citizen is involved in the judicial process is regarded by most people as being only for the good of society. Indeed, in this country, in the lower courts the vast bulk of criminal trials are presided over by lay justices, a system which is virtually unknown in any other part of the world. Whatever may be the idiosyncrasies and peculiarities of individual jurors, it is argued, these are subsumed in the general reliability and stability of the total jury, but the same situation does not obtain where a judge or judges are sitting alone. As Lord Denning has said:

> Continuously over the last 800 years the people of England, by sitting as jurors, have taken an active part, indeed, a decisive part, in the administration of justice. They have always had the last word on the guilt or innocence of their fellow men. This participation in justice has, I believe, done more than anything else to establish the English habit of obedience to the Law which a great historian has described as "the strongest of all forces making for the nation's peaceful continuity and progress."

Lord Devlin has described trial by jury as "the lamp that shows that freedom lives," and has expressed the view that were a tyrant to arrive in this country, his first objective would be to abolish trial by jury.

Indeed, we might add that 1,000 years of history have shown that even at the time when it was possible for the Crown to control the judiciary, it found it exceedingly difficult, and often impossible, to control the jury. Whatever doubts may exist as to the need to make some improvements in the methods of trial by jury, there is one aspect about which most citizens of this country would entertain little doubt, namely that a system which has worked well for the preservation of freedom and liberty over a long period of this country's history must not lightly be impaired or abrogated for considerations of time, money, or expediency.

EXTRATERRITORIAL JURISDICTION: THE GENERAL THEORY

London Sessions
ABA Annual Meeting 1985
Ballroom, Dorchester Hotel
London, England

Wednesday, July 17, 1985
2:00 P.M. - 4:00 P.M.

Prof. Detlev Vagts
Harvard Law School
Cambridge, Massachusetts 02138

One who remembers the days of the great alliance under Churchill and Roosevelt cannot help feeling concern that two nations and two legal systems with as much in common as ours should be locked in a contest over extraterritorial jurisdiction. My paper is aimed at exploring, first, how we came to be on this collision course, then how the controversy impinges on particular areas of our economic life and, finally, a few thoughts about how we might get to work on improving things.

A Touch of History

A reasonable way to begin a survey of the developments leading to the current dispute over extraterritorial jurisdiction is with a review of the events of 1927, the year of the S.S. Lotus case, the World Court's one and only stab at resolving the extraterritoriality problem. Also in 1927, a Belgian law professor did a study of extraterritorial criminal jurisdiction in which he concluded that the United States and the United Kingdom were the two conservative states on the matter, in contrast to the continental states. At that time, the chief American contribution to the debate on extraterritoriality had been the State Department correspondence by J. B. Moore on the Cutting case, rejecting the Mexican claim to try a Texas editor for libel affecting Mexicans. Moore, who was the U.S. member of the World Court in 1927, dissented from the Lotus judgment on the ground that Turkey's prosecution was explicitly based on the passive personality principle, an illegitimate ground. Concurrently, Judge Lord Finlay took a more sweeping view of the matter, ruling that it was not necessary for France to prove the existence of an international rule specifically outlawing Turkey's practice.

The Anglo-American harmony of 1927 was soon eroded. American courts began to decide cases, particularly in the antitrust field, that went further and further in their outward reach. At the same time, U.S. theoretical statements about extraterritoriality, in the Harvard Research Draft Convention of 1935 and the Restatement of Foreign Relations Law of 1962, both stated versions of the "effects" principle in broader terms and, in the latter case, applied standards used in "common" criminal cases to more complex matters of economic regulation. Meanwhile, British theory tended to dig in behind the proposition that territoriality (and nationality) are the only bases supported by international law. The British position in the process became further removed not only from the American but also from the continental version.

One cannot help speculating as to why our courses diverged so much. Partly it must be due to relative power positions. After 1918 the United States increasingly felt itself to be the central power in the free enterprise, democratic world and responsible for mobilizing that world against Nazism (and the German-based cartel system), and then against Communism. Britain on the other hand became more intent upon defending a territorially diminished base against all comers. One would also guess that U.S. courts, which are accustomed to reaching across state frontiers that are less formidable barriers than international ones, are less impressed by national frontiers than are the British. Finally, there is simply the fact that the American judiciary are, by long tradition, freer to depart from 1909 precedents than are their British counterparts.

Antitrust

Developments in the antitrust field have been key to the problems of extraterritoriality in British-U.S. relations. Although Justice Holmes had stated a "pure" territoriality theory in the American Banana case in 1909, by the mid-1920s the Supreme Court had approved prosecution of antitrust violations in cases where little of the action took place in America. Finally, in 1945, the Aluminium case carried matters to the extreme where none of the actions, but only their effects in the form of price increases, took place in America. Episodically, antitrust cases involving British interests have flared up, and there is a well-known string of controversies--ICI-Dupont, Westinghouse-Rio Tinto, Laker Airways, etc.--that have enflamed relations between the two governments. Let us note that there were also, before Britain's accession to the Common Market, cases of conflict over like issues with the European Economic Community.

Securities

British-U.S. relations seem to have been less damaged by American activity in the field of securities regulation. This is true even though the theoretical claims on which some securities cases have been based are rather far-reaching. The U.S. securities law cases have not in general worked against British interests; fraud is, after all, against British law as well as American. Furthermore, British fraud prosecutions cases have occasionally reached fairly far afield in cases where Britons were the victims. Only in a situation in which the demands of U.S. regulation would have required British firms doing business in the U.S. and having U.S. shareholders to conform their disclosure patterns to U.S. models was Britain moved to protest (and the Securities and Exchange Commission to make a strategic retreat).

Boycott Legislation

American legislation of the type that has provoked conflict over trade with the People's Republic of China and the U.S.S.R. dates to 1917 when the United States entered World War One. A year earlier there had been a civilized but sharp exchange between Ambassador Page and Secretary of State Sir Edward Grey about the scope of the 1915 Act to Provide for the Extension of the Restrictions Relating to Trading with the Enemy. Let us remember that even before 1914 there was a long history of differences between the United States and Britain about the extent of a belligerent's powers to interfere with neutrals' trading with the enemy. Finally, the United States learned about the technique of blacklisting neutrals from the British 1939 Act. What is significantly different about post-1950 events is the attempt by the United States to interfere with trade in time of (relative) peace rather than of war. To the extent that U.S. and western European states collaborated in COCOM to establish common lists of forbidden items, relative harmony prevailed during the 1950s and most of the 1960s. At times, however, substantive policies on trade have differed, most conspicuously in the pipeline episode, and conflicts have emerged.

Unitary Taxation

Matters of income tax are special, and the theory of jurisdiction to tax has developed specially. However, the parallels between other jurisdictional conflicts and the unitary tax question are too significant to overlook. The normal method of allocating taxes between states internationally is to attempt to divide up a complex multinational enterprise into local components and conceive of each as trading at arms' length with the other components. A separate income statement and tax bill is computed for each unit. Internally it has become common to divide up income between the states of the United States by applying a formula--based on property, payroll, and sales--to the unitary income of the entire enterprise. Thus California, with one-third of a firm's property, payroll, and sales, would tax one-third of its net revenue. While that system works fairly satisfactorily within the United States, where there is a fair amount of uniformity in state practice, its application abroad involves hardships and has aroused protests. The United States and the United Kingdom included the matter in their tax treaty negotiations though one can hardly say they put the matter to rest.

Other

There are quite a few other areas in which the United States asserts a right to regulate acts abroad. For example, our rules on addictive drugs can be applied to processors and vendors operating overseas. The same was true of alcohol during the noble prohibition experiment of the 1920s. So far as a reasonably alert journal reader can tell, these cases arouse little difficulty. One guesses that it is because the activities thus repressed are regarded as contrary to British interests as well (and those who engage in them lack political influence here in London).

British Reactions

The description of British reactions to U.S. actions is best left to British observers. Let me say a few things about the U.S. counter-reaction. The diplomatic protest is the time-hallowed minimum reaction to a foreign action seen to be an affront. For a British court to refuse to enforce a U.S. court's judgment on the grounds that it violates Britain's public policy is well within its discretion. So long as the treaty on the recognition of judgments initialled by the two states languishes unratified, there is no international delinquency there. For a British court to refuse the aid of its processes in gathering evidence for a case where U.S. interests are antagonistic to Britain's violates no American right, given the escape clauses in the Hague Convention on the topic. When a British executive order directs a British subject to disregard a U.S. command, the action may be unfriendly but it is not unlawful, it does not go beyond any international jurisdictional boundary.

Where there is a problem is in the British statutory "clawback" scheme under which penal damages assessed and collected by U.S. courts might be retrieved through the British courts. As final actions by officers of the U.S. government completed within its territory, the U.S. award and execution thereon seem entitled to more respect than that. It may be hard to arrange a body of authority to prove that the "clawback" violates international law but the factors which have caused each of our judiciaries to develop an "act of state" doctrine point to the notion that it is undesirable to frustrate a foreign state's policy so uncompromisingly.

Resolutions

Here let us review the possible mechanisms through which future episodes of conflict may be resolved. One need not take the more pessimistic views of the seriousness of the episodes to date to judge that it is worthwhile to take advantage of a period of relative calm to think about ways of forestalling the next crisis.

Unilateral U.S. Restraint

Clearly the problem would be less if the U.S. executive exercised more restraint in initiating proceedings with extraterritorial effect. Contemplating the pipeline fracas, one wonders if the U.S. government's institutional memory had wholly erased such episodes as the *Fruehauf* affair in 1965. Congress can play a role in cutting back, as it did in the 1982 Sherman Act amendment limiting jurisdiction to "direct" effects; it may do so again in the Export Administration Act revisions pending in 1984. Even with better internal decision-making in Washington there will be problems. Private American plaintiffs can initiate litigation in antitrust or other fields that causes problems. Sometimes the need for action will seem to the executive, even after sober second thoughts, to be overwhelming.

The courts can and do exercise some restraints. But one must recall that U.S. courts have no power to set aside statutes or executive actions as violating international law; they have only a power to interpret those rules restrictively if such a reading is intellectually respectable. Scholars have advocated that U.S. courts apply some version of an interest-balancing test to curtail excesses. Judges have responded by doubting that they have the ability to make such judgments in an internationally even-handed way. Such doubts arise from the limits on the intelligence resources of courts but, beyond that, from modesty about national judges posing as supranational balancers.

Bilateral Negotiations

The United States is a party to bilateral agreements with Australia, Canada, and the Federal Republic of Germany that contain commitments to consult prior to initiating antitrust proceedings. Experience under the senior agreement, the Canadian-U.S. arrangement, seems to indicate that the course of cordiality has not been smooth at all times. Nor can the agreement stand in the way of forays by litigious private parties. Occasional crises will come on so quickly as to preclude advance cooperation. Still, one judges that an attempt to develop a reliable, confidential channel between the antitrust authorities of our two governments would be worth the effort. Other pairs of agencies might be similarly linked. We should remember that our governments _do_ share many attitudes towards policies--although obviously not in all details. Secret price-fixing talks or frauds on stock purchasers should evoke cooperative, not antagonistic, reactions.

Conceivably, agreements might go beyond the procedural/consultational level and try to define either the reach of each state's authority or even the substantive rules involved. One event that suggests that surprising things are possible is the treaty between the United States and Switzerland that committed Switzerland not only to tolerate but to assist U.S. efforts to repress certain types of international criminal activity. The treaty draws tight lines around the types of issues involved, specifically excluding antitrust. However, it does suggest what two systems that have struck sparks when they collided with each other in the past can do with a sufficient will to accommmodate each other's most basic interests.

Multilateral Cooperation

Sometimes it is easier to work out differences in a larger body representing more shades of opinion and varieties of interest than between two protagonists of polar positions. One example of such a group is the Organization of Economic Cooperation and Development. The OECD provides a forum within which representatives of the industrialized states can meet to exchange views and to enumerate principles of conduct, generally nonbinding ones. In its more specialized way, COCOM has served to coordinate the national policies of the western states on strategic goods. Recent events have shown that it does not have the power to contain major differences of opinion.

International Litigation or Mediation

With the new American enthusiasm for "dispute resolution," one is led to try to imagine some form of body to resolve the type of dispute we have been discussing. Straightforward adjudication seems inapt for the role. The issues are not likely to be sufficiently sharp-edged to lend themselves to resolution in the way that courts function. The question of whether a given U.S. action violates international law because of its extension is going to find judges or arbitrators short of tangible legal materials with which to build answers. Unless the apparent British position that the effects of an action within a territory can never be a basis for jurisdiction, no matter how clearly intended or specially severe those effects may be, is sustained, the task of drawing lines is basically nonjusticiable. In a domestic setting, one might imagine courts with a large flow of cases gradually developing a body of law that provided some predictability in at least standard types of cases. It is rather hard to visualize this happening in an international setting. A special trans-Atlantic tribunal might get three or four cases a decade--in comparison with the World Court's one in sixty years. Even if the diplomatic demarches and correspondence can be counted as part of the customary international law background, these sources will be thin. Unless the basic agreement could itself lay down very explicit (and likely arbitrary) rules for the tribunal to apply, the judges' task would be impossible to fulfill satisfactorily.

Finally, one looks at dispute resolution by less sharp-edged methods than arbitration, that is, by conciliation, good offices, etc. One might invent a panel of neutral fact finders who could examine a situation and produce a report, setting forth the facts, assessing the national interests involved, and recommending a course of action. If the panel were impressive enough, its report, though not binding, would be highly persuasive.

Conclusion

Considering the differences in background, culture, and interest between the United States or the United Kingdom and many other nations, the gulf between our two countries is relatively narrow. It would be a bad sign indeed for the prospects of the international legal order if we failed to cope with this set of problems.

SELECTED BIBLIOGRAPHY

The development of U.S. general extraterritoriality theory can be traced through the Research in International Law under the Auspices of the Harvard Law School, Jurisdiction with Respect to Crimes, 29 Am. J. Int'l L. Supp. 435 (1935); the Restatement (Second), Foreign Relations Law of the United States §§6-43 (1965); Restatement, Foreign Relations Law of the United States (Revised)§§401-418 (tent. draft 2, 1981).

Efforts to explore possibilities of reconciliation of U.S. and European views include D. Rosenthal & W. Knighton, National Laws and International Commerce: The Problem of Extraterritoriality (1982); Symposium, The European Business World and the Extraterritorial Application of United States Economic Regulation, 35 Wirtschaft und Recht 67 (1983); Symposium, German Yearbook of International Law (at press). For a 1927 review, see Bourquin, Crimes et delits contre la surete des etats etrangers, 16 Hague Academy, Receuil des Cours 117.

For an exchange on the British blocking statute, see Lowe, Blocking Extraterritorial Jurisdiction: The British Protection of Trading Interests Act, 1980, 75 Am. J. Int'l. L. 257 (1981), Lowenfeld, Sovereignty, Jurisdiction and Reasonableness: A Reply to A.V. Lowe, id. at 629.

For recent reviews of extraterritoriality in U.S. practice as applied to specific areas, consult, J. Atwood & K. Brewster, Antitrust and American Business Abroad (2d ed. 1981); Abbott, Linking Trade to Political Goals: Foreign Policy Export Controls in the 1970s and 1980s, 65 Minn. L. Rev. 739 (1981); Kaden, State Taxation of Multinational Corporations, 32 Catholic Univ. L. Rev. 829 (1983); Johnson, Applications of Federal Securities Laws to International Securities Transactions, 1980 Fordham Corp. L. Inst. 89.

EXTRATERRITORIALITY: THE BROADER CONTEXT OF THE CONFLICT

London Sessions
ABA Annual Meeting 1985
Ballroom, Dorchester Hotel
London, England

Wednesday, July 17, 1985
2:00 P.M. - 4:00 P.M.

William Beckett
Department of Trade and Industry
Room 11.10
Ashdown House
123 Victoria Street
London SW1E 6RB

Whilst it is fashionable these days to perceive jurisdictional conflicts and to suspect extraterritoriality in almost every legal subject matter, in this paper I intend to concentrate on a very few areas where such conflicts are perceived in the regulation of economic activity other than antitrust enforcement. Although antitrust still occupies the centre stage, other areas, such as trade boycotts, export and re-export controls, and securities law enforcement, have recently attracted the excessive jurisdiction spotlight.

Whilst in principle excessive prescriptive jurisdiction may be exercised equally by the judicial as well as by the legislative authorities of a state, the approaches and mechanisms for resolving conflicts are very different in each case. Antitrust law in the United States, although founded in statute, is essentially case law. It is the courts which have fashioned the statutes into such an instrument of torture, and it is the courts which have directed them at conduct outside the United States. Of course, the courts will say that they are merely giving effect to the intentions of the legislature--but can they really say what those intentions were in relation to the modern-day complexity of international economic relations?[1] The legislature, if not in accordance with the declaring zeal of the courts, always has the power to amend the antitrust statutes to reflect its present-day policies. With statutes that are hallowed, however, such as the Sherman Act, the reality is that the courts are not interfered with, and the executive branches of government dealing with foreign responses can only lament that they are powerless to act. Once the transnational litigation process has started, despite the use of blocking laws which might be said only to make matters worse, the only way to settle is for the defendants to reach for their cheque books.

In those other areas of conflict apart from antitrust, the courts are not in the front line. It is the economic regulatory authorities that are perceived to be exercising excessive prescriptive jurisdiction in pursuit of their present-day policies. Foreign government responses may thus be made directly to the authorities who have the power to change their policies and to accommodate foreign sensitivities to their methods of implementation.

I speak about perceived excessive jurisdiction not only to adopt a neutral stance in the debate between states as to what under international law is permissible or not, but in order to explore the question whether it is not just the form and manner in which jurisdiction is exercised which is objectionable rather than the substance of what is done. As Alan Neale has demonstrated in his analysis of antitrust cases, the United States does not need to rely on a questionable use of the effects doctrine and could, without much difficulty, abandon its claims to jurisdiction on this ground. I, too, would like to show that in these other areas there is no real need to set about regulation in ways which give rise to objections based on principles of international law.

What are these principles of international law around which the debate between states takes place? They are the territoriality principle and the nationality principle, the latter being stated as an exception to the former. The territoriality principle permits a state to regulate the conduct of all persons present within its territory, but not to bind persons outside, except its nonresident nationals. Leaving aside the Lotus-like attacks on these Huber-Storyan principles, the relevant debate in recent nonantitrust cases is centred more on the relationship between territory and nationality. That jurisdiction may be based either on the territoriality principle or on the nationality principle presupposes that problems of concurrent jurisdiction may or will arise. Self-evident examples may easily be given to show that the nationality principle must yield to the jurisdiction to prescribe on the territoriality principle and. of course, the nationality principle can never extend to a jurisdiction to enforce outside the nationality state. Where the conflicts arise, nationality as a principle is not unlimited but must yield in the face of contrary mandatory requirements imposed by the state of residence.

The United Kingdom has consistently taken the view that a jurisdiction to prescribe based on the nationality principle must yield to a jurisdiction to prescribe based on the territoriality principle. In 1948, commenting on the drafts of the Declaration on the Rights and Duties of States, the United Kingdom stated:

> It is, they consider, not correct that a state's jurisdiction over foreigners within its territory is exclusive. International law recognises both territorial jurisdiction over all persons and things within the territory and a personal jurisdiction over nationals wherever they may be. In general, in cases of conflict, the personal jurisdiction cedes to the territorial jurisdiction.[2]

Again in 1969, to the Commission of the European Communities, in the ICI Dyestuffs case, the United Kingdom's aide memoire said:

> The nationality principle justifies proceeding against nationals of the state claiming jurisdiction in respect of their activities abroad only provided that this does not involve interference with the legitimate affairs of other states or cause such nationals to act in a manner which is contrary to the laws of the state in which the activities in question are conducted.

There are two sides to the relationship between the territoriality and nationality principles when considering extraterritoriality: the extent to which extraterritoriality jurisdiction over one's nationals conflicts with local law and, from the other point of view, the extent to which extraterritoriality jurisdiction over aliens within the territory conflicts with the law of their own nationalities. In the first case, jurisdiction over one's nationals abroad is an accepted form of extraterritoriality limited in the case of conflicts with local law, but in the second case it may be said that there is an inherent limitation on jurisdiction not dependent on any conflict with the law of nationality. United States courts, however, do allow the defence of foreign sovereign compulsion, and it is this which has perhaps encouraged other states to adopt their powers of direction in their blocking statutes.

Actual conflicts with local law do not, as a matter of principle, give rise to much difficulty. The trouble starts with statements, as in the Dyestuffs case quoted above, about interference with the legitimate affairs of other states. From this there is a kind of quantum leap to the proposition that jurisdiction to prescribe based on the nationality principle cannot be allowed to affect adversely a liberty left to the individual by the local law. As Jennings puts it, "the ethos of a system of law is to be collected as much from what it leaves to individual freedom as from what it requires or forbids, or guarantees.[3] Thus we move from conflicts of law to conflicts of policies, and State A is said to break international law by exercising jurisdiction over its nationals by requiring them to do or not to do things in State B, whose law is silent on the matters in question. This is indeed a questionable proposition because, if true, it might be asked whether there really is anything left in the principle of the state's right to prescriptive jurisdiction over the acts of its nationals abroad. Or is it only in respect of conflicts of economic policy that such a limitation on the nationality principle exists when a state is to be castigated for seeking to impose its own economic policy on another state or to thwart that state's own economic policy?[4] Or again, as Rosenthal and Knighton argue, is it that a limitation is only justified in the field of economic regulation for political purposes on the ground that other states need not co-operate with a state which is pursuing a political purpose to which they do not subscribe?[5] Reduced to this level, the leap from conflicts of laws to conflicts of policies hardly leads to a sound basis for asserting principles of international law in support of objections.

The United States, it seems, would accept that, in a conflict-of-law situation, the law of the territorial state must prevail, but it is less certain that the United States would do so when the conflict is between the policy of states. Tests of reasonableness may moderate U.S. claims that primary jurisdiction rests with the state where the corporation is doing business, but such balancing tests are likely to be even more uncertain than they are in antitrust cases when applied to trade embargoes and political boycotts. However, if these matters are so uncertain, it might be asked how they can be asserted as principles of international law in the first place.

Before leaving the international law principles, there is the basic question of the nationality of the corporate body. The United Kingdom stands firmly on the principle that the nationality of a corporation is determined by the place of incorporation and that a state is not entitled to regulate the activities of a company incorporated in another state on the basis that the whole, or substantial part, of its shareholding is owned or controlled by nationals of the state concerned. Although more concerned with the discretionary nature of diplomatic protection, this proposition is claimed to be supported by the dicta in the Barcelona Traction case.[6]

The Pipeline Case

It is out of the conflict of policies that the pipeline case arose. This conflict stemmed not so much from a difference in the basic policies of the United States and the United Kingdom but rather from a difference in the method of their implementation. The root cause of the difference was what was seen on this side of the Atlantic as a retrospective change in rules relating to the re-export of goods already exported from the United States. Given the traditional U.K. attitude to retrospection and the desire to exempt existing contracts, the dispute flared to the point of the United Kingdom invoking its so-called blocking legislation to protect the interests of U.K. companies caught in the middle. Without the retrospective element it is more than likely that the United States and its European allies could have united behind a common policy and objections would not have been made to the form of the U.S. actions. As it was, battle was joined, and the principles of international law were trotted out to make yet another jurisdictional dispute.

United Kingdom objections and those of other European states, co-ordinated in the European Communities comments on the Amendments of 22 June 1982 to the Export Administration Regulations, began from the premise that the only accepted bases of jurisdiction were territorial and nationality and argued that neither were present to justify the restraints placed on European companies. The Regulations claimed an effect over companies incorporated in European states which were not considered to be U.S. nationals notwithstanding their U.S. parenthood, and any claim to jurisdiction over U.S. goods and technology was rejected because they could not have any nationality. Even the effects doctrine, which was not recognised as having any general acceptance as a basis of jurisdiction, was rejected on the ground that there could be no direct effects in the United States arising out of the performance of the contracts in Europe.

But was it really necessary for the United States to legislate in such a form and manner which afforded its European allies the opportunity to complain of breaches of international law? Was there really a need to purport to legislate directly for overseas subsidiaries of U.S. parents? Could not a control have been exercised simply over the U.S. parents, as U.S. nationals, and over their activities abroad? There was no conflicting local law, and it is difficult to say that there was a conflicting policy other than the point about retrospection. The United Kingdom left its companies to conduct their business as they wished, and this was still the position even after use of the blocking legislation.

The real difficulty concerned the U.K. companies trading in the United States, trading that is at least to the extent of seeking licences to export goods of U.S. origin. For these companies the introduction of a new prohibition on re-export after they had acquired the goods presented them with the dilemma of offending against the U.S. regulations for failing to fulfill their contractual obligations. Notwithstanding that they had accepted export licences subject to compliance with future changes in the re-export conditions, and accepted the same as a term in their contracts of purchase, the resulting prohibition seemed an extraterritorial attempt to control the right to export goods from the United Kingdom. But is it an example of offending extraterritoriality to grant export licences subject to conditions limiting re-export with or without any element of retrospection, whether contracted for or not?[7] A state can surely choose, as a matter of its own law, to control the export of goods from its territory, and to any ultimate destination whether directly or indirectly. Most states, including the United Kingdom, actually do so.[8] There may well be a basis of objection if such controls are to be enforced in the face of contrary mandatory requirements to re-export imposed by the licensee's home state. In such a case the U.S. courts perhaps would allow a foreign sovereign compulsion defence to any proceedings for breach, but it is difficult to see any international law objection to consequent administrative action such as black listing.

Blocking Statutes

In the United Kingdom we prefer to call blocking statutes protective legislation--hence the title of the Protection of Trading Interests Act 1980. In so far as the application and enforcement of foreign law requires the active assistance or the passive acquiescence of the United Kingdom, then regard must be had to the trading and economic interests of the United Kingdom. No breach of international law is involved here, although there is a departure from the traditional assistance and co-operation ordinarily given to other states in commercial litigation. Such statutes do not, of course, solve the underlying dispute. They are invoked at the stage after diplomatic protest and negotiation has failed to produce a satisfactory response. Once invoked the confrontation becomes public and complete. No longer is objection based on a failure to recognise conflicting policies but on a conflicting local law which the blocking statute deliberately creates.

The first use of the United Kingdom's present statute was in the pipeline case. It was directed at those provisions of the Export Administration Regulations relating to the re-export or export of goods from the United Kingdom. The effect, as a matter of English law, was to free the U.K. companies from the shackles of the U.S. prohibition of re-exports or exports to the Soviet Union. The United Kingdom was prohibiting its companies from complying with the U.S. prohibition. The double negative, however, did not produce a mandatory requirement to effect exports to the Soviet Union, and thus, in a sense, there was no conflicting law. The only effect, if litigation had ensued in the U.K. courts, would have been to give the companies a defence against actions by their U.S. contracting partners but to deny them the opportunity of setting up the U.S. prohibition against their Soviet Union contracting parties--hardly a solution to the company's dilemma.

Solutions

In the broader context of the conflict where private litigants do not regularly engage the court, the solutions are not to be found in an appeal to the principles of international law. The conflicts are unnecessarily dressed up as infringements of international law when in fact they are disputes about policies. Given harmony on policies, then co-operation would be restored and arguments about the bases of jurisdiction would not be heard. Discussions, bilateral and unilateral negotiations, and above all early warnings, are the only way to smooth out differences in the application of policies. Efforts may be made on both sides not to enflame differences and present them as basic conflicts of law. Particularly welcome in this direction from the U.S. side are the efforts of the Securities and Exchange Commission to consult widely with foreign governments and agencies before embarking on new proposals--waiver by conduct--which, if not handled carefully, might once again lead to debates about the principles of international law.

FOOTNOTES

1. See the remarks of Judge Wilkey in the Court of Appeals in one of the Laker actions describing the U.K. blocking statute as having no visible purpose except to defeat the policies of the doctrine branches of the U.S. government. Laker Airways Ltd v. Sabena, 731 F.2d 909 (D.C.Cir.1984).

2. U.N. document A/C N 4/2 of 15 December 1948.

3. British Year Book of International Law (1957) p. 151.

4. Akehurst, Jurisdiction in International Law--British Year Book of International Law (1972-3), p. 189.

5. National Laws and International Commerce--The Problem Extraterritoriality (1982), p. 58.

6. International Court of Justice Reports (1970).

7. For an analysis of the U.S. export controls, and in particular the use of submission clauses, see A.V. Lowe--International and Co-operative Law Quarterly, 1984, p. 575.

8. The U.K. courts have recognised the right of foreign states to control their exports indirectly to particular destinations. See Regazzoni v. Sethia [1958] A.G.301.

THE CASE MANAGEMENT DEBATE IN THE UNITED STATES

London Sessions
ABA Annual Meeting 1985
Audley Suite, Grosvenor House Hotel
London, England

Wednesday, July 17, 1985
2:00 P.M. - 4:00 P.M.

U.S. Magistrate Wayne D. Brazil
Northern District of California
450 Golden Gate Avenue-Box 36008
San Francisco, California 94102

Our goal here is to provide an overview of the current debate in America about case management as it relates to civil litigation. There are three fundamental tensions that permeate this debate.

The first is the tension between the values of fairness and of efficiency. Some opponents of case management accuse some of its proponents of elevating concern over efficiency above concern over fairness--of being too prepared to sacrifice thoroughness (the search for truth) for the sake of speeding up dispositions and reducing docket backlogs. In this view, there is a great danger that judicial officers will become too responsive to pressures to generate flattering statistics about their productivity and too insensitive to the subtle forms of misbehavior that can be exposed only by tenacious and complete discovery. On the other hand, proponents of case management reject the view that fairness and efficiency are locked in a simple bipolar tension. Instead, the case management people insist that one of the major sources of unfairness in our system is its inefficiency. They point out, for example, that parties who must wait five years for a jury trial (as they must in some urban court systems) can be discouraged even from trying to enforce their rights. And backlogs of that duration can give defendants economic incentives not to make serious efforts to settle claims or to promptly acknowledge liabilities. There are larger implications of these facts: when parties are discouraged from trying to enforce their rights because doing so would take too long and cost too much, and when the system's slowness and ineptitude discourage defendants from acknowledging their obligations, the rule of law itself is jeopardized. The system's failure to provide meaningful law enforcement encourages people to break the law. It rewards the unprincipled at the expense of the law-abiding.

The second major tension at the center of this debate pivots on strongly held views about the adversary system. Opponents of case management fear that it threatens to eviscerate our traditional form of dispute resolution and to replace it with an essentially inquisitorial system. Opponents fear a massive (if gradual) shift of primary responsibility for the system away from litigants and counsel and toward the judiciary and its minions. They fear that the judiciary will usurp the freedom of litigants by extending and concentrating its own power, and that the system will become further bureaucratized and rigidified. These fears are cast in big words that provoke big emotions. We will explore whether they are justified in a moment.

The third tension at the center of the case management debate is between the proponents of the two principal forms of organization of civil courts in the United States: the master calendar system, which is associated primarily with state courts, and the single assignment system, which is the dominant form in federal trial courts. In the sections that follow we will discuss the virtues and the problems associated with each of these systems. We will use that discussion to explore the other two tensions that we identified above. En route we will describe some of the principal tools American courts use for case management.

Before turning to these matters, however, it is important to point out why the movement toward case management began. The problems that inspire this movement seem to be as old as litigation itself. They include the high cost of adjudication, the slow pace of dispute resolution, delays and docket backlogs, the convoluted and often clumsy procedures by which cases are moved toward trial, and the sense of powerlessness and frustration that clients, even sophisticated institutional clients, often feel when they are involved in the system. These problems are easy to describe. They are not easy to attack. They have shown a distressingly remarkable capacity to survive even the most determined and conscientious efforts at procedural reform. Deep concern about cost, delay, and convolution inspired the great reformers of the mid-nineteenth century who led the movement away from common law pleading and toward the codes. The same concerns inspired the protracted efforts that resulted in the reformulation of the federal equity rules in 1912. They inspired the 30-year campaign that culminated in the merger of law and equity in the federal system and the adoption of a radically expanded system of pretrial discovery, both accomplished through the promulgation of the Federal Rules of Civil Procedure in 1938. Most recently, they inspired the substantial changes in Federal Rules 7, 11, 16, and 26, changes that simultaneously impose greater responsibility for management on federal judges and greater duties to demonstrate restraint, reasonableness, and a sense of proportionality on lawyers. In a real sense, case management is simply the most popular recent idea to which reformers have turned to assault hoary problems that have eluded other kinds of procedural solutions. No one thinks case management can completely solve these problems. The best it can do is reduce their sway.

We should bear in mind two points about these problems when we examine criticism of case management and evaluate options. One is that the magnitude and character of the needs that underlie the case management movement vary considerably from jurisdiction to jurisdiction in the United States. In some less densely populated regions, for example, litigants have ready access to early trial dates. Early trial dates seem to be the best single source of discipline in our system. Where they are available, there is less room for other problems to grow. Moreover, lawyers who practice in rural areas or smaller towns are more likely than their urban counterparts to know each other socially and to expect to see each other in subsequent lawsuits. These facts can temper adversarial excesses and create an environment that rewards civility and reasonableness. The combination of an early trial date and social pressure toward restraint can reduce the need for assertive management by the judiciary.

In major urban centers, however, problems tend to be much more severe. There are fewer socio-professional restraints on lawyer behavior. Lawyers are less likely to know each other, less likely to have confidence in each other, less likely to expect to need to get along with each other in subsequent cases. It is in this environment that the backlogs are most severe and the economic stakes in lawsuits tend to be greatest. Not suprisingly, it is in this environment that the discovery system is most abused and that the case development process is most unwieldy and expensive. These facts lead to a second point we must bear in mind when thinking about case management: in the jurisdictions where it is needed, it is sorely needed. The problems to which it is responsive are real, immediate, large, and have ominous implications. That means we must be prepared to take some risks and tolerate some imperfections when we fashion remedies. The fact that case management poses potential threats to some values is important; but it is even more important to ask whether the benefits delivered by case management outweigh the actual damage it does to other interests.

The Master Calendar System

Under the master calendar system, courts divide responsibility for various parts of the adjudicatory process: certain judges hear only pretrial or discovery matters, other judges rule on requests for equitable relief, others host settlement negotiations, and yet others preside at trials. Some courts also compel some of their judges to develop expertise in certain substantive areas of the law; e.g., family law or probate. These substantive-area specialists are largely confined to cases that fall in their specialties.

The principal case management virtues of this kind of system are the efficiencies that come with highly developed expertise among the judges. When a judge or commissioner handles virtually nothing but discovery problems for a substantial period of time, that officer learns the relevant law inside and out. He or she also learns a great deal about how lawyers behave in that part of the litigation world and about the nature of the problems that arise in it. Such judges are adept at applying the law to particular disputes and may become important sources of ideas about how to improve the law in the areas they master. Many people also think that the master calendar system is the only system capable of mass-processing a large volume of litigation. Apparently the theory behind this thinking has two central elements: one is that expertise makes for the most efficient resolution of discrete disputes; the other is that judges whose responsibilities are confined to pieces of suits are not likely to get caught up in time-consuming oversight of matters that turn out to be inconsequential.

The principal disadvantage of the master calendar system is that it gives the courts no means to oversee each lawsuit as a whole. Because different judges are responsible for different parts of each suit, no one judicial officer is responsible for the entire evolutionary development of each civil action. That makes it difficult for the court to set a tone for the case, to monitor the progress of an action, to learn the personalities of counsel and litigants, to respond with management tools that fit the needs of given cases. No one judge is in a position to help counsel develop and execute a management plan; no one judge can help counsel adjust as original plans fail to fit evolving situations. There is no judicial officer to whom counsel can turn as a resource to help prevent problems from arising in the first place, and no one who knows the case well enough to provide expeditious solutions when the unanticipated occurs (e.g., no one familiar enough with the case to fairly resolve disputes that arise during discovery through the simple device of a phone call).

Lawyers handling cases in court organized under the master calendar system spend most of their time in wholly unsupervised activities. Most of what happens in each case remains invisible to the judges. That means that lawyers have considerable room to overprepare, underprepare, misfocus, meander, postpone, or overcharge. The magnitude of these problems varies with the integrity and competence of counsel and with the sophistication of clients. Some institutional clients, for example, can look out for themselves and can discipline their lawyers. But parties who have little or no experience with litigation and who do not understand its subleties can be vulnerable. The court (in a master calendar system) is in a poor position to intercede on their behalf.

Another management problem associated with the master calendar system is that each judge who must resolve a discrete problem in his or her part of the litigation must learn the case from scratch. It follows either that there is considerable duplication of learning effort or that the judges who resolve discrete disputes know relatively little about the whole case environment in which they are acting. In other words, there is a real risk that each judge who interacts with the case will have only the most superficial knowledge of it and of the principal actors in its drama. Superficiality increases the risk of error and of failure to detect problems. Moreover, when lawyers can predict that the judge won't thoroughly understand the situation they might be more tempted to play it loose with the rules.

The magnitude of the kinds of problems associated with the master calendar system also can be a function of the size, complexity, or spleenfulness of particular suits. In smaller, less-complex matters, where the lawyers are proceeding in basic good faith, there is no obvious need for judicial intervention. Simply providing a forum for resolving disputes and setting an early trial date may be all that is required to optimize delivery of service to clients. Similarly, in less complex matters, judges handling discrete parts of a suit will not have great difficulty mastering enough of the situation to render efficient and reliable decisions. Nor will there be a great deal of room for undetected maneuvering or for shenanigans by counsel.

On the other hand, the master calendar system is less well-suited to handle matters that are more complex, or in which lawyers are not competent or are not proceeding in good faith. Some state courts have recently acknowledged this fact by creating special management tracks for complex cases and assigning each case on such a track to just one judge, who handles all pretrial aspects of it.

The Single Assignment System

Under the single assignment system, a court has the capacity to avoid most of the shortcomings that can plague the master calendar system. One judge is assigned responsibility for virtually all phases of an action as soon as the complaint is filed. Once so assigned, the judge can (1) use a meaningful early status conference to help counsel identify the core issues and to develop a plan and a schedule for acquiring the information needed to assess the strengths and weaknesses of positions and to conduct meaningful settlement discussions; (2) help counsel conduct settlement negotiations or find another host for such negotiations; (3) explore with counsel the advisability of using some alternative mode of dispute resolution (e.g., mediation, mini-trial, summary jury trial, or neutral expert) or an innovative procedural technique (e.g., joint fact finding or use of a special master to orchestrate a search for stipulations or to resolve privilege claims); and (4) isolate key legal issues whose early resolution through summary judgment or bifurcated trial might terminate the dispute or establish the basis for serious settlement discussions. A judge in the single assignment system also has the capacity to help pace case development--to fix sound schedules and keep things moving by resolving disputes quickly. A judge who has kept in contact with the suit as it has developed also is in a better position to know when a lawyer or party is misbehaving and when it would be appropriate and constructive to impose sanctions. Finally, the single assignment system lends itself better to <u>grouping</u> similar cases so that they can be litigated in one integrated procedure that permits pooling resources and information (e.g., in the asbestos and other mass tort cases).

Since there are so many management advantages in the single assignment system, why don't all American courts use it? One answer is that it is perceived as being much more expensive than the master calendar alternative. Whether this is true or not must depend in part on how much time the judges commit to each case assigned to them. If judges were to become heavily involved in developing and supervising execution of case preparation plans for every suit assigned to them, the single assignment system would be quite costly (whether its <u>net social cost</u> would exceed that of the alternative system might remain an open question). But deep judicial involvement in every matter is neither necessary nor desirable. Thus the real question in this area should be: is it preferable to have a system that carries the <u>capacity</u> for this kind of involvement in selected matters?

The Challenge to the Philosophy of Management

To answer this question, one must squarely confront the negative inplications of the kind of assertive and involved case management that the single assignment system permits. Early, deep involvement by a judge in the developmental stages of a lawsuit can threaten important values. If the judge who is so involved is the judge who will hear potentially case dispositive motions (e.g., for summary judgment) or who will preside at trial, there is a risk that the decision-maker will lose his or her impartiality, or at least the appearance of that impartiality, by being exposed to information or arguments prematurely, or in a light different from the light that would be cast if the rules of evidence were being enforced. Of course there is a way to avoid this kind of problem: give responsibility for pretrial case management to a judicial officer (another judge, magistrate, or special master) who will <u>not</u> try the case or decide potentially dispositive motions. Some would reject this suggestion on grounds of efficiency, arguing that each case would have to be learned by two judicial officers. Since only about 10% of all civil cases that are filed actually go to trial, however, this "inefficiency" might not amount to much. Moreover, the judge who presides at trial can learn the case efficiently through the detailed submissions counsel must make in connection with a final pretrial conference.

Nor is it clear that managing a case's development and discovery is an efficient way for the judge who will preside at trial to learn what he or she needs to know about the action. Much of what occurs during the pretrial period turns out to be irrelevant or of marginal consequence. Especially in large, complex cases, discovery often involves a great deal of blind and fruitless groping. The percentage of the information that emerges from this process that is truly significant is very small. And in smaller, less-complex cases, the trial judge can master the relevant material relatively easily on the eve of trial.

The idea of dividing judicial responsibility for the pretrial period and for trial might trigger fear that judges would become less "statistically accountable." One of the reasons for converting federal courts to the single assignment system was to improve administrators' ability to allocate workloads evenly among judges and to "subtly" pressure judges to do their share by keeping track of the number of matters assigned them and the rate of their case terminations. One way to retain a significant level of accountability in a system of bifurcated judicial responsibility would be to assign individual cases to specified teams of two judges (or a judge and a magistrate) and to keep "statistical track" of each such team.

Another possible ground for objecting to splitting the pretrial case management function from the trial function might be fear that the judicial officer who is involved only at the pretrial stage would have substantially less "clout" with counsel than would a judge who would preside at trial. For example, lawyers who know that the judge who hosts their settlement conference will have nothing to do with the trial might pay less attention to that judge's views about the merits of positions or the settlement value of the case. While this might be true, it is not necessarily bad. It is not clear that, as a matter of policy, it is healthy for judges to have a great deal of "informal" influence over lawyers and litigants. The line between that kind of influence and coercion can be thin.

This point raises a larger issue about the whole notion of case management. Does a judge who assertively "manages" the full pretrial development of a case acquire too much unrestrainable power? Some commentators fear that the managerial judge can make decisions during the pretrial period that effectively fix both the character and outcome of the case--and that many time such decisions are essentially immune from appellate review. Some argue, for example, that through rulings on what discovery can be had, a judge can exercise great power over the shape of a case and over litigants' rights--but that since most such rulings are interlocutory, they escape meaningful scrutiny by appellate courts. Moreover, the cost of petitioning or appealing to an appellate court can deter parties from challenging all but the most clearly significant pretrial rulings--even though the aggregate effect of a series of nondispositive pretrial rulings might be devastating.

It is difficult to assess the seriousness of this problem. We have no data about how often judicial officers abuse or (in good faith) misuse their power in the case management process. The fact that relatively few voices have sounded warnings or reported problems of this kind raises a suspicion that instances of abuse are rare. In fact, a much larger number of lawyers and commentators join the chorus complaining about the judiciary's general failure to play an active case management role.

Another challenge to the case management philosophy is based on fear that when judges get involved in planning and monitoring case development they threaten the creativity, industry, and morale of the litigation bar. Some writers fear that outside "management" will be heavy-handed and clumsy, forcing confrontations that otherwise probably would not occur, raising issues that otherwise would lay dormant, pressing litigants into needless expense in the name of thoroughness and maintaining a predetermined pace. Some commentators elevate these kinds of fears to a higher level of abstraction by analogizing judicial management to political systems that feature rigid, centralized, exterior control. They contrast this specter of case management with the individual freedom and creativity they associate with laissez faire economic systems and open democratic political organization.

To permit the debate about case management to be cast as a contest between the relative virtues of Social Darwinism and Eastern-block forms of socialism disserves the realities of the situation and introduces a whole school of emotionally powerful red herring.

Case management need not involve usurpation of the lawyers' central role by judges. In fact, most judges are so busy and have so few resources relative to the demands on their time that they could not displace counsel even if they wanted to. Moreover, rational and responsible lawyering reduces even the most assertive managerial judge to a role that consists of occasionally lubricating the machine, suggesting fresh perspectives or new approaches, and providing a forum for discussing sensitive matters. When the lawyering is not rational and responsible, the purpose of case management is simply to help counsel bring their work closer to that ideal. Good judicial case management <u>begins</u> by <u>listening</u> to the lawyers and their clients. It is "situation-specific"--<u>responsive</u> to the special needs of particular cases. Its goal is to <u>help all</u> participants in the process understand the dispute as clearly as possible, focus on what is central to it, develop expeditiously the information needed to resolve it, and either facilitate a negotiated disposition or deliver up the matter promptly and tidily to a trial court. Toward these ends, a good case manager encourages and capitalizes on the creativity and industry of counsel. The judge invites the lawyers to lead--and only moves beyond an essentially advisory role when the lawyers decline the invitation. Thus, there need be no tension between case management and litigators' morale. Only the lawyers whose interest is not in the "just, speedy, and inexpensive determination of every action" need be demoralized by confronting a managerial judge. By contrast, lawyers whose interests conform to the purpose of the adjudicatory system can look to the managerial judge as a valuable resource and ally--someone who will help refine and execute plans that are well tailored to the case at hand.

APPENDIX A-1

CASE MANAGEMENT IN ENGLAND AND AMERICA DIFFERENCES TO FOCUS DISCUSSION

AMERICA	ENGLAND
Single assignment (federal courts); judges responsible for specified cases from filing to disposition.	Bifurcated judicial responsibility; masters handle all pretrial matters; judges assigned day before trial.
Judges control scheduling, fix trial date early in pretrial period; pace case development by setting discovery cut-off dates, times for key motions, pretrial and settlement conferences.	Counsel control scheduling, often waive limits set by rules for completing various pretrial steps, have considerable discretion in setting trial date.
At early status conference, judge (or magistrate) can help parties identify issues, reach stipulations, focus discovery, plan informal information exchanges, get case into posture conducive to meaningful settlement negotiations by scheduling key motions (e.g., partial summary judgment).	Involvement of judicial officer varies with type of court. In commercial court, judge active in pre-trial matters. In general civil litigation, extent of masters' involvement depends on counsel's initiative.
Judge alerts counsel to alternative dispute resolution procedures or helps counsel fashion special procedures appropriate to the peculiar needs of a given case, e.g.: private attorney as special master to resolve privilege disputes, facilitate fact finding, orchestrate discovery, etc. neutral expert early neutral evaluation mini-trial summary jury trial	No analogue??

arbitration

mediation

Rules do not provide for automatic disclosure of any kind of information (rare exception: motion for more definite statement) (but see South Carolina experiment).

Rules compel disclosure of all relevant, unprivileged documents when pleadings are closed. [What are the sanctions for failure to disclose? prohibiting use at trial would not be sufficient re inculpating documents.]

Broad and adversarial discovery; substantial use of oral depositions; cost and delay and contentiousness can be serious problems; burden of dispute resolution on courts can be substantial.

Voluntary inspection of documents. Little use of oral depositions or other discovery (rely for most part on documents and affidavits of parties). Burden on judiciary very small.

Substantial disclosure of evidence and witnesses at least by final pretrial conference; at this conference, judge in good position to help counsel identify areas of agreement, enter stipulations, focus and streamline trial.

All evidence often remains undisclosed. Procedures are available to identify most other kinds of evidence before trial.

Judges and magistrates play active role in facilitating settlement (often a judge or magistrate who would not preside at trial hosts settlement negotiations).

Neither judges nor masters participate actively in efforts to reach settlement.

Large, fractionalized bar in which (urban areas) peer pressure and professionalism not significant sources of restraint.

Professionalism and peer pressure serve as more significant restraints on abuses in specialized courts.

Cost shifting not a significant source of restraint or discipline.

Routine shifting of expenses of litigation to losers or abusers is a key source of discipline.

	Clients protected by right to review by taxing master of fee client paid own lawyer. Ample legal aid guarantees that fear of costs will not unjustifiably deter inpecunious claimants, but the availability of that aid also dilutes somewhat the effectiveness of cost shifting as a source of discipline.
Only analogue in federal courts is bankruptcy; in state courts probate and family law matters often sent to judicial specialists.	Some specialized courts, e.g., official referees in construction cases; the Commercial List.

APPENDIX B

QUESTIONS FOR THE AMERICAN SIDE INSPIRED BY ELEMENTS OF THE ENGLISH SYSTEM

1. Should the federal courts follow the English lead and move toward bifurcation of judicial responsibility for civil actions: pretrial assigned to magistrates, trial to judges? (note adoption of essentially this system in the federal district court in San Diego, California).

2. Should we move toward the English fee-shifting system? Would such a move require substantial expansion of the legal services system for indigents?

3. Should we follow the English lead and establish a system (like the taxing masters) which would enable clients to secure expeditiously an independent review of the reasonableness of the fee charged them by their own attorney?

4. Should we follow the English lead by compelling disclosure of all relevant, unprivileged documents when pleadings are closed (or perhaps earlier, e.g., when pleadings are served?) (note local rule to this effect in the federal district court in South Carolina).

5. Should we cut back on the use of oral depositions and, like the English, rely more on affidavits by parties?

6. Should we develop more specialized courts; e.g., comparable to the English Commercial List?

7. Should we restrict access to the litigation bar and attempt to make it a more specialized and more thoroughly professionalized group?

CASE MANAGEMENT

London Sessions
ABA Annual Meeting, 1985
Audley Suite, Grosvenor House Hotel
London, England

Wednesday, July 17, 1985
2:00 P.M. - 4:00 P.M.

The Hon. Mr. Justice Woolf
Royal Courts of Justice
Strand, London WC2A 2LL

and

Sir Max Williams
Clifford Turner
Blackfriars House
19 New Bridge Street
London EC4V 6BY

In England, "Case Management" has not attracted the same attention as it has in the United States. On this side of the Atlantic, the parties and their legal advisers are largely left to manage their litigation as they please; the Court only becomes involved when one or more of the parties seeks judicial intervention. Changes have, of course, been made over the years, but they have been of modest dimensions. Even the scrutiny of Law Reform Committees has not revealed a desire for fundamental change. However, attitudes are beginning to alter, and there is growing appreciation that perhaps a more fundamental reappraisal is needed.

To make the position in the English courts understandable, it is necessary to outline certain important features of English procedure that have a significant impact on management of cases, which may be unfamiliar to many American lawyers. In giving the outline, we will focus mainly on the ordinary nonjury action in the Queen's Bench Division of the High Court (since these actions form the bulk of the cases in the High Court.)

The Queen's Bench Masters

The trial judge is normally allocated to a case the afternoon before the trial begins. Up to that stage, when interlocutory decisions are required, they are made by Masters who are Officers of the Court and who play a central role in the working of the Court.

Prior to appointment, the Masters are almost invariably, but not necessarily, barristers who've had considerable practical experience of litigation in the High Court. Subject to the right of appeal to a judge, the Masters can make virtually all the decisions which are necessary prior to a case being ready for trial. They deal with arguments over the adequacy of the pleadings (which are only required to identify the issues, and do not set out the arguments of the parties.) They deal with extension of time for taking various interlocutory steps laid down in the Rules of the Supreme Court (RSC). They rule on the adequacy of discovery, i.e., have the parties disclosed all documents which are relevant to the issues set out in the pleadings? They give directions for trial. When there is no defence they can give summary judgment. The main opportunity of the Master to give directions is on what is known as the Summons for Directions under Order 25. On the hearing of this summons, the parties should seek all the directions which are needed to make the case fit for trial. It is, however, one or other of the parties who brings the case before the Master. He does not take action on his own initiative, and it is almost universal for the parties to waive compliance with the time limits laid down in the Rules for taking the various steps prior to the hearing. As the role of the Master is reactive rather than active, his influence is less than it could be. Many cases will only come before him on the Summons for Directions; a large proportion of the cases never come before a Master because in personal injury actions the RSC provide that standard directions apply unless the Master otherwise orders.

In the ordinary way, as long as an action is not vexatious or an abuse of the process of the Court, the approach is that if a party wants to come to Court and is prepared to pay for the privilege, he is perfectly entitled to do so, and what is more, conduct the action as rapidly or slowly as his opponent will permit. The Court has a power, which is normally exercised by a Master, to strike out actions for undue delay, but an order will only be made in a case where the delay has been substantial and could prejudice a defendant, and then only on the defendant's application. If the parties do not complain, the Court is normally only concerned by delay if a date has been fixed for a hearing, or a case is warned for hearing, and the Court will be inconvenienced in its disposal of other cases if an adjournment is granted.

Costs

The normal rule is that the party who loses should pay the other side's costs as well as his own. Such costs are all the costs properly incurred by the winning party and in particular include the costs of the lawyers acting on behalf of that party. The normal order for costs (the party and party order) does not provide an indemnity in respect of all the costs that a winning party incurs because a Taxing Master will scrutinise the Bill of Costs, and if he considers that a particular expenditure is not justified, "tax off" or reduce that item. However, if it is felt that there are particular circumstances justifying this, the Court can make more generous orders for costs where the litigant will recover almost his entire costs (a solicitor and client order). In general, the decision as to which party has to pay costs is dealt with by the Judge at the end of the trial when he knows which party has succeeded. He can make special orders in relation to specific issues, and if he is of the view that a party has incurred costs unnecessarily, he can disallow the costs on that issue or even award the costs to the successful party's opponent. The Master can also deal with the question of costs of the hearings which take place before him in a similar manner.

The power to have the other party's Bill of Costs taxed before a Taxing Master, and the knowledge that the Judge at the trial and the Master on an interlocutory hearing have a very wide discretion to make the other side pay the whole or part of the costs, can act as valuable sanctions against default, delay, and oppression. A client is also protected against his own solicitor overcharging by the right to have his bill taxed by the court.

The Court can also make an order that the solicitors personally pay the costs of the other side in respect of a particular issue. Such a penal order is, however, only made where there has been some serious professional default on the part of the solicitor--and such orders are rarely sought.

If the Court has formed an adverse view of the professional conduct of the lawyers of a particular party, it can take the initiative in making such an order on its own volition. A defendant can also obtain valuable protection by making a payment into Court. If such a payment is not accepted the other party usually has to pay all the costs after the date of payment into Court if he does not recover a larger sum.

Discovery

No doubt the English approach to costs explains why, on the whole, discovery takes place with limited intervention, even of the Master. When the pleadings are closed, each party is required to make a list of documents which are, or have been, in his possession, custody, or power relating to any matter in question raised by the pleadings in the action, and to indicate whether or not the other party is permitted to inspect the documents or whether this is refused (e.g., because of legal privilege). If there is a dispute then it is largely confined to whether or not particular documents should be disclosed, or as to whether or not certain categories of documents which have not been disclosed should be. Although oral evidence is technically possible on issues as to discovery, it is rarely required, and the affidavit of a party as to the position in relation to documents is not challenged.

The Role of the Profession

In the heaviest of litigation, the greatest control of the interlocutory stages of an action is needed if the litigation is not going to mushroom out of control. Such litigation is normally conducted by a small specialist bar and solictors who are all jealous of their reputation. This means that they are reluctant to waste time making unnecessary points because their reputation is of considerable professional value. In the informality of Chambers, the Judge or Master can be appropriately robust if he feels that these standards are being departed from.

The Problems

There are two principal explanations for the dissatisfaction with the present situation. First of all there is the effect of Legal Aid. If a litigant is of limited means, and can satisfy the Legal Aid Committee that he has a prima facie case, his legal costs can be met by the State. He will have to make a contribution according to his means, but in a large proportion of the actions in which private individuals are involved, one or more of the litigants will be likely to be legally aided. Whilst the Legal Aid Fund pays the costs of a party who is eligible, it normally is not liable to pay the costs of the other party if that other party is successful. Futhermore, the legally aided litigant's personal liability to pay the other side's costs, if he loses, is normally limited to the same amount as he contributes to his own costs. Quite apart from this effect of Legal Aid, its existence means that the Government and the public have an interest in keeping the costs of litigation as low as possible. It is one thing for the parties to squander their own wealth, it is a different thing if they are squandering unnecessarily the wealth of the State, at the taxpayers' expense. Futhermore, some legally aided litigants are ill equipped to control their lawyers and unacceptable delays on the part of lawyers can impede justice.

The other factor is the pressures on the High Court. For the size of the population, High Court litigation and the most serious crimes have been tried by a remarkably few Judges. In the three Divisions of the High Court, there are 77 High Court Judges who try the High Court civil cases, and various criminal cases, not only in London but throughout England and Wales. The increase in litigation means that there is a considerable pressure both on civil court space and Judge power. Until recently, attention was diverted from this problem by the even greater problems of the criminal courts. However, remedial steps having been taken to deal with the criminal problems, attention has now begun to focus on the High Court and the need for more positive management has become apparent.

Possible Improvements

Monitoring of Progress

With the use of computers, it should now be a relatively easy and inexpensive task to chart the progress of actions once they are commenced and, where there appears to have been a predetermined period of inactivity, to bring this to the notice of the parties and seek an explanation. If no satisfactory response is forthcoming, the case could then be listed before a practice Master to give any directions necessary. This interventionist approach would need to be backed up by a different attitude in relation to the making of orders for costs. Unlike the present situation, in the case of delay which is the responsibility of the legal advisers, the Master should take the initiative in requiring to know why an order for costs should not be made to be met personally by the solicitors. Fixed dates for trial could be given at an early stage of the action and this could overcome the present approach which tends to condition too many legal advisers to progressing their litigation at an unacceptable slow pace.

Exchange of Evidence

It is already the practice to require the parties to share medical and other expert evidence. Unless there are exceptional reasons for not doing so, a much more extensive and forceful approach should be adopted with regard to the exchange of expert as well as other evidence. There should be a requirement, unless the Court otherwise directs, (e.g., in fraud cases), that no evidence can be called at the trial unless at an appropriate time prior to the trial the evidence has been submitted to the other side. Openness with regard to the evidence should facilitate more settlements. It then should be possible for the Master to ensure that only those issues which are "alive" go for trial.

Compromise

Except in defamation cases, it is extremely rare to have a jury action in the High Court. Where the trial is before a Judge alone it would be undesirable for the Judge to bring pressure on the parties to compromise, and the Judge, to protect his image of impartiality, should hold himself aloof from becoming involved in the negotiations. This does not mean that a different Court official such as the Master could not play a most useful role. In many cases, the intervention of an objective conciliator into the process, will result in agreement being reached where otherwise this would not be possible.

Special Masters

It is difficult to see a place for the role of a Special Master of the sort envisaged by Magistrate Wayne Brazil in the interlocutory process on this side of the Atlantic. Whatever the dimensions of a case, it has not been found that there are problems in Masters, or if necessary Judges, being in a position to adjudicate on issues as to discovery.

Discovery

Although the discovery process in English Courts is limited compared with other jurisdictions, there is no doubt that in many cases it is still unnecessarily burdensome and expensive. The parties have the right, at present, to apply to limit their obligations as to discovery. However, this right is not sufficiently exercised. It may be that what is needed is for categories of cases to be identified where discovery is not to take place without the leave of a Master.

Pre-trial Examination of Parties and Witnesses

This is not part of the English system. On the whole, it is felt that the added expense and delay which could result from this, outweighs the possible advantages (particularly if evidence were to be exchanged prior to trial as suggested previously).

Court Experts

The Court already has the power to appoint its own experts, but this power is not frequently exercised except in the Family Division when dealing with questions in relation to infants. There are many cases, however, where the employment of separate experts by each of the parties, and the resulting conflicts as to expert evidence, prevents settlement and prolongs the trial. In the ordinary case, considerable advantages could accrue from the parties being required to appoint an expert nominated by the Court, and then their being bound by his opinions, except in so far as the Court otherwise orders.

The general approach that we would advocate is that once the jurisdiction of the Courts is invoked, the conduct of the litigation should no longer be left almost entirely in the hands of the parties. Instead, the Court should take charge of the proceedings and regard it as its duty to ensure that as far as practicable, the parties conduct their litigation in a speedy, economical, and practical manner.

Special Lists

In three areas of specialised work steps have already been taken to try and improve the situation and an interesting experiment is also being tried in family work.

Crown Office

A Crown Office list has been established to deal with administrative law cases on applications for judicial review. Initially, it was still open to a party to seek declaratory relief in an ordinary action as an alternative to applying for judicial review. However, in O'Reilly v. Mackman (1983) 2 A.C.237, the House of Lords radically changed the position from a case management point of view by making it clear that it would be contrary to public policy, and as such an abuse of the process of the Court, for a person to seek to establish that a decision of a public authority infringed rights that he was entitled to have protected under public law by an ordinary action. Nearly all public law cases will therefore now be dealt with on an application for judicial review. It is part of this procedure that an application can only be made with leave of the Court. The application is made ex-parte and the proposed respondent does not appear. The application for leave has to be made promptly, and unless the Court extends the time, in any event within three months from the date when grounds for the application first arose[1]. The applications are usually determined within six to nine months from the date on which leave to make the application was granted. In the majority of cases there is no oral evidence or discovery but a Judge will allow it in the minority of cases where the Judge is of the opinion that discovery and cross-examination is necessary if justice is to be done. A nominated panel of Judges hears the applications for judicial review and the hearings tend to be short, because the evidence, being in the form of affidavits, is available to the Judge before the hearing and he is fully familiar with the issues and the evidence before he commences the hearing.

It will be appreciated from this summary that when compared with the ordinary procedure, the litigants' rights could be said to be curtailed. However, the popularity of the procedure confirms that the restrictions in practice are more theoretical than real. They are justified because the applications being in the public law field, it is not only the litigants who are concerned as to the outcome. Furthermore, the requirement that an applicant who wishes to challenge a decision made in the public sphere requires leave, means that the Court can be more generous on issues such as locus standi since the filter of leave excludes frivolous applications.

Official Referees

Official Referees are Crown Court Judges who specialise in the type of work which is often the subject of arbitration. Nowadays, the Official Referee has to deal with very large claims arising out of disputes in respect of vast building and engineering projects. Cases which are tracked "to Official Referees" are allocated to a particular Official Referee, and he will, at the outset of the action, give directions and fix a date for trial. The Official Referees are a highly specialised and efficient tribunal, and the fact that they have control of the interlocutory stages of their cases means that they can encourage or direct the parties to take steps which they might not take on their own initiative which lead to a substantial saving in costs. More and more, they are succeeding in encouraging the parties to exchange evidence before the hearing and obtaining the co-operation of the parties to a meeting of experts with a view to narrowing the issues. The result is that cases, which would otherwise have proved almost unmanageable, become capable of resolution. The success of the procedure is again confirmed by its increasing popularity.

The Commercial List

The third category of special cases are those which are disposed of in the Commercial List. This list was devised to provide a speedy remedy in commercial matters. The Judges, who deal with the commercial cases, are Judges who had experience of dealing with these cases at the Bar before they became Judges. There are special rules relating to pleadings in the Commercial List, designed to keep the pleadings as short and as simple as possible. Once a case is in the Commercial List, again directions are given by a Judge rather than a Master, this being designed to streamline the procedure.

Mediation

In family work, a novel and interesting experiment--mediation--has been introduced. This takes place both as an in-Court and out-of-Court service. It is not conducted by Court officials but by officials of voluntary organisations or the social services. Mediation is not concerned with reconciliation but conciliation, the object of the exercise being to sort out the consequences of a broken marriage without the necessity for the adversary Court process which could aggravate the situation. First indications are that very considerable savings in Court time, and consequently money, can result from the parties agreeing to use the service.

Additional Suggestions

The initiatives which have resulted in improvements in specialised situations are not necessarily appropriate to apply to the general run of cases.

The Assignment of Cases to Individual Judges

Unless High Court Judges cease spending part of their time on Circuit, it would be wholly impracticable to assign all or even the majority of cases to an individual Judge. Individual assignment would no doubt enable the Judge to play a greater part in the pre-trial management of the case and would probably also give the Judge greater motivation in the disposal of his list of cases. However, the proportion of cases that are ineffective, or settle at the last minute, means that unless there is a flexibility in listing, which is impossible with individual allocation, extensive judicial time will be wasted.

Channelling of Cases

In general, the English approach is against Judges becoming too specialised. There are obvious dangers in a blinkered approach to the law. However, the Special Lists which already exist indicate there are cases where familiarity with particular problems is of assistance, and there are other areas of the law which could benefit from specialised treatment. For example, cases involving assessment of damages for personal injuries can be dealt with more satisfactorily by a Judge who deals with those sort of cases frequently and is, therefore, fully familiar with the tariff. Such cases could be channelled to a panel of Judges for trial. What is needed is the regular monitoring process so that cases can be identified which should be allocated to specialist Judges.

Control of Progress

The passive role of the Court in relation to the time which elapses before a case comes to trial is no longer acceptable. The number of cases in the system is affected by the time they take to come to trial, and much greater use should be made of giving a date for trial or for listing for trial at the outset of the litigation to which the parties will have to work and for the Court to police each case's progress, and only allow departure from a laid down timetable for good reason.

Conclusion

We conclude by expressing the hope that the discussion on Case Management as part of the A.B.A. Conference in London in 1985 will stimulate overdue interest in the subject in the United Kingdom, and that our attempt to give an indication of the English dimension will assist our American colleagues.

COMPUTERS AND PRIVACY IN THE UNITED STATES

London Sessions
ABA Annual Meeting 1985
Ballroom 2, Hilton International
London, England

Wednesday, July 17, 1985
2:00 P.M. - 4:00 P.M.

Robert P. Bigelow
100 Tower Office Park
Woburn, Massachusetts 01801

A "legal" right to privacy is a comparatively new phenomenon in American society. Until the western frontiers were settled--an event that did not really occur until the 20th century--the individual who wished to be anonymous or to get away from his own past had the option of going into the wilderness. Indeed, American tradition has it that he who asked too many questions might make the acquaintance of the business end of a Colt revolver.

American Developments to 1966

The American law of privacy has developed on two bases--tort and constitutional. Legal recognition of a right to personal privacy can be traced in England at least to (and perhaps beyond) Prince Albert v. Strange, 1 McN. & G. 23 (1849), which held that common law prohibited even the attempted publication of a description of etchings made by Queen Victoria and her consort for their personal enjoyment. Justice Thomas Cooley is believed to have originated American concepts of the right to privacy when he suggested that there is protection against invasion of privacy under the Fourth Amendment of the United States Constitution in A Treatise on Constitutional Limitations (1868). In A Treatise on the Law of Torts (2d Ed., 1888), Cooley asserted a right to a civil remedy for interference with "the right of one's person...said to be a right to complete immunity; to be let alone" (1888). This was followed in 1890 by the famous law review article, "The Right to Privacy" by Warren and Brandeis, discussed in Professor Tapper's paper.

Prosser has classified four distinct kinds of invasion of privacy as developed by decision, sometimes aided by statute:

- o Use for the defendant's benefit or advantage of a person's name or likeness;
- o Intrusion on the person's solitude;
- o Public disclosure of private facts; and
- o Publicity that places a person in a false light in the public eye.[1]

Development of a constitutional right to privacy, relying primarily on the Bill of Rights, has had a much rockier road.[2] For example, in a 1967 case, the United States Supreme Court, in the course of condemning sophisticated surveillance equipment, said, "...the protection of a person's _general_ right to privacy--his right to be left alone by other people--is, like the protection of his property and of his very life, left largely to the law of individual states.... What a person knowingly exposes to the public, even in his own home or office, is not a subject of Fourth Amendment protection."[3] This, despite a decision earlier holding unconstitutional a state law prohibiting the dissemination of contraceptive information on the ground that the statute violated marital privacy.[4] In _Roe v. Wade_, 410 U.S. 113 (1973), the case which held that abortions could not be prohibited, the Court held that while the right to privacy is a constitutional right, it is not unqualified and is subject to important governmental interests. Other cases have not clarified this right for privacy, either constitutionally or under federal statutes.[5]

The Computer as a Legislative Catalyst

The development of the computer, and man's ability to merge electronically records previously kept in many places, has given rise in the last twenty years to the concept of "information privacy"--a combination of the latter three of Prosser's concepts noted above.

The question of personal privacy and the computer came to public notice following a recommendation by a committee of the Social Science and Research Council for the establishment of a Federal Data Center to gather machine-readable information in numerous federal departments and agencies. The Committee identified some 600 repositories of data with 30,000 computer tapes and 100,000,000 punched cards that might be eligible for inclusion. As citizens became aware of the implications of this proposal, committees of the Senate and the U.S. House of Representatives began hearings on problems of the computer and privacy invasion.

In 1971, the Subcommittee on Constitutional Rights of the Senate's Judiciary Committee, chaired by Senator Sam Ervin, Jr. of Watergate fame, held major hearings on Federal Data Banks, Computers and the Bill of Rights; in addition to testimony about Army surveillance techniques of Vietnam dissenters, the Subcommittee also heard testimony from the computer industry on possible abuses of computerized information systems.

In February 1972, then Secretary of Health, Education and Welfare Elliot L. Richardson established an Advisory Committee on Personal Data Systems to "analyze the consequences of using computers to keep records about people." Its report, released on July 30, 1973 with considerable publicity at a press conference presided over by then Attorney General Richardson and his successor at HEW Caspar W. Weinberger, recommended federal legislation:

- Allowing an individual's right to find out what information is maintained about him in computerized systems, to obtain a copy on demand, and to contest the accuracy, pertinence, and timeliness of information about him in a computer-accessible record;

- Requiring recordkeeping organizations to inform individuals on request of all uses made of their personal information kept in computerized files; and

- Giving each individual the right to refuse to disclose his or her social security number to any person or organization not authorized by federal statute to collect and use the number.[6]

A presidential committee, the Domestic Council Committee on the Right of Privacy was also established to study the problem.

The Privacy Act of 1974

Numerous bills concerning personal privacy were filed in both Senate and House; finally, at the end of the 1974 Session, Congress passed the Privacy Act of 1974.[7] In addition to regulating the development and maintenance of records on individuals, the Act also established a Privacy Protection Study Commission and limited the use of social security numbers as identifying numbers.

The main body of the Privacy Act prohibits most agencies of the federal government from disclosing information contained in personal "records" except with the written consent of the individual to whom the record pertains unless the disclosure comes within one of eleven exceptions. "Record" includes "any item, collection, or grouping of information about an individual that is maintained by an agency, including, but not limited to, his education, financial transactions, medical history, and criminal or employment history and that contains his name, or the identifying number, symbol or other identifying particular assigned to the individual, such as a finger or a voice print or a photograph."

When obtaining such information, the agency must tell the individual the authority under which the agency solicits the information, whether the disclosure of information is mandatory or voluntary, the principal purpose for which the agency is planning to use the information, the routine uses that may be made of the information (a routine use is defined as "the use of such record for a purpose which is compatible with the purpose for which it was collected"), and what can happen to the individual who does not provide all the requested information. Agencies may maintain information only when relevant and necessary to accomplish agency purposes defined by law, and records cannot be kept describing an individual's exercise of his First Amendment rights unless specifically authorized by statute.[8]

The disclosure of records to any person in any manner or to another agency is generally prohibited unless the subject individual gives written consent or makes a written request for the disclosure. There are a number of exceptions, such as to employees of the agency maintaining the records and who need them to perform their job, when disclosure is required under the Freedom of Information Act, to the Census Bureau, and, in certain instances, to other agencies or instrumentalities of any American governmental jurisdiction (federal, state, or local) for civil or criminal law enforcement. Records may also be disclosed to a person who shows a compelling circumstance affecting the health or safety of the subject of the record, to Congress, its committees and subcommittees, and when required by court order.

Agencies are required to give public notice of the existence of their record systems, changes therein, and the procedures and rules under which they conduct the systems. These are periodically published in the Federal Register. For a few years after the Act became effective, each agency published notices of new systems and an annual compilation of these systems. During the first five years, the total pages published exceeded 17,250, at a cost in excess of $4,275,000. Since 1982, only changes to the compilations have been published, although the requirements for publication of new systems and changes in old systems still exist.

Agencies are also required to record and retain for at least five years records of disclosures other than those made to employees in the course of their duties and disclosures made under the Freedom of Information Act. These records contain the date, nature, and purpose of the disclosure and the person or agency to whom the disclosure was made; this information must be given to the individual upon request except when disclosure is made to another governmental agency in connection with law enforcement.

An agency that maintains records subject to the Act is required to adopt rules for the conduct of its personnel in the operation of the system and establish appropriate security safeguards and procedure for disclosing information to an individual upon his request and for reviewing denials of access.

The Act's basic philosophy is that the individual be allowed access to his record and may request correction when he believes the record incorrect. If the agency does not agree with the alleged correction, the individual has a right to file a statement of disagreement or to seek a change by order of court.

In addition to the exceptions to disclosure, a number of records and record systems are completely exempt from the operation of the Act, even if the agency is covered (as Congress and the judiciary are not). The first exemptions are for systems maintained by the CIA or a law enforcement agency in its investigatory or enforcement capacity. Certain information can be deleted in other records that are classified for national security purposes, used in law enforcement, as statistical records, or related to employment or promotion.

Civil remedies, including injunctive relief and damages, are available to individuals whose records are not kept properly; violations of the Act by government officers or employees are misdemeanors with fines of up to $5,000. Employees of a private contractor which maintains a system of records for a covered agency are considered government employees for purposes of the Act and subject to all of its sanctions.

Social Security Numbers

Section 7 of the Act prohibits any federal, state, or local government agency from denying to an individual "any right, benefit, or privilege provided by the law because of such individual's refusal to disclose his social security account number." Exempted from this provision are disclosures required by federal statute or under certain governmental systems in existence and operating before January 1, 1975. This section also requires all government agencies asking for a social security number to tell the individual whether disclosure is mandatory or voluntary, under what authority it is solicited, and what uses will be made of it.

Because one state determined that this provision prohibited the Registry of Motor Vehicles of that state from requiring social security numbers for drivers' licenses, the law was revised in 1976 to permit a state or political subdivision in administering any tax, general public assistance, driver's license or motor vehicle registration law to use a social security number and require the individual to furnish it. The 1976 revision also provides that whoever discloses, uses, or compels the disclosure of a social security number of any person in violation of the federal law is guilty of a misdemeanor.

The Privacy Protection Study Commission

Section 5 of the Privacy Act of 1974 established a seven-member Commission to study the data banks, automated data processing programs, and information systems of governmental, regional, and private organizations to determine what standards and procedures protected personal information, and to recommend to the president and the Congress the extent (if any) to which the requirements and principles of the Act should be applied to information practices of those organizations, either through legislation, administrative action, or voluntary adoption of requirements and principles.

The Commission delivered its 641-page report to President Jimmy Carter and the Congress on July 12, 1977, making a number of recommendations. It concluded "that an effective privacy protection policy must have three concurrent objectives," and based its recommendation on these objectives:

- To minimize intrusiveness;
- To maximize fairness; and
- To create legitimate, enforceable expectations of confidentiality.

To implement these recommendations and ensure that its work continue, the Commission recommended the establishment of an independent entity within the federal government to (1) monitor and evaluate how privacy statutes and regulations are working; (2) participate in federal administrative proceedings where privacy would be affected; (3) continue privacy research; (4) issue rules interpreting the Privacy Act and its revisions; and (5) act as an advisory board on privacy to the federal government and the states.

Following the Commission's report, a number of bills were introduced into the Congress, primarily by Representative Barry Goldwater, Jr. and Representative Edward Koch (now Mayor of New York City), both of whom had been members of the Commission. To date, these proposals have not been enacted by Congress, although other federal statutes do touch upon a number of privacy issues.[9]

State and Local Acts

Individual states have taken steps to enact and implement their own privacy acts applying to governmental records. The first was Minnesota in 1974. Since then, a number of states have passed what are called Fair Information Practices Acts, generally relating to the right of an individual to examine governmental records about himself. In addition to state privacy acts, some municipal governments have enacted analogous ordinances.

However, access by the public to governmental records is a fundamental feature of American policy, and most jurisdictions have such statutes. Like the federal Freedom of Information Act, 5 U.S.C. Section 552, these statutes provide general access to the public for governmental records, subject to certain exceptions.

The Computer and Privacy in the United States

American laws relating to privacy, public records, and the like, whether at a federal, state, or municipal level, do not ordinarily distinguish between manually kept records and those kept in computer-readable form. This differs from European data protection acts which usually apply only to automated systems, sometimes including as "personal information" data on fictitious persons such as corporations and unions. Therefore, decisional law on privacy in the United States is not concerned with whether the records in question are maintained in a computer or in manual files.

However, the computer's ability to match records of one agency against another has been the subject of some controversy within the United States. In one case, it was held that the Privacy Act of 1974 was inapplicable to a computer matching project under which the records of persons receiving Veterans Disability Pensions and those receiving Social Security Disability benefits were matched in order to locate those who had failed to report social security benefits to the Veterans Administration.[10] In 1979, the Office of Management and Budget issued specific guidelines for the performance of computerized matching programs, and the practice continues to this day--between July 18 and August 13, 1984, nine federal agencies commenced such matching programs.

The United States and International Privacy

While fear of the all-knowing government computers was a major force in the passage of the Privacy Act of 1974 and analogous state laws, and the law of privacy has developed through decisional law throughout this century, the basic philosophy of limited governmental controls has led, as a general matter, to statutory recognition of the problem only with respect to governmental records and to specific records of private employers and organizations that have been perceived by the legislatures to pose particular problems.

Unlike the European data protection laws, which apply in most part only to automated records and create a governmental authority without whose permission automated data banks cannot be maintained, the United States philosophy has been to encourage voluntary participation by private industry to preserve personal privacy in nongovernmental areas.

While the Privacy Protection Study Commission recommended a governmental entity to monitor and interpret the Privacy Act, the powers of this agency would not be comparable to the powers of a European data protection authority, and, in any event, no such agency has been established in the United States. For this reason, provisions of European data protection acts prohibiting the transfer of automated personal information across national borders except to nations meeting specified criteria may create problems for American business.

Yet surveys have shown that American citizens are highly aware of the potential of the computer for abuse of personal privacy, as more and more records become computerized. Alan Westin of Columbia University, in a presentation to the International Federation for Information Processing in 1983, pointed out five particular areas as important privacy issues: (1) automation of the workplace with monitoring of terminal operators and workers' health conditions; (2) interactive consumer information systems in the home; (3) use of electronic cards for identification and credit; (4) camera surveillance for computer security; and (5) expansion and consolidation of government data bases, particularly in law enforcement, taxation, welfare, and health.

The increasing computerization of American society requires ever-increasing attention to the potential for privacy invasion with resultant diminution of citizens' rights by government and private industry. Steps have been taken to improve the rights of the citizen vis-a-vis the large organization, and the implementation of strict European data protection acts may encourage American business and government to pay even more attention to this area in order that American business may compete abroad. The common law philosophy of "Let us not do something until the need has been clearly demonstrated" militates against enactment of broad legislative controls. The "right to be let alone" is an underlying philosophy of American life. It means not only the right to personal privacy, but the right of the individual not to be bothered by government or business, and the right of business not to be bothered by government.

FOOTNOTES

1. Prosser on Torts, 5th Edition, 1984, West Publishing Company, pp. 849-868.

2. The first ten Amendments to the United States Constitution.

3. Katz v. United States, 389 U.S. 347, 350-351 (1967).

4. Griswold v. Connecticut, 381 U.S. 479 (1965).

5. E.g., United States v. Miller, 425 U.S. 435 (1976); Paul v. Davis, 424 U.S. 693 (1976); Department of the Air Force v. Rose, 425 U.S. 352 (1976).

6. Social insurance numbers.

7. Public Law 93-579, 88 Stat. 1897, most of which is codified in 5 U.S.C. Section 552a.

8. The First Amendment includes freedom of speech, freedom of religion and assembly, and the right to petition the government.

9. For example, Fair Credit Reporting Act, 15 U.S.C. Section 1681l et seq.; Right to Financial Privacy Act, 12 U.S.C. Section 1301 et seq.; and Electronic Funds Transfer Act, 15 U.S.C. Section 1693c(a)(9).

10. Jaffess v. Secretary of HEW, 393 F.Supp. 626 (S.D.N.Y. 1975).

FROM PRIVACY TO DATA PROTECTION

London Sessions
ABA Annual Meeting 1985
Ballroom 2, Hilton International
London, England

Wednesday, July 17, 1985
2:00 P.M. - 4:00 P.M.

Colin Tapper
All Souls Reader in Law
Magdalen College
Oxford

This paper comments upon the transition in the terminology of the debate in England about the handling of personal information from that of "privacy" to that of "data protection." Such a transition can be discerned by comparison of the titles of the first bill dealing with this topic, Lord Mancroft's "Right of Privacy Bill" introduced into Parliament on 14 February 1961, and the most recent "Data Protection Act" passed by the Parliament in the summer of 1983. It may also be discerned by comparison of the terms of reference and title of the first departmental committee to report upon the subject, the Committee on Privacy, chaired by Kenneth Younger, which was to "consider whether legislation is needed to give further protection to the individual citizen and to commercial and industrial interests against intrusion into privacy by private persons and organisations, or by companies;"[1] and that of its successor, the Committee on Data Protection, chaired by Sir Norman Lindop, which was to "advise the Government on the permanent control machinery needed to secure that all existing and future computer systems holding personal information, in both the private and public sectors, are operated with appropriate safeguards for privacy; and to consider and refine the objectives to be incorporated in legislation establishing permanent safeguards."[2]

It is here proposed to examine briefly the genesis of the legal embodiment of a concept of privacy, the legal implications of that embodiment, some reasons for the change of focus to data protection, and finally its legal implications, especially as embodied in the current Act.

Privacy

It is far from mythological that the legal concept of privacy sprang new-born, but encased in doctrinal justification and protection, from the heads of Samuel Warren and Louis Brandeis in 1890.[3] Like its successor, data protection, it found its original justification in the development of a new technology, and in the commercial exploitation of that technology. The technology in question involved photography and the rotary press; its commercial exploitation, popular newspapers. Warren and Brandeis were upset by the unauthorized reporting of Warren's daughter's marriage in Boston's yellow press. They set to work upon a mish-mash of mainly English precedents, and produced a new right--"privacy"--and a new tort, its invasion. Their new concepts corresponded in their essence to the popular notion of invasion of privacy. They were designed to vindicate the emotion of violation experienced by those whose intimate secrets are intruded upon and broadcast. It was not long before innovative courts began to expand the doctrine in a number of different directions, some of them quite antithetical to its original orientation. Thus, in one line of cases, the gist of the complaint was not that intimate personal information had been broadcast, but that the information which had been broadcast was misleading because it was insufficient, and so placed the subject in a false light. It was largely in response to such disparate development that Prosser reclassified the tort into four separate subdivisions.[4] It has been argued that in so doing he was dissipating the unity of the doctrine created by Warren and Brandeis.[5] While it is doubtful whether the torts cobbled together in 1890 were really susceptible of unification, and while it is unfair to blame Prosser for doing no more than categorise the dissipation of the tort, it must be conceded that its legal apotheosis had departed from the popular sense of privacy as an intrusion into matters of personal intimacy.[6] That sense was however preserved in Lord Mancroft's bill of 1961. In the explanatory memorandum, stress is laid upon the maintenance of human dignity, and the thrust of the bill is encapsulated in clause 4, which in considering factors affecting the measure of damages laid stress upon the distress or embarrassment caused to the plaintiff, and to the means by which the sensitive material was obtained. It may also be noted that the bill was concerned solely with the publication of such material, subject to defences along the lines of privilege and reasonable public interest. In essence, it complemented the law relating to trespass so far as acquisition was concerned, and that of defamation so far as dissemination was concerned.

Legal Implications of Privacy

In the hindsight of the controversy that developed in the two decades following the introduction of Lord Mancroft's bill, it is worth noting not only the matters subsumed within such an approach to the protection of privacy, but also those excluded from it. Perhaps the most significant omission in that perspective is any reference whatever to dissemination by modern technological means apart from cinematography or television. There is no reference whatever to computers, nor would the bill apply to information disseminated by computerised means.[7] In part, this may reflect the primitive technology of the time, which was unable to handle very large amounts of information, but it is still more reflective of the bill's concentration upon the publication of information rather than upon its storage and use. This also explains the absence of any reference to complaints associated with such matters, namely the inaccuracy of information, or its use for purposes, not involving publication, other than that for which it was originally compiled. Nor does the bill make any provision for the transmittal of the information in question to its subject; perhaps, in its concentration upon material capable of causing embarrassment or distress upon publication, it assumed that the information would either already be known to the subject, or else would cause some embarrassment or distress by being revealed even to him.

As noted above, the bill was not concerned with inaccurate information. It left the law of defamation to deal with that. It did however import some defences from the law of defamation, such as those of privilege. It further added defences based upon reasonable public interest. It was left unclear exactly how far the fact that the information had already been made public would provide a defence. It could perhaps have been argued that once information had been made public it could not again be published, in the sense of being made known to the public for the first time. There was, however, no definition of "publish." It could also, perhaps, have been argued that such prior publication might itself create sufficient public interest in the subject to attract the statutory defence. It is also possible, however, that the popular sense of privacy connoting an element of intrusion in the acquisition of the information was not thought appropriate to a situation in which such intrusion would be at best nominal, and the thrust of the complaint would be the harassment of the subject by republication. Another grey area dealt with the relevance of the consent of the subject to the acquisition of the information. Here, too, the special statutory defence refers to the conduct of the plaintiff in creating reasonable public interest. The central situation is presumably that of the publicity-seeking individual who cannot then reasonably complain of the publicity he achieves, which may be less flattering than he would wish.[8] It is less clear how far the conduct of the plaintiff in voluntarily having released the information of which he subsequently complains is relevant to liability, though it is clear that it is at least a factor to be taken into account in the assessment of damages.

A further implication of the focus upon the popular conception of privacy is that the bill applied only to protect individual human beings. It would be strained to regard corporate bodies as capable of being distressed or embarrassed.

The first paragraph of the explanatory memorandum, explaining the objects of the bill, suggests that protection of the right of the public to be kept informed in all matters in which it may reasonably be concerned must be balanced against the main goal of protecting privacy. As noted above, there is no provision for an individual to secure access to the distressing and embarrassing matters about himself with which the bill was concerned, still less is there the slightest hint of a right to secure access to any other information either from private or public sources. Although in many jurisdictions, for example Sweden and the United States, legislation to provide for freedom of information preceded legislation to protect privacy, in the United Kingdom there has been, until recently, relatively little pressure for the introduction of such measures. It is possible, however, that such an inclination underlay some of the pressure to change direction in favour of subject access to information, and towards the inclusion of governmental records in any scheme of privacy legislation.

As noted above, the decade which began with Lord Mancroft's bill ended with the appointment of the Younger Committee on Privacy. During that decade there was an exponential growth in computing technology, and with it an inexorable advance of the computer into the area of personal information. Nineteen eighty-four seemed no longer very far ahead. The Committee was itself concerned that its terms of reference excluded the public sector, and noted the growth of interest in the protection of personal information held on computers. It now seems clear that the publication of the report of this Committee first signified the watershed between privacy and data protection. The Committee rejected proposals to create a unified right to privacy as essentially incoherent and practically unjusticiable. It concentrated instead upon particular areas of concern. One of these was the use of computers, and it gave rise to a separate chapter of the report. Perhaps the most striking feature of this topic was the disparity between the evidence of abuse of privacy in this respect, and fear of such abuse. A special survey commissioned by the Committee found that "Of all the forms of invasion of privacy which have been cited in evidence to us, that involving the use or misuse of computers has been the least supported in concrete terms."[9] On the other hand, it topped the list of matters which people felt should be prohibited by specific legal provision.[10] It also appeared that these fears were, so far as they had any rational basis, concentrated upon public, rather than private, misuse of computers.[11] The Committee interpreted the concept of privacy more widely than Lord Mancroft's bill had done, and elaborated a number of principles that it felt should govern the handling of personal data by computer, though even on its own wide approach it was constrained to admit that some of these had little real connection with privacy.[12]

This realisation had become so clear by 1976 that the next departmental committee was in terms concerned with Data Protection rather than privacy, had no members in common with the Younger Committee of only four years before, and devoted its first substantive chapter to the distinction between privacy and data protection. Its concerns differed in a number of very significant respects. It dealt only with automated systems; it was not limited to questions of privacy; it recognised the impact and importance of continental European influence in relation to data protection; and most important of all, it was responsive to economic considerations.

In this latter respect, it followed the lead established in an earlier white paper.[13] Since it also accepted the view that a number of variable factors affect each particular application, the approach of the Committee was merely to recommend guidelines of general application, any detailed implementation to be made by codes of practice essentially peculiar to each application. The Committee stated that:

> The information which we have illustrates that any attempt to apply a simple universal requirement would be fraught with difficulty and could lead, in some cases, to disproportionate effects. High costs could be incurred simply from the inappropriateness of rules applied to particular cases. But not only could costs be high; the inflexible application of rules could also lead to unnecessary procedures, serious hindrance to the functioning of some organisations, and, at times, even the impossibility in practice to comply with the requirements. In other cases, although it might not be impossible to comply, to do so could mean that a particular application could become uneconomic;...All this shows the unsoundness of any regulatory scheme that includes the universal application of any single requirement.[14]

Unfortunately this wise approach was rejected. The new Act does adopt a universal set of principles, subject to modification or supplementation by order of the Secretary of State, and to various exemptions, including a number of governmental applications, and those of a trivial character.[15] The reason for this stance was avowed in the white paper announcing the government's intentions.[16] After a somewhat unconvincing nod in the direction of protecting privacy it was stated that:

> Without legislation firms operating in the United Kingdom may be at a disadvantage compared with those based in countries which have data protection legislation. When the Council of Europe Data Protection Convention comes into force it will confirm the right of countries with data protection legislation to refuse to allow personal information to be sent to other countries which do not have comparable safeguards. <u>This could threaten firms with international interests operating in this country and the activities of British computer bureau which increasingly process data for customers in many different countries.</u> Accordingly, in order to conform with international standards of privacy protection and to avoid possible barriers to trade, the Government has decided to introduce legislation which will apply throughout the United Kingdom and will enable the United Kingdom to ratify the Convention. The legislation will be designed to impose no greater burden on our resources than is necessary.[17]

It is thus apparent that the abandonment of Lindop was prompted largely by commercial considerations, by the need to move fast, and by a desire to economise. The implications of an Act dictated by such policies will now be considered.

There are many possible regimes of data protection. The new Act embraces a continental European model. Its hallmarks are the width and ambiguity of its definitions, and the indicative character of its guidance. In some respects, the current form departs from its predecessor, which was lost when the general election was called.

The Act is intended to apply only to the automatic processing of personal information. This is presumably why the term "data" is used. It is defined to mean "information recorded in a form in which it can be processed by equipment operated automatically in response to instructions given for that purpose."[18] Nowadays automatic character reading systems have progressed far enough to enable automatic processing of almost any conceivable variety of typeface, and even handwriting. It was therefore necessary to restrict the ambit of the Act by subsequent interlocking definitions of a "data user" and of "processing." This complicates matters, and it is by no means completely clear that the scheme will achieve its aim.

One of the complaints frequently levelled against the legislation is that it applies only to automated information, and not to that held in manual files.[19] Two further definitions in section 1 of the Act define "personal data" and "data subject." A key element is that data becomes personal by relating to a living individual, who must be capable of being identified from the information, and then becomes its data subject. Since "relating" is left undefined, and identifiability only is required, it would seem that the number of items of personal data and of possible data subjects is virtually infinite. It does, however, exclude the dead, and corporate bodies. Here, too, neither the Convention nor the Council's Guidelines require both of these. It should be noted that the professed aim of avoiding penalisation under foreign laws may be prejudiced by the availability of so many options, since both international documents permit restriction of dissemination across national boundaries notwithstanding adherence to the provisions of the Convention or Guidelines if the restriction is in support of more restrictive domestic legislation.

The Act is based upon the principle of compulsory registration, and registration is governed in general terms by principles of data protection, subject to a scheme of exemptions either from some of the principles, especially that of disclosure to the data subject, or from the whole application of the Act.

FOOTNOTES

1. Committee on Privacy, 1972, Cmnd. 5012, para. 1.

2. Committee on Data Protection, 1978, Cmnd. 7341, appendix 1.

3. Warren and Brandeis, The Right to Privacy (1890) 4 Harvard L.R. 193.

4. Prosser, Privacy (1960) 48 California L.R. 383.

5. Bloustein, Privacy as an Aspect of Human Dignity: An Answer to Dean Prosser (1964) 39 New York University L.R. 962.

6. It could easily be argued that Prosser was, in fact, preventing further dissipation by channelling the tort into no more than four more highly defined lines of development.

7. It is interesting that the currently fashionable term, "information," does not appear in the bill either.

8. Compare *Woodward v. Hutchins* [1977] 2 All ER 751, CA.

9. Committee on Privacy, 1972, Cmnd. 5012, para. 580.

10. *Ibid*., appendix E(II) Table 14.

11. *Ibid*., para. 582.

12. *Ibid*., para. 598 (the principles related to the temporal life of the information, its accuracy, and the coding of value judgments).

13. White Paper, Computers and Privacy, 1975, Cmnd. 6353.

14. Committee on Data Protection, 1978, Cmnd. 7341, para. 22.05.

15. See part IV of the Act.

16. White Paper, Data Protection, 1982, Cmnd. 8539, para. 2.

17. *Ibid*., emphasis added.

18. Cl. 1(2), emphasis added.

19. Both the Council of Europe Convention and the Guidelines proposed by the Council of the Organisation for Economic Cooperation and Development, appended to the government White Paper, make application to manual files optional.

ALTERNATIVE DISPUTE RESOLUTION IN THE UNITED STATES: AN OVERVIEW

London Sessions
ABA Annual Meeting 1985
Westminster Room, Inter-Continental Hotel
London, England

Wednesday, July 17, 1985
2:00 P.M. - 4:00 P.M.

Prof. Frank E. A. Sander
Harvard Law School
Cambridge, Massachusetts 02138

Beginning in the late 1960s, American society witnessed an extraordinary flowering of interest in alternative forms of dispute settlement. Following a decade or so of virtually unabashed enthusiasm, serious questions and doubts are now beginning to be raised. In addition, we are slowly starting to accumulate some limited data concerning viable models and empirical effects, making this an opportune time for taking stock and exploring promising future directions.

Initially, it is important to realize that current interest in alternatives to the courts is not a new phenomenon. Arbitration has been used to resolve commercial disputes for hundreds of years, and mediation was commonplace in religious communities in colonial New England (Auerbach, 1983). It appears, however, that alternatives are now being used more broadly than at any other time in American history. It may therefore be useful to speculate on the confluence of events that have led to the current renewal of interest in alternatives.

The 1960s, it will be recalled, were characterized by considerable strife and conflict, emanating in part from the civil rights struggles and the Vietnam War protests. An apparent legacy of those times was a lessened tolerance and a greater tendency to turn grievances into law suits. While the reasons for this are not clear, surely one factor was the waning role of some of society's traditional mediating institutions--the family, the church, and the community. At the same time that our capacity to resolve disputes outside the courtroom was diminishing, the grounds for going to court were expanding. Initially, both state and federal legislatures were rapidly creating new causes of action to remedy some of our oldest woes, such as race and sex discrimination. Additionally, advances in technology increased the imposition of harm (in the form of chemicals and other toxic substances) while at the same time enhancing our capacity to detect and seek redress for such harm.

The net result of all these factors was the assertion of an increased volume of legal claims, many of which had not been previously recognized. Courts began to find themselves inundated with new filings, triggering cries of alarm from the judicial administration establishment. At the same time, judicial congestion, with its concomitant delay, led to claims of denials of access to justice.

One response to these problems was a demand for more judges and more courtrooms; another was a search for alternatives to the courts. In part, this search was a product of disillusionment with courts as dispute resolvers in many types of cases (child custody disputes come quickly to mind); in part it was a product of a growing mood of antiprofessionalism.

---

*This paper will appear in somewhat modified form as Chapter 1 of S. B. Goldberg, E.D. Green, and F.E.A. Sander, Varieties of Dispute Resolution (Little Brown 1985).

This movement was also supported by contemporaneous intellectual developments. Over the past 15-20 years, cultural anthropologists have sought to apply to disputes in the United States their studies of dispute resolution in other cultures. At times, the influence of the cultural anthropologists has been indirect; at times, as with the transformation of the Kpelle tribal moot into the neighborhood justice center, it has been direct (Danzig, 1973). Legal scholars, too, most notably the late Lon Fuller, were active in the 1960s and 1970s, in analyzing the characteristics of various dispute resolution processes, such as mediation and arbitration, with a view to reaching useful conclusions about their strengths and limitations for particular types of disputes (Fuller, 1963, 1971, 1978).

The early interest in resolving disputes outside the courts received important support from a variety of sources. In the 1964 Civil Rights Act, Congress established the Community Relations Service to aid in the settlement of racial and community disputes. The Ford Foundation established the National Center for Dispute Settlement to bring to bear accumulated learning on dispute settlement in the solution of newly emerging disputes. Again with the help of the Ford Foundation, Ted Kheel, a noted labor arbitrator and mediator, set up the Institute of Mediation and Conflict Resolution in an attempt to apply to newer conflicts the techniques long successfully utilized in labor disputes. Finally, the Law Enforcement Assistance Administration (LEAA) took a firm interest in developing and testing alternatives, even if the required statutory nexus to the criminal justice system at times frustrated a wide-ranging approach.

From this brief summary, there emerge four contrasting goals of the alternatives movement, each with its own constituency:

- To relieve court congestion, as well as undue cost and delay;
- To enhance community involvement in the dispute resolution process;
- To facilitate access to justice; and
- To provide more "effective" dispute resolution.

Quite obviously these goals may overlap and conflict. For example, measures aimed at relieving court congestion would take a very different form from measures designed to enhance community control over dispute settlement. The point is that in any particular situation it is essential to think clearly and precisely about the reasons for pursuing alternatives.

As regards the goal of relieving court congestion, the literature of dispute processing has made it plain that only a small proportion of disputes result in court filings, and only a similarly small proportion of the latter consume significant amounts of judicial resources. Disputes that cannot be readily adjusted through negotiation may be resolved by mediation or arbitration; of those disputes that do lead to a court filing, somewhere around 90-95 percent are settled without the need for a full-blown trial. In view of this substantial winnowing-out process, it is unlikely that an expansion or more appropriate use of alternatives will significantly reduce still further the number of filings or the proportion of filings that lead to a full-blown trial. This is not to say that a cautious and informed use of ancillary mechanisms to screen (and stimulate the settlement of) court cases is not worth undertaking; on the contrary, such a program appears to hold considerable promise. But the notion that a pervasive use of alternatives can hope to solve "the court crisis" seems misguided.

One must be similarly skeptical regarding the communitarian goal of the alternatives movement. While the proponents of this goal view community participation in the dispute resolution process as a means by which a lost sense of community can be regained and community power enhanced, critics have questioned the feasibility of this goal in today's highly mobile American society. Moreover, if dispute settlement is to be a community function, unconnected to the justice system, funds to operate such programs may be difficult to find. Finally, these programs, which were stimulated by the perceived inadequacies of the justice system, will themselves give rise to comparable questions, such as how they can prevent denials of due process or the latent coercion that is implicit in group decision making. Thus, the principal promise of the alternatives movement would appear to lie in facilitating access to justice and providing more effective dispute resolution processes.

As one thinks about the goal of increasing access to justice, one is immediately struck by the paradox that providing more accessible means of dispute resolution may result in more disputes being brought forward to be resolved, thus further clogging the dispute resolution machinery and causing further delays. Today, some people who believe that they have legitimate claims do not assert those claims, choosing either to avoid the person they believe has wronged them, or simply to "lump it" (as in "like it or lump it"). With the advent of dispute resolution forums more accessible than the courts, such people may flock to those forums. Whether or not this result is desirable depends on the costs of providing alternatives, compared with the costs, real but difficult to measure, of having no means at all of resolving some grievances. The important thing to note is that there is a trade-off: The price of increased access to dispute resolution mechanisms may be a substantial increase in the number of disputes brought forward for resolution.

It is also important to note that the goal of increasing access to justice is not necessarily met by providing access to a dispute resolution mechanism other than the courts. Indeed, one of the criticisms of the alternatives movement is that it serves to screen out of the courts some disputes that can be resolved effectively only by judicial intervention. Hence, the access goal of the alternatives movement should be that of ensuring access to a dispute resolution mechanism that is appropriate for the dispute.

This redefinition or clarification of the access goal of the alternatives movement both relates that goal to the goal of providing more effective or appropriate dispute resolution, and highlights the importance of the latter goal. The central question in implementing the latter goal is what dispute resolution process or combination of processes is appropriate or effective for resolving different types of disputes. Preliminarily, there would appear to be general agreement that an effective dispute resolution mechanism is one that is inexpensive, speedy and leads to a final resolution of the dispute. At the same time it should be procedurally fair, efficient (in the sense of leading to optimal solutions), and satisfying to the parties. Indeed, one of the notable contributions of the alternatives movement has been a renewed emphasis on process as a way of underscoring the importance of the values cited above. In addition to looking at outcomes, dispute resolution scholars now ask: Did each disputant have a fair chance? Given a specific outcome, what was the quality of the process? Were the parties satisfied with the process utilized? In short _how_ parties won or lost may often be as important as _whether_ they _did_.

Alternative Dispute Resolution Processes: Description, Taxonomy, and Applications

Description

It may be useful at this point to consider the extent to which the various dispute processes further the values noted above.

The most common and familiar form of dispute settlement is bargaining or negotiation. Compared to processes utilizing third parties, negotiation has the great advantage of allowing the parties themselves to control the process and the solution. If the parties cannot settle the dispute themselves, and bring in a third party, the critical question is whether the third party has power to impose a solution or simply to assist the disputants in arriving at their own solution. The latter process is commonly referred to as mediation; the former is referred to as adjudication, whether performed by a court or by a private adjudicator, known as an arbitrator. These three primary processes--negotiation, mediation, and adjudication--can of course, be combined in a variety of ways, and one of the achievements of the alternatives movement has been the rich variety of hybrid dispute resolution processes it has spawned. For example, an adjudication-like presentation of proofs and arguments is combined with negotiation in the Mini-Trial, arbitration is combined with court adjudication in a procedure known as rent-a-judge, and mediation is combined with arbitration in med-arb. Other well known hybrid processes are the ombudsman (which involves a mediator/investigator) and the neutral expert. These processes are further considered below.

Taxonomy

While no empirically validated determination of which process is appropriate for a particular dispute has yet been developed, a variety of considerations appear relevant. First among these is the relationship between the disputants (i.e., is the dispute between individuals with an ongoing relationship or is it the product of a single interaction, such as an automobile accident). In the former situation, it is important to have the parties seek to work out their own solution, for such a solution is more likely to be acceptable to them than an imposed solution, hence more long-lasting. Thus negotiation, or if necessary, mediation, appears to be a preferable technique in these situations. Another advantage of such an approach is that it encourages a restructuring of the underlying relationship so as to eliminate or mitigate the source of conflict, rather than simply dealing with each manifestation of conflict as an isolated event.

Another criterion is the nature of the dispute. Lon Fuller (1978) has pointed out that "polycentric" problems are not well suited to an adjudicatory approach. These are allocational disputes, in which no clear governing guidelines for decision are available and where any particular solution has proliferating ramifications. One example of such a dispute, given by Fuller, is where two museums received a bequest of a collection of paintings in equal shares, with no directions for apportionment. The problem, as Fuller points out, is that the disposition of any single painting has implications for the disposition of every other painting, as each museum seeks a complete and well-rounded collection. For disputes such as this, a negotiated or mediated solution that seeks to accommodate the desires of the disputants is far better than any externally imposed solution.

Another important distinction is between novel disputes requiring a definitive precedent (and hence a court decision), and recurring applications of the same issue, which can be readily handled by some less-sophisticated and elaborate adjudicatory mechanism, such as arbitration.

The amount at stake in a dispute has generally been thought significant in determining the appropriateness of a particular dispute resolution procedure. Indeed, the small claims court movement had as its premise that small cases are simple cases, and that therefore a pared-down judicial procedure was what was called for. Yet there is no necessary connection between amount in controversy and appropriate process. Quite obviously a small case may be complex, just as a large case may be simple. Thus, a more sensible approach would be to analyze disputes in terms of the novelty or complexity of the issues presented. Those disputes presenting novel or complex issues would be appropriately referred to a dispute resolution forum in which there was ample opportunity for the full presentation of evidence and argument; those presenting simpler or more routine issues would be referred to a more truncated procedure.

Speed and cost also appear to be relevant factors in determining the appropriate dispute resolution process. From the perspective of the disputants, if a speedy and inexpensive resolution is desired, then negotiation may be ideal since it requires no involvement of third parties. But if negotiation fails, simplified adjudication may be preferable to mediation, in view of the latter's emphasis on thoroughly probing the conflicts in the underlying relationship, rather than simply seeking to resolve the dispute. Alternatively, the parties might choose mediation, but advise the mediator that their goal was limited to dispute resolution, and did not encompass a wide-ranging effort to restructure their relationship.

Where public funds are involved, the public interest in the fisc must also be taken into account. From this perspective, even if the parties are unconcerned with the costs of dispute resolution, the state is, and should provide only that procedure which is appropriate in light of the relevant characteristics of the dispute. In the United States, this statement of the ideal must, of course, be qualified by such considerations (where applicable) as the constitutional right of access to the courts and to a jury trial.

Finally, attention must be paid to the power relationship between the parties. Where one disputant has notably less bargaining power than the other (e.g., a habitually deferential or financially naive wife dealing with her experienced businessman husband, or a pollution victim faced by a powerful corporation), an adjudicatory mode in which principle, not power, will determine the outcome may be preferable. In some situations, the mere availability of adjudication is important as leverage to bring the more powerful party to the bargaining table and to reduce inequalities of bargaining power. For example, a threatened challenge to the adequacy of an environmental impact statement may both bring the alleged polluter to the bargaining table and encourage it to take more seriously the claims of the pollution victim.

Applications

Both primary and hybrid processes have been used in a number of contexts, some for many years, others only recently. Arbitration, for example, has been used to resolve commercial disputes for hundreds of years, and to resolve disputes about the interpretation of collective bargaining contracts, at least on a large-scale basis, since the 1940s. Recently, arbitration has been used in a host of new areas, such as consumer disputes and medical malpractice claims. While a submission to arbitration is normally voluntary, and the outcome final and binding (except for limited judicial review), nonbinding arbitration has been used in prison and other institutional disputes, where the authorities are unwilling to delegate total decision making power to outsiders. Compulsory, nonbinding arbitration of cases filed in court, but falling below a fixed value (court-annexed arbitration) has also become increasingly widespread in recent years.

Mediation, which was used for many years to help employers and unions arrive at mutually acceptable contract terms, is today used in a wide variety of disputes, particularly among persons with an ongoing relationship. Indeed, California requires that all child custody disputes be mediated prior to judicial disposition.

Another type of interpersonal dispute frequently resolved by mediation is the neighborhood squabble. There are now almost 200 neighborhood justice centers, which receive civil and minor criminal cases from court, prosecutor, or police (and sometimes on a walk-in basis), and which attempt to resolve those cases primarily by mediation. In addition to its use in interpersonal disputes, mediation has also been used to resolve large-scale public disputes involving a multiplicity of parties and interests. Among these are environmental disputes, disputes over the content of government regulations, and disputes over the allocation of public funds.

Many hybrid processes have also been used with considerable success. Med-arb, in which issues unresolved by mediation are submitted to arbitration, typically with the same person serving first as mediator and then as arbitrator, is used to resolve contract negotiation disputes between public employers and their unionized employees.

Perhaps the most publicized of the hybrids has been the Mini-Trial, in which the lawyers for each party are given a brief period (typically no more than a day) in which to present the essence of their case to senior executives of both parties. After the presentation, the executives try to negotiate a settlement of the case, sometimes assisted by a neutral advisor who has heard the presentations. If settlement does not come about, the advisor provides the parties with his opinion of the likely outcome if the dispute were litigated, and sometimes that dose of reality helps to break the deadlock. The Mini-Trial has been utilized in a number of major inter-corporate disputes in recent years, and appears to have led to settlements in nearly all.

Perhaps the most valuable by-product of the recent resurgence of interest in dispute resolution has been the renewed interest in negotiation that it has stimulated. Obviously, negotiation as a means of dispute resolution long antedates the alternatives movement, and would stand as the preeminent mode of dispute resolution even without such a movement. Nonetheless, the interest in resolving disputes outside the courts has focused attention on negotiation as a basic means of dispute resolution. This is apparent in the number of "how-to-negotiate" books that have been published in recent years, the spate of negotiation workshops and seminars, the appearance of scholarly works on negotiation, and the introduction of negotiation into the curriculum of law schools and business schools. Although it is too soon to tell, these developments may improve the practice of negotiation sufficiently that more and more disputes will be resolved by negotiation, with less and less need for third-party involvement.

Concluding Cautions

It would be inappropriate to conclude this brief survey of recent dispute resolution developments in the United States without at least summary reference to some of the critical questions that are now beginning to emerge. Detailed consideration of any of these issues would necessitate a callous disregard of the limited scope of this overview paper, and is in any event premature. But it does seem appropriate at least to take note of these questions by way of lending focus and direction to future research and inquiry relating to alternative modes of dispute resolution.

If the alternatives to adjudication have all the advantages claimed for them why are they not more widely used? Are there aspects of the legal system that deter the use of alternatives? Or does the lack of demand for alternatives reflect the fact that the alternatives movement is primarily a product of the self-interest of the alternatives providers, rather than an expression of the needs of alternatives consumers?

Is there an adequate empirical basis for the claimed advantages of the alternatives? How, for example, can one adequately measure the asserted advantages of mediation over adjudications? Is it possible to develop a sophisticated cost-benefit analysis of alternative processes?

Is there a risk that the availability of alternatives will shunt low and middle-income disputants to a form of second-class justice, consisting primarily of semi-coerced compromise settlements, while the so-called first-class justice offered by the courts becomes available only to the rich and powerful? In thinking about this question, the reader should be aware that the neighborhood justice center clientele consists primarily of low-income disputants referred by courts and prosecutors as an alternative to criminal proceedings.

Is there a danger that mediation, with its emphasis on accommodation and compromise, will deter large-scale structural changes in political and societal institutions that only court adjudication can accomplish, and that it will thus serve the interests of the powerful against the disadvantaged?

To the extent that new modes of dispute resolution call for new practitioners, with skills different from those who practice in the judicial system, what steps should be taken to ensure that these practitioners have the requisite skills? Should there be regulation of the practice of dispute resolution similar to that of the practice of law?

Can the alternatives movement survive success? If alternative dispute resolution processes become widely used, will they suffer from the woes common to other heavily-used institutions--increasing costs and delay, bureaucratization, and perfunctory performance?

In light of the prominent place of the courts in American society, and the free dispute resolution services provided by the courts, how can other forms of dispute resolution, even if more appropriate for a particular dispute, succeed in attracting users and adequate funding? Does the answer lie in integrating alternative dispute resolution processes into the public justice system? One model for public institutionalization of alternative dispute resolution is the Multidoor Courthouse. This concept calls for a multi-faceted intake center where disputes are analyzed according to their salient characteristics and referred to that process, or sequence of processes, most appropriate for their resolution. This proposal is now being tested under ABA auspices in Houston, Tulsa, and Washington, D.C. The results of that experiment should help to tell us whether this idea is indeed a promising herald for more effective dispute resolution.

REFERENCES

1. Auerbach, J., Justice Without Law? (1983).

2. Council on the Role of Courts, The Role of Courts in American Society (West 1984).

3. Danzig, R., Toward the Creation of a Complementary Decentralized System of Criminal Justice, 26 Stanford L. Rev. 1 (1973).

4. Fuller, L., Collective Bargaining and the Arbitrator, 1963 Wisc. L. Rev. 3.

5. Fuller, L., Mediation: Its Forms and Functions, 44 So. Calif. L. Rev. 305 (1971).

6. Fuller, L., The Forms and Limits of Adjudication, 92 Harv. L. Rev. 353 (1978).

7. Marks, J.B., Johnson, E., and Szanton, P.L., Dispute Resolution in America: Processes in Evolution (Nat. Inst. Disp. Res'n. 1984).

8. Paths to Justice: Major Public Policy Issues of Dispute Resolution (Nat. Inst. Disp. Res'n. 1984).

ALTERNATIVE DISPUTE RESOLUTION: CONTEMPORARY DEVELOPMENTS IN BRITAIN

London Sessions
ABA Annual Meeting 1985
Westminster Room, Inter-Continental Hotel
London, England

Wednesday, July 17, 1985
2:00 P.M. - 4:00 P.M.

John Griffiths, Q.C.
1 Brick Court
Temple, London EC4Y 9BY

and

Dr. Simon Roberts
Reader in Law
The London School of Economics and
Political Science
Houghton Street
London WC2A 2AE

The general label "alternative dispute resolution" embraces potentially an almost endless variety of forms. In this paper discussion is limited to two kinds of departure from state-sponsored adjudication. In the first, an essential characteristic of formal adjudication remains, in that the dispute is still taken to a third party for decision--but in a procedural environment chosen by the parties themselves. Here commercial arbitration is the example we consider. In the second, the power to make a decision is retained, so the efforts of third parties remain auxilliary to those of the disputants. Community and family conciliation provide the cases examined.

In preparing this paper we have been conscious that, while there may be particular enthusiasm for alternative forms of dispute resolution at present, the advocacy and growth of such alternatives has a history as long as state-sponsored adjudication itself. Some procedures (commercial arbitration is an example) are well established and have long taken on a definite shape; others, such as family conciliation, represent only embryonic forms. We also recognise that the interest now shown here in alternatives to formal adjudication comes somewhat behind similar movements in the United States; so we are in the fortunate position to profit from recent trans-Atlantic experience.

Commercial Arbitration

The main theme of this part of the paper is the extent to which the wishes of disputants as to the resolution of justiciable disputes (in particular, commercial disputes) are, and can be, accommodated by the law.

In England, arbitration has long been an acknowledged and effective method of resolving disputes. No doubt this very fact may reflect a failure or deficiency in the system or practice of the courts adequately to provide for disputants either the remedies they desired or those means of achieving those remedies which the disputants felt was appropriate. On the other hand, the very toleration and recognition of arbitration as an alternative to litigation in the courts is itself evidence of the law's response to the desires of disputants.

Nevertheless, arbitration and the process of the courts are inextricably intertwined. This inter-dependence owes its existence partly to the jealous preservation by the courts of their jurisdiction. A rationale for this jealousy can easily be found in the possibility, and undesirability, of there arising an arbitral body of law separate and distinct from that of the courts, or, even, several such bodies, each peculiar to the trade or commodity in question. Such a development could also invite the arbitrators themselves, fortified by their known expertise and experience in the relevant trade or commodity, to rely upon their intuitive response to the merits of the case before them. Inevitably consequent on such practices would be uncertainty and injustice : the fallibility, even of arbitrators, requires adherence to a body of authority universally accepted within a system of law. Reliance on the unfettered instinct of an arbitrator would be unwise.

The dependence of arbitrations on court process has another reason. That is, the preference of the disputants themselves for the buttressing of their own agreement for arbitration by a developed and coherent legal system. To this extent, the interrelation, and means of resolution, themselves evidence flexibility in the law in responding to the wishes of disputants.

Indeed, it is presumably partly because the disputants themselves wish it, that the courts have powers of enforcement of an arbitration, and have the right and duty to ensure that the arbitration is conducted in accordance with the requirements of natural justice. Similarly, while an arbitrator may, and often will, have considerable latitude as to procedure, he must apply the relevant legal principles as if he were a judge.

Historically, there have been statutory provisions and regulations relating to arbitrations from as long ago as 1698; however, the response to disputants' needs by the law has been imperfect.

One major area of deficiency, prior to the passing of the 1979 Arbitration Act, was the extent to which the pre-1979 system, or the way in which it was operated, failed adequately to cater to disputants' needs. Prior to 1979, the losing party had a virtually absolute right of appeal in all cases where a question of law had arisen. There was always the possibility, therefore, of the prolongation of a dispute, far beyond its reasonable timespan, by the exercise of that right. The extent to which abuse of the right actually caused frequent and considerable delay is not clear. Nevertheless, the existence of the possibility must have been a deterrent to resort to English arbitration.

Moreover, there were a number of developments which rendered the existing system unsuitable. In the 1970s, commercial disputes of a magnitude hitherto unknown, which were not well suited to resolution in the courts, were arising. Yet they involved issues of fact and law which were so complex and interrelated that their separation (by application to the courts for resolution of the legal questions) was both impracticable and undesirable. The arbitrations consequent on the embargo of the export of American soya bean meal were examples. Another important aspect was the fact that foreign organisations, while wishing to resolve disputes by arbitration according to English law in England, were reluctant to have the issues of the dispute so readily exposed to the scrutiny of English courts. This reluctance was perhaps particularly marked, and understandable, in the trading agencies of sovereign states.

A third major concomitant deficiency was the increase in cost and delay (these being, of course, directly correlated in any event) resulting from the system and its operation. After all, among the major advantages of arbitration over litigation in the courts are speed--in that the disputants do not have to await a space in the Court's lists--and cost--in that arbitrations may dispense with formalities. Even the advantages of London as a place for arbitration, being without par in its combined expertise in finance, banking, insurance, commodity markets--and, indeed, arbitration--were insufficient compensation, increasingly, for these difficulties.

The implications and operation of the 1979 Act have yet to be worked through fully, but the Act has done much to ameliorate the position. The much-reduced prospects of appeal--indeed, the difficulty of even obtaining leave to appeal--have reduced the uncertainty as to the finality of the Arbitrator's Award and thereby also removed many of the difficulties set out above. While there is still no obligation to provide a reasoned award (which was a further objection of some to English arbitration, for in some places an Award without reasons cannot be enforced), the practice of providing one is more prevalent. At the same time, it is quite plain that arbitration really is intended to be more free of formalities: Lord Justice Donaldson (as he then was) stressed the absence of any technical requirements in the writing of an Award (Bremer Handelsgesellschaft v. Westzucker [1981] 2 Ll.R.130 and 132).

Nevertheless, these reforms are necessarily somewhat piecemeal and are not made on the basis of one coherent view of the interrelation between resolution by the courts and resolution by arbitration. For example, in that an agreement to go to arbitration rather than to litigate in the courts is consensual, the parties to it might be thought entitled to exclude the jurisdiction of the courts altogether. Yet they cannot.

However, the reason for this is that different disputants have different needs and desires as to how arbitration is to work out their disputes and to what extent they wish to retain resort to the courts. Inevitably, a statute cannot simultaneously reflect the inconsistent--often contradictory--wishes of disputants. That there has been change shows flexibility to the pressures of disputants' needs.

There are many other ways in which the law relating to arbitration could, nevertheless, provide more adequately for disputants. For example, cases could be heard in camera, and there could be edited judgments, in response to the desire of some disputants for privacy (over and above that to have justice to be seen to be done). There could be power to proceed with an arbitration in default of the appearance of the other party, or any other default, including the power to strike out wherever there has been delay and the interests of justice so require. There could be an option to exclude the right to judicial review. A court could have power to appoint an arbitrator where the arbitration agreement provides for a stranger to make an appointment, but he has failed to do so. On a reference to three arbitrators, the award of any two could be binding. There could be a right of consolidation where there is a string of interrelated arbitrations, provision for payment-in, and a rules committee like the Supreme Court Rules Committee. Arbitrators could allow the costs of foreign lawyers.

That these are possible is shown by their incorporation in the Arbitration Ordinance of Hong Kong. A further possibility reflecting the desires of many disputants, and included in the Hong Kong legislation, is provision for conciliation, the arbitration only to proceed on its failure, while protecting the disputants against any possible difficulties or embarrassment consequent on the failure of the conciliation. This must be a development which many disputants would welcome.

Indeed, it is central to the resolution of labour disputes. The degree to which elaborate machinery for conciliation is required, whether the identity of the conciliator should be stipulated, and whether the conciliation agreement should be enforceable, are matters as to which, again, there will be wide divergence of disputants' views. The relative equality or otherwise of the disputants may be a guiding factor.

Nevertheless, there are many other ways in which the law plainly does not provide for disputants' needs. The second major area is that it simply leaves out of account disputants who do not want, or cannot afford, arbitration on the scale and at the cost at which it is available. There is no option as to the scale of arbitration process available. There may indeed be an objection, that a two-tiered system might lead to a second class of justice being dispensed, for those choosing the second tier. But this is to adopt an absolute and rigid notion of justice, which is not one in any event necessarily dispensed at present. Lengthy and exhaustive enquiry may be obfuscatory. A crude light, albeit briefly shone, may be more illuminating.

The satisfactory resolution of disputes, subject only to the requirements of natural justice, must be dependent on the taking into account of those variables, the needs and resources of the disputants. It must be conceded that the law cannot comprehensively provide for infinite variety. However, plainly, it falls short of the potential it possesses for adequate account of such permutations.

Embryonic Forms

While the growth of commercial arbitration can credibly be presented as a simple struggle of disputants to disengage from the perceived constraints of formal adjudication, the characterisation of contemporary developments in the areas of community and family mediation is more complex. A notable feature of the position in Britain is the wide variety of sources from which the demand for institutional reform comes: from government, as a means of reducing the load of court business and as a way of handling "tension" within particular communities; from utopian reformers anxious to bring dispute resolution procedures back to "the people"; from professional groups, such as lawyers or family therapists, looking for business; and from grass-roots sources, disputants dissatisfied with what they are getting from existing agencies. We have to remember the possibly contradictory interest which these diverse viewpoints represent.

New forms of alternative dispute resolution have recently been advocated, and have now begun to appear, in two principal fields: general community conciliation and family conciliation. Agencies in the former category (there is one, for example, in the London Borough of Newham) claim to provide "help" with a wide range of disputes. The precise nature of this intervention is not always clearly articulated in the prospectus, but in general it appears that assistance is of a mediatory character, a matter of promoting a negotiated solution rather than offering a third-party decision. Prospective business may cover such matters as minor crime, disputes between neighbours, disputes between suppliers of goods or services and their customers, disputes between members of different ethnic groups, and disputes between police and public. None of these agencies in Britain has been in operation long enough for a general assessment, but experience of similar projects in the United States suggests some pitfalls which might be avoided. American commentators seem to have agreed that such agencies are seldom "successful" in the sense of satisfying their customers where there are large disparities of power between the two disputants. Such disparities arguably separate large commercial concerns and individual litigants, e.g., police and members of the public, employers and employees. In short, alternative agencies are most appropriate in a relatively egalitarian context. There also seems to be a consensus that the disputants themselves have got to want the new agency, and that the procedures introduced must "make sense" to members of the community concerned. Such conditions are less likely to be met where the "demand" comes from above, rather than from within the group(s) involved. There is a real danger that institutions imposed by government can come to represent an auxilliary tier of "second class" justice into which certain categories of troublesome business will be filtered.

Agencies of community conciliation in Britain have been established too short a time for it to be clear whether these dangers have been avoided. However, institutions of "family conciliation" are both more numerous and have been in operation for longer periods, some since 1979, so the shape of their development is more distinct. The broad objective of these agencies appears to be agreed. This is to assist with joint decision making by the parties themselves. They aim to help with the construction of an agreed solution, rather than by offering a decision from a third-party standpoint. These are <u>not</u>, therefore, processes of arbitration. However, the procedural forms encountered under this form of intervention are extremely varied, and there appears no clear consensus on a range of crucial questions.

First, while the kind of help extended to the parties clearly falls under the generic head of mediation, practices range from unobtrusive aids to communication to heavily directive forms of intervention. Most family mediators seem to conceive of their role as extending beyond that of the go-between (passing messages backwards and forwards between the parties) and the convener (setting up a forum in which the parties can meet). But beyond that little is clear. Some mediators appear to limit themselves to identifying options; some go further and offer an evaluation of available choices as they see them; others make active efforts to persuade the parties to accept a preferred solution, even putting pressure upon them to do so. Differences of view also exist as to whether it is appropriate for the mediator to intervene in protection of a weaker party or to safeguard the interests of children. All of these doubts really resolve themselves around the question of the extent to which power is to remain with the disputants themselves, or pass to a third party. Some argue that the essence of family conciliation is that, for better or worse, this form of dispute resolution should aim to yield a solution which the parties themselves have reached.

A second imponderable surrounds the relationship of family conciliation to the work of existing professional groups, notably lawyers, social workers, and therapists. Are family mediators to emerge as an autonomous group of specialists, or will they remain within existing professions? English lawyers have, on the whole, been much more reluctant to hold themselves out as mediators than their American counterparts, preferring to confine themselves to the roles of partisan (albeit one with a responsibility to the legal system itself), or adjudicator. However, the recent development of "in-court" and "court-related" schemes under which judges and registrars participate in, or at least supervise, mediation (often as a first step in disputes brought to court for adjudication) reveals one way in which lawyers are already becoming implicated in this form of alternative dispute resolution. There are obvious hazards in such arrangements, in that adjudicatory roles will tend to get muddled in the minds of disputants in a manner that may damage both types of process. Is it in anyone's interest that judges should come to be seen, even in a limited way, as promoters and managers of negotiation? Given the authority that judges rightly enjoy in this society, it can be argued that they are the wrong kind of people to offer unobtrusive help with joint decision making.

Were barristers and solicitors to overcome their present doubts as to the desirability of acting in mediatory, as opposed to partisan, roles, there remains the drawback that they also enjoy an authority which must diminish the freedom of many disputants to negotiate before them. Even if lawyers do not mediate, problems still surround their role in processes of family conciliation. Clearly, many who take their disputes before a mediator will want and need the advice and support of lawyers as skilled partisans. But should lawyers be "there," directly supporting their clients when efforts at mediation are made, or should they confine themselves to giving advice in advance and then wait on the sidelines to help evaluate any potential agreement? If lawyers are directly involved in mediatory processes, many disputants will seek to use them as champions. Where they do so, the distinctive quality of joint decision making, as putting power back into the hands of disputants themselves, will be lost.

Equally controversial is the proper relationship of family mediation to "social work," "counselling," and "therapy." It is notable that family therapists in Britain are already holding themselves out as possessing the skills necessary to train "conciliators," as well as to act as conciliators themselves (see, for example, the current prospectus of the Institute of Family Therapy (London) Ltd). Here again, it seems desirable that proper boundaries be maintained between these different, if complementary, disciplines. Mediation and therapy are not the same, and should be performed on separate occasions by different people.

A tendentious argument is being advanced here. It is that family mediation should develop as a form of dispute resolution distinct from legal processes, and that only harm can come to both modes of resolution by relating them too closely to each other. Family mediation must also be distinguished from those forms of intervention associated with counselling and therapy. Mediators should be low-key figures, closer in image to the neighbour than the dominant professional. It follows, too, that while many disputants may choose to have their quarrels adjudicated upon; those who do not should be encouraged through the institution of mediation to retain as much of the responsibility for decision making as is possible. Finally, we argue that family mediation will only work where the parties wish to experience it, and where a relative equality of bargaining power is present. "Power," of course, is found in many forms, and economic muscle on one side may be off-set by different forms of strength (e.g., physical control of the children) on the other. It follows from this last point that mediation should be addressed to the whole complex of matters demanding decision on family breakdown, rather than one isolated element (such as custody or access) alone.

TAXPAYER COMPLIANCE:
THE ROLE OF THE PROFESSIONS IN THE UNITED STATES AND THE UNITED KINGDOM

London Sessions
ABA Annual Meeting 1985
Ballroom, Dorchester Hotel
London, England

Thursday, July 18, 1985
10:00 A.M. - 12:00 Noon

Frederic G. Corneel
1 Post Office Square
Boston, Massachusetts 02109

and

Stewart T. Bates, Q.C.
4 Pump Court
Temple, London EC4Y 7AN

and

John F. Avery Jones
Speechly Bircham
Bouverie House
154 Fleet Street
London EC4A 2HX

The requirements of modern society are so costly that a majority of citizens must contribute to their support. If the mechanism used for this purpose is an income tax, then the gross receipts, deductions, and exemptions of the individual taxpayer become essential to the determination of the tax. Since no government can check into the situation of each of the scores of millions of taxpayers, the whole system functions only if there is a high level of voluntary compliance. In this respect, the satisfactory operation of a tax code is no different from the law generally in a democratic society: It requires the agreement of the members of the society.

Many observers are of the view that in the United States and the United Kingdom there has been a decline in the level of tax compliance, and that more and more taxpayers are using doubtful or plainly illegal means of reducing their contribution. There is concern that the increasing leakage in the income tax system will lead to other tax systems such as sales and excise taxes, which can be more easily enforced, but which will not be as fair in reflecting the individual's ability to contribute. Further, lawlessness in any important area of our lives is likely to lead to lawlessness elsewhere.

The level of taxpayer compliance depends upon many factors, including enthusiasm or distaste for the government, the relative levels of patriotism and selfishness, honesty and greed, the fear of punishment, and the rate and subject of the tax. Many of these factors are beyond the control of the professions. But certainly one major consideration bearing on the level of tax compliance is our sense of what others are doing. If taxpayers have the sense that all but a few crooks pay their taxes, they will not strain to avoid paying their fair share. But if the taxpayers have the sense that people generally cut corners, they will think, "Why should I be a patsy?"

Clearly, this is one of the factors bearing on taxpayer compliance that is much influenced by the professions. The ordinary citizen will gain some insight into the general level of compliance from the press, from advertisements by those who make their living promoting investments designed to reduce taxes, and the tales of corner cutting told by friends and acquaintances. But it is the attitude of the professional that best conveys to the ordinary citizens what "goes" and what is beyond the pale.

The attitude of the professional informs the client not only as to the standard of conduct of other taxpayers but of the standard of the profession itself. No reputable professional would advise conduct involving a clear violation of law, and this rejection of lawlessness gives some boost to compliance.

Where compliance does suffer at the hand of professionals is in connection with the thousands of situations not specifically dealt with by the law. The professional knows that the legislature intended a certain economic result to produce a given amount of taxes, but because the law in many ways turns on form rather than substance, the professional is able to recommend another way for the taxpayer to achieve the same economic result with a lesser tax. From the national point of view, these professional efforts are undesirable. Either income that was meant to be taxed escapes taxation or an already overly complicated law must be further refined in order to close the particular loophole.

Compliance also suffers because in many cases the imposition of a tax turns on elusive standards, such as "reasonable" compensation, "ordinary and necessary" business expenses and, most elusive, the "fair market value" of goods and services for which no market exists. Certain transactions will clearly meet the test of such standards, and others will just as clearly fail to meet it. But there are also many transactions of which it cannot be said with certainty whether or not they will meet the particular test. And if the professional is of the view that it is up to the client to decide how thin or thick the ice on which he wants to skate--and that is, generally speaking, the view of the professionals--then the professional may suggest transactions and return-reporting positions that are likely, although not certain, to result in a violation of law.

Finally, there may come to the attention of the professional facts which either indicate a clear violation of law by the client or which, if known to the tax collector, would be seen as strong evidence adverse to the client's position. Compliance might be advanced if the profession made these facts known to the tax authorities. But here the value of the taxpayer compliance runs head-on into the value of having the lawyer be the client's friend, confidant, and loyal advocate.

The situation of the taxpayer and the tax professional is reminiscent of the "tragedy of the commons." The farmer knows that the village green will be overgrazed and become useless if each farmer grazes more than one cow. But each farmer also knows that in the short run he can become richer if he grazes several cows. Many tax reduction stratagems that professionals devise will, in the long run, lead to a more complicated or a less fair law; indeed, very likely one which will require less professional services. But in the short run the client and, therefore, the individual lawyer will prosper by showing to his clients ways to overgraze.[1]

Preventing a tragedy of the commons in taxation is a challenge for each individual lawyer in deciding upon specific choices facing him in his practice but more so for the profession as a whole in working toward professional standards that will assure that our zeal to promote the interest of the individual client will not undermine the system that serves clients, lawyers, and society generally.

In this paper we will try to demonstrate by example how the tax professions in our two countries deal with the perplexing problems created by seeking to accommodate two conflicting demands: the client's desire to reduce his taxes and the need of "the system" for taxpayer compliance. We begin with a brief overview of that aspect of the system in each country that relates to tax returns.

Efforts to Ensure Compliance in the United States

The United States has an exceedingly complex income tax law, so complex that a majority of the taxpayers use professional assistance in reporting their income. This professional assistance may be rendered by lawyers, accountants, or commercial income tax return preparation services. The latter surely account for the larger number of returns, but the older professions, particularly the accountants, are responsible for the more important returns. There is no requirement to employ an independent lawyer or accountant for even the most complicated returns, and probably a majority of all corporate returns are done by the staff of the corporation.

If a professional does prepare a return, he must sign it, and he is subject to various laws and regulations applicable to "tax return preparers." This very concept is recent in the law, and with it have come various penalties applicable to the preparation of negligent or wilfully erroneous returns for others.

While some lawyers prepare or supervise the preparation of tax returns, the major part of their tax practice tends to lie in other areas. First, there is tax planning--structuring transactions in such a way as to reduce or postpone taxes. Second, lawyers may be called upon to represent clients who are being audited by the Internal Revenue Service and, if no agreement is reached in connection with such audit, further to represent them in any resulting litigation.

The Internal Revenue Service audits only a very limited number of returns (although it is hoped that through improved utilization of computer matching of various information returns with income tax returns, the audit process may become more productive). The frequently used term "playing the audit lottery" refers to the practice of taking clearly improper or highly questionable positions on a tax return on the chance that noncompliance will not be discovered on audit. The combination of limited audit with the complexities of the tax law is thought to give the taxpayer strong odds against detection of his noncompliance. This in turn leads to temptation for the taxpayer and his adviser.

Concern with taxpayer compliance has recently led to a tremendous outpouring of punitive legislation addressed to taxpayers, return preparers, and others having information relative to the taxable income of third parties. This legislation establishes penalties for negligent or intentional understatement of taxes, penalties for valuation errors, "no fault" penalties where the understatement is substantial, penalties specifically addressed to those involved in abusive tax shelters, and penalties for failure to report relevant information. It is still too soon to judge the effectiveness of this effort.

Lawyers involved in tax matters are subject to regulation from many different sources. There is the tax return preparer legislation already mentioned, enforced by the Internal Revenue Service. The Internal Revenue Service also has adopted and administers rules of conduct for those who practice before it, not specifically relating to returns, but to such matters as tax shelter opinions, audit representation, and the like. The various states have rules for the conduct of their attorneys, which may be applied either directly or by analogy to practice before the Internal Revenue Service. From time to time, the American Bar Association issues standards of professional conduct, which have no legal force of their own, but which may be taken into account by the states in formulating their own rules. Committees on Ethics of the American, State, and local bar associations advise with respect to the application of these rules. Disciplinary committees, either of bar associations or under court supervision, enforce the rules by penalties ranging from reprimands to disbarment. Finally, there is an increasing amount of malpractice litigation which tends to indicate the legal limits to permissible conduct by lawyers with respect to their obligation to the client or others with whom the client may be doing business.

Efforts to Ensure Compliance in the United Kingdom

Much of what is said about efforts to ensure compliance in the United States is equally applicable to the United Kingdom. The complexity of English tax law is such that professional assistance, usually by accountants, or other tax practitioners such as Members of the Institute of Taxation, is frequently required. There is, however, no equivalent of the commercial income tax return preparation services. The adviser is not required to sign the return.

The role of the lawyer is again similar, although the lawyer's role in the nearest equivalent to audit, the in-depth investigation of business accounts, is probably much less than in the United States. The audit lottery, although not known by that name, is a familiar concept. In the year to 31st March 1984, 3 percent of unincorporated businesses and 1 percent of company accounts were investigated in-depth, and 4.5 percent of unincorporated traders' accounts and 25 percent of company accounts were reviewed for technical points. The balance would be accepted after a brief scrutiny.

Penalties for negligent or intentional understatement of taxes are part of our system, and no fault penalties have been suggested in a recent report of a committee under the Chairmanship of Lord Keith, on similar lines to the U.S. model. It is too early to say whether this is likely to be accepted.

There seems to be a great deal less regulation of lawyers' conduct than in the United States. The only penalty which could be incurred by the adviser is for assisting in the making of a return which he knows to be incorrect. No rules of conduct are issued by the Inland Revenue. Neither branch of the legal profession has issued any practice statements specifically relating to tax matters. Professional negligence actions in the courts are infrequent as these tend to be settled by insurers.

There is one difference between the U.S. and the U.K. systems, which should be mentioned at this point, which is that self-assessment is unknown in the United Kingdom, although an experiment into its use for corporation tax is currently being undertaken. The importance of this can be exaggerated because, of course, the facts must come initially from the taxpayer, but the tax return can be looked on as giving the inspector information which he can accept or reject, rather than putting forward a precise figure which the taxpayer is saying is correct. Accountants will, therefore, frequently highlight doubtful areas and leave it to the inspector to disagree if he thinks fit. This attitude probably encourages the taxpayer to take the benefit of a doubt particularly when, at the same time, the Inland Revenue are given sufficient information to challenge the taxpayer's position.

1. May a Lawyer Suggest Steps Having No Economic Significance Merely in Order to Change the Tax Consequences?

Example

A large multinational corporation decides to enter into the fast-food business. It feels its chances for success would be much improved if it could use the name of a famous nouvelle cuisine chef. It offers the chef a $5,000,000 sign-on bonus to come to work. The chef consults his tax counsel who advises him that he will be subject to income taxes totalling more than 50% because this would be compensation income. Asked to recommend a way of improving the tax situation, the lawyer suggests that the chef "incorporate himself," setting up, perhaps, a small restaurant or cooking school, becoming its employee and having this corporation function as consultant to the multinational company with the thought that after more than six months, the stock might be sold at a capital gain.

When the chef learns that the capital gains taxes will still take more than $1 million, he asks for a yet less-expensive recommendation, and the lawyer suggests an eventual tax-free exchange of the stock of the chef's corporation for stock of the multinational company.

The American approach. Although the point of this exercise is to convert compensation for services, namely, payment for use of the chef's name and possible advice, to a capital gain or tax-free transaction, few American lawyers would hesitate on ethical grounds to give just this advice.

Depending upon how certain it is at the outset that the chef's corporation will merge with the multinational, there are varying degrees of risk that the transaction would be challenged if reviewed by the Internal Revenue Service. A careful lawyer might suggest that the transaction not take place in the same year as the year in which the company is formed, so that the I.R.S. is less likely to note the series of steps and seek to collapse them into a single tax-avoidance scheme. He may suggest that the transaction be with a newly formed subsidiary of the multinational so that the chef's corporation will be the surviving company and not have the short life that often gives rise to "step transaction" attacks. The lawyer may urge against making a definite agreement at the outset which would assure that the merger will take place, but rather suggest some approach like cross-options under which the chef has a right to put his stock to the multinational at one price and the multinational has the right to acquire the chef's stock at a somewhat higher price. Given those cross-options, it may be argued that neither side might exercise the option and that, therefore, at the time of the formation of the chef's corporation, the merger was not a foregone conclusion.

But all these precautions are taken only in order to increase the chance of success of this particular plan. In a great number of cases that apply the step transaction doctrine, corporations having a relatively short independent life are disregarded and in the case just posited, there is certainly a chance that the chef may, in spite of all of the planning, be taxed at ordinary income rates; but the courts which may disregard "sham" transactions of this kind do not criticize the lawyer who suggested it.

The United Kingdom approach. Until recently, arrangements which had no economic significance but were implemented in order to change the tax consequences would be likely to be accepted by the U.K. courts, so long as the arrangements did not contravene express anti-avoidance statutory provisions. But in a case in 1982 (Ramsay v. CIR), a new approach was adopted by the House of Lords. If the arrangements are a pre-ordained series of transactions, which include steps which have no commercial purpose apart from the avoidance of liability to tax, such steps may now, under the new approach, be disregarded for fiscal purpose.

It is interesting that in formulating the new approach the House of Lords referred, inter alia, to some decision of U.S. courts. For example, they referred to the following passage in the judgment of Judge Learned Hand in Gilbert v. Commissioner of Internal Revenue[2]:

> The Income Tax Act imposes liabilities upon taxpayers based upon their financial transactions...If, however, the taxpayer enters into a transaction that does not appreciably affect his beneficial interest except to reduce his tax, the law will disregard it...

As there is an inevitable, substantial gain in money or money's worth arising out of the proposed transactions, it seems likely that the new approach would be invoked by the Inland Revenue. The risk would still be there even if there was no definite agreement at the outset which would assure that the merger would take place; and, in this respect, cross-options would be dangerous and therefore unsatisfactory. It would be the risk of the application of the new approach rather than ethical reasons that would dissuade U.K. lawyers.

However, if the chef would be prepared to take his chance and simply trust that in due course his success would force, so to speak, the multinational corporation to acquire the shares in his corporation on a "takeover" basis, the new approach could not be validly applied and there would be no tax liability, income tax or capital gains, unless and until the chef disposed of his shares in the multinational corporation.

2. Suggesting an Approach Likely to be Taken to an Improper Extreme

Example

A client complains that he is helping to support his elderly mother with income on which *he* has to pay taxes. Can the lawyer properly suggest to the client that he put his mother on the payroll of the client's corporation, perhaps, as a member of the Board of Directors and as Assistant Secretary, positions that she can fill with very little effort, and then claim a business expense deduction for the compensation paid to her? Mother is 70, of reasonably sound mind and health, and could conceivably give a few hours to the business each month for which she might receive a very modest amount of "reasonable compensation" although, of course no other 70-year-old woman would be offered the job.

The danger with this suggestion is that if the compensation paid to mother is in fact limited to a "reasonable" amount, it would be so low as not to provide more than a very limited help to the client. Therefore, in all likelihood, the client would be inclined to extrapolate this suggestion and pay his mother a great deal more than reasonable compensation. Such excessive compensation would clearly result in tax understatement and might conceivably result in tax fraud since what would in fact be involved here would be: 1) an overstatement of deductions by the corporation, 2) a dividend from the corporation to the son on which the son should pay taxes, and 3) a taxable gift from the son to the mother.

The American approach. If the corporate return claimed a deduction for clearly unreasonable compensation paid to the mother, the lawyer could not sign the return of either the corporation or his client. Even if the lawyer did not sign the return, it would not be proper for him to suggest to the client the payment of unreasonable compensation. Although we are not aware of any rule barring a lawyer from making a suggestion merely because it is likely to be taken to an improper extreme by the client, this approach appears dubious at best and most reputable American tax advisers would not make it.

It may be asked why should it be ethical to suggest ways for the chef to disguise his compensation as a tax-free exchange of shares but be unethical to suggest ways of disguising the client's dividend and gift in this case as compensation to the mother? Do not both raise the same question of a form chosen to disguise the substance of a transaction?

The difference may be that in the case of the mother's compensation, the return makes what amounts to a factual assertion, namely, that the compensation paid to the mother is in line with what would be paid to an unrelated person rendering the same services. In the case of the chef, on the other hand, what the return will at most represent is a legal conclusion, namely, that the exchange of shares is entitled to tax-free treatment. American lawyers inevitably feel more comfortable asserting legal conclusions--whose validity may be challenged--than making serious doubtful assertions of fact.

This example also raises the question of valuation which is pervasive throughout the tax system. There is a general feeling that in matters of valuation, clients can give themselves the benefit of the doubt--claiming a high value for charitable contribution purposes and a low value for estate tax purposes. The Internal Revenue Code in recent years has introduced various valuation penalties, and it will have to be seen how effective they are. They address, however, the valuation of property rather than the valuation of services. Reputable counsel will tend in these matters also to give to the client the benefit of the doubt but, at least when it comes to the valuation of property rather than services, make sure that there is a persuasive appraisal by a reliable appraiser to back up the position taken.

The United Kingdom approach. Again the U.K. approach would be similar, although if the remuneration were not so great as to be clearly unreasonable, there would probably be more willingness in the United Kingdom to put it forward as a deduction and let the Inland Revenue argue if they thought fit. It is equally true that lawyers in the United Kingdom feel more comfortable asserting legal conclusions whose validity may be questioned than making seriously doubtful assertions of fact.

There are no equivalent valuation penalties in the United Kingdom and, indeed, the Keith Committee has suggested excluding valuation differences from the no-fault penalty regime, on the basis that the Inland Revenue tend to check valuations independently in any case and, therefore, they are not being misled by the taxpayer giving himself the benefit of the doubt in questions of valuation.

While in the instant case the issue of the reasonableness of the mother's compensation is most likely to be raised by the Inland Revenue if the Revenue knows of the relationship, U.K. lawyers would not volunteer the existence of the relationship. Of course, the relationship may be obvious from the names and the Revenue is always free to ask.

3. Structuring Transaction to Avoid Audit

Example

A client wants to give shares in his corporation to his son, assuming for this purpose quite a modest value for the stock, but he is afraid that the Internal Revenue Service will place a high value on the stock and charge him with a taxable gift. Is it proper for the lawyer to suggest to the client that instead of giving the stock to his son, the father sell the stock to the son against the son's note? In later years, the father can forgive portions of the note annually or give cash to the son with which the son can pay off the note.

By using this approach, the father need report only gifts of note forgiveness or gifts of cash, as to which there can be no valuation controversy, even if the gifts are so large as to require the filing of a gift tax return. In effect, this plan will have deprived the I.R.S. of the opportunity to audit the gift value of the stock the father transferred to his son.

The American approach. In the United States, reputable attorneys would not shrink from making a recommendation along these lines, although just like the mother's compensation in the preceding example, it may lead to abuse since a sale for less than adequate consideration clearly involves a gift. Therefore, the reputable attorney will caution the client that prior to making the sale he should obtain an appraisal from a qualified appraiser, since a sale at any unreasonably low price would in itself constitute a taxable gift. The lawyer would also counsel the client against any commitment to the son to forgive the note in the future or to provide the cash with which to pay off the note, since such commitments might by themselves convert what was in form a sale into a gift.

This type of transaction raises the question whether it is ethical for the lawyer to originate plans designed to prevent the Internal Revenue Service from becoming aware of transactions that may at least in the eyes of the Internal Revenue Service involve underpayment of taxes. In the view of American attorneys, there is no opprobrium attached to devising plans to reduce the risk of audit; what cannot be done is to suggest a plan that will clearly result in an underpayment of taxes.

The United Kingdom approach. The answer would be exactly the same in the United Kingdom. The advice about obtaining a valuation would certainly be given because of the requirement for avoiding a taxable gift that the sale was at a price such as might be expected to have been freely negotiated at the time of the sale.

Because of the method of calculating the value of the gift under the U.K. tax system, of the loss in value to the donor, this would be a dangerous exercise if the effect of the sale of a small part of the shares was that the donor lost control of the company or lost having a significant stake. In such a case, the danger of there being a taxable gift would be considerably increased and far greater caution would be required in fixing the price.

4. Calling Government Errors to Attention of Authorities

Examples

(a) The tax authorities have begun a detailed and potentially very troublesome audit of a client but have evidently failed to notice that the period for assessment of deficiencies is about to expire.

Should the lawyer inform the client of the situation? Should he request the client's permission to call the matter to the attention of the tax authorities? What should he do if the client refuses to authorize action?

(b) The tax authorities have insisted on what both lawyer and client deem quite an unfair settlement of a controversy which the client has accepted only because of the costs of litigation. When the authorities send the bill to the client for the additional tax, they have evidently made a mathematical mistake and the bill is too low.

The American approach. In the United States, lawyers feel no sense of obligation to call to the attention of the adversary legal oversights likely to work to the disadvantage of the adversary. For this purpose, the Internal Revenue Service would be regarded as an adversary. That this is clearly the accepted view is evidenced by the fact that books on tax practice recommend that if any amended return claiming a refund is to be filed, such filing should take place immediately prior to the time that the period of limitations for assessment of deficiencies expires. In this way, the government would be barred on audit of the amended return from recovering any additional taxes based on issues not raised in the refund claim.

While a lawyer should properly call the expiration of the period of limitations to the client's attention--since after all it is the client's case and not the lawyer's case, reputable lawyers would feel no obligation to advise the client to call to the government's attention the fact that as a result of a clerical oversight it is about to lose the entire case.

The second question, involving Internal Revenue Service computational mistakes favorable to the client, is a composite of several questions, some that are easy to answer and some that are more difficult.

First, it is clear that the lawyer should call the government error to the attention of the client. Second, it is clear that without the client's consent the lawyer cannot disclose information adverse to his client to the other side. Therefore, without the client's permission the lawyer would not disclose the error.

Now to the more difficult aspects: Many reputable lawyers would urge disclosure of the error to the Internal Revenue Service and might well, if the client refused to give permission, resign. This conclusion would be particularly clear in the event that the erroneous computation resulted in a refund to which the client was not entitled. But even if the error means the client will not pay a debt he has in principle agreed to pay, a lawyer would be uncomfortable to continue in the representation.

The consideration that argues the other way here is that client and lawyer consider the settlement unfair. What has been agreed to here is not the tax as it might be owed under the law fairly applied, but a sum of money to have relief from the government's threat, akin to blackmail, to litigate the matter. Surely there is no ethical obligation to call the blackmailer's attention to the fact that he has made a computational error.

The United Kingdom approach. In the first example, dealing with the expiration of the government's right to assess deficiencies, the practice in the United Kingdom would be identical. Guidance issued by the Institute of Chartered Accountants would require the client to be informed in these circumstances and lawyers would probably act in the same way.

The second question is less likely to matter in the United Kingdom because of the Inspector's ability within a six-year period, to "discover" the mistake and send another assessment. The lawyer's approach would be the same as in the first case. While he would inform the client, he would probably not go as far as urging disclosure, and he would be most unlikely to consider resignation. It should perhaps be added that if the error led to an excessive repayment of tax, the client could be committing a criminal offence by keeping the excessive repayment and a lawyer would be bound to disclose the fact to the Inland Revenue, at least, if the repayment were made to the lawyer on behalf of the client.

5. Calling Taxpayer Errors to Attention of Government

Example

A father who owns a shoe manufacturing company has sold some shares in his corporation to a corporation owned by his son which owns a number of retail shoe stores. The father made the sale on the basis of advice from his accountant that it would result in capital gain.

The lawyer becomes aware of this but knows that the transaction almost certainly resulted in a dividend. (Under U.S. law, a sale of stock to the issuing corporation which the seller continues to control is taxed as a dividend. A sale to another company under common control is taxed in the same way. Companies owned by father and son are deemed to be under common control.)

(a) If the tax return has not yet been filed, would it be proper for the lawyer to suggest that the transaction be undone?

Would it be proper to suggest filing a return which reported the transaction as capital gain but in an attached statement gave all of the relevant facts?

(b) If the return has already been filed, what should the lawyer do?

The American approach. In the United States, reputable counsel would suggest that the transaction be reversed and undone only, if as a matter of law, such undoing might be effective for tax purposes. There is some tax law that suggests that tax consequences depend upon the situation at the end of the year so that prior to year-end it may be possible to make changes which could not be made later on. There are also cases which permit the undoing of transactions because they were based on factual error, that is, if I buy Whiteacre based upon my belief that it has 10,000 acres and in fact it has only 1,000, I may be able, as a matter of law, to undo the purchase. But if my error is one that relates to the legal consequences of what I am doing, as was the case here, the courts do not permit revocation of the transaction--this is so even though a legal error may be vastly more important in its adverse consequences than a factual error.

In sum, the ethical question as to whether to advise revocation turns on the legal question whether such revocation might have the effect of undoing the tax consequences. If there is some reasonable chance that it would be effective, the lawyer can give the advice. If, on the other hand, it is clear that any revocation should, as a matter of law, be disregarded, the revocation would serve only the purpose of concealing from the Internal Revenue Service facts indicating that tax liability is owing. A lawyer should not recommend or participate in the implementation of a plan that will "work" only if a clearly erroneous return is filed.

If the transaction cannot be revoked, then, unless some "reasonable basis" argument can be made that the tax is not owing, the transaction will have to be reported and the tax paid.[3] (A "reasonable basis" position is one that is somewhat stronger than "frivolous" although not as strong as one having "substantial authority," which in turn is not as strong as one having at least an even chance of succeeding.)

The suggestion of giving the correct facts in a rider to a return that draws the wrong legal conclusion, has no merit. Indeed, there is no recognized ethical obligation to attach riders or explanatory memoranda to any return, although responsible lawyers generally feel that the weaker their "reasonable basis" position, the stronger is the argument to disclose at least some of the relevant facts. But where there is no basis at all in the law for the position taken, the return cannot be saved by attaching a factual statement.

If a clearly erroneous return has already been filed, then the attorney is under an ethical obligation to inform the client of the error and may also be under an ethical obligation to urge correction of the error if it was innocently made. However, the client is not required as a matter of law to file a corrected return.[4]

In any event, lawyers may well be concerned about the difficulties they may get into in representing a client who refuses to correct a clear and material error, either in connection with the audit of the erroneous return, or in the audits of future returns, or in connection with responses to auditor's request for information relating to contingent liabilities. Therefore, they may decide to withdraw from future representation of the client, either altogether, or in tax matters, unless the client corrects the error. Probably, in practice, whether a lawyer withdraws or not will depend on the lawyer's judgment whether difficulties along the lines mentioned are likely to arise.

The United Kingdom approach. The revocation of the transaction is equally unlikely to be effective in the United Kingdom and the advice would be the same.

In the United Kingdom, the adviser is much more likely to make the suggestion of reporting the transaction as a capital gain, but giving all the relevant facts, not including, however, the vital fact of the control of the companies. However, as in the case of the mother on the company payroll, the relationship may be obvious from the names and the Inland Revenue is always free to ask. The attack by the Revenue would be under a particularly obscure anti-avoidance provision, section 460 of the Taxes Act 1970, and it would be perfectly proper to leave it to the Revenue to make the contention that the proceeds of sale were taxable as income. Had the facts been slightly different and the father had sold to a company which he controlled, the likelihood of the anti-avoidance section applying would be more of a certainty, but it might still be possible to show that the sale was carried out for bona fide commercial reasons and did not have the main object of avoiding tax.

The United Kingdom does not, as such, recognize a reasonable basis argument. The legal obligation is to make a return of income "computed in accordance with the Income Tax Acts." This is generally understood to mean that the taxpayer must have some basis, presumably higher than a frivolous one, for making the contention and this may equate to the U.S. reasonable basis. Although it is difficult to find a legal reason to support it, there is a fairly generally held view that so long as all the facts are disclosed, one may in practice take quite an unreasonable legal position. The Keith Committee proposed that where the taxpayer had taken the benefit of a doubt and disclosed that he had done so, he should be exempt from the no-fault penalty.

The law is clearer in the case of the return which has already been filed and it comes to the notice of the taxpayer that it is incorrect. The taxpayer is treated as having made a negligent return for which there are penalties, unless he corrects the error without unreasonable delay (section 97, Taxes Management Act 1970). It is likely that the lawyer's duty would be to cease to act for the client if he refused to correct the error. However, the sort of error which is in mind here, is much more the omission of some income rather than taking an extreme legal view. Provided the facts were properly disclosed, the lawyer is unlikely to recommend correction of the return because the client's view of the law is almost certainly wrong. It is thought, however, that, as before, the strict legal position is that one should not put forward a position without any legal backing, but it seems to be accepted in practice that this is done so long as the facts are disclosed. This may in part reflect the degree of legal uncertainty in the absence of regulations or a rulings procedure.

Conclusion

Tax lawyers lead a Jekyll-and-Hyde existence. Their very livelihood depends upon people playing according to the rules of the game. Some of the most distinguished tax lawyers from time to time work in the government or directly or through bar association committees contribute to the improvement of our tax system and its administration.

On the other hand, in representing individual clients, we are frequently adversaries both of the Revenue Service and the system in general. Like the warhorses in Job, we love the smell of battle, of finding a new and undiscovered path that avoids all the traps so carefully laid by the government. All of this is not only profitable, but it is good fun, and we would not want it differently.

While these activities for individual clients may be seen as running counter to the goal of compliance, that is so superficially only. What is needed is not compliance with the legislature's wish or that of the Revenue Service to collect taxes. What is needed is compliance with the tax law as it is written. As long as the professions make it clear that they will advance the goals of their clients only by legal means, they enhance respect for law including the least popular of laws, the tax laws.

FOOTNOTES

1. The authors are indebted to James Lewis, Esquire, of the New York bar, for the following quotation indicating that the problem here under discussion is rather older than American village greens:

   Meanwhile each fancies that no harm will come from his neglect [of the common good], that it is the business of somebody else to look after this or that for him: And so, by the same notion being entertained by all separately, the common cause imperceptibly decays. [Thucydidus, The History of the Peloponnesian War, Book I, Section 141.]

2. Gilbert v. Commissioner of Internal Revenue 248 F.2d 399 at p. 411.

3. Some lawyers might counsel the client against engaging counsel, "I am very concerned that if I looked into all of the facts and researched the applicable law, I would have to advise you to report the transaction as a dividend. You might, therefore, consider just handling this matter with your accountant who told you you could report the sale as resulting in capital gain."

4. If the error was intentional and the lawyer, as return preparer, was an unwitting tool to his client's improper schemes, the lawyer would certainly urge correction and absent correction would resign. On the other hand, the lawyer owes it to the client to inform him that correction of intentional errors may led to civil and even criminal penalties, and though the client alleges his error was innocent, the I.R.S. may not believe him and seek to impose the penalties for intentional errors. Under these cirucmstances, the proper course for a lawyer who prepared what he now knows to be an incorrect return may be not only to urge correction but also consultation with another counsel who does not have the same personal interest not to be party, even unwittingly, to client misconduct.

LAW OFFICE MANAGEMENT SYMPOSIA

London Sessions
ABA Annual Meeting 1985
Ballrooms 1-2-3 and Crystal Palace
Hilton International, London, England

Thursday, July 18, 1985
10:00 A.M. - 12:00 Noon

Section of Economics of Law Practice
American Bar Association
750 North Lake Shore Drive
Chicago, Illinois 60611

Law Office Management Symposia

Summary

The Annual Meeting Symposia, sponsored by the American Bar Association Section of Economics of Law Practice, have been enthusiastically received by lawyers for the past several years. Panelists, like the attendees, will not be merchandised as experts. We will merchandise panelists as people who have substantial experience in the delivery of quality legal services.

The objective of the Symposia is to present a forum where all attendees (audience and panelists) share their ideas, problems, and solutions for the delivery of quality legal services. The moderator will guide attendees and panelists through the various areas of discussion itemized in the attached outline.

The audience will be divided into discussion groups according to law firm size: Solo practitioners; 2-4 lawyer group; 5-15 lawyer group; and over 15 lawyer group. Each discussion group will be led by a moderator. His or her supporting panel will consist of lawyers, solicitors, barristers, and administrators. The moderator and panelists will be selected according to firm size, specialty interest, and their knowledge of effective operation of a law practice.

This will be an audience participation event. We are looking for the unique, the creative, the <u>new use</u> of an old technique or technology. Our effort is to keep the <u>audience involved</u> without permitting monopoly by any participant.

Law Office Management Symposia

Topics for Discussion

Firm Organization

Goals and Philosophy
1. Total organization.
2. Attorneys.
3. Staff.

Structure and Selection of Management Form
1. Solo practice.
2. Professional corporation.
3. Partnership.
4. Partnership of corporations.
5. Shared space.

Accepting Change
1. Inflation.
2. Competition.
3. Changing goals of people.
4. Changing role of the law practice.

Facilitating Firm Organization
1. Long range planning.
2. Office meetings:
    a. Attorneys
    b. Staff.
3. Retreats:
    a. Frequency
    b. Format
    c. Planning.
4. Office manual:
    a. Operational
    b. Procedural
    c. Organization chart.

Other Topics

People

How to Attract Clients
1. Reputation.
2. Specialization.
3. Advertising.

Building Good Client Relationships
1. Rapport building.

Lawyers
1. Recruiting.
2. Testing.
3. Motivating.
4. Educating.
5. Training.

Staff
1. Recruiting.
2. Testing.
3. Motivating.
4. Educating
5. Training.

Ratio of Staff to Attorneys
1. Changes in ratio.
2. Equipment assistance.

Team Approach to Practice of Law

Staff Composition

Other Topics

Physical Plant

Office Location

Building Ownership

Office Design

Technology

Communication Equipment

Word Processing Equipment

Computers
1. In-house.
2. Out-house.
3. Consultation.

Copy Equipment
1. Regular copy equipment.
2. Facsimile gear.
3. Telephone terminal flexibility.

Dictating Equipment
1. Stationary.
2. Central system.
3. Portable.

Filing Equipment
1. Micro filming.
2. Location.
3. Retention policies.
4. Types of systems.

Library Facility

Video Equipment
1. For training.
2. For witness preparation.
3. For preservation of events.

Calendar Control

Conflicts Check

Tickler Systems

Other Topics

Systems

Analysis
1. Management.
2. Substantive.

Development

Delegation

Financial Management

Budgeting
1. Historical data.
2. Application.
3. Testing.

Time Keeping

Bookkeeping

Unbilled Time

Work in Progress

Billing and Accounts Receivable

Cash Flow Management

Management Controls and Reports

Fee Arrangements
1. Written.
2. Mandatory.
3. Client confidence.

Collection

Compensation
1. Attorneys.
2. Staff.

Fringe Benefits

1. Attorneys.
2. Staff.

Termination of Lawyer Services
1. Retirement.
2. Disability.
3. Death.

Termination of Staff Services
1. Retirement.
2. Disability.
3. Death.

Other Topics

JUDICIAL REVIEW OF ADMINISTRATIVE ACTION
IN THE UNITED STATES AND BRITAIN

London Sessions
ABA Annual Meeting 1985
Westminster Room, Inter-Continental Hotel
London, England

Thursday, July 18, 1985
10:00 A.M. - 12:00 Noon

The Hon. Malcolm R. Wilkey
U.S. Court of Appeals for
the District of Columbia
5832 U.S. Courthouse
Washington, D.C. 20001

I. Administrative Agencies in the United States

In drafting the Constitution, the Framers attempted to prevent the abuse of state power by apportioning it among three branches of government. The emergence of administrative agencies presents an embarrassing variation to the separation of powers that was the genius of the original constitutional plan, because, in a single organizational entity, the capacity to legislate rules, to implement those rules, and to penalize individuals who do not follow those rules may be combined.

To guard against the dangers inherent in this admixture of functions, each of the three traditional branches of government has developed mechanisms to restrain the "fourth branch." The tripartite functions of administrative agencies are thus subjected to tripartite controls. For example, the legislature can limit agency activity by appropriate language in the authorizing statute, and by monitoring agency performance in appropriation and oversight hearings. The executive branch can exercise the supervisory power commanded by a bureaucratic superior, at least over agencies that are not "independent," and even over independent agencies there is executive budget control. Finally, the judiciary can review agency decision making to ensure conscientious consideration of the issues within the authority of the agency, and a modicum of logical quality in the ultimate decision.

This paper focuses on the aspirations, the mechanics, and the practical limits to the third--the judicial--check on administrative action. My reason for discussing this subject with a British audience was well-expressed by David Williams, President of Wolfson College, Cambridge, when he referred to the 1957 report of your Franks Committee to point out the benefits of international cross-fertilization of ideas: Although "translation of the [administrative] practice of one country into the procedures of another is not likely to be appropriate,...since the basic issue, the relationship between the individual and the administration, is common, there will continue to be advantage in comparative study."[1]

II. The Aim of Judicial Review

The purpose of judicial review is to uphold the rule of law so that the aggregated and tripartite powers of an agency are not subject to abuse. Admittedly, agency personnel have discretion in choosing how to carry out their assigned tasks; some freedom of action is essential if the agency is to perform its duties in a way that best achieves the goals Congress set out when it established the agency in the first place. Yet the purview of agency expertise is limited by statutes and by constitutional requirements of due process.

The trick to judicial review, then, is to supervise agencies closely enough to make sure that they are doing their job but not so closely that courts do the agencies' job for them. In the United States, courts have gone much further than the requirements of British (and even Canadian) notions of "natural justice" and the limited duty to give reasons, and have required agencies to state their factual findings and to reason to defensible conclusions. The requirement of findings and conclusions serves two purposes, one procedural and one substantive. From a procedural standpoint, the requirement ensures that agencies evaluate the available evidence, apply the governing law, and <u>think</u> their way to a conclusion. From a substantive standpoint, findings and conclusions provide a basis for meaningful judicial review.

Because the objective of judicial review is to get the agencies to do <u>their</u> jobs, a reviewing court will not infer findings or supply a rationale not employed and cited by the agency. If it were otherwise, courts would invade the sphere reserved by Congress for the agency and would depart from the sphere of their own expertise.

An analysis of judicial review produces a "summing up" of all the rules of administrative law, both procedural and substantive, for if an agency violates any of the fundamental rules, the agency action is sure to be challenged and ultimately nullified by the courts.

III. Standards of Review by Type of Agency Action

Under the Administrative Procedure Act of 1946, courts evaluate agency decision making under two general rubrics. Review of informal rule making is governed by the "arbitrary and capricious" standard, while review of agency adjudication and formal rule making is governed by the "substantial evidence" standard of review. Under the latter standard, the agency must compile a paper record, and its conclusions must be supported on consideration of the record as a whole, including the evidence against the agency's position as well as that in support. "Substantial evidence review" thus holds the agency to a stricter standard of performance.

Notwithstanding the superficially equal treatment of all informal rule makings on the one hand, and all adjudications and formal rule makings on the other hand, precedents pertaining to one agency or function are not necessarily transferable to another. In practice, courts apply variable values and standards to different agencies, even to different functions in the same agency. The reason for this is that agencies perform at least six different functions, each of which merits more or less deference to agency expertise, subjects individuals and businesses to more or less risk of arbitrariness, and is more or less susceptible to judicial review after the fact. A court will review activity within each function with the <u>purpose</u> of that function in mind.

The functions may be isolated as follows: (1) simple enforcement calling for sanctions, (e.g., orders issued by the Federal Trade Commission (FTC) and the Securities and Exchange Commission (SEC); (2) rate making and licensing, (e.g., that performed by the Interstate Commerce Commission (ICC), the Federal Energy Regulatory Commission (FERC), and the Federal Communications Commission (FCC); (3) environmental and safety regulation, (e.g., rules promulgated by the Environmental Protection Agency (EPA) and the Occupational Safety and Health Administration (OSHA); (4) the granting of benefits, loans, grants, and subsidies by such agencies as the Department of Health and Human Services (HHS), the Department of Housing and Urban Development (HUD), and the Veterans Administration (VA); (5) the inspecting, auditing, and certification of potentially dangerous facilities and equipment performed by agencies like the Nuclear Regulatory Commission (NRC) and the Federal Aviation Administration (FAA); and (6) policymaking and planning such as that undertaken by the Civil Aeronautics Board (CAB), the NRC, and HHS.[2]

IV. How the Court Goes About It: The Method of Evaluating Agency Action

In spite of the different functions reviewed, our procedure is--or should be--a four-step analytic process. Although thousands of pages have been written about it, the essence of judicial review can be distilled into four simple stages:

1. Was the action taken within the agency's powers under its authorizing statute?

2. Were the parties accorded procedural due process, that is, notice, followed by an appropriate opportunity either to comment or to participate in a hearing?

3. Was there evidence (substantial evidence in an adjudicatory proceeding or formal rule making on the record) to support the agency's action?

4. Was the rationale by which the agency reached its results logical; in other words, was there a connection between the evidence adduced and the conclusion reached by the agency that is both discernible and defensible?

Understand these four steps, and you understand judicial review.

In reviewing an agency's decision for authority, procedural due process, evidentiary support, and cogent reasoning, a court should not substitute its view for the agency's judgment, even if, as is not uncommon, there is substantial evidence to support either of two inconsistent conclusions. Judicial restraint should be the order of the day. As we put this standard in more than one case, "while we may not have reached the same conclusion the Commissioner did if we were to decide the matter ourselves, there need be only a rational nexus between the facts found and the decision made to sustain the agency's determination."

My formulation of the appropriate inquiry is, I submit, simpler to execute and less intrusive than that of some of my colleagues on the District of Columbia Court of Appeals. I am inclined to agree with Jack Beatson, Fellow and Tutor in Law of Merton College, Oxford:

> [T]he dispute between members of the District of Columbia Circuit Court of Appeals...revolved around the question of whether judges determine the rationality of a decision by "steeping" themselves in the technology or by requiring more and more elaborate procedures. Neither approach seems particularly palatable. The first deprives the agency of a substantial role in the decision on the merits, while the second invites the high costs of delay and the distortion of issues as well as indirect interference with the determination of the merits of the case.[3]

The wisdom of judicial restraint becomes evident when we see how judicial review works out in practice.

V. Current Specific Issues

Deregulation

President Reagan took office in January, 1981, with the idea that we could no longer look to government as the solution to our problems; in many instances government was the problem. Accordingly, in the truck, railroad, and airline transportation industries, agency rate making and regulation is being scaled back drastically (or eliminated entirely, in the case of domestic airlines).

The President's deregulatory initiatives have led to some interesting paradoxes. In the case of the Civil Aeronautics Board, for instance, more administrative effort has been expended trying to phase out the agency than was found necessary to install it originally. Moreover, it is surprising to observe who are among the most vehement opponents of deregulation: those who prefer not to feel, but to view from a sheltered industry the cold winds of competition elsewhere.

Some of these opponents have successfully sought the aid of courts to block rescission of previously adopted regulations. In *Motor Vehicle Manufacturers Association v. State Farm Mutual Automobile Insurance Co.*, the Supreme Court held that the National Highway Safety Administration's attempt to rescind a regulation mandating passive restraints in automobiles was subject to the same standard of review as would be applied to a regulation to require such restraints in the first place. The Court in State Farm vacated the judgment of a panel of our court and instructed us in turn to remand to the agency for further proceedings. In Public Citizen and Center for Auto Safety, at the behest of a public interest (not industry) group, a similarly constituted panel of our court held that the same agency's suspension of a tire treadwear grading standard was "arbitrary and capricious" and went so far so to reinstate the standard.

While litigants in the two cases just mentioned sought judicial review to block agency attempts to reduce the burden of regulations, other litigants have invoked the jurisdiction of our courts to compel agencies to embark on regulatory campaigns. Environmentalists, for example, sued the Interior Department under Secretary Watt and the Environmental Protection Agency under Commissioner Gorsuch, demanding the exercise of enforcement discretion to their liking. But perhaps the most controversial example of this stratagem is Chaney v. Heckler, in which a divided panel of our court held that the administration of drugs in lethal quantities to execute condemned prisoners violated the "misbranding" and "safety and effectiveness" provisions of the Food, Drug and Cosmetic Act. The plaintiffs apparently wanted a label similar to that required on cigarette packages--"The Surgeon General has determined that this drug may be dangerous to your health." Not surprisingly, the Supreme Court granted certiorari and will hear argument this coming term.

The Breakup of AT&T and Judicial Review of Consent Decrees

Perhaps the most widely publicized "deregulatory" act in recent memory was the government's entry into a consent decree with American Telephone and Telegraph (AT&T), which removed restrictions imposed on AT&T by a previous consent decree. The earlier consent decree essentially limited AT&T to the provision of common-carrier communications services.

In exchange for the right to enter the fast-growing information and data-processing fields, AT&T agreed to divest its local telephone operating companies. As a result, there is now a new competitive situation, internationally, nationally, and regionally, as giant AT&T attempts to compete against discount long distance carriers and to establish a bridgehead in the market for microcomputers. Regulatory adjustments will spawn new controversies with new antagonists, and with old antagonists in new positions.

The AT&T breakup revives troubling questions about judicial review of consent decrees. Ordinarily, extrajudicial settlements of outstanding litigation are a welcome alternative to an expensive and lengthy trial, but when one of the parties is the United States, the possibility of unilateral executive lawmaking is raised. For example, an industry or public interest group may sue, reach agreement with a regulatory agency, and persuade a court to enter a consent decree settling the suit. The decree may be binding on the agency forever, govern all other parties positioned to raise similar issues, and severely constrict agency discretion granted by statute. If courts do not engage in a searching review of these consent decress, "sweetheart deals" between a sympathetic administration and a public interest group or corporation may take place, as apparently happened in the early 1950s with AT&T, and in the early 1970s with International Telephone and Telegraph. If a court does engage in searching review--as District Judge Harold Greene in our circuit did when he reviewed the proposed AT&T consent decree in a meticulous 103-page opinion--the court of necessity becomes both super-legislature and super-agency, an unelected and unguided guardian of the "public interest."

Legislative Veto

Unreviewed consent decrees present the risk that the executive branch will unilaterally bind the government as effectively as any piece of legislation; legislative veto provisions raise the similar risk that the legislative branch will unilaterally exercise executive or judicial power or take legislative action without the required presentation of legislation to the president.

The Supreme Court's holding in *Immigration and Naturalization Service v. Chadha*--that a provision authorizing one House of Congress to veto the attorney general's suspension of an alien's deportation--was prefigured by two decisions in our circuit that also held various legislative veto provisions unconstitutional. These holdings stand in sharp contrast to the unquestioned constitutionality of acts in Britain providing that rules be laid before one or both Houses of Parliament and that such rules be annulled either automatically or by resolution. The different constitutional result in our countries stems from the importance of the constitutionally prescribed separation of powers principle in the United States.

The *Chadha* decision left open a number of questions. Because over 200 statutes contain legislative veto provisions, one immediate question is whether these unconstitutional provisions are severable or whether whole statutes must be invalidated. If a statute does not state that unconstitutional sections are severable, there will inevitably be a series of challenges to agency authority on the theory that the nonseverable legislative veto clause invalidates the agency action. If the legislative veto clause is severable, however, the remainder of the statute exists with "no strings attached." Conceivably, there could now be an excessive and therefore unconstitutional delegation of legislative power. Even assuming that the severability problem is satisfactorily resolved, one wonders what Congress can do to reassert its authority over administrative agencies. Before *Chadha*, Congress had been moving in the direction of reducing agency discretion by providing for legislative veto of overzealous agency action. With a similar goal, Senator Bumpers went so far as to propose de novo court review of agency action. After Chadha, Congress is even more inclined to assert control, but what some thought its most effective tool has been taken away. Some academics suggest that Congress could mimic the legislative veto by conditioning the legal effect of a regulation on Congress's passage of a confirmatory law (presented to the President) pursuant to expedited internal rules. Although feasible, this approach would require Congress to reopen the uneasy compromise reached over its internal procedures and devote much more attention to proposed regulations. It remains to be seen whether Congress values the legislation veto sufficiently to adopt this more costly surrogate.

Risk Assessment

Another question deserving the attention of Congress, as well as the consideration of agencies and courts, is how risks of various governmental acts should be assessed and by whom. The nuclear industry presents this problem in perhaps its most acute form.

Broadly written congressional enactments provided the occasion for judicial activism in recent years. In *People Against Nuclear Energy*, for example, the Supreme Court reversed a panel of our court for requiring an environmental impact statement assessing the *fears* local residents might have about the reopening of a nuclear power plant. Likewise, in *Vermont Yankee*, the Supreme Court twice reversed our court for usurping the policymaking prerogatives reserved for the political branches of government.

Regulation of nuclear power, like selection of energy sources in general, necessitates resolution of complex issues far beyond the technical capacity of most judges. Aside from the lack of facilities, lack of expert staff, inadequate training, and institutional inability to mandate public expenditures, judicial forays into delicately woven regulatory schemes are episodic--they disrupt the agency's attempt to manage its affairs in a coordinated fashion.

Rather than arrogate policy decisions for itself, the judiciary would be better advised to require agencies to assess risk in an appropriate manner, assuming that risk assessment is authorized by Congress. Commendably, the executive branch has instituted its own regulatory analysis review program pursuant to President Reagan's Executive Order 12,261. Although the agency responsible for implementing the program, the Office of Management and Budget, can review only a small percentage of regulations, Harvard Professor Richard Stewart reports that "[i]ts analysts have often identified unnecessarily costly or clumsy elements in proposed regulations and secured useful modifications in them."[4]

Sound decision making suggests that agencies consider *total risk*; that is, the sum of the risks manifest at each stage of the process by which a service or good is produced. By comparing nuclear energy to its real, available alternatives instead of some imaginary cheap, safe, and inexhaustible energy source, even courts might conclude that their penchant for remanding to agencies for further fact finding has jeopardized America's energy security. I hasten to add, however, that the most enlightened cost/benefit analysis must remain unavailing in many fields because Congress has laid down an all-or-nothing approach. Accordingly, agencies responsible for protecting the snail darter or banning carcinogens like saccharin must act oblivious to the costs their regulations impose on the economy or the consuming public.

VI. The Problem of Judicial Activism, or "The Seizure of Abandoned Swords and Purses."

The problem of snail darters and carcinogens, however, is the exception and not the rule. In the last few decades, Congress has deliberately passed the difficult decisions to the judiciary far more often than it has legislated an overly rigid rule. The most acute issue facing reviewing courts today is what they should do when the two political branches leave the task of policy making to the unelected members of the judiciary.

By abdicating its duty to legislate public policy, Congress makes the position of the judiciary untenable. Without congressional guidance, how can a court tread the line between deference to agency decision making and correcting deviations from congressionally mandated policy? The courts are supposed to do both. Where the line is drawn will decide many a case but line drawing is frequently plain policy making.

By identifying the source of administrative law's current affliction, we have also identified where lies its cure. Reform of the administrative process is primarily the duty of Congress and the agencies. The ability of the courts to reform the agencies is limited by the nature of their review function only, and by statute (as we saw in _Vermont Yankee_ and _People Against Nuclear Energy_). Moreover, because courts can decide only "cases and controversies" under our Constitution, judicial reform would be piecemeal, costly, and slow in coming--even if it did not violate statutory and constitutional norms.

The inability of courts to reform the administrative process underscores the theme of this paper--the necessity of judicial restraint. Only by keeping within the bounds set by the Framers, Congress, and our institutions can judges keep faith with the oaths of their office and, by refusing to exercise the prerogatives of Congress and executive, force them to live up to their constitutional obligations as well.

FOOTNOTES

1. Williams, The Donoughmore Report in Retrospect, 60 Pub. Admin. 273,284(1982).

2. Verkuil, The Emerging Concept of Administrative Procedure, 78 Colum. L. Rev. 258,294-303(1978).

3. Beatson, A British View of Vermont Yankee, 55 Tul. L. Rev. 435, 446(4).

4. R. Stewart, The Limits of Administrative Law 19 (June 1983) (unpublished manuscript).

SELECTED BIBLIOGRAPHY

Cases

American Federation of Government Employees v. Pierce, 697 F.2d 303 (D.C. Cir. 1982)(per curiam)

American Textile Manufacturers Institute, Inc. v. Donovan, 452 U.S. 490 (1981)

Baltimore Gas & Electric Co. v. Natural Resources Defense Council, Inc., 103 S. Ct. 2246 (1983), rev'g. Natural Resources Defense Council, Inc. v. Nuclear Regulatory Commission, 685 F.2d 459 (D.C. Cir. 1982)

Chaney v. Heckler, 718 F.2d 1174 (D.C. Cir. 1983), cert. granted, 104 S. Ct. 3532 (1984)

Citizens for a Better Environment v. Gorsuch, 718 F.2d 1117 (D.C. Cir. 1983), cert. denied, 104 S. Ct. 2668 (1984)

Consumer Energy Council of America v. Federal Energy Regulatory Commission, 673 F.2d 425 (D.C. Cir. 1982), aff'd mem. sub nom. Process Gas Consumers Group v. Consumers Energy Council of America, 103 S. Ct. 3556 (1983)

Consumers Union, Inc. v. Federal Trade Commission, 691 F.2d 575 (D.C. Cir. 1982) (en banc), aff'd mem. sub nom. Process Gas Consumers Group v. Consumers Energy Council of America, 103 S. Ct. 3556 (1983)

Immigration and Naturalization Service v. Chadha, 103 S. Ct. 2764 (1983)

Industrial Union Department, AFL-CIO v. American Petroleum Institute, 448 U.S. 607 (1980)

Metropolitan Edison Co. v. People Against Nuclear Energy (PANE), 460 U.S. 766 (1983), rev'g sub nom People Against Nuclear Energy (PANE) v. Nuclear Regulatory Commission, 678 F.2d 222 (D.C. Cir. 1982)

Motor Vehicle Manufacturers Association v. State Farm Mutual Automobile Insurance Co., 103 S. Ct. 2856 (1983), aff'g in part and rev'g in part, State Farm Mutual Automobile Insurance Company v. Department of Transportation, 680 F.2d 206 (D.C. Cir. 1982)

Public Citizen and Center for Auto Safety v. Steed, 733 F.2d 93 (D.C. Cir. 1984)

Tennessee Valley Authority v. Hill, 437 U.S. 153 (1978)

United States v. American Telephone and Telegraph, 552 F. Supp. 131 (D.D.C.), aff'd mem., Maryland v. United States, 460 U.S. 1001 (1983)

Vermont Yankee Nuclear Power Co. v. Natural Resources Defense Council, 435 U.S. 519 (1978), rev'g Vermont Yankee -- Natural Resources Defense Council v. Nuclear Regulatory Commission, 547 F.2d 633 (D.C. Cir. 1976)

Statutes

Administrative Procedure Act of 1946, 5 U.S.C. §§551-559, 701-706 (1982)

Delaney Amendment, 21 U.S.C. §348(c)(3)(A)(1982)

Endangered Species Act of 1973, 16 U.S.C. §1533 (1982)

Tunney Act, 15 U.S.C. §16(e)(1982)

Other Writings

Beatson, Jack, A British View of Vermont Yankee, 55 Tul. L. Rev. 435 (1981)

Beatson, Jack, Legislative Control of Administrative Rulemaking: Lessons from the British Experience?, 12 Cornell Int'l L.J. 199 (1979)

Breyer, Stephen, The Legislative Veto After Chadha, 72 Geo. L.J. 785 (1984)

Edwards, Harry T., Judicial Review of Deregulation, 11 N. Ky. L. Rev. 229 (1984)

Frug, Gerald, The Ideology of Bureaucracy in American Law, 97 Harv. L. Rev. 1276 (1984)

Jaffe, Louis, Judicial Control of Administrative Action, (1965)

Law Reform Commission of Canada, Administative Law: Independent Administrative Agencies 143-57 (1980) (Working Paper 25)

McGowan, Carl, Reflections on Rulemaking Review, 53 Tul. L. Rev. 681 (1979)

Note, Severability of Legislative Veto Provisions: A Policy Analysis, 97 Harv. L. Rev. 1182 (1984)

Stewart, Richard, The Limits of Administrative Law (June 1983) (unpublished manuscript)

Stewart, Richard, The Reformation of American Administrative Law, 88 Harv. L. Rev. 1667 (1975)

Tribe, Laurence, The Legislative Veto Problems: What Does INS v. Chadha Really Mean?, in 5 J. Choper, Y. Kamisar & L. Tribe, The Supreme Court: Trends and Developments--1982-1983, at 179-203 (1984)

Wilkey, Malcolm, Activism by the Branch of Last Resort: Of the Seizure of Abandoned Swords and Purses (1984)

Williams, David G. T., The Donoughmore Report in Retrospect, 60 Pub. Admin. 273 (1982)

Verkuil, Paul, The Emerging Concept of Administrative Procedure, 78 Colum. L. Rev. 258 (1978)

JUDICIAL REVIEW IN THE UNITED KINGDOM - 1976 TO 1984

London Sessions
ABA Annual Meeting 1985
Westminster Room, Inter-Continental Hotel
London, England

Thursday, July 18, 1985
10:00 A.M. - 12:00 Noon

The Hon. Mr. Justice Vinelott
Royal Courts of Justice
Strand, London WC2A 2LL

and

Sir Michael Kerry, K.C.B., Q.C.
South Bedales
Lewes Road
Haywards Heath
West Sussex

Almost a decade has passed since (at the meeting of the ABA in Atlanta in 1976) papers were read explaining current developments in administration law in England and the United States. It can be seen in retrospect that 1976 was a watershed year in the development of administration law in England.

In the decade preceding 1976, there had been a series of landmark decisions. In Ridge v. Baldwin [1964] A.C.40, the House of Lords made it clear that the supervisory jurisdiction of the High Court exercising the prerogative remedies of mandamus prohibition and certiorari extended beyond the control of bodies having judicial or quasi-judicial duties to many bodies or persons having authority conferred by statute to make administrative decisions. Such persons were thereby made amenable to the power of the Court to quash a decision for error of law or for a failure to act fairly towards a person adversely affected by the decision. In Anisminic Limited v. Foreign Compensation Commission, [1969] 2 A.C.147, the old inhibiting distinction between errors of law, which went to jurisdiction and were reviewable by the Courts, and those which did not, was for practical purposes abolished. In Padfield v. Minister of Agriculture, [1968] A.C.997 and in The Secretary of State v. Tameside M.B.C. [1976] A.C., the House of Lords reviewed decisions of Ministers made under powers which, it was claimed, conferred an unfettered discretion on the Minister and affirmed the power of the Court to evaluate the factual basis on which the discretion was exercised to ensure that it was exercised in good faith in pursuance of the policy to be inferred from the legislation. These radical changes in substantive law were accompanied by a judicial challenge to the power of a Minister of the Crown to refuse to disclose official documents on the ground of Crown or public-interest privilege. In Conway v. Rimmer [1968] A.C.910, the House of Lords held that it was open to the Courts to weigh the interests of justice in compelling disclosure of relevant documentary evidence against the interests of government in retaining confidentiality.

However, in 1976, the power of the Court to review administrative action and control abuse was hampered by procedural limitations. The traditional machinery for instituting review of a decision by an inferior tribunal or of a decision by a public body was an application for leave to issue one of the prerogative writs--in particular the writ of certiorari. But the Court had no power to order discovery at the suit of the applicant. If, therefore, the decision was one which did not state the reasons for it, it was difficult to challenge it on the ground of error of law. This defect was mitigated by the Tribunal and Enquiries Act 1958 (now the Tribunals and Enquiries Act 1971) which required many of the more important tribunals to state the reasons for their decisions. However, there are tribunals and, more importantly, public bodies outside the scope of that Act. Strikingly, in the Anisminic case, the error of law upon which a decision of the Foreign Compensation Commission was quashed was only revealed in the course of discovery in an action for a declaration; if the proceeding in that case had been by way of application for the issue of certiorari, it would never have come to light. Furthermore, evidence in an application for leave was given by affidavit, and the rules contained no provision for cross-examination of the deponents. These and other practical disadvantages to which the applicant for leave to issue one of the prerogative writs was subject led to a great increase in actions for declaratory relief in which discovery and, in an appropriate case, cross-examination could be obtained, although the plaintiff suffered from the disadvantage (of little importance in practice) that the Court could not reach out and quash a decision declared to be invalid.

Order 53

In 1976, the Law Commission in a valuable review of the state of administrative law, recommended the introduction of legislation which would simplify and improve the machinery of the Courts. The reform was initially carried out by the introduction of a new rule, Order 53, made under powers for regulating procedure in the High Court. Doubts have been expressed from time to time whether the new rule was intra vires this rule-making power. Those doubts have been set at rest by subsequent legislation--Section 31 of the Supreme Court Act 1981.

The new Order, which is headed "Application for Judicial Review," is designed to create a uniform, flexible, and comprehensive code of procedure for the High Court's exercise of its supervisory jurisdiction over the proceedings and decisions of tribunals and public authorities. All such applications, whether they would formerly have been made by an application for leave to issue one of the prerogative writs or by an action for a declaration or an injunction, may now be made by a single application for judicial review in which the Court has the same powers that it would have had if the application had been made in any of these ways.

As in the case of the prerogative writs, the application for review under the new Order 53 is in two stages. First, the applicant without notice to the respondent, applies ex parte for the leave of the Court. If leave is given, the application proceeds as an inter partes suit in the ordinary way. The initial stage is designed to create a sieve to exclude baseless applications and applications by persons who clearly do not have an interest in the subject matter of the application, even within the broad principles governing standing in public law review. To this extent, Order 53 follows the procedure of the old prerogative writs and extends them to cases where what is sought is declaratory or injunctive relief.

Under the new Order 53, there is express provision for discovery of documents, the administration of interlocutories, and the cross-examination of deponents to affidavits. Discovery is not automatic as it would be in an ordinary action commenced by writ;

discovery is obtainable on application when and to the extent that the justice of the case requires. The ordinary rules of Court apply to the cross-examination of deponents upon affidavits. It is too early to say how far these powers will be used in practice; in a recent case, O'Reilly v. Mackman [1983] A.C.237, Lord Diplock, while making it clear that the grant of leave to cross-examine deponents on application for judicial review is governed by the same principles as in other proceedings, also stressed that "to allow cross-examination presents the Court with a temptation not always resisted to substitute its own view of the facts for that of a decision-making body upon whom the exclusive jurisdiction to determine facts has been conferred by Parliament".

Two other points should be noted. First, if in an application for judicial review the Court concludes that the complaint is properly not one of infringement of rights entitled to protection in public law but of rights entitled to protection in private law, the Court may order the proceedings to continue as if commenced by writ. This is a one-way street. An application commenced by writ cannot be turned into an application for judicial review. Secondly, an application for judicial review must be made promptly. The rules require the application to be made within three months after the decision or act of which complaint is made. or within such longer period as the Court may in any particular case allow.

These formal changes in procedure have been accompanied by administrative changes in the way in which the business of the Courts is organised. Applications for judicial review falling within the field of civil law are normally heard by a single Judge of the Queen's Bench Division. In practice, these applications are heard by one of a number of Judges with experience of administrative law. This administrative change is reminiscent of the creation of a list of Judges with special knowledge of commercial law from which has emerged what is now officially known as the Commercial Court. Thus the creation of the new procedure for judicial review has been accompanied by the creation of something very like an administrative Court. Together these changes have provided a framework within which the substantive principles of administrative law can be further developed.

Substantive Law

Lord Diplock recently described the three grounds upon which administrative decisions may be open to judicial review as "illegality," "irrationality," and "procedural impropriety." In considering developments since 1976, the first two of these grounds can be taken together. Cases of "illegality" (that is, where a decision is based upon a wrong view of the applicable law) most frequently turn upon the interpretation of particular statutory provisions and yield no generally applicable principle. The category of "irrationality" comprises those cases where the decision is so outrageous that it is in itself evidence that the person making it must have been influenced by some improper motive, or must have taken into account matters which he ought not to have taken into account or have failed to take into account matters which he ought to have taken into account, or has more simply taken leave of his senses. Recent cases have taken the Courts closer to politically charged decisions. In the Tameside case, the Labour administration tried to force through, at short notice, a reorganisation of schools in the Manchester area; it was held to have misunderstood its powers under the Education Acts. More recently in Bromley Borough Council v. G.L.C. [1982] A.C.768, the G.L.C. was held not to have given sufficient attention to the interests of ratepayers generally in exercising its powers in relation to fare fixing on the London Transport system.

Procedural Impropriety

It is in the field of procedural impropriety that the most striking advances have been made. The basic rule of fairness, particularly where pre-existing rights of an individual are affected by administrative decision, are well settled. The individual must be given the opportunity of knowing what is alleged against him and of making representations as to why his rights should not be taken away or restricted. Where there is no initial requirement for consultation or for a hearing, it was formerly doubtful whether such a requirement could be created by the conduct of the party making the decision. Two very recent cases (the decision of the Privy Counsel in A.G. of Hong Kong v. Ngunuyen Shiu [1983] 2 A.C.629, and of the House of Lords in re The Council of Civil Service Unions and Others [1984] 3 All ER 935, commonly called the G.C.H.Q. case) have made it clear that a course of conduct may give rise to such a "legitimate expectation." In the former of these two cases, an announcement by the immigration authorities in Hong Kong that before an illegal immigrant from Macau was repatriated he would be interviewed, and that each case would be treated on its merits, was held to give rise to a legitimate expectation (though not amounting to an enforceable legal right). An order made without following that procedure was quashed. Lord Fraser stated the principle in the following short passage:

> The expectations may be based upon some statement or undertaking by or on behalf of the public authority which has the duty of making a decision, if the authority has, through its officers, acted in a way that would make it unfair or inconsistent with good administration for him to be denied such an enquiry.

In the G.C.H.Q. case, new conditions of service for staff at G.C.H.Q. (the Government Communications Head Quarters) were introduced on instructions from the Prime Minister issued under a prerogative order in Council. The new conditions denied staff the right to belong to a national trade union. It was held unanimously by the House of Lords that the practice followed for a very long time of consulting the unions before introducing changes in relationship between management and staff gave rise to a reasonable expectation of consultation before an action as drastic as the curtailment of trade union rights that was imposed was decreed, and that the denial of that reasonable expectation would by itself have invalidated the action complained of.

The action failed because the Crown successfully argued that the interests of national security overrode the principle of good administration that would otherwise have invalidated the decision. It should be noted in passing the the G.C.H.Q. case is also of importance in the field of administrative law because the House of Lords made it clear that the power of the Court to review administration decisions extends to some decisions made under instruments promulgated under the royal prerogative--though there may be sound reasons of public policy why the Courts should not trespass on all powers derived from the royal prerogative--for instance, the Crown's treaty-making powers.

Remedies in Public and in Private Law

The division which has emerged between public and private law has been thrown into sharp relief by a trio of recent decisions by the House of Lords.

In O'Reilly v. Mackman (supra), prisoners were charged with disciplinary offences before a Board of Visitors. The Board held enquiries, found charges proved, and imposed penalties. The prisoners brought separate actions in the High Court against the Board, claiming declarations that the findings and penalties were void. It was held by the House of Lords that it was contrary to public policy and an abuse of the process of the Court for the actions to proceed; the proper procedure was that prescribed by Order 53. It should be noted that the plaintiffs had not suffered any infringement of rights derived from private law; their complaint that they had forfeited part of remission of sentence was a complaint that they had been deprived of a privilege which they had a reasonable expectation of enjoying, but even if well founded, the complaint would not have given rise to a claim for damages. It should be noted also that before the new Order 53 came into force, an action by the prisoners for declaratory relief would have been allowed to proceed. The decision of the House of Lords was based in part upon the fact that the disadvantages which formerly attached to a review of administrative action by the prerogative writs had been removed, and in part upon the necessary protection afforded by Order 53 to public authorities by the requirement for leave to institute proceedings and by the limited period within which review must be sought. These restrictions Lord Diplock considered to be essential if the administration of a modern state is not to be hampered by groundless, unmeritorious, or tardy claims.

In Cox v. Thanet District Council [1983] 2 A.C.287, the plaintiff applied to his local housing authority for accommodation relying upon the authority's duty to house homeless persons under the Housing (Homeless Persons) Act 1977. The House of Lords, in declaring that the plaintiff was not entitled to institute proceedings otherwise than by application for judicial review, stressed that the authority's duty to house homeless persons arose only after the authority had made a preliminary determination that a person was homeless or threatened with homelessness and was in priority need and was not intentionally homeless. Thus the applicant had no antecedent rights in the field of private law. Rights in public law could only arise in consequence of the discharge by the authority of its administrative functions. The exercise of those functions was the subject of administrative review and that review could be conducted only in accordance with the provisions of Order 53. Lord Bridge expressed this point in a short passage:

> It is inherent in the scheme of the Act that an appropriate public law decision of the Housing Authority is a condition precedent to the establishment of the private law duty.

The recent, and as yet unreported, decision of the House of Lords in London Borough of Wandsworth v. Winder stands in striking contrast. That case concerned the tenant of a flat held on a weekly tenancy from the local authority. The tenant had a secure tenancy, and under the Housing Acts the local authority could only repossess the flat in specified circumstances which included the persistent nonpayment of rent. The authority gave him notice under the 1980 Act increasing his rent. He paid what he regarded as a reasonable increase and refused to pay the balance. The same thing happened a little later when the rent was increased. The local authority took proceedings, claiming possession of the premises on the grounds that the rent had not been paid. The tenant defended his action on the ground that the decisions to increase the rent were ultra vires and void. The question was whether it was an abuse of process for him to challenge the local authority in his defence to the action instead of applying for judicial review under Order 53. The House of Lords, deciding that it was not, drew a sharp distinction between the case where (as in O'Reilly and in Cox) the plaintiff has no pre-existing private law right and relies upon a decision or act in the field of public law to create a right. There a challenge to the decision or act, or failure to act, lies wholly in the field of public law and a challenge must be made, if at all, under Order 53. In the Winder case, the defendant had a pre-existing right under private law--the right to a secure tenancy at the rent he had agreed to pay--and he could not be called upon to pay any additional rent except as a result of a lawful increase resulting from a decision properly made by the local authority. He was entitled to rely upon his private right and in an action by the local authority to challenge the validity of the decision to increase the rent. As Lord Fraser pointed out, the tenant:

did not select the procedure to be adopted. He is merely seeking to defend proceedings brought against him by the local authority--in so doing he is seeking only to exercise the ordinary right of any individual to defend an action against him on the grounds that he is not liable to the whole sum claimed by the plaintiff. Moreover, he puts forward his defence as a matter of right, whereas in an application for judicial review success would require an exercise of the Court's discretion in his favour.

The Limits

These decisions have emphasised the divergence between what is now seen as the function and procedure of the Court when reviewing decisions of tribunals and public authorities and the function and procedure of the Court when adjudicating on disputes between citizens or between a citizen and an organ of central or local government on matters concerning private rights. Within the field of public law, the applicant has no right to judicial review; he must first obtain the leave of the Court. Evidence in the first stages is by affidavit, and the applicant is subject to uberrima fides. The applicant has no right to discovery or to interrogate or to cross-examine on his opponents' affidavits; these are available only at the discretion of the Court. The time within which the application must be brought is narrowly circumscribed. On the other hand, the applicant is not subject to the same strict rules of standing. In the field of public law, standing is afforded to anyone who can show a "sufficient interest" and there are indications in the decision of the House of Lords, in Inland Revenue Commissioners v. National Federation of Self Employed etc., [1982] A.C.671, that the Courts will give a wide interpretation to "sufficient interest" and will not confine it to the interest formerly necessary to support an application for leave to issue one of the prerogative writs. More importantly, the House of Lords in that case held that standing ought not to be decided as a preliminary issue but considered in the light of the gravity of the case, and, in particular, whether it appeared that there was a possibly serious charge of illegality against a public body.

It is nonetheless important to recognise the boundaries beyond which the English Courts do not trespass. First, the system that has been established represents a pragmatic extension of existing institutions and procedures. The legislature has not intervened to create a separate Court structure to review administrative decisions; judicial control over powers conferred by statute or otherwise on ministers, public authorities, and tribunals are exercised through the ordinary Courts of Law. Secondly, a closely related point: administrative decisions are not reviewed on their merits. As Lord Brightman observed in Chief Constable of the North Wales Police v. Evans [1982] 1 W.L.R. 1155, "Judicial review is concerned, not with a decision, but with the decision-making process."

The Courts in England have not so far felt able to go as far as some of the U.S. Courts in entering into a "substantial evidence review" of the grounds of a decision of a public authority. It is inconceivable, for instance, that the Courts in England would attempt not merely to quash but to supplant a decision of a public authority. The Lord Chancellor recently emphasised that review by the Courts is not intended to take away from tribunals and public authorities "the powers and discretions properly vested in them by law and to substitute the Courts as the bodies making the decisions" (see Chief Constable v. Evans, [1982] 3 All ER 141).

AN AMERICAN PERSPECTIVE OF LEGAL MALPRACTICE: TWO DECADES OF LITIGATION

London Sessions
ABA Annual Meeting 1985
Ballroom, Grosvenor House Hotel
London, England

Thursday, July 18, 1985
10:00 A.M. - 12:00 Noon

Ronald E. Mallen
Suite 1800
Four Embarcadero Center
San Francisco, California 94111

The Profile of Legal Malpractice Liability

The concern of the American lawyer about legal malpractice claims is a relatively recent phenomenon. Liability claims were virtually unheard of until the late 1960s. There were few reported appellate decisions and very little literature on the subject. The price of a professional liability policy was often less than that for automobile and homeowner's insurance

Since the late 1960s, the changes have come rapidly. In just the last ten years there have been as many reported legal malpractice decisions as in the entire history of American jurisprudence. In fact, during the last ten years there have been four times as many decisions as in the previous decade. There are no signs at either the appellate or trial levels that the frequency of litigation has lessened. Today, the new lawyer is likely to be the subject of three or more claims in his or her career. Some dubious solace may be found in that only one of three claims is likely to result in a liability payment.[1]

Professional liability insurance has been particularly cyclical, fluctuating in price and availability. In the mid-1970s, when legal malpractice claims appeared to be exploding, insurers suddenly found themselves with an unexpectedly high number of claims of uncertain exposure. Losses were difficult to evaluate, often unliquidated. Liability evaluation required analysis of a rapidly developing and unsettled area of law. Defense costs soared. The then common occurrence policy seemed to portend timeless exposure.

Many insurers reacted by leaving the market. Those who stayed were able to substantially increase their rates, sometimes as much as 500 percent. Others entered the market because they saw the opportunity to write bar associations, providing attractive cash flow in a high-interest economy. Cash flow appeared to be the primary attraction. The product became priced more by the competition than by underwriting.

The losses, spurred by the increasing frequency of litigation and the growing severity and high cost of defense, continued to escalate into the early 1980s. Another factor contributing to the losses was that many of the underwriters and claims services were managing general agent operations, inexperienced in the lawyers' professional liability field. Newcomers, however, enthusiastically appeared to replace those departing the market. That enthusiasm to write legal malpractice policies, however, appears to be diminishing.

As we reach the middle of this decade, the legal malpractice insurance market again appears to be changing. In many American jurisdictions, such as California, few of the insurers writing today were in the marketplace only several years ago. Premiums over the last year have uniformly increased from 25 to 50 percent, with another 50 to 100 percent increase projected within the next year or two. The tightening of the market has resulted in careful screening of applicants for legal malpractice insurance, and a lack of insurance or inadequate insurance (such as exclusions for prior acts) for many lawyers. As they did almost ten years ago, state bar associations are investigating bar-sponsored or owned insurance programs for their members. Those programs started a decade ago still exist, some successfully, others with uncertain futures.

American lawyers are now concerned about understanding and controlling their liability. In the mid-1970s, the American Bar Association appointed a task force to study the problem. Today it has a Standing Committee on Lawyers' Professional Liability. One of the Committee's initial projects, the National Legal Malpractice Data Center, is now bearing fruit. The purpose of the statistical studies is to analyze the causes of professional liability claims and to develop loss prevention programs to minimize or avoid the risks. The Data Center consists of a computerized data bank containing detailed information on over 25,000 nationally reported legal malpractice claims. Insurers have supported the Data Center financially and have also provided information on both open and closed claims.

Even though the project is in its relative infancy, significant information has been disclosed and is starting to be analyzed. The major obstacle to accurate analysis is the need to match demographic information on the profiles of the lawyers who practice as against the profiles drawn off the data bank. Until this information is available, it is difficult to determine if one group of lawyers or a particular area of legal practice is disproportionately at risk. The publication of data, however, has had the salutary effect of alerting lawyers to the reality of legal malpractice claims. The publicity alone, regardless of what the statistics mean, has created an interest in loss prevention.

Although the Center's data require careful study, several areas seem to merit special attention. First, analysis by area of law reveals that real estate and personal injury plaintiff's practice combined, in equal shares, produce almost 50 percent of all claims against lawyers. Next (but with only half the exposure) are collection-bankruptcy matters. Then follow, respectively, family law, estates and probate, corporations-business organizations, and criminal law, leaving an "others" category producing about 15 percent of the claims. Unfortunately, we do not know how the losses compare to the percentage of lawyers who practice in those areas.

Over 50 percent of all legal malpractice claims arise from litigation activities. We do not know, however, what percentage of the lawyer population engages in litigation. The predominant error is of inadvertence, the failure to comply with time limitations. Those should be avoidable.

In looking at the profile of the lawyer charged with malpractice, we find that 80 percent of all claims arise from firms of five or fewer lawyers. We do not know whether that figure is skewed because large firms tend not to report all claims because of their sizable deductibles, nor do we know what percentage of lawyers practice in firms of five or fewer lawyers.

When demographics are applied, however, areas for loss prevention are disclosed. Information on the ages of lawyers subject to claims, for example, revealed some dramatic discrepancies. The young lawyer, who accounted for only four percent of the claims, constituted 22 percent of the lawyer population. The experienced, ten-year lawyer who gave rise to 68 percent of the claims population, constituted only 43 percent of the lawyer population. While the claims information is biased towards insured attorneys, and therefore towards attorneys who can afford insurance, the discrepancies appear too great to be so easily discounted. The experienced lawyer, skilled, busy, and maybe now sloppy, incurs a disproportionate number of legal malpractice claims and therefore is a target for loss prevention efforts.

The product of the National Legal Malpractice Data Center will enable the American Bar Association and the state and local bar associations to tailor their limited resources more efficiently to loss prevention programs to minimize, and perhaps control, legal malpractice claims. The project, however, as the field of lawyers' professional liability, is still quite new.

Liability Trends--Liability to Nonclients

Several newly developing areas of exposure seem to portend serious problems for the American lawyer. One such area concerns claims from persons with whom a lawyer has never had an attorney-client relationship and who, in fact, may have been his client's adversary. The latter group, comprising about 50 percent of all claimants, assert various theories of intentional torts. The other claimants seek to establish a negligence duty within the parameters of an attorney-client relationship owed another.

The concept of a duty of care to a person who is not a client is very new, originating in a 1961 California Supreme Court decision concerning an error in the execution of a will which deprived the plaintiff, a designated beneficiary, of the specified bequest.[2] In this case, the attorney's error not only frustrated the intent of his client but also caused an injury which both the client and the beneficiary would have wished to avoid. The court's decision was based upon a duty in tort. Some jurisdictions have a predicated duty upon a third-party beneficiary contract. Although most courts have found a duty in the will-beneficiary situation, this initial creation of duty has had a minimal intrusion in the attorney-client relationship.[3]

Not surprisingly, establishment of a duty of care to a person who is not a client has led to an assault on the citadel of privity. Many of the claims have been made by persons never intended to be benefited by the attorney, and a duty would have resulted in obvious conflicts of interest with the client, for example in situations involving buyer and seller and mortgagor or mortgagee.[4] Duty has been rejected because such situations are analogous to that involving adversaries in litigation.[5] Some situations involving adversity, however, are more subtle. For example, should an attorney for a spouse in a divorce proceeding protect the children's interests? The Illinois Supreme Court refused to imply such a duty, recognizing the potential of conflicting interests since the wife's and children's interests in the division of marital property and income may significantly differ.

Another type of claim has come from persons dissatisfied with the American legal system who sue their former opponent's attorneys. With the exception of alleged securities violations, most claims are brought against lawyers who represented plaintiffs in litigation. The common theory is for malicious prosecution, and most claims have been by physicians either seeking vindication or pursuing the belief that suing lawyers will deter future medical malpractice suits.[6] Other professionals have shown a similar intolerance to unsuccessful malpractice suits. Lawyers have been as equally unforgiving as their medical counterparts.[7]

Few malicious prosecution actions, however, ever succeed. Only rarely has an appellate court affirmed a judgment against a lawyer acting in a representative capacity for malicious prosecution.[8] Several, often unsurmountable, obstacles portend failure. The strong public policy of access to the judicial system has preserved strict requirements of pleading and proof that the proceeding was prosecuted with malice and without probable cause and that it terminated in the claimant's favor.[9] Probable cause not only presents a question of law, but is based upon an ethical standard which only requires that the claim not be "frivolous." A substantial minority of jurisdictions further require "special" injury, a type of damage other than that normally incident to being sued.[10]

The intentional tort remedies have not been successful. A response to the high frequency of tort litigation, and the many perceived groundless lawsuits has been new judicial and legislative remedies. In 1980, the United States Supreme Court, in <u>Roadway Express, Inc. v. Piper</u>, expanded the inherent power of a federal court to award attorneys' fees against a party who litigated in bad faith to also include that party's attorney.[11] Said the Supreme Court, "If a court may tax counsel fees against a party who has litigated in bad faith, it certainly may assess these expenses against counsel who willfully abused judicial processes."[12]

The Supreme Court did not delineate whether conduct less than "bad faith," such as "vexatious" litigation, would suffice. A 1983 amendment to Rule 11, however, imposes a duty upon lawyers to conduct a reasonable legal and factual investigation.[13] Bad faith has been defined as being without a "colorable basis in law," the same inquiry for probable cause in a malicious prosecution action.[14]

"Shotgun" pleadings and unmeritorious legal theories or claims may warrant the exercise of sanctions power.[15] Harassment, delay, or other improper tactics may also suffice.[16] A court found sanctions appropriate against a law firm which stubbornly resisted a motion to disqualify it for having previously represented the party it was now suing.[17] On the other hand, an unmeritorious motion to disqualify may itself incur sanctions if brought in bad faith.[18] Intentional misstatements and miscitations of law have been held to constitute evidence of bad faith.[19]

Some states have acknowledged a similar inherent power of their courts. Other states, such as California, have concluded that their courts did not have the inherent power to award attorneys' fees as sanctions for bad faith proceedings.[20] The California legislature responded with a statute for tactics or actions not based in good faith which are frivolous or cause unnecessary delay.[21]

These new judicial and legislative remedies seek to distinguish between weak but justifiable claims on one hand, and vexatious conduct and inadequate investigation on the other hand. The line between innovation and stupidity, however, is in the eyes of the beholder. These restraints will have some chilling effect. The more appropriate question is whether the ultimate price for improving the quality of litigation will be the cost of depriving some individuals of access to the courts.

Liability Trends--Judgmental Errors

As the sophistication of lawyers in prosecuting legal malpractice cases increases, and as the consumer expectation of clients also increases, lawyers are seeing their judgment decisions challenged more frequently than ever before. The immense legal malpractice exposure of lawyers for judgmental decisions, whether as advisor or advocate, arises from the constant need to make decisions where, simply stated, the "law is not a science." Judges have on occasion observed that the certainty an attorney would need to assure that no one would ever disagree with his advice could only come from equipping his library with a crystal ball.[22]

To understand the present dilemma facing the American lawyer we start, coincidentally, with the seminal legal malpractice decision originating in England in 1767, Pitt v. Yalden.[23] A solicitor retained to collect his client's debt directly caused the court to imprison the debtor but erroneously interpreted a statute, thereby enabling the debtor to be freed and the debt to be discharged. The legal malpractice case proceeded to the House of Lords, where the major issue concerned the lawyer's responsibility in interpreting an ambiguous and unclear statute. Said Lord Mansfield:

> Not only counsel, but Judges may differ, or doubt, or take time to consider. Therefore an attorney ought not to be liable in cases of reasonable doubt.[24]

This doctrine, as accepted in the American jurisdictions, protected both advisor and advocate from errors arising out of an exercise of judgment on propositions which were debatable or uncertain.

A major qualification to judgmental protection was imposed by the 1975 California Supreme Court decision of Smith v. Lewis.[25] The issue concerned an attorney's failure to advise his client to claim a community property interest in her husband's military pension in a divorce proceeding. Although the Court concluded that the legal proposition was unsettled, it also observed that the attorney had not discussed the issue with his client or conducted any legal research. The Court granted that an attorney advising a client that she had no interest in her husband's military pension could be entitled to judgmental protection. Here, however, the lawyer did not investigate, research, or counsel the client and therefore did not exercise judgment. As a consequence, said the Court, the lawyer was not entitled to the protection of the rule.

This decision involved conduct by an advisor, a lawyer seeking to counsel a client regarding appropriate future conduct. A lawyer exercises judgment when acting as an advisor or as an advocate. There is, however, a marked distinction. The advocate typically deals with past conduct whereas the advisor seeks to assist the client in determining future conduct and relationships. The advocate is result-oriented and success is usually measured in hindsight. In the litigation process, the advocate seeks those steps that will maximize the likelihood that the client will prevail. Thus, an advocate's judgment is not necessarily based on what is morally right or wrong but rather on what is tactically most likely to achieve the client's objective. This involves the art of persuasion and consideration of each circumstance for its likely effect upon the desired goal.

Judgmental protection for the advocate was recognized and expounded upon in two Tennessee decisions in the late 1970s. The initial decision was by the Tennessee Court of Appeal in Strickland v. Koella.[26] A lawyer was charged with a series of judgmental errors, such as failing to seek a change of venue, failing to have a jury trial, and failing to use discovery depositions at trial. Although some of the claims were clearly speculative, the Court analyzed the English rule of immunity for barristers and set forth the policy conclusion that, "there can be no cause of action against an attorney arising out of the manner in which he honestly chose to present his client's case to the trier of facts."[27]

The similar federal case of Woodruff v. Tomlin[28] was pending at the same time and was ultimately decided by the Sixth Circuit in 1980. The attorney was charged with failing to change venue, failing to object to jury instructions, not using a traffic reconstruction expert, and not calling witnesses. The court in its analysis distinguished between whether the lawyer was acting as an advisor or an advocate. For example, in determining the propriety of jury instructions, the court found Tennessee law to be unsettled at that time and therefore the lawyer was not liable for an error of judgment. When functioning as an advocate, the lawyer was not liable for errors in tactical decisions. For example, whether to use a traffic reconstruction or demonstrative evidence was a matter of strategy. Similarly, the lawyer could not be liable for failing to have impeached an adverse witness by cross-examination.

These decisions provided some comfort for litigation attorneys concerned about the judgmental vulnerability where virtually every decision could be second-guessed. That sense of security, however, was short-lived when in 1980 the Minnesota Supreme Court decided Togstad v. Vesely, Otto, Miller & Keefe.[29] The attorney had been consulted concerning a possible medical malpractice claim which he recommended against after interviewing the prospective client for almost an hour. Later, another lawyer reached a different opinion regarding the merits of the medical malpractice action and, as the legal malpractice action, a jury concluded that the claim would have resulted in a judgment for almost $650,000.

One of the lawyer's defenses was that his advice was a "mere error" in judgment. A lawyer expert, however, testified that he would have done different and more research than the defendant before rendering advice. Thus, said the Court, the lawyer's error was not a matter of judgment but rather a failure to adequately research and investigate.

The Togstad opinion portends a serious exposure for attorneys concerning the quantity and quality of their research and investigation. Few lawyers ever research and investigate with the same approach and to the same extent. A distinction in style may portend the basis for a legal malpractice claim should the client receive a dissatisfactory result. This exposure may adversely impact the public if lawyers decline to provide prospective clients with a candid opinion regarding the merits of the claim. An incentive for equivocation is the risk that another lawyer may disagree and that disagreement may take the form of a legal malpractice suit.

A possible solution to the attorney's dilemma can be found in the 1978 California Supreme Court decision of Kirsch v. Duryea,[30] which involved a decision by a lawyer not to pursue a lawsuit he had filed. After several years of litigating a medical malpractice action, and after consulting with physicians, the attorney decided that there was insufficient evidence to proceed. The attorney withdrew from the case upon Court order; but before the client could find new counsel, a statute of limitations expired because the case had not been brought to trial.

In the legal malpractice action, a jury concluded that the attorney's decision was erroneous and that the claim would have resulted in a judgment of $237,000. When presented to the California Supreme Court, the principal issue was whether the lawyer could be liable for an erroneous evaluation of the merits of the cause of action. The Court observed that liability depended upon the resolution of conflicting policy considerations. On one hand, the attorney was obligated to protect and pursue his client's claim. On the other hand, the attorney had an ethical responsibility not to pursue a cause in which he no longer believed. These considerations were part of the judgmental process and were not to be measured by the standard of care but rather by whether the attorney's decision to honor his obligation to the judicial system was "so manifestly erroneous that no prudent attorney would have done so."[31]

The liability of the American lawyer for judgmental decisions remains unsettled. In that lack of uncertainty itself abides a serious exposure for legal malpractice claims and a reluctance to provide candid advice where excuses may suffice. Ethical aspirations induce candor, but self-protective instincts encourage caution. The American courts will need to better define the parameters of judgmental protection. Using the marketplace of the jury system to resolve issues pertaining to judgmental errors may not be in the best interests of prospective clients who, as a consequence, may find that the advice they seek is replaced by equivocation, caveat, or excuse.

FOOTNOTES

1. The legal malpractice statistics cited in this article are drawn from the National Legal Malpractice Data Center. The Data Center recommends caution in analyzing the data. The information is based upon claims made against insured lawyers provided only by contributing insurers. We are uncertain whether claims experience of the total lawyer population differs from that of the insured lawyer. Nor do we know whether the demographic profile of the insured lawyer differs from that of the uninsured lawyer.

   Coding of a claim involves some degree of judgment. Some fields of data require more subjectivity than others, and there may be some inaccuracy because of differences in classification. The information is, however, thoroughly screened by edits in the system at the time of input to the data base and is then reviewed by the American Bar Association's staff through the National Legal Malpractice Data Center. Although there may remain some small degree of coding error, the National Legal Malpractice Data Center believes that the data base is sufficiently accurate and representative to support valid conclusions.

   Probably the greatest danger in misinterpretation is the limited information available on the demographic characteristics of the lawyer population. There is a strong temptation to draw inferences concerning what appears to be disproportionate areas of error, areas of law, or profiles of the errant practitioner without knowing whether the apparent distinctions still exist when compared to the lawyer population as a whole. As the project continues to develop, not only will such demographic information be made available, but it will also be applied and interpreted by the Data Center.

2. Lucas v. Hamm, 56 Cal.2d 583, 364 P.2d 685, 15 Cal.Rptr. 821 (1981).

3. See Mallen & Levit, _Legal Malpractice_, §622, General Principles--Privity (2d ed. 1981) (hereinafter _Legal Malpractice_).

4. _Legal Malpractice_, §602, General Principles--Privity.

5. _E.g._, _Madrasatul-Watania, Inc. v. Halperin_, 88 App.Div. 2d 503, 449 N.Y.S. 736 (1982); _Heyer v. Flaig_, 70 Cal.2d 223, 74 Cal.Rptr. 225, 449 P.2d 161 (1969).

6. See _Legal Malpractice_, §45, Malicious Prosecution--Introduction, n.56.

7. _E.g._, _Pettigrew & Bailey v. Pickel_, 429 So.2d 340 (Fla. Dist.Ct.App. 1983); _Lasswell v. Ehrlich_, 416 N.E.2d 423 (Ill.App.Ct. 1981); _Wilson v. Brooks_, 369 So.2d 1221 (Ala. 1979).

8. See _e.g._, _Peerman v. Sidicane_, 605 S.W.2d 242 (Tenn.Ct.App. 1980); _Raine v. Drasin_, 621 S.W.2d 895 (Ky. 1981) (judgment affirmed against one of two attorneys).

9. See _Legal Malpractice_, §49, Malicious Prosecution--The Cause of Action--Generally, n.87.

10. _Legal Malpractice_, §60, Malicious Prosecution--The Cause of Action--Damage.

11. 447 U.S. 752 (1980).

12. _Id._ at 766.

13. _Kuzmins v. Employee Transfer Corp._, 587 F.Supp. 536 (N.D. Ohio 1984).

14. _Analytica, Inc. v. NPD Research, Inc._, 708 F.2d 1263 (7th Cir. 1983). _Cf. Smith v. Smythe, Cramer Co._, 571 F.Supp. 58 (N.D. Ohio 1983) ("willfully abused the judicial system"). See also _Davison v. Idaho Department of Health & Welfare_, 105 Idaho 784, 673 P.2d 384 (1983).

15. _Kuzmins_, _supra_ (one of two theories held groundless).

16. _Tedeschi v. Smith, Barney, Harris Upham & Co., Inc._, 579 F.Supp. 657 (S.D.N.Y. 1984) (no "reasonable attorney" could have believed the claims could be proved).

17. _Analytica, Inc._, _supra_.

18. _Rains v. Superior Court_, 150 Cal.App.3d 933, 198 Cal. Rptr. 249 (1984).

19. Malhiot v. Southern California Retail Clerks Union, 735 F.2d 1133 (9th Cir. 1984).

20. Sun v. Langston, 170 Ga.App. 60, 316 S.E.2d 172 (1984); Berthelsen v. Hall, 194 N.J.Super. 22, 475 A.2d 1275 (1984).

21. West's Ann.Cal.Civ.Code Proc. §128.5.

22. Denzer v. Rouse, 48 Wis.2d 528, 180 N.E.2d 521 (1970).

23. 4 Burr. 2060, 98 Eng.Rep. 74 (K.B. 1767).

24. Id at 2061, 98 Eng.Rep. at 75.

25. 13 Cal.3d 349, 118 Cal.Rptr. 621, 530 P.2d 589 (1975). See also Attorney--Malpractice--Attorney's Liability for Failure to Research--Smith v. Lewis 1 Glendale L.Rev.280 (1977).

26. 546 S.W.2d 810 (Tenn.App. 1976), cert. denied, id. (Tenn. 1977).

27. Id. at 814.

28. 423 F.Supp. 1284 (W.D.Tenn. 1976).

29. 291 N.W.2d 686 (Minn. 1980).

30. 21 Cal.3d 303, 146 Cal.Rptr. 218, 578 P.2d 935 (1978).

31. 21 Cal.3d at 309, 146 Cal.Rptr. at 222, 578 P.2d at 939.

PROFESSIONAL NEGLIGENCE

London Sessions
ABA Annual Meeting 1985
Ballroom, Grosvenor House Hotel
London, England

Thursday, July 18, 1985
10:00 A.M. - 12:00 Noon

Michael Ogden, Q.C.
2 Crown Office Row
Temple, London EC4Y 7HJ

and

Sir Denis Marshall
Barlow Lyde & Gilbert
1 Finsbury Avenue
London EC2M 2PJ

Throughout discussion of this topic, one important difference between the United States and the United Kingdom must be borne in mind, namely that in this country all such cases are tried by judges sitting without juries. The practical consequences of this cannot be overstated. It affects the time taken to try cases and consequently the cost of doing so; it affects the size of damages, and liability as well. Judges are less sympathetic to plaintiffs than are juries. In practice, in this country, the only civil actions determined by juries are actions for defamation and, less commonly, false imprisonment, being usually actions against the police. It is noteworthy that even in cases in which juries specifically say that they are not awarding exemplary or punitive damages, the size of the award plainly reflects the jury's view of whether the plaintiff is a pleasant person or not.

We now turn to consider the position generally in England and Wales and the problems which exist or which we foresee will arise in the future. Unless we specifically say so, all references are confined to the position in this country.

The standard of care in such cases is that enunciated by McNair J. in Bolam v. Friern Hospital Management Committee, 1957, 1 WLR 582 at 586:

> ....where you get a situation which involves the use of some special skill or competence, then the test whether there has been negligence or not is not the test of the man on top of the Clapham omnibus, because he has not got this special skill. The test is the standard of the ordinary skilled man exercising and professing to have that special skill. A man need not possess the highest expert skill at the risk of being found negligent. It is well established law that it is sufficient if he exercises the ordinary skill of an ordinary competent man exercising that particular art...there may be one or more perfectly proper standards; and if a medical man conforms with one of those proper standards then he is not negligent...a mere personal belief that a particular technique is best is no defence unless that belief is based on reasonable grounds...a doctor is not negligent if he is acting in accordance with...a practice (accepted as proper by a responsible body of medical men skilled in that particular art), merely because there is a body of opinion that takes a contrary view. At the same time, that does not mean that a medical man can obstinately and pig-headedly carry on with some old technique if it has been proved to be contrary to what is really substantially the whole of informed medical opinion.

This, however, must be subject to the proviso that it may still be open to a court to decide that some practice adopted by most members of a profession is a negligent practice. Obviously, such cases will be rare, but a good example is the case of Edward Wong Finance Co. Ltd. v. Johnson Stokes and Master 1984 2 WLR 1 in which, in effect, the Privy Council, in an appeal from Hong Kong, decided that a conveyancing practice adopted by most solicitors in Hong Kong was negligent.

While it is clear that a professional person will not be able to avoid a finding of negligence on the ground that he fell below the general standard because of inexperience, it is not yet clear to what extent an expert in a given sphere within the profession will be expected to exercise a higher standard than others who are not specialists in that sphere. Of course, a neurologist to whom a patient is referred by his family doctor must be expected to exercise the standard of the ordinary skilled neurologist rather than the lower standard of a family doctor, who by definition does not hold himself out as being a neurologist. However, in other professions the matter is far less clear; lawyers are a good example. Most solicitors and most barristers regard themselves as experts in one or more branches of the law. Solicitors will ask advice from a particular barrister because they know that he is an expert in a particular sphere; certainly in actions against solicitors, the fact that a solicitor is generally regarded, and would himself say that he is an expert in a particular branch of the law, has not resulted in a higher standard of care being required of him by the court. Paradoxically, it seems very likely that a solicitor who instructed a counsel whom the court considered unsuitable for the task might himself be held liable to the lay client for having done so. We have in mind a young, inexperienced barrister being instructed on his own in a very complex case of a recondite nature, there being large sums at stake. In recent years barristers have been able to indicate in the Bar List that they are specialists in certain fields. Recently, The Law Society has decided to permit solicitors to advertise, and when this occurs, it is likely that solicitors will indicate spheres in which they hold themselves out as willing to accept instructions. It is difficult to see how lawyers who do this do not put themselves into exactly the same category as the neurologists, thereby holding themselves out as possessing particular expertise in the subject and being required to exercise a higher degree of expertise than other lawyers. Of course the contrary argument is that any lawyer who undertakes a case is impliedly asserting that he will conduct it with the same degree of expertise as anyone else.

At this stage, it is convenient to consider the interlined problems of fear of litigation and the availability and cost of insurance. In this country, fear of litigation does not appear to have affected the conduct of doctors and, certainly, not to the same extent as is the case in the United States. In part, this may be due to the fact that all doctors are insured under their own Professional Indemnity Scheme as are all solicitors in private practice. However, it is common to find in surveyors' reports, and to a lesser extent in accountants' and auditors' reports, disclaimers and provisos of such a nature as in some cases to water down the value of the advice given to negligible proportions.

We understand that insurers generally throughout the world are becoming increasingly wary of writing professional indemnity insurance. This is true in part because this type of insurance is written on what is termed "long tail" business (meaning that it is normal for years to elapse from the date a claim on the insured person is made, and the final closing of the file on that claim). In the meantime, increases in awards of damages, and the effects of inflation, make the accurate estimating of an economic premium to cover the ultimate cost of claims both difficult and financially hazardous. On the other side, where many years may elapse between the making of the claim and its final adjudication or settlement, there have, we believe, been cases where insurers regarded as thoroughly secure and reliable at the time the insurance is effected, going into liquidation before the claim is resolved.

Particularly affected are architects and consultant engineers. Sums claimed against architects, accountants, and consulting engineers where something has gone wrong are in some cases very large indeed, and of such amounts that even the largest firms may well be unable to obtain adequate cover.

In the case of architects in the United Kingdom, the insurance market is in an extremely difficult state because of the unhappy experience of insurers over claims. A small-to-medium-sized firm with a good claims record may well be required to pay around 7 percent of the gross fees of the firm for a year to obtain coverage of £750,000 in the aggregate for all claims in that year, and a deductible in respect of each claim of £5000. We are advised that experienced brokers have recommended their clients to maintain cover of not less than two-and-a-half times the amount of the firm's gross fees. In this country, architects as a result of the economic climate have had a very difficult time in recent years, and many cannot afford to maintain adequate cover.

Accountants are in a more favourable position. As with architects, they are recommended to take out cover for some two-and-a-half times the gross fees of the practice. For cover of £1 million pounds each and every claim, and a deductible of £10,000 each and every claim, and an aggregate deductible of £250,000 for all claims in the year, the premium might well be 1.6 to 2 percent of gross fees for the first £250,000 of cover and 1 percent of gross fees for the next £750,000. For coverage of £4 millions excess of £1 million (bringing the total of £5 millions cover), the rate would be 50 percent of the premium payable for the first £1 million pounds. The very large firms of accountants, however, can and do insure for very much larger amounts. Only the larger firms take out, or can afford to take out, cover for £10 millions, and only the very largest take out £100 millions. It will be seen that accountants' premiums are substantially lower than architects. Indeed all professions are separately rated according to underwriters views of the exposure, but in the case of most professions the statistics available are far from complete.

The problem is very real and is likely to get worse. Decent, respectable, large companies do not bankrupt their own professional advisers if something goes wrong and will usually be content to settle for the full extent of the insurance cover. However, not all plaintiffs are decent or respectable. Some, who have a grudge against their lawyer, would be only too delighted to see him bankrupted. In our view, it is extremely unsatisfactory that the present situation exposes professional men to the risk of bankruptcy in circumstances in which it is either completely impossible or financially impracticable for them to obtain adequate insurance cover.

It may be said that it is always possible for the professional man to exclude liability. In practice this is an unsatisfactory solution. Professional men are reluctant to act in this fashion and it is very difficult for some people to do so when their competitors do not do so. Equally, it is very unsatisfactory to find professional men excluding or limiting liability in cases in which the resultant claim is for a small sum especially when the claim is being made by a private person of only moderate means.

The sensible solution for the United Kingdom may well be one which would prevent exclusion of liability in respect of small claims, and therefore go further than the Unfair Contract Terms Act 1977 (which subjects exemption clauses to a test of reasonableness), while, at the same time, protecting professional men from catastrophic claims which would bankrupt them. In this country, the limit would protect people of moderate means would not be more than £500,000, since this exceeds the value of an ordinary house and also is roughly the size of the highest sum of damages awarded in a personal injuries or fatal accident case, although it may well be that personal injury and fatal accident cases could simply be excluded from the limiting provision. The basis of the necessary legislation would be that it would be made impossible to exclude liability for sums less than £500,000 or whatever other figure is fixed upon, that professional men should be obliged to insure in respect to all claims up to that figure, and that in return they should not be liable for sums in excess of that figure unless they specifically contract to be so liable. These were the main recommendations of a Sub-Committee of the United Kingdom Inter-Professional Group, consisting of a barrister, solicitor, doctor, and an architect in 1979. In our view, these proposals would find ready acceptance by the public and also commercial institutions. In this connection it must be remembered that insurance premiums constitute an overhead of which regard must be taken when the client is charged for the services rendered and the payment of very large premiums are bound to increase the prices charged and, particularly so, if additional insurance cover is being obtained for a particular job, e.g., the design of a very expensive bridge or building. However, it must be said that at the present time no professional body has come out in favour of the recommendations in the Sub-Committee's Report, and none have adopted them.

Traditionally, professional people in this country practised on their own or in small partnerships. As a result of legislation permitting larger partnerships, these have now come into being. The combination of larger partnerships and the insurance problems already mentioned are causing suggestions that professional people should be able to form limited companies. A further factor leading to such demands is that large claims can arise from the negligence of an employee, for whose conduct all partners are legally liable, even where they had no personal knowledge or involvement in the matter. In passing, it is noteworthy that in this country employers do not sue their employees unless they have been dishonest.

The pressure for these changes is strongest in those professions concerned in construction work, where the claims may be enormous, and members of which may find themselves in competition with limited liability companies, employing professional people as salaried employees and whose directors are likely to be immune from suit should the company go into liquidation through inability to meet a substantial claim arising from negligence. It seems extremely unfortunate that the basis upon which professional people have long worked, with its attendant advantages to clients, should be endangered by the extraneous factors mentioned. Having said this, there does not appear to be any general pressure from the professions taken as a whole towards limitation or exclusion of liability for negligence, and this may be due to the availability of insurance cover even though as mentioned before at increasing cost.

The scope of the duty of care has been much extended by the courts in recent years. Insofar as the professions are concerned, this has largely mirrored the attitude of the courts in negligent cases generally. However, the persons to whom the duty of care is owed include those whom lawyers would not have contemplated as being within the scope of duty in former times. Liability for negligent misstatement (Hedley Byrne, 1964 AC 465) has added widely to the number of prospective claimants. An example of the extension of the scope of duty can be seen in Anns v. Merton, 1978 AC 728, in which a local authority was held liable to lessees of flats which suffered damage because of the local authority's failure to ensure compliance with building bye-laws during construction of the building. (For an interesting combination of the two concepts in which a valuer for a building society was held liable to the mortgagor, see Yianni v. Edwin Evans and Sons, 1982 QB 438).

The Limitation Acts continue to cause problems, not only to professional people, but also to their insurers and are contributory factors to the reluctance of insurers to write such risks as already mentioned. Between 1963 and 1980, no less than three statutes were enacted by Parliament, all of which made significant alterations to the law. Inevitably, these statutes themselves resulted in considerable and complex litigation. By definition, the effect of a Limitation Act is to exclude from recovering damages some plaintiffs who would have been able to do so had they commenced their proceedings in time. Inevitably there is a tendency for courts to view benevolently a plaintiff who, through no fault on his part, may be excluded because he started his proceedings too late. The maxim that hard cases make bad law is seldom more apparent than in such cases. The combination of Parliament's legislation and the very natural sympathy of the courts to plaintiffs in such cases have undoubtedly caused difficulties in this country. An example of the problem is when a person of unsound mind suffers bodily injury, in which event the limitation period will be extended until three years after he ceased to be under the disability, which for practical purposes may extend the period indefinitely (Limitation Act 1980 Section 28). Of course, the problems involved in trying such a case fairly are enormous.

The problem just mentioned, relating to personal injury cases involving minors and persons of unsound mind does not arise very frequently. However, great difficulties are being experienced in cases involving the construction industry. The origin of the problem can probably be seen to be the reversal of the court's view that if a contract existed a party to the contract had rights only in contract and not in tort (Groom v. Crocker, 1939, 1 KB 194,205). In a series of cases decided in the past ten years, the courts have made decisions proving the correctness of J. A. Weir's observation in 1963 C.L.J.216 that since Hedley Byrne v. Heller, 1964 AC 465, "All breaches of contract which might with reasonable care have been avoided became torts overnight" (Batty v. Metropolitan Realisations Ltd., 1978, 2 WLR 500: Midland Bank Trust Co. v. Hett, Stubbs & Kemp, 1978, 3 WLR 167 Junior Books Ltd. v. Veitchie Co. Ltd., 1983 AC 520. This has had profound effect upon actions under the Limitation Acts, in that whereas time begins to run in contract at the date of the breach, in tort time starts running at the date when damage is caused by the tortious act. The consequences of this, particularly in the construction industry, are obvious in that defects may not occur for many years after the building has been completed. Of course, this has given rise to extremely difficult factual problems concerning the date upon which it could be said that damage occurred. The problem was considered by the House of Lords in Pirelli General Cable Works Ltd. v. Oscar Faber & Partners, 1983, 2 AC 1. The House decided that the cause of action accrues from the moment when the building suffers damage even if such damage cannot be seen with the naked eye. The exception to this general proposition was said to be cases where the defect is so gross that the building is "doomed from the start," in which event the cause of action accrues as soon as the building is built. The precise ambit of this latter point has been the subject of litigation at first instance and, at the time of writing this paper, the point remains to be decided.

Of course, the difficulty at the heart of the problem lies in the fact that whereas in one case it might be advantageous to a plaintiff to say that his cause of action did not accrue until later, in another case it would be advantageous for him to say the reverse. A plaintiff whose claims would otherwise be barred by the

Limitation Acts will obviously wish to say that the cause of action accrues at a time when the limitation period has not expired. However, a building owner who discovers shortly after the building has been completed that there are defects which will cause damage or may do so (and the distinction is important) will wish to be able to sue as soon as possible for fear that, if he delays, the person responsible, for example the builder, may have gone into liquidation, thereby leaving him with doubtful remedies against the architect or consulting engineer.

The position of lawyers in this country differs from those of other professional people in one important respect. Both barristers and solicitors are immune from suit for negligence when undertaking certain types of work (Rondel v. Worsley, 1969, 1 AC 191 and Saif Ali v. Sydney Mitchell & Co., 1980 AC 198). For many years it had been generally assumed that barristers were immune from suit but that solicitors were not. This supposed general immunity was of such antiquity that it is difficult to be certain upon what grounds it rested in former times. Certainly one of them was that, since a barrister cannot sue for his fees, there was no contractual relation between barristers and the litigant. Furthermore, it was thought that there could not be liability for negligent misstatement. However, in recent years, as in most common law countries, the boundaries of negligence have been considerably extended, while in Hedley Byrne & Co. Ltd. v. Heller & Partners, 1964 AC 465, it was firmly established that a person is liable for damage caused by negligent misstatement.

In the cases cited, the House reconsidered the problem afresh and decided that barristers were immune from suit when conducting cases in court and for some pre-trial work. Insofar as the extent of the immunity for pre-trial work is concerned, in the majority of speeches in the Saif Ali case, part of the judgment of McCarthy P. in the New Zealand Court of Appeal in Rees v. Sinclair, 1974, 1 NZLR 180, 187, was cited with approval. He said as follows:

> I cannot narrow the protection to what is done in Court: it must be wider than that and include some pre-trial work. Each piece of before trial work should, however, be tested against the one rule; that the protection exists only where the particular work is so intimately connected with the conduct of the cause in Court that it can fairly be said to be a preliminary decision affecting the way that cause is to be conducted when it comes to a hearing. The protection should not be given any wider application than is absolutely necessary in the interests of the administration of justice and that is why I would not be prepared to include anything which does not come within the test I have stated.

In the course of the two cases in the House of Lords which are cited above, consideration was given to the position of solicitors. Although the observations made are technically obiter dicta, it can be said with confidence that they represent the law, which is to the effect that solicitors who are conducting litigation are protected to the same extent as if a barrister had been acting.

The reason for the decision was put fairly and squarely on the basis of public policy. This concept has been much canvassed in recent years (Dorset Yacht Co. Ltd. v. Home Office, 1970 AC 1004, Anns v. Merton London Borough Council, 1978 AC 728, and McLoughlin v. O'Brian, 1983 AC 410) and it is undoubtedly now a well-established reason for withholding a remedy in appropriate cases. A number of reasons were advanced in the Rondel and Saif Ali cases for the proposition that immunity ought to exist in such cases, such as the fact that it is part of the general immunity from civil liability which attaches to all persons in respect to their participation in proceedings before a court of justice, judges, court officials, witnesses, parties counsel, and solicitors alike; the fact that a barrister owes a duty to the court as well as to his client and should not be inhibited through fear of an action by his client from performing it; long usage; and the fact that a barrister is obliged to act for any client, however difficult, who sought his services in the type of work which the barrister was accustomed to do for a fee for which he would usually ask for doing such work. However, the present writers consider that the reason given by the House of Lords which, even if standing alone, would entirely justify the decision is what Lord Diplock described in Saif Ali as "the need to maintain the integrity of public justice."

There was a time when criminals, however reluctantly, would accept that, if the Court of Appeal dismissed their appeal against conviction, that was the end of the matter. It is certainly not so today. As it is, some convicted persons will try every possible and many impossible avenues to attempt to reopen their cases. There can be no doubt that if they were able to sue their lawyers for their conduct of the case, they would do so in large numbers. Nearly all such cases would be utterly without merit, and as Lord Salmon put it in Saif Ali, Rondel's complaint against his counsel was that the shocking injuries in respect of which he had been convicted had been inflicted with his teeth and bare hands rather than with a knife, admitting to the judge who heard the application that he was not alleging that had counsel cross-examined the witnesses as he had wished he would have had any chance of being acquitted. This is a fair measure of the kind of case which would ensue had the House of Lords reached a different conclusion about the public policy point. So too, the same kind of thing would undoubtedly arise in civil actions in those cases in which a litigant was not prepared to accept any final determination of the case against him. In the experience of the writers of this article, the present system works well and without complaint from the public.

The division of the legal profession in England and Wales into two branches, barristers and solicitors, creates situations which may not be immediately apparent to those accustomed to a jurisdiction where all lawyers are in a fused profession and subject to the same disciplines, as in the United States. The barrister is the specialist lawyer who alone has rights of audience before the higher courts, whereas both barristers and solicitors may each appear as advocates in the lower courts.

By Rules of Conduct, a barrister may not receive instructions from lay persons in England and Wales directly, and must do so through instructions from a solicitor, although he may be instructed directly from overseas. Again, by Rule of Conduct, a solicitor who thus instructs a barrister to perform legal work is himself liable for payment of the barrister's fees, even though for any reason he may not be able to recover these from his lay client. Thus, the relationship between the lay client and the barrister being at one stage removed through the intermediary of a solicitor, coupled with the absence of any contractual relationship between them, has to be borne in mind.

It is, of course, now established that despite this absence of any direct contractual relationship, the barrister owes a duty in tort to the lay client not to act negligently, subject, of course, to his immunity from suit in conducting advocacy which has been discussed earlier.

Where the solicitor has instructed a barrister in a particular matter, one might think that by reason of his taking this action he would be released from liability to the client should something go wrong. This is by no means necessarily so. As has already been made clear, the solicitor in the performance of his obligations has to exercise that standard of care and skill which is demanded from a reasonably competent and diligent solicitor, and he cannot divest himself of his duties to his client by instructing a barrister, even where the client has approved. However, errors of judgment or ignorance on some point of law, which will occur from time to time, do not necessarily constitute negligence of a solicitor unless it be established that an ordinarily competent solicitor would not have made the error or would have been unaware of the relevant law.

Solicitors are, however, responsible for the consequence of ignorance or nonobservance of rules of practice, for the want of care in the preparation of the cause for trial, and for the mismanagement of so much of the conduct of the cause as is usually and ordinarily allotted to the solicitors' branch of the Profession (Montriou v. Jeffreys-1825 2 C & P 113).

A solicitor is not required to know every statute, but he must be familiar with those which would be known to the competent solicitor, particularly the Statutes of Limitation. If he is ignorant of the law on a point, he must either inform himself of it, or if it is difficult or doubtful must recommend that counsel's opinion be obtained. Having taken this step, if the lay-client then refuses the advice, the solicitor will only be liable in negligence if it is shown that he should have had the requisite knowledge of the law himself. Even when counsel's opinion has been obtained, he must still exercise care in checking the advice received, and will not be absolved from responsibility for failing to observe obvious errors.

Professional indemnity insurance is not a popular form of protection in the insurance market, and as has been said about certain professional groups, particularly architects and consulting engineers, there is no doubt that the potentially very large liabilities, which first come to light sometimes many years after the professional services in question have been performed, have created a difficult situation.

Nevertheless it is contended that in the conditions of the 1980s, the existence of adequate and reliable professional indemnity insurance is an essential element to the carrying on of professional practice, and while professional indemnity insurance continues to be available, then the case for exclusion or limitation of liability by contract obviously is diminished. Indeed, it is not, of course, possible for professional persons to evade their liability in tort for negligence in those cases where there is no contractual relationship with the claimant, unless by statute some form of limitation of liability were to become applicable in all cases.

To summarise, in this country there are real fears that the continued availability of adequate and secure cover at reasonable cost, particularly in cases where the amount of cover required is substantial, may not continue, and that the unlimited potential exposure of the professional person and firms requires serious consideration, perhaps along the lines of the proposals in the U.K. Inter-Professional Group Sub-Committee's Report.

WHAT AN ARBITRATOR CAN DO TO OVERCOME DELAYS IN INTERNATIONAL ARBITRATION

London Sessions
ABA Annual Meeting 1985
Haberdashers' Company
London, England

Thursday, July 18, 1985
2:00 P.M. - 4:00 P.M.

The Hon. Howard M. Holtzmann
Iran-U.S. Claims Tribunal
Parkweg 13, 2585 JH The Hague
The Netherlands

Several comments are needed at the outset: first, while this program focuses on the need for "Overcoming Delays in International Arbitration--by Courts, Parties and Arbitrators," it must be remembered that not all international commercial arbitrations suffer from that problem. In many cases, those concerned admirably live up to the traditional motto of the American Arbitration Association: "Speed, Economy and Justice." The problem of delay is, nevertheless, sufficiently prevalent and serious to warrant our attention. Second, any discussion of this topic must recognize that international commercial arbitration encompasses a wide variety of disputes in which the procedures range from casually informal to highly structured. I will concentrate on the conduct of relatively complex commercial cases of the type that have become increasingly important in world trade. Third, my remarks are not intended to relate to the Iran-United States Claims Tribunal. That arbitral body presently sitting in The Hague operates in unique circumstances upon which I, as one of its Members, hesitate to comment at this stage of its history. Lastly, to put our subject into perspective, it is only fair to observe that delay is endemic to most litigation, be it in courts or before arbitral tribunals. How many of us have known a defendant who was in a hurry, or a lawyer in a large case who did not have a busy schedule elsewhere?

I start from the premise that an effective system of international commercial arbitration is important in facilitating world trade, and that world trade is one of the building blocks of world peace. We are thus dealing not only with the concerns and costs of particular litigants, but also with matters of broader public significance. As the American Bar Association and the American Arbitration Association jointly have stated, "The use of commercial arbitration to resolve a wide variety of disputes has grown extensively and forms a significant part of the system of justice which our society relies upon for the fair determination of legal rights." Preamble to ABA-AAA Code of Ethics for Arbitrators in Commercial Disputes (herein called "Code of Ethics").

The cures for delay that I will discuss relate mainly to the attitudes of arbitrators. My thesis is that more arbitrators in complex international cases should recognize that they have a responsibility for the pace of the proceedings. In my view, adopting an activist attitude is the most important contribution an arbitrator can make toward overcoming delay. John Locke wrote that a man makes progress by "steadily intending his mind in a given direction." If arbitrators will steadily direct their attention to achieving more efficient conduct of their cases, the procedural techniques to be used need not be revolutionary. Indeed, a number of demonstrated techniques already exist. See, e.g., Poppleton, The Arbitrator's Role in Expediting the Large and Complex Commercial Case, Arbitration Journal, Dec. 1981, at 6.

The subtitle of this essay might well be "Ten Easy Ways for an Arbitrator to Avoid Delay." I say "easy ways" because the steps I suggest do not depart from either the traditions of the Anglo-American adversarial system or the inquisitorial system that characterizes civil law procedure; they do not require legislative reform in any country I know; and they can be accommodated within most sets of arbitration rules that parties are accustomed to adopt in international commercial contracts. Nor do the attitudes of activism and the techniques that I advocate run against the grain of the common law, although some might occasionally require the sympathetic understanding of the courts--which I am confident they will receive.

Here are my suggestions of a number of practical ways arbitrators can help to overcome delay in complex cases.

1. Always Remember the Sloth and the Dinosaur

While I have characterized my advice as being "easy ways," I do not underestimate the resistance to changing ingrained attitudes and habits of mind. One widely accepted attitude is that arbitrators have a relatively passive role, influencing the pace of proceedings only by deciding disputes between the parties on such matters as setting schedules and granting adjournments or extensions, and even then being quite permissive. The prevalent attitude in England--and it has not been very much different in the United States--is described by Sir Michael J. Mustill and Stewart C. Boyd in their perceptive book, <u>The Law and Practice of Commercial Arbitration in England</u> 17 (1982):

> [T]he procedural initiative lies entirely with the parties.... Unless invited to decree what is to happen next, the arbitrator need not, and in most cases does not, do anything at all. The responsibility for maintaining the momentum of the reference rests entirely with the parties.

The authors were describing one existing practice, not necessarily advocating it. Indeed, the quoted passage is followed by the comment that, "This is not to suggest that the role of the arbitrator is merely supine. On the contrary, a good arbitrator will stamp his personality on the proceedings in such a way as to ensure that the proceedings are conducted with the minimum of effort, delay and expense." <u>Id</u>.

The all too typical attitude that the responsibility for the momentum and pace of arbitral proceedings rests solely with the parties is the first thing that must change if delay is to be overcome. A strong stimulus to changing that attitude could come if arbitrators were to look at arbitration as others see it. I recently received a letter from a young woman who works in a law firm that handles a number of complex international arbitration cases. She observed:

> That little Sloth called Arbitration is a slow animal. People often study the Sloth's habits, but its motions are

> difficult to see from far away. Actually, motion is difficult to perceive from close up. This muddled creature sits all day (and all night) eating what the caretakers heap before its big, gaping mouth, but it rarely rises or makes distinct motions, aside from swallowing. The Sloth has a mouth larger than the rest of its body, and yet it hardly makes a noise. You would think that an animal who is all mouth, would consequently be all sound. And yet, this peculiar species seems only capable of ingesting large quantities of paper fibers with no supplemental nourishment. Its talents have degenerated into some of the most basic activities of life--indiscriminately eating all heaps in sight and processing them thoroughly. Our little analogy could be stretched further, to a point beyond tasteful boundaries. But, let it suffice to say that the arbitration Sloth, must be waited on, and waited for, for indefinite periods of time.

(In deference to my correspondent's cases, I will not reveal her name.)

Assuming that arbitrators are prepared to recognize the slothfulness of some arbitrations, how do we overcome the common notion that it is up to the parties, not the arbitrators, to take procedural initiatives? I suggest that if you accept my premise that international commercial arbitration has an important role in facilitating world trade, and consequently in promoting world peace, you will agree that it is not for the parties alone to determine how it should be conducted, because there is a broader public interest to be served. Thus arbitrators have a responsibility to assure that the acceptability of arbitration is not undermined by a persistent reputation for costly delay. This is not a new or radical idea. For example, the Code of Ethics begins by stressing that:

> [f]air and just processes for resolving disputes are indispensable in our society. Commercial arbitration is an important method for deciding many types of disputes.... <u>Therefore, an arbitrator has a responsibility not only to the parties but also to the process of arbitration itself</u>....

Canon I, para. A (emphasis added). The Code of Ethics goes on to enunciate specifically the arbitrator's professional responsibility to avoid delay:

> An arbitrator should perform duties diligently and conclude the case as promptly as the circumstances reasonably permit.

Canon IV, para. B.

In addition to remembering the sloth, arbitrators would also do well to recall the fate of the dinosaur. The dinosaur is the beast that became so large, cumbersome, and slow that it could no longer survive. As arbitration cases become larger and slower, the process faces a similar danger of obsolescence. Any such development would create serious practical difficulties in world trade, for trade is hampered when a prompt and economical method of resolving disputes is not available. That is because businessmen then consider that the risk in the transaction is increased, and they react by either refusing to enter into what they consider an overly hazardous arrangement, or they increase the price.

For these reasons, I suggest that the first step for arbitrators to take in developing the necessary activist attitude is to resolve always to remember the sloth and the dinosaur.

2. Don't Accept To Serve If You Are Too Busy

Chronologically, the first opportunity for an arbitrator to avoid delay arises when he or she is approached to serve. If you are too busy, say "No." That is not merely avuncular advice. It is an ethical obligation, laid down in the Code of Ethics in the light of practical experience. The ethical mandate of Canon I is:

> Persons should accept appointment as arbitrators only if they believe that they can be available to conduct the arbitration promptly.

3. Don't Just Schedule the Proceedings, Plan Them

There is a profound difference between merely establishing a schedule and thoughtfully planning a proceeding. Scheduling involves setting dates; planning requires analyses of what must be done, the sequence in which actions will be taken, and making informed guesses as to how long each of the necessary steps will take. On the basis of a plan, a schedule ensues. As the poet Robert Burns has taught us, the best laid plans of arbitrators go "aft agley." But the important thing is that the arbitrator establish a comprehensive plan against which to measure progress, recognizing always that the plan will need to be modified in the light of developing circumstances. The fact that things may change is no excuse for not making a plan. Businessmen recognize that plans are indispensable, even in an uncertain world; arbitrators should do no less.

A realistic plan not only provides coherence for the proceedings, but also aids the parties and their lawyers in preparing the case and scheduling their other activities.

4. Arrange for the Parties to Submit Complete Written Statements of the Case in Advance of the Hearing

The modern trend in international commercial arbitration favors submission by the parties at an early stage of a full written statement of the claim and defense, including each party's description of the basis of arbitral jurisdiction, the points at issue in the case, the facts and law supporting the claim, and the amount and basis of the relief sought. Submission of the relevant contracts and supporting documentary evidence at an early stage is also encouraged. Examples of this trend can be seen in the UNCITRAL Arbitration Rules, arts. 18, 19, and the International Arbitration Rules of the London Court of Arbitration, art. 6 & sched. B, para. 8. On the other hand, the American Arbitration Association's Commercial Arbitration Rules do not require detailed written submissions by the parties (*see* sec. 7), although in practice extensive written submissions are usually made in complex cases. Mustill and Boyd describe a typical English practice in *ad hoc* arbitration in which:

> [t]he parties do not by written means set forth their case in advance of the hearing. They exchange "pleadings"; but these are not statements of fact or evidence, and often are not sent to the arbitrator. There is therefore nothing in the nature of the *dossier*, built up by the contributions of the parties, and kept under continuous review by the arbitrator.... Instead the presumption is that the arbitrator will come to the hearing with a completely fresh mind, and will reach his conclusion on the basis of what is then laid before him, and nothing less.

M. Mustill & S. Boyd, *supra*, at 18.

In view of the wide variations in practice and possible differences in the expectations of the parties, particularly when they have different national backgrounds, it is important that an international arbitrator should very soon inform them that he wishes to receive complete statements of their cases and describe what he wants the statements to include. Article 6 of the International Arbitration Rules of the London Court of Arbitration are a convenient guide in this respect. Arbitrators can make their wishes known by correspondence or at an informal pre-hearing conference with all the parties. It may be desirable to determine from the parties the time each will reasonably need to comply. The investment of time at the start of the process to secure complete statements of the case will avoid delays later by preventing surprise, and will assist preparation by the parties and the arbitrators for a complete and effective hearing. The power of arbitrators in this respect is explicit, or implied, under most rules and laws, and, in any event, parties will normally consent to make written submissions requested by the arbitral tribunal.

5. Make Effective Use of Pre-Hearing Conferences

There is increasing use of pre-hearing conferences in complex cases. The power of arbitrators to call such conferences is at least implied in applicable arbitral rules or under governing law. Even if it is not explicit or implied, there is little likelihood of legal questions arising concerning the appropriateness of such a conference, because the parties can be expected to consent to participate in a pre-hearing conference when invited to do so by the person who will decide their case. The principal pre-hearing conference is usually held soon after both parties have submitted statements of their cases but in some situations might well be held even earlier. Of course, all parties must be given adequate notice of the conference and be treated equally.

The only list of topics for a pre-hearing conference included in any arbitral rules that I know is the Guideline prepared by the Iran-United States Claims Tribunal. 1 Iran-U.S. C.T.R. 98 (1983). That list, although unique in that it is codified, reflects practice successfully followed in various courts and in *ad hoc* arbitrations. Use of this Guideline has generally been helpful, and the following discussion is based in part on it.

The matters that might be considered at a pre-hearing conference include:

- Clarification of the issues presented and the relief sought. This is particularly helpful if previous written statements fail to result in a clear joinder of issues;

- Identification of any issues to be considered as preliminary questions. This is important because it may be possible to dispose of all, or part, of a case on the basis of a prompt decision on a preliminary question;

- Determination of whether any further written statements will be required (*e.g.*, an exchange of pre-hearing briefs). This leads to early consideration of the completeness of the previous written statements;

- Getting an early idea as to what additional documents or other evidence the parties intend to submit or the arbitral tribunal might consider helpful, and fixing a schedule for submission prior to the hearing. Establishing the procedure that the authenticity of all such documents is admitted, and that all letters and telexes submitted by the sender were received by the addressee, unless challenged in advance of the hearing. This will avoid formally proving points that are not contested and save time at the hearing. Determining which, if any, documents will require translation;

- Determining whether voluminous and complicated data should be presented through summaries, tabulations, charts, graphs, or extracts in order to save time and costs. Arranging for the other party to have an opportunity before the hearing to review the underlying data on which the summaries, tabulations, etc., are allegedly based;

- Considering the extent to which testimony of witnesses can appropriately be presented in the form of sworn written statements, while recognizing that the affiant would also normally be expected to be available at the hearing for cross-examination. This can greatly expedite the hearing;

- Discussing whether the parties intend to present experts, and, if so, the qualifications of, and the areas of expertise to be covered by, any such experts. In some cases, particularly where arbitrators have civil law backgrounds, the arbitral tribunal may wish to appoint its own expert. Exploration of that possibility is desirable at an early stage.

- Determining the earliest date when the parties can be ready to submit lists of their witnesses, together with an indication of the subject on which each will testify. See, e.g., UNCITRAL Arbitration Rules, art. 25, para. 2; and

- Discussing whether the parties can stipulate their agreement on any issues of fact or law. There are usually some matters on which the parties can agree. Identification of these can save time at the hearing.

On the basis of the information elicited at the pre-hearing conference, it should be possible for the arbitrators to make a comprehensive plan for the proceedings. To the extent possible, a schedule of specific dates should be included in the plan, but it may be that in some cases all dates cannot be determined at so early a stage.

An additional advantage of the pre-hearing conference in an international case is that the occasion brings the parties to the same city, providing them with a convenient opportunity to discuss among themselves the possibility of settlement. The discussions at the pre-hearing conference can help to impart realism to settlement negotiations. Settlement is, of course, the best way to overcome delay.

6. Streamline The Hearing

A major factor in streamlining the hearing is to assure that the case--and the arbitrators--are well prepared before it takes place. Various steps that will contribute to that have been referred to above in my discussion of statements of the case and pre-hearing conferences. It is also helpful to arrange for the hearing to be held on consecutive days rather than as sporadic episodes. A certain momentum tends to build up in continuous hearings; memories are fresher and repetition is avoided. In the arithmetic of arbitration, an uninterrupted whole is usually less lengthy than the sum of separated parts.

Perhaps the greatest spur to an efficient hearing is an arbitral tribunal that is able tactfully to convey that, while it wishes each party to have full opportunity to present its case, it is impatient with repetition, irrelevance, and rhetoric. Maintaining a calm atmosphere also helps. Overly contentious statements and provocation by counsel are not only time-consuming in themselves, but they breed similar responses from opposing counsel, thereby at least doubling the time wasted.

7. Don't Be Afraid To Speak Up

It is conventional wisdom that the safest way for arbitrators to avoid having their awards vacated by the courts for misconduct or bias is to say little and to accept all evidence and argument, no matter how irrelevant or repetitive. While that is the most cautious conduct, it is the least expeditious. In my view, arbitrators can and should help speed a case by indicating, where appropriate, what they consider to be the key issues, any provisional views they may have reached, what additional evidence or legal argument they think is needed, and when they feel submissions are irrelevant or repetitious. Mustill and Boyd sum up this position with characteristic directness:

> [I]f the arbitrator has come to provisional conclusions on an individual issue or issues there are occasions on which "showing his hand" can produce tangible saving in time, and hence in expense, and the arbitrator should not be inhibited from doing so, in a proper case, by the fear that the Court might afterwards find evidence of bias. Moreover, although patience is an important attribute of any person acting judicially, there is no call for it to be limitless. Provided he displays courtesy and moderation, an arbitrator does not display bias by making it clear that he disapproves of the manner in which, or the length at which, a party is putting forward his case.

M. Mustill & S. Boyd, <u>supra</u>, at 219.

8. Don't Let One Party Paralyze the Proceedings

Arbitration rules typically empower arbitrators to proceed with the arbitration if a party who has been duly notified of a hearing fails to appear without showing good cause; they also generally permit arbitrators to make an award on the evidence before them if a party invited to produce evidence fails to do so in a timely fashion and does not show sufficient cause for the failure. <u>See, e.g.</u>, UNCITRAL Arbitration Rules, art. 28, paras. 2, 3; AAA Commercial Arbitration Rules, sec. 30; International Arbitration Rules of the London Court of Arbitration, sched. B, para. 9. Such powers may well exist under the applicable law, even in cases not governed by such rules. Arbitrators should remember this vital power and not hesitate to remind parties that they intend to use it when the circumstances so dictate. Such a warning discourages dilatory conduct. The eventual use of the power is the ultimate means by which arbitrators can prevent paralysis of the proceedings.

9. Don't Be Afraid of the Courts

Courts accustomed to the sloth and the dinosaur may be surprised when they see a gazelle leap swiftly out of the jungle of arbitration, but I believe they will welcome the sight. Judges who are themselves wrestling with the problem of overcoming delay in their own cases can be expected to be sympathetic to arbitrators trying to do the same thing. Moreover, there is a strong trend in the law in the United States, the United Kingdom, and elsewhere to uphold arbitral awards. Therefore, I think that arbitrators need not fear that an activist attitude and the use of techniques such as those that I have described will result in courts overturning their awards, provided, of course, that the arbitrators treat the parties equally, give each a fair opportunity to present its case, and follow any procedural requirements prescribed by contract or applicable rules.

This is, however, a topic that is more for the distinguished judges on this program to comment on than for me, and I eagerly await their views.

10. Decide Promptly

This point needs no elaboration.

Conclusion

Arbitrators in international commercial cases have a professional responsibility to work to overcome delay. They can best accomplish this by adopting an activist attitude and by utilizing a number of available procedural techniques. The task is important in order to preserve arbitration as a viable element in a worldwide system of justice, to facilitate international trade, and thereby to contribute to world peace. Activist arbitrators can help to achieve this goal.

DELAYS IN ARBITRATION: THE ROLE OF THE COURT

London Sessions
ABA Annual Meeting 1985
Haberdashers' Company
London, England

Thursday, July 18, 1985
2:00 P.M. - 4:00 P.M.

The Rt. Hon. Lord Justice Mustill
Royal Courts of Justice
Strand, London WC2A 2LL

So far as concerns the effect, in terms of delay, of the supervisory powers exercised by the English courts over the arbitral process, three topics must be considered:

- o The power of the courts to intervene during the reference;
- o The power of the courts to prevent the reference of a dispute from being a source of delay in the enforcement of valid claims; and
- o The effect of recourse to the courts as a source of delay in the completion of the reference and the enforcement of the award.

By way of introduction, it is necessary to describe briefly the origin, nature, and mode of exercise of the supervisory power.

The relationship between the courts and the arbitral process in England has always been close. One form of arbitration sprang from proceedings in court. If an action involved complex accounts or technical issues, the court had power to refer these matters to an arbitrator for a report. The action continued in existence, but was temporarily abated. The court retained control over the proceedings, in two major respects. First, it lent its coercive powers to the parties so that the order referring the matter to arbitration, and any resulting award, could be enforced. Second, the court has a right to intervene by setting aside the award in various situations, notably if there was procedural injustice ("misconduct") or if the award displayed on its face an error of law by the arbitrator.

It was recognised at an early date that voluntary arbitration out of court was less satisfactory than arbitration stemming from an action in court, because of the absence of any mechanism for compelling the parties to arbitrate and to honour the award. Accordingly, a series of statutes extending over more than 200 years enabled the parties to an arbitration which did not stem from court proceedings to have the reference nevertheless treated as if it took place pursuant to a "rule of court," thus entitling them to call for the exercise of the court's coercive powers. This did, however, bring with it a subjection to the supervisory powers of the court.

Even today, arbitrations are treated as if they were governed by the old system, and the court retains its old inherent powers (except for the abolition by statute of the power to set aside for error on the face of the award).

In addition to these inherent powers, derived from the long-standing and intimate relationship between arbitration and the courts, there has been a process of legislation whereby individual powers have been conferred on the courts. One of these powers, which enables the court to remit an award to the arbitrator as an alternative to the more far-reaching remedy of setting-aside, is concerned with judicial control of the reference. The remainder have the object of sustaining and reinforcing the arbitral process, by empowering the court to exercise rights which either cannot be, or have not been, conferred on the arbitrator by the contract to arbitrate. These include powers to grant injunctions; to order the inspection and preservation of property; to compel the attendance of witnesses; to prevent the dissipation of the respondent's assets before an award is made against him; and to order certain categories of respondents to give security for any award of costs which may be made against them.

Two important points must be made on the inherent and statutory powers thus summarised. In the first place, they do not include any general jurisdiction to intervene where the reference is still in progress to correct any actual or threatened procedural injustice. During the 1970s, certain decisions asserted a novel power to this effect, but this concept was firmly repudiated by the House of Lords in Bremer Vulkan v. South India Shipping.[1-2] At first sight, it may seem anomalous that a court which does have power to remedy an injustice after an award is made should deny itself the opportunity to intervene at the moment when the injustice is ripe. Nevertheless, I suggest that it would have been unfortunate if any such power had been upheld, since even if in practice the court had only rarely exercised the power, there would have been opportunity for repeated delays in completing the arbitration, whilst one party or another applied to the court for the redress of real or imagined grievances.

Secondly, the absence of any express limit on the powers of the court to set aside or remit the award may appear to offer ample scope for judicial meddling, and consequent delay.[3] In practice, the use of the powers is circumscribed by a long history of judicial decision, emphasising that the court will grant relief only in the clearest cases of injustice, and will not account it an injustice if the arbitrator, consistently with the express or implied terms of the arbitration agreement, adopts a procedure markedly different from those prevailing in the courts of justice.[4] Moreover, provided that the arbitrator has shown an intention to act fairly, and has given the parties proper notice of what he proposed to do, and proper opportunity to present their case, the court is very reluctant to interfere.[5] In practice, although the powers of the court are very wide, they are very rarely exercised.[6]

The same statement applies to a power of the court which has received unfavourable comment abroad: the jurisdiction to entertain appeals from arbitrators on questions of law. Space does not permit me a rehearsal of the arguments for and against the right of appeal. It is sufficient to say that it was created in the first part of the nineteenth century by the choice of parties who expressly provided for it in their arbitration agreements; that it was given statutory force in 1854 and progressively enlarged during the next 100 years; and that the tide of opinion turned in the 1960s and 1970s, with the result that a new balance was struck by the Arbitration Act 1979. This gives the parties a right to exclude an appeal by prior agreement, except only in the case of commercial, maritime, and insurance contracts. Even where the possibility of appeals subsists, the losing party cannot exercise it as of right, but only with the leave of the court. Since the enactment of the new system, two decisions of the House of Lords have laid down the principles according to which leave will be granted in such narrow terms that the number of appeals brought before the courts is likely to be small, and possibly very small.[7]

Against this background I turn to the three topics previously mentioned.

Intervention to Prevent Delay

Delays in the reference may be due to lack of proper activity by the arbitrator; to a simple failure by the claimant to take any steps to prosecute his claim; and to failure by the parties to cooperate in the efficient conduct of the reference, or to comply with the arbitrator's directions.

Delays by the arbitrator rarely arise from laziness or deliberate inactivity. More commonly, they result from the demands either of his own business activities, or of other pending arbitrations. There is little that the court can do to remedy this source of delay. Having no general power to intervene in the reference, the court cannot order the arbitrator to accelerate. The only possibility is to remove the arbitrator, under powers conferred by section 13(3).[8] This is an unattractive remedy because it entails that in addition to the delays already experienced there must be added the further waste of time (and costs) involved in beginning afresh before a new arbitrator.[9] No doubt for this reason, attempts to invoke the jurisdiction are very rare, and there appears to be no reported instance in recent years where the court has actually granted relief.[10]

The second situation, where the claimant takes no steps to prosecute the arbitration, has been the subject of considerable litigation and controversy in recent years. It is well-established law that where the plaintiff in a High Court action neglects to pursue it to such a degree that the resulting delay makes a fair trial impossible, the court can order the action to be dismissed. Repeated, but in the main unsuccessful, attempts have been made to transfer this salutory remedy to the sphere of arbitration. The suggestion that the arbitrator might himself have power to dismiss for want of prosecution was ruled out in 1973. It was, however, argued that the court could intervene, two grounds being cited.

First, it was said that the court could grant an injunction to restrain the further conduct of the arbitration by virtue of a general inherent supervisory power. This argument was laid to rest when the House of Lords decided in the Bremer Vulkan case that no such power existed.

Second, an analysis was developed on the following lines. An arbitration agreement is a contract, albeit of a special kind. It is subject to termination in the same way as any other contract, notably by repudiation, frustration, and express or implied consent. Each of these modes of termination is relevant, so the argument ran, where the claimant's long delay has made it impossible to try the issues fairly. This line of argument received its first severe set-back in the Bremer Vulkan case, where the House of Lords held, for reasons which cannot adequately be discussed in a brief address, that a respondent in an arbitration is not entitled to treat the contract to arbitrate as repudiated, simply by prolonged and inexcusable delay on the part of the claimant. The second version of the argument was ruled out when the House of Lords held in Paul Wilson & Co. v. Partenreederei Hannah Blumenthal that prolonged delay by the claimant, acquiesced in by the respondent, did not bring about discharge by frustration.[11] The House did, however, leave open the possibility of discharge by consent, in the shape of an implied mutual abandonment. At present this seems unlikely to provide a solution in more than a minority of cases, but it is hoped that by the time this paper is read a decision of the Court of Appeal will have shed some light on the problem.

The final source of delay is a failure by one or other party to proceed at reasonable speed with the arbitration and, in particular, to obey the orders of the arbitrator. It will be plain from what has been said that there is little the court can do to help. There are, however, three points to be made.

First, the court has power, under section 5 of the 1979 Act, to give the arbitrator power "to continue with the reference" in the same manner as a judge of the High Court might continue with proceedings in that court. It is unnecessary to enter in detail into the many procedural problems created by section 5. Plainly a power to "continue with the reference" cannot enable the arbitrator to bring the reference to an immediate end by dismissing the claim or making a summary award in favour of the claimant. Whatever the intent of the section, it appears to have missed the mark in practice. At the time of going to press, no record has been found of any order being made under this section.

Second, there is reason to hope that the legislature may decide to create a statutory power permitting the dismissal of claims in arbitrations for want of prosecution. Whether this new power, if created, will entrust the choice to the arbitrator or the court remains to be seen. Moreover, on any view, even if the court is given powers of dismissal, this will not amount to anything approaching a general power to intervene in the reference.

Third, it is quite plain that although the court is not able, by virtue of its own powers, to prevent delay, it will be solicitous not to interfere when the arbitrator takes proper steps to this end. A desire to be fair, and a proper understanding of what the arbitrator has in mind, and an opportunity to put the party's point of view, are what is required. If these requirements are complied with--and they are not in the least inconsistent with the procedures suggested by Mr. Holtzmann--the taking of a strong line by the arbitrator is not a ground for the court declaring him to be guilty of misconduct, in fact, it is quite the reverse.

Prevention of Arbitrator from Causing Delay

All of us are familiar with the situation where the collection of a legitimate claim is held up by a debtor who raises spurious defences. The arbitrator may feel some inhibition when wondering whether to cut through the debtor's smokescreen by making a summary award in favour of the claimant, because of the possibility that he will be held to have infringed due process, with the result that the creditor will have to begin the arbitration again. This would leave the creditor in a worse position than if a more leisurely procedure had been adopted. English arbitration law offers a really substantial advantage in this situation.

In a High Court action there exists an effective and widely used procedure for dealing with delays of this kind. Under Order 14, Rules of the Supreme Court, a plaintiff can depose that there is no defence to the claim, and thereby require the defendant to show cause on affidavit why there is "an issue in dispute which ought to be tried." If the judge finds no such issue, the plaintiff will obtain an immediate judgment, without the need for a trial. There is nothing exceptional in a summary procedure of this nature, although the approach of different legal systems may differ in matters of detail. One particular feature is, however, unique to English law. The reasoning is this. The arbitration agreement contemplates that an arbitrator will be appointed to adjudicate upon disputes. If an action in the High Court raises an arbitable dispute, the action will be stayed so that an arbitrator can be appointed to adjudicate upon it. If, however, there is no genuine defence, the claim is in reality undisputable; there is, therefore, no arbitable dispute, no reason why the court proceedings should yield to an arbitration, and equally no reason why summary judgment should not be given for the plaintiff. Accordingly, a summary judgment can be given in favour of the plaintiff, even where his claim is to enforce a contract which includes an arbitration clause.

This effective means of preventing the injustice which results from the defendant holding up proceedings with spurious defences enables the court to provide cheap and speedy justice that the arbitration process cannot always match. It deserves to be more widely known.

Delays Caused by Recourse to the Court

A complaint often made by those unfamiliar with the English system is that proceedings in arbitrations are held up by recourse to the court. In the light of what is stated above, this complaint may be answered as follows.

First, the most frequent occasion of recourse to the court, namely the involving of ancillary procedural powers, cannot be accounted a source of delay. Of course, it takes time--not much time--to apply to the court for orders attaching the defendant's assets, requiring a witness to attend to give evidence, preserving the property for inspection, and so on. Since the court will not grant an order unless satisfied that it will make the conduct of the reference more efficient, the delay involved in the preparation and hearing of the application can scarcely be regarded as unacceptable.

Second, if the parties have not chosen to exclude the right of appeal to the court on questions of law, they can hardly complain about the delay resulting from the exercise of this right. Furthermore, the mesh of the filter which the court applies when deciding whether to grant leave to appeal is so fine that even where a right of appeal is in principle available, the party is only rarely allowed to exercise it. The right of onward appeal from the Commercial Judge to the Court of Appeal is also so circumscribed as to be available only in the most exceptional of cases. Thus, whatever may have been the strength of the complaints about the delays created by the right of appeal under the former procedure--and my personal view is that they were in general exaggerated--there can now be no justification for treating the court as a source of delay in this particular respect.

Third, the existence of a wide discretion to set aside or remit arbitration awards gives the court the opportunity for flexibility in its approach to questions of alleged procedural injustice, which is not possessed by courts in other countries where the power to intervene is more explicitly defined. In practice, the power is rarely exercised. For example, during the three years 1981-1983, there were only ten reported decisions arising from applications to set aside or remit an award, and in not all of these did the court actually grant relief. Set against the background of the many thousands of arbitrations commenced each year, this is surely a small price to pay for the retention of a right which enables the party to be confident that if he really does suffer a substantial procedural injustice, means exist to have it put right.

Conclusions

Whatever the formal breadth of its power, in practice the English court adopts a noninterventionist role in the arbitral process. In consequence, there is little that it can or will do to reduce delays in arbitration, or to create delays. The responsibility for inhibiting delay rests squarely with the arbitrator. He is entitled to take a firm line, and provided he acts judicially, the court will support him.

FOOTNOTES

1. In Japan Line v. Aggeliki Charis [1980] 1 Lloyd's Rep. 288 and Bremer Vulkan v. South India Shipping (Court of Appeal) [1980] 1 Lloyd's Rep. 255.

2. [1981] A.C. 909.

3. Except that setting aside is available only where the arbitrator "has misconducted himself or the proceedings, or where an arbitration or award has been improperly procured": section 23(2). (All references are to the Arbitration Act 1950, unless otherwise stated.)

4. Examples are much too numerous to cite. Acceptance of this approach was certainly complete by the time of French Government v. Tsurushima Maru (1922) 8 Ll.L.Rep. 403.

5. A high proportion of the few instances where the court has granted remission or setting aside in recent years have arisen from misunderstandings or lack of communication.

6. At the time of going to press, detailed statistics are still in the course of collection. It is hoped they will be available when this paper is read. For the present, it is safe to say that successful applications to set aside or remit represent only a handful of the many thousands of cases arbitrated in England every year.

7. Pioneer Shipping v. B.T.P. Tioxide (The "Nema") [1982] A.C. 724; Antaios Compania v. Salen (The "Antaios") [1984] 3 W.L.R. 592.

8. The arbitrator then forfeits his fees.

9. For a discussion of the problems raised by section 13(3), see Succula v. Harland and Wolff [1980] 2 Lloyd's Rep. 381. There is a possible alternative remedy under section 1, of giving leave to revoke the authority of the arbitrator, but in practice this adds little or nothing to section 13(3), and is even more difficult to obtain.

10. Crawford v. Prowting [1973] 1 Q.B. 1, approved in the Bremer Vulkan case.

11. [1983] A.C. 854.

COHABITATION WITHOUT FORMAL MARRIAGE

London Sessions
ABA Annual Meeting 1985
Ballroom 1, Hilton International
London, England

Thursday, July 18, 1985
2:00 P.M. - 4:00 P.M.

Michael S. J. Albano
311 W. Kansas Avenue
Independence, Missouri 64050

and

Donald C. Schiller
100 West Monroe, 6th Floor
Chicago, Illinois 60603

Many American couples who live together without marrying fail to realize the impact that their cohabitational status has on their legal rights. In a social climate that has, since the early 1960s, spawned such developments as palimony, alimony for men, do-it-yourself divorce, test-tube babies and embryo transplants, surrogate mothers and putative fathers, American courts have grappled with reconciling traditional doctrine with modern mores. To complicate matters, there is no federal domestic relations law; each state has its own set of statutes and judicial interpretations. Thus, a cohabitating couple in California may well have different rights and obligations than a similar couple in Illinois.

This paper first addresses the enforceability of contracts between unmarried cohabitants in the United States. The first section discusses such barriers to enforcement of express and implied contracts as the illegality of consideration doctrine and considers some of the remedies that state courts and legislatures are fashioning to better meet the needs of a growing class of litigants. The second section focuses on certain consequences of a divorced person's decision to live out of wedlock with another partner, such as loss of alimony or even loss of child custody.

I.

Unlike their single counterparts, legally married couples enjoy certain benefits that derive solely from their married status, including the right of a non-income-earning spouse to share in the distribution of property acquired during the marriage, even if title is placed in the other partner's name. Similarly, putative spouses (those who reasonably believe they have been legally married but in actuality have not) are treated as married for most purposes. See, for example, Ill. Rev. Stat. Ch. 40, §305 (1983); Succession of Marinoni, 183 La. 776,164 So. 797 (1935). Some states also recognize common-law marriage, which confers legal rights upon those who prove both an agreement to marry and cohabitation as husband and wife. E.g., Smith v. Smith, 257 S.W. 2d 335 (Tex. 1953). See generally Stein, Common-Law Marriage: Its History and Certain Contemporary Problems, 9 J Fam. L. 271, 296 (1969).

Those who live together without a legally recognized marital status, however, cannot expect to acquire property interests by reason of the cohabitational relationship alone. The term "meretricious cohabitation" has been applied to those relationships "in which partners live together with full knowledge and belief that they are not legally married." Note, Property Rights of Non-Marital Partners in Meretricious Cohabitation, 13 New England L. Rev 453 (1978). One of the consequences of such a relationship is that the parties must look to traditional contract theories that may not adequately protect their true expectations and interests.

Express Agreements

Historically, many express agreements between cohabitants were held unenforceable on the ground that the meretricious character of the relationship itself contaminated the agreement. If all or part of the consideration for the contract was viewed to be illicit sexual relations, civil courts held such agreements void as against public policy. See Stevens v. Anderson, 256 P. 2d 712 (Orig., 1911); Wallace v. Rappleye, 103 Ill. 229 (1882). A contract between two cohabitants could be viewed as payment for sexual services, violating statutes against prostitution. Alternatively, the cohabitational status could be viewed as violative of criminal statutes prohibiting fornication or other sex offenses. Even if no criminal laws were broken, courts often found unmarried cohabitation to be immoral.

Perhaps in recognition of changing social mores, a few courts have virtually rejected the illegality doctrine as a bar to agreements between cohabitants. Latham v. Latham, 274 Or. 421, 547 P. 2d 144, (1976); Tyranski v. Piggins, 44 Mich. App. 570, 205 N.W. 2d 595 (1973). In Latham, defendant had defaulted on his promise to share all accumulated property equally when the parties separated. Although the agreement was based on the consideration of plaintiff's living with defendant and providing him with "all amenities of married life," the Oregon Supreme Court held that such agreement was not void as against public policy, despite the general rule that cohabitation agreements were void because it was necessary to protect the expectations of the innocent party. In Tyranski, the Michigan Court of Appeals affirmed the trial court's judgment granting specific performance of the decedent's oral agreement to convey a house to plaintiff, holding that the agreement was not void despite the fact the parties had cohabited for several years and were legally married to other parties at the time.

Faced with the potential harshness of the illegality concept, but unwilling to abrogate traditional doctrine, increasing numbers of American courts are creating a middle ground between voiding all contracts between cohabitants and abolishing the illegality concept entirely. A logical approach is to separate, if possible, the illicit sexual relationship from other agreements between the parties based on other considerations and uphold the "untainted" portions of the agreement. This concept has long been supported by such authorities as Corbin, Williston, and the Restatement of Contracts. See 6A Corbin on Contracts §1476 (1962 ed.); 15 Williston, A Treatise on the Law of Contracts, §1745 (3d 1972); Restatement of Contracts §589 (1932).

In accordance with this severability approach, express agreements have been held void only if illicit sexual relations are held to be the sole or primary consideration for the agreement. See Marvin v. Marvin, 18 Cal. 3d 660, 557 P. 2d 106, 116, 134 Cal Rptr. 815 (1976). The New Jersey Supreme Court stated in Kozlowski v. Kozlowski, 164 N.J. Super. 163,403 A. 2d 902, 908 (1978), that "society's mores have changed" and "an agreement between adult parties living together is enforceable to the extent it is not based on a relationship proscribed by law, or on a promise to marry." Similarly, the Wyoming Supreme Court has held that only if a contract has meretricious sexual services as its consideration will it be violative of public policy and therefore unenforceable. Hence, an out-of-wedlock living arrangement does not, by itself, make parties incapable of contracting. Kinnison v. Kinnison, 627 P. 2d 594 (Wyoming 1981). The Kinnison court upheld an oral agreement between the parties to settle plaintiff's claims for quantum meruit based on her housekeeping services.

In Carlson v. Olson, 256, N.W. 2d 249 (Minn. 1977) the Supreme Court of Minnesota affirmed the trial court's holding that despite the male partner's contribution of the actual monies for the acquisition and improvements to the parties' property, one-half share of all property constituted an irrevocable gift to the female partner in consideration of the "wifely and motherly services" she performed during the cohabitation. Accordingly, the plaintiff was granted a partition of all property acquired during the 21 years the parties lived together and held themselves out as husband and wife.

In sharp contrast, however, the Supreme Court of Georgia barred any recovery by a woman who for 18 years cooked, cleaned and cared for the decedent and also contributed money for the purchase of their home. Rehak v. Mathis, 238 S.E. 2d 81 (Ga. 1977). The Rehak court ruled that it would not aid either party to a contract founded upon illegal or immoral consideration. Since the parties were not married, their cohabitational status constituted illegal consideration.

In Hewitt v. Hewitt, 77 Ill. 2d 49, 394 N.E. 2d 1204 (1979) the Illinois Supreme Court noted that allowing cohabitants to enter mutually enforceable contracts would threaten the institution of marriage by allowing parties to gain benefits incident to marriage without assuming some of the burdens, and would, in effect, sanction the return of common-law marriage which has been illegal in Illinois for over 70 years. The Hewitt court did not explicitly rule out the enforceability of some cohabitant contracts involving "independent matters" (presumably those not based in any part on sexual relations), but did not further explain this possible exception. While Wyoming and Minnesota have abolished common-law marriage also, neither the Kinnison decision, supra, nor Carlson v. Olson follow the Hewitt court's apparent fear that recognizing cohabitant's rights will signal a return of common-law marriage.

The various states do not agree on the extent to which express contracts between cohabitants should be enforced; the Minnesota case of Carlson v. Olson, and the Georgia case of Rehak v. Mathis, points up the polarity of approaches. Nevertheless, more and more state courts are taking the middle ground and finding ways to sever the sexual component of cohabitants' agreements in order to uphold important property rights.

Once past the illegality hurdle, unmarried cohabitants may enforce express oral agreements arising out of such business-related circumstances as agreements to pool earnings and share in accumulations; agreements of partnership; or joint ventures or enterprises. Generally, a partnership or joint enterprise is less onerous to establish than other types of oral agreements between cohabitants, Fernandez v. Garza, 88 Ariz. 214, 354 P. 2d 260 (1960); Mitchell v. Fish, 97 Ark. 444, 134 S.W. 940 (1911), presumably because of well-established principles of agencies and partnership, which can be applied to any business dealings.

Express oral agreements of any type, of course, are subject to other legal barriers such as the Statute of Frauds and problems of proof. If one of the parties to an express oral agreement has died, dead man's statutes may preclude the only proof that could establish such agreement, the survivor's testimony. For unmarried partners, there is no counterpart to the intestacy laws, which give surviving spouses rights based on their marital status. Moreover, written contracts between cohabitants that avoid some of the proof problems may be as unenforceable as oral ones, either for previously discussed illegality doctrine, or, in a state such as Illinois, if the written agreement attempts to put the cohabitants in a situation comparable to marriage, thereby violating the public policy expressed in legislation governing marriage and dissolution of marriage. See Grant and Hyinck, Caveat Amator: The State of Affairs in Illinois, 29 De Paul L. Rev. 493 (1980).

Implied Agreements

Although at times reluctant, state courts have enforced express agreements made between cohabitating adults. However, until very recently, courts would not intervene in disputes between cohabitants who failed to make or even allege an express agreement; courts refused to imply them from the circumstances.

Implied contracts may be of two types, implied in fact or implied in law. See D. Dobbs, Handbook on Law of Remedies, §§4.2, 4.3 at 234 and 240-48 (1973). For practical purposes, the distinction between an express agreement and one implied in fact or in law is that the former is based on an actual "meeting of the minds," while the latter two are premised on equitable considerations that compel judicial recognition of the intent or expectations of at least one of the parties. For example, courts have not had a problem in recognizing an implied agreement that a party requesting certain services, such as a doctor's care, will pay for the services, even if no discussion of price has preceded the service. In the unmarried cohabitant context, however, a person claiming payment for cooking and cleaning services based on an implied contract has not fared well in court.

The landmark decision of the California Supreme Court in Marvin v. Marvin, 18 Cal. 3d 660, 557 P. 2d 106, 134 Cal. Rptr. 815 (1976), virtually eliminated the distinction between express contracts and implied or equitable relief in that state, recognizing that unmarried partners should not be treated significantly different from other contracting partners. Consequently, the path should be clear for cohabitants to employ such traditional contract and quasi-contract theories of recovery as quantum meruit, constructive trust, resulting trust, or estoppel if the facts warrant such a recovery.

The facts warranting recovery, however, are not so easily categorized as the legal theories and it remains to be seen whether many other state courts will follow the lead of Marvin. Although some post-Marvin courts have found implied contracts between unmarried cohabitants where the parties lived together for an extended period of time, Carlson v. Olson, supra (21 years); McCullon v. McCullon, 410 N.Y.S. 2d 226 (1978) (28 years), long duration is not of itself dispositive and is in fact immaterial if the court refuses to recognize an implied agreement. See Hewitt v. Hewitt, supra (parties held themselves out as married for 18 years).

Assuming that state law does not bar implied agreements between cohabitants, proof problems remain significant. A party asserting an implied contract to pool and share earnings must establish that the parties' conduct constituted a joint enterprise or partnership. What conduct evidences such a relationship is not altogether clear, but pooling of resources alone is probably insufficient to establish the partnership agreement or joint venture. Other factors, such as duration of the cohabitational relationship, birth of children to the couple, and the contributions, financial or otherwise, that the parties make are likely to influence a court's findings as to the existence of one or more theories of relief. In addition, if a party seeks compensation for certain services (cooking and cleaning, for example), he or she may have to overcome a presumption that the services were gratuitous and therefore constituted insufficient consideration.

As suggested by the Marvin decision, some of the proof problems germane to express or implied contract theories can be overcome through quasi-contractual theories grounded in preventing unjust enrichment. Quantum meruit, for example, would permit one partner to claim compensation for services that benefitted the other, absent any actual agreement between them, as long as the claimant had a reasonable expectation of payment for the services. Dobbs, supra, §4.2, at 234-38. Other equitable theories such as constructive or resulting trust may be appropriate in some circumstances, for example, where one partner gives the other money to purchase a house or car and the other puts legal title in his or her own name. See Dobbs, §4.3, at 240-41; Albae v. Harbin, 249 Ala. 201 30 So. 2d 451 (1947).

There would seem to be no reason to deny unmarried cohabitants access to the courts for enforcement of agreements that are entirely separate from their living arrangements, as in the case of partners in business transactions who also happen to live together. The thornier problems have arisen in the more typical case where the dissolution of the cohabitational relationship resembles a "divorce," and the partner contributing no income, but perhaps substantial services, seeks property or financial support from the other.

In response to the wide-ranging and often inconsistent theories that the various state courts have employed to grant or deny certain rights to unmarried cohabitants, some state legislatures have proposed laws that deal directly with actions between unmarried partners. A proposed Connecticut bill, for example, would require a written document to sustain a civil action for support. An Oregon proposal would define the property and alimony rights of unmarried cohabitants. The Virgin Islands' legislature has enacted an innovative "Vesper Marriage" law which recognizes as an enforceable contract the agreement of two adults over 60 to live together as husband and wife without acquiring any interest or claim in the marital estate, property, or income of the other and without any legal right of inheritance from the other.

Although there is still a great deal of confusion concerning the rights of nonmarital partners to sue each other, and there is little uniformity as to theories of recovery between unmarried partners, California has once again forged ahead of her sister states by recognizing tort actions against third parties for the loss of consortium between unmarried parties. In Butcher v. Superior Court of Orange County, (Ct. App. January 11, 1983), the California Court of Appeals held that a marital relationship is not a prerequisite for loss of consortium recovery. The Butcher court noted, however, that there must be sufficient proof to show a stable relationship with the characteristics found in a de facto marriage.

II.

The Effect of Cohabitation on Prior Marital Relations

Apart from threatening their property interests, unmarried partners' living arrangements may adversely affect their rights to alimony, child custody, and visitation. The majority of state courts employ a traditional approach to determine whether an ex-spouses's right to alimony should be terminated because of his or her cohabitational relationship with another. Generally, a divorce decree is modifiable, if either the earning capacity of the obligor substantially changes or if the recipient's needs substantially change. Therefore, it is not the mere fact of cohabitation that determines whether alimony should be modified; it is whether cohabitation has diminished the financial need of the recipient that is determinative. Wight v. Wight, 284 S.E. 2d 625 (W. Va. 1981). Proof of more than mere co-tenancy is essential; there must be actual evidence that the co-tenant "supports" the ex-spouse financially. The California appellate case of In Re Marriage of Teib, 80 Cal. App. 3d 629, 145 Cal. Rptr. 763 (1978) held that the fact of cohabitation creates a significant enough change of circumstances in and of itself to require a reexamination of whether the need for support continues.

Seemingly rejecting the traditional approach, a few states have enacted statutes which compel the court to terminate alimony if the recipient moves in with another and has conjugal relations. See Ala. Code §30-2-55 (1981); Ga. Code §30-220 (1980); and Ill. Rev. Stat. Ch. 40 §510 (h) (1980). The Illinois statute requires termination "if the party receiving maintenance cohabits with another person on a resident, continuing conjugal basis." Because this legislation is new, it is difficult to foretell whether the courts will consider any factors, other than the mere fact of the cohabitation, such as the wealth of the person paying alimony, the support needs of the recipient, or the length of the cohabitation. At least one court refused to inquire whether the alimony recipient's financial circumstances had in fact changed as a result of her cohabitating.

Perhaps the most challenging issue the courts face with respect to the rights of unmarried cohabitants centers on custody and visitation rights. No other concept in child custody matters is more familiar or important than that of the "best interests" of the child. Whether the issue is initial custody or a change of custody or a modification of visitation rights, the courts look primarily to the effect of the change on the child's best interests. Unavoidably, this test grants the trial court broad discretion and not surprisingly, different states have reached conflicting decisions and rationales.

The Supreme Court of Illinois upheld the trial court's grant of a father's petition for a change of custody based on the fact that the children's mother was cohabitating with another man, finding that the judgment was not against the manifest weight of the evidence. Jarrett v. Jarrett, 78 Ill. 2d 337, 400 N.E. 2d 421 (1979), cert. denied 449 U.S. 927, 66 L.E. 2d 155 (1980). The court expressed concern over the example that the mother was setting for her female children in living with a man outside of a marital relationship, the fear being that the mother was in effect encouraging the children to engage in immoral activities in the future. While the reasoning of the court is certainly open to criticism on social and moral, as well as legal grounds, the result in Jarrett is consistent with the Illinois Supreme Court's Hewitt decision in that both reflect the court's concern for the preservation of marriage in accordance with the legislative policy expressed in the Illinois Marriage and Dissolution of Marriage Act. Ill. Rev. Stat. Ch. 40, §102(2).

In contrast to the Illinois Supreme Court's reasoning, the Washington Appellate Court held in a situation similar to that in Jarrett that a custodial father who was the cohabitating parent would be allowed to retain custody even though the children "knew the sleeping arrangements." Grieger v. Grieger, 8 Fam. Law Rptr. 2199 (Wash. App. 1982). Considering a somewhat less traditional sleeping arrangement, where the mother had a female lover, an Oklahoma court agreed with the noncustodial father that the circumstances had sufficiently changed to warrant removing custody from the mother. M.J.P. v. J.B.D., 8 Fam. Law Rptr. 2217 (Okla. 1982).

For the same reasons that courts may change custody upon a determination that the child's interests are affected by the custodial parent's cohabitation, courts will also impose restrictions on the visitation rights of the noncustodial parent who is cohabitating. In Drum v. Drum, 397 A. 2d 1192 (Pa. Super. Ct. 1979), the court ordered that the father's live-in companion be absent during his children's visit because of their expressed religious concern about his conduct. Still another court ruled that the children could visit their cohabitating father only during the day and not stay overnight. Gallo v. Gallo, 7 Fam. Law Rptr. 2499 (Conn. Sup. Ct. 1981). If the court finds that there are no adverse effects on the children, however, restrictions on visitation will not be granted merely because of the existence of a cohabitational relationship. Sorace v. Sorace, 344 A. 2d 553 (Pa Super Ct. 1975).

Conclusion

The contractual and property rights of Americans who live together without marrying continue to evolve as courts adopt outmoded doctrines to fit contemporary needs. While some states continue to view cohabitation as immoral and against public policy favoring marriage, and deny relief on that basis, most courts are concluding that unmarried partners should not risk losing vital rights because of their lifestyles.

When child custody or visitation matters are in issue, however, the courts may face greater challenges in assessing whether a parent's cohabitational status adversely affects their children. In following the flexible and creative tradition of American jurisprudence, state courts are meeting the challenges and balancing competing legal, social and moral considerations.

COHABITATION WITHOUT FORMAL MARRIAGE

London Sessions
ABA Annual Meeting 1985
Ballroom 1, Hilton International
London, England

Thursday, July 18, 1985
2:00 P.M. - 4:00 P.M.

Robert Johnson, Q.C.
Queen Elizabeth Buildings
Temple, London EC4Y 9BS

and

Blanche Lucas
Theodore Goddard & Co.
16 St. Martins Le Grand
London EC1A 4EJ

COHABITATION WITHOUT FORMAL MARRIAGE

The concept of cohabitation encompasses a wide range of relationships. This paper is concerned with the legal implications of a seemingly permanent and stable relationship between a man and a woman who are not married to each other and who are living together.

In England, legal rights and obligations of cohabitees toward each other are determined by a mixture of judicial discretion exercised in the courts and a hotchpotch of unrelated and uncoordinated legislation. There is no legislation comparable to the matrimonial legislation in relation to property and maintenance which recognises mutual rights and obligations emanating from contributions towards the relationship and "joint enterprise," in addition to those of a financial nature. The absence of such legislation causes numerous anomalies and injustice to the cohabitees. A comprehensive legislative code to govern all legal aspects of cohabitation might, however, cause additional problems due to its inevitable rigidity and inability to cater to the wide variety of circumstances and differing relationships. The question posed is whether the rights of cohabitees would be better served by retention of the existing position or by a single legislative code.

Property

Despite the many legal consequences arising from cohabitation, on the breakdown of the relationship, litigation has centred on the division of the home. Naturally if one or both of the parties own the home, the main consideration is the division of the beneficial shares in their principal asset. On the breakdown of a marriage, the Matrimonial Causes Act 1973 gives the Court power to redistribute the parties' assets according to specific criteria (now redefined by a 1984 Act) and the circumstances of the case, irrespective of the property rights of the parties. There is no equivalent legislation governing the property rights of cohabitees, and the present position is that their rights are governed by ordinary principles of property, contract, and trust laws, which are, arguably, too rigid and not particularly appropriate to the resolution of disputes between cohabitees.

In dividing the property there are three important factors to consider:

- Their beneficial shares;
- The sale of the property; and
- The date of valuation.

Beneficial Shares

If the cohabitees' house was purchased in joint names, there is a presumption that the parties intended joint beneficial interest in the property. The Court will give effect to an express declaration of trust. If there is no such declaration, Lord Denning stated,

> "In ascertaining the respective shares, the courts should normally apply the same considerations to couples living together (as if married) as they do to couples who are truly married." (Bernard v. Josephs 1982 Ch 391 at page 3.)

This approach, which takes into account the nonfinancial contributions of the parties, demonstrates Lord Denning's willingness to equate the rights of a female cohabitee with those of a married woman. As the property in that case was in joint names, the court could have simply apportioned the beneficial interest according to the amount of contribution. It is this approach that we believe should be applied in the future.

Often the home is purchased in the sole name of the man. The woman can then acquire a beneficial interest if there is an express agreement or declaration. Direct and indirect contributions in money or money's worth to the purchase and improvement of the property will create a resulting trust in her favour. Alternatively, a common intention may be imputed in the absence of such contribution (Pettit v. Pettit 1970 AC 777 and Gissing v. Gissing 1971 AC 886).

To what extent does the present law confer an interest on the woman cohabitee who has made no financial contribution? The most recent Court of Appeal decision is Burns v. Burns 1984 1 All ER 244. It was held that a cohabitee cannot acquire a beneficial interest in the property without direct or indirect contribution to the property in money or money's worth. This decision marked a considerable retreat from previous dicta in earlier cases, and we believe has left the woman cohabitee in a weaker position than formerly. The relevant facts were that the house was in the man's sole name; the parties had lived together for 19 years, during which time the woman had raised a family, looked after the home, and had done everything that a wife would have done in similar circumstances. During the last five years she had earned a living and was able to contribute to the joint household expenses, but it was held that an intention that she should receive an interest in the property could not be imputed by the performance of domestic duties alone. As to her financial contributions in the latter years, these were not sufficient to have enabled the man to pay the mortgage. She had no claim.

In contrast, in Gordon v. Deuce 1983 1 WLR 563, the woman acquired an interest in the property on the basis that her financial contributions to household expenses allowed the man to pay the mortgage, and so her contribution indirectly helped to purchase the property.

The Court of Appeal in Burns v. Burns criticised earlier dicta of Lord Denning, particularly his dicta in Hall v. Hall 1982 3 FLR 379. There he had stated that nonfinancial contributions by the woman in raising a family could confer an interest in the property itself. Lord Justice May said:

> When the house is taken in the man's name alone, if the woman makes no "real" or "substantial" financial contribution towards either the purchase price, the deposit or the mortgage instalments by means of which the family home was acquired, then she is not entitled to any share in the beneficial interest in that home even though over a very substantial number of years she may have worked just as hard as the man in maintaining the family, in the sense of keeping house, giving birth to and looking after and helping to bring up the children of the union.

He said that the injustice should be remedied by legislation and not by the court.

In Walker v. Hall 1984 FLR 126, the woman's share in the property was assessed in exact proportion to the amount of her financial contribution to the acquisition of the property. Her contribution to general household expenses did not increase her share.

These two decisions reflect the approach taken today by the the English courts in respect of the position of a woman cohabitee. The departure of Lord Denning has made her position significantly more precarious. Lord Denning had created devices to protect her by adapting principles of equity and contract, the implied or constructive trust, equitable estoppel, and contractual licence. It is valuable to examine briefly these concepts to determine whether protection could still be afforded to the woman in the light of the more recent decisions.

1. Trusts. In Cooke v. Head 1972 1 WLR 518, the Eves v. Eves 1975 1 WLR 1338, contribution by means of actual physical labour on the property ("much more than most women would do") was held to create an implied or constructive trust to confer an interest in the property. Today, significant physical contributions of this kind would constitute an indirect contribution in money's worth and would confer an interest in the property.

2. Equitable estoppel. A woman was held entitled to the entire beneficial interest in the property by having spent all her capital on improvements to the property in reliance on a promise that the home belonged to her (Pascoe v. Turner 1979 2 All ER 945). In contrast, such contribution may be regarded as a mere loan (Richards v. Dove 1974 1 All ER 888). Today, the size of the beneficial share would be calculated in strict accordance with the size of the financial contribution. Another woman who had contributed to the care of the household, relying on a promise that

she could live in the home rent-free for life, was allowed to do so (Greasley v. Cook 1980 1 WLR 1306). Thus, a nonfinancial contribution of this kind cannot confer a proprietary interest, although it may constitute the "detriment" suffered by a woman for the purposes of her invocation of the doctrine of estoppel.

3. Contractual licence. A contractual licence can arise if there is evidence of an agreement or intention to create a legally binding interest and contribution or other consideration to support the promise (Tanner v. Tanner 1975 1 WLR 1346). A contractual licence may be terminated with reasonable notice (Chandler v. Kerley 1978 1 WLR 693). Accordingly, there is no proprietary interest as such, and these decisions are not affected by Burns. The effect of Burns and Walker v. Hall is devastating for the woman cohabitee who has effectively stunted the development of her own earning capacity by enabling her partner to work whilst she has brought up their family and looked after their children. Lord Denning had adapted legal principles to recognise that such a woman could acquire an interest in the property since her female role dictated that she could not contribute in a financial way. The Court in Burns recognised the injustice in denying her a right but felt constrained by precedent not to follow Lord Denning's approach. There is no doubt that a woman who has contributed to a joint enterprise in raising the family should not be denied a beneficial share in the property that she has helped, and indeed enabled, her partner to purchase by releasing him from his household duties.

The Sale of the Property

Any party who can prove a legal or beneficial interest in the property can apply for an order for sale under section 30 of the Law of Property Act 1925:

> If the trustees for sale refuse to sell or to exercise any of the powers .... any person interested may apply to the court for a vesting or other order for giving effect to the proposed transaction or for an order directing the trustees for sale to give effect thereto, and the court may make such order as it thinks fit.

One cohabitee may apply to the court for an order for sale of the property even if the other cohabitee refuses to allow a sale. In deciding whether or not to order a sale, the court looks to the underlying purpose of the trust. If the property was bought as a home for the family, the sale may be postponed until the home is no longer needed for that purpose and the children have grown up (Re Evers 1980 1 WLR 1327). The cohabitee remaining in the property may have to pay an "occupational rent" to the other cohabitee as compensation for exclusion from the property.

The problem with section 30 is that usually the court can only regulate the sale of the former home and cannot deal with other assets belonging to the cohabitees. It also merely affects the distribution of the realised value of the house and cannot readjust the beneficial interest in the property. Although it is a useful mechanism for cohabitees, its limitations are considerable.

The Date of Valuation

The property is valued at the expiration of the trust purpose. Generally this is on the separation of the parties (Hall v. Hall and Bernard v. Josephs). However, the trust does not end if the house was purchased as a family home. Valuation will then not be until the home is no longer needed for the family (Cousins v. Dozers 1982 FL 36 and Gordon v. Deuce 1983 1 WLR 563).

Changes are needed to rectify the injustice and inconsistency in the present law. Legislation enacted on a contractual basis would help only those sufficiently cynical and educated to conceive of a contract of separation before embarking on the relationship. The majority of women would be in no better position than they are today. Alternatively, legislation could be enacted on a basis of mutual dependency; i.e., a woman acquires a right in property on the basis that her partner could not earn a living without her contribution to the joint household.

However, any legislation in the field can be resisted on the basis that it is an imposition of rights and obligations on people who often have deliberately chosen to opt out of those responsibilities by not entering into marriage. They may want to accept the responsibilities during their relationship but not to do so on its breakdown.

In our view, legislation for cohabitees in respect of their property rights should not impose rights and duties. There should be legislative guidelines but the particular decision should ultimately be one of judicial discretion. The criteria, reflecting the amended section 25 of the Matrimonial Causes Act 1973, should take account of all the aspects and circumstances of the relationship.

Occupation

A cohabitee has no statutory right of occupation, as does a spouse under the Matrimonial Homes Act 1983. A cohabitee with a proprietary interest has a right of occupation by virtue of such interest. If her name is not on the title deeds, the cohabitee must register a "caution" or obtain an injunction to protect her occupational interests. If there is no beneficial interest, the cohabitee must prove a licence to occupy; otherwise, the owner is free to sell the house with vacant possession (Tanner v. Tanner).

If one cohabitee is violent towards the other, the innocent cohabitee may apply to the court for an injunction to exclude the violent one from the home or to require him to allow the other to enter and stay in the home and not to molest the other. Protection is the same for spouses as for cohabitees, and it is afforded to "a man and a woman who are living with each other in the same household as man and wife" (section 1, Domestic Violence and Matrimonial Proceedings Act 1976). This is irrespective of property rights (Davis v. Johnson 1979 AC 264). The right to exclude, is a temporary right (Davis v. Johnson and Hopper v. Hopper (1979) 1 WLR 1342). It is less than the statutory right of occupation of the spouse, but it is nevertheless an advance towards the equality of rights for battered women, regardless of their status.

Maintenance

An unmarried couple are under no legal duty financially to support each other during their relationship or on their separation. On separation, it is argued, a moral obligation surely exists upon the man to continue to support a woman who has freed him of domestic responsibilities and the upbringing of their family so as to enable him to earn a living. A woman should not be deprived of continued support merely because there is no marriage, when the obligations performed by her are equivalent to those of a married woman.

The validity of contracts to maintain each other on separation has not been determined (compare Marvin v. Marvin (1976) 18 CAL (3d) 660). It is unlikely that they would be considered contrary to public policy in view of the pressing demand for legislation to protect the position of the female cohabitee.

Welfare Benefits

The position concerning welfare benefits leads to numerous anomalies. By virtue of the "cohabitation rule," an unmarried couple living together are treated as a married couple for the purpose of claiming supplementary benefit. The rule was formulated on the basis that an unmarried couple should not be in a financially better position than a married couple. However, in effect, a woman loses her right to claim benefit as an individual, even if the man is in fact not supporting her. As mentioned previously, the man is under no legally enforceable duty to support her.

For other welfare benefits, cohabitation is taken into account, seemingly at random when it suits the Government budget. Cohabitation is not taken into account for entitlement to contributory benefits; e.g., retirement benefit, sickness benefit, invalidity benefit, and maternity benefit. A woman is not entitled to claim these benefits on the basis of her partner's contributions, despite the performance of quasi-marital duties during the relationship and on separation.

In contrast, cohabitation is taken into account to deprive a cohabitee of certain benefits; e.g., noncontributory invalidity benefits and the extra child benefit for single parents. Based on assumed and not de facto dependancy, these rules lead to a Catch 22 situation. During the relationship, the female cohabitee may not be able to claim supplementary benefit even if the man is not adequately financially supporting her. If she has raised a family to enable her partner to earn a living, she cannot claim benefit based on his contributions. Nor can she enforce a maintenance claim against him.

Illegitimacy

The mother of an illegitimate child has exclusive parental rights and duties over the child (section 85 (7) of the Children Act 1975) unless the father successfully applies to the court for custody or access, under section 9 (1) or section 14 (1) of the Guardianship of Minors Act 1971. Parents of legitimate children enjoy equal rights over their children (see section 1 (1) of the Guardianship Act 1973). In determining custody on a father's application, the child's welfare is the first and paramount consideration (see section 1 of the Guardianship of Minors Act 1971).

Parents have a legal duty to maintain their children. The married parent with custody can apply for maintenance for the child from the other parent in chamber proceedings in the High Court or County Court (section 9 (2) of the 1971 Act). In the absence of an agreement for maintenance of the child (which is legally enforceable), the mother of an illegitimate child must apply to the Magistrates Court under the Affiliation Proceedings Act 1957. The procedure is embarrassing, cumbersome, and public. There is no provision for discovery of documents or prior notice of the other side's case. Its quasi-criminal character deters many applicants. Illegitimate children must be given equality with legitimate children in respect not only of the rights but also of the machinery to enforce rights of financial support. The consent of the father of an illegitimate child is not required before its adoption. He has only the right to make general submissions as to whether an adoption would be in the child's interest.

Financial Provision on Death

In the absence of a testamentary disposition, "any person...who immediately before the death of the deceased was being maintained, either wholly or partly, by the deceased" may apply for reasonable financial provision from the deceased's estate (Inheritance [Provision for Family and Dependants] Act 1975). Paradoxically, the duty to support a dependent cohabitee may therefore be enforced on the death of the other, although it is not enforceable while the parties are alive. A cohabitee is only entitled to maintenance, to be provided by a lump sum or periodic payments or both, whereas a spouse is entitled to a reasonable provision above what is strictly necessary for maintenance.

Conclusion

The existing legislation fails to deal adequately with the legal rights and duties of cohabitees in relation to each other. It is illogical and arbitrary for cohabitees whose relationship may accord with marriage in all but name. True, they may have chosen not to be subject to the legal duties and responsibilities that marriage imposes, but injustice and inequality abound. The position of the putative father is tenuous and insecure. The position of illegitimate children is unequal and unfair. A woman cohabitee who has contributed regularly to joint household expenses is denied legal redress on all fronts. She was not dependent upon her partner and therefore has no financial claim against his estate on his death. However, such contribution is not directly referrable to the acquisition of the property in his sole name, and she is denied a proprietary claim in that.

In our opinion, there should be innovative legislation to consolidate the law relating to cohabitation that would remedy the injustice and anomalies highlighted in this paper. The protection of cohabitees afforded by the legislation should reflect the length and quality of the individual relationship. A cohabitation relationship, which mirrors marriage, should be governed by the criteria that govern marriage.

The question we posed was whether the rights of cohabitees would be better served by a single legislative code. Our answer is yes. The further and more controversial question is whether the introduction of such legislation would be seen as undermining the status of proper legal marriage.

BIBLIOGRAPHY

1. Rayden on Divorce.

2. Martin Parry, Cohabitation.

3. Butterworths Family Law Service.

4. Cretney, Family Law.

5. "The Legal Implications of a Relationship Outside Marriage" Pearl 1978 CLJ 252.

6. "Formality and the Family; Reform and Status Quo."

7. Zuckerman 1980 96 LQR 248.

8. "Section 30 of the Law of Property Act and Unmarried Cohabitees" Schuz 1982 FL 108.

9. "Rationalizing the Cohabitation Rule" Oliver 1979 9 FL 10 "Cohabitants their Haves and the Winds of Change" Parker 1983 FL 40.

THE UNITED STATES AND INTERNATIONAL HUMAN RIGHTS

London Sessions
ABA Annual Meeting 1985
Ballroom, Park Lane Hotel
London, England

Friday, July 19, 1985
10:00 A.M. - 12:00 Noon

Prof. Louis Henkin
Columbia University
School of Law
435 W. 116th Street
New York, New York 10027

Before the Second World War, how a nation treated its own inhabitants was deemed a matter of "domestic jurisdiction," and not anyone else's business. Today, the human rights of all people, everywhere, are of deep international concern, the stuff of international politics, and a subject of international law. There are human rights commitments in the U.N. Charter, an international treaty to which virtually all of today's 160 states are parties. The Universal Declaration of Human Rights, adopted by the U.N. General Assembly in 1948, has been universally accepted. Some international human rights principles have entered the stream of customary international law and are binding on all states. International human rights convenants and conventions--e.g., on genocide; civil and political rights; economic, social and cultural rights; and the elimination of racial discrimination--have been adhered to by many states. Every U.N. organization includes human rights issues on its agenda, and some U.N. groups focus exclusively on human rights. Human rights are also a preoccupation of regional organizations--e.g., the Organization of American States, the Council of Europe, and the Organization of African Unity--and there are regional human rights conventions, commissions, and courts as well. At Helsinki in 1975, 35 states, including the United States, the Soviet Union, and their allies, made a major political bargain in which arrangements on security and cooperation in Europe were exchanged for commitment to human rights.

The United States, which has been dedicated to the idea of human rights since its national beginnings, has played a major part in the international human rights movement. It helped write human rights into the Nuremberg Charter and into the U.N. Charter; it helped draft the Universal Declaration and numerous other international human rights covenants and conventions. Although the United States has not yet adhered to the principal international agreements, international human rights standards have entered U.S. law and influenced U.S. politics and domestic policy. Congressional legislation denying aid, prohibiting arms sales, and otherwise dissociating the United States from governments that are gross violators of human rights, has become a permanent, if unsteady, plank in U.S. foreign policy.

International Human Rights Standards

The Universal Declaration of Human Rights recognizes a series of individual rights and proclaims them "a common standard of achievement" so that states will strive to promote respect for them and "secure their universal and effective recognition and observance." With some variations, the same rights were later included in two comprehensive international agreements, the International Covenant on Civil and Political Rights and the International Covenant on Economic, Social, and Cultural Rights. Particular rights were also made the subject of special conventions--e.g., the Genocide Convention and the Convention on the Elimination of All Forms of Racial Discrimination.

The Universal Declaration recognizes the familiar rights to life, liberty, and property; equal protection of the laws; freedom from killing, torture, slavery, and arbitrary detention; fairness in the criminal process; freedom of movement and residence within one's country and freedom to leave and return to it; privacy and "personhood"; and poltical and religious freedom. The Declaration also recognizes economic and social rights to education, work, rest, and leisure; social security; and an adequate standard of living. These rights are not subject to distinctions on the basis of race, religion, sex, or other invidious grounds. They are subject only to limitations necessary to secure the rights of others and the "just requirements of morality, public order and the general welfare in a democratic society" (Universal Declaration of Human Rights, art. 29(2)).

The same rights and limitations recognized in the Universal Declaration are restated in greater detail and with legal precision in the International Covenant on Civil and Political Rights, and the International Covenant on Economic, Social, and Cultural Rights. In the former, each state party "undertakes to respect and to ensure to all individuals within its territory and subject to its jurisdiction the rights recognized in the present Covenant" (International Covenant on Civil and Political Rights, art. 2(1)). In the International Covenant on Economic, Social, and Cultural Rights, each state party "undertakes to take steps...to the maximum of its available resources, with a view to achieving progressively the full realization of the rights recognized in the present Covenant" (International Covenant on Economic, Social, and Cultural Rights, art. 2(1)). The international standards articulated in these international instruments are to be implemented by states through their own laws and institutions. The international covenants and some of the special conventions, however, also provide some international "machinery" to monitor adherence to human rights standards and induce compliance. (More effective systems, including a commission and a human rights court, with defined authority to consider and resolve complaints of violations, are established by the European and American conventions.)

Human Rights and Constitutional Rights

The United States is one of the progenitors of the modern idea of human rights. Because the United States was also a principal mover in the international human rights movement, it is not surprising that much in the International Bill of Rights--the Universal Declaration and the principal international covenants--reflects the U.S. Bill of Rights and its constitutional jurisprudence. There are small differences, however, principally, in articulation.

While the rights of U.S. citizens are formally contained in Delphian eighteenth century instruments, much of U.S. constitutional jurisprudence has had to be distilled from a confusion of Supreme Court opinions reading between the lines and penetrating the penumbra of the Constitution and filling out its euphonious generalities--liberty, due process of law, privileges and immunities, and equal protection of the laws. Americans often forget that some of their most precious and confirmed rights--the presumption of innocence, the freedom of travel, the right to marry and found a family, the right of parents to ensure the moral-religious education of their children, even the right to vote--are not plainly stated in the Constitution. The right to equal protection of the law, missing from the original U.S. Constitution and the Bill of Rights but added by the Fourteenth Amendment, applies literally only to the states; that the federal government must not deny any person equal protection of the laws has been inferred, much later, by historically and intellectually questionable constitutional interpretation, intoning "due process of law."

International human rights instruments, on the other hand, are of contemporary vintage, and spell out specifically rights only inferred to be in the U.S. Constitution by the Supreme Court. For example, the Constitution forbids only "cruel and unusual punishment" for a person convicted of committing a crime; the International Covenant on Civil and Political Rights forbids torture and cruel, inhuman, or degrading treatment or punishment in any circumstances. The International Bill of Rights also includes what we have come to call civil rights, not all of which are constitutionally protected, but which are part of the web of life and law in the United States. On the other hand, some U.S. rights--e.g., the right to a jury trial, and the prohibition on establishment of religion--are peculiar to U.S. politics and history, and do not commend themselves as a universal necessity. Within the U.S. as within the international system of rights, there are conflicts between rights and other values, which may be resolved differently--e.g., the International Covenant on Civil and Political Rights requires states to prohibit by law propaganda for war or incitement to racial or religious hatred; in the United States, such a law might violate the freedom of speech or press.

Another major difference between international human rights and U.S. constitutional rights reflects another influence, not, as is commonly suggested, that of socialism, but of the Western commitment to the welfare state. The Universal Declaration and the International Covenant on Economic, Social, and Cultural Rights take a few small, important steps beyond equality of opportunity in declaring that it is society's responsibility to ensure fulfillment of every person's basic human needs. The Covenant recognizes a right to food, clothing, housing, and education; to work, leisure, a fair wage, decent working conditions, and social security; to physical and mental health; to protection for the family, for mothers and children; and to participation in cultural life. Although states adhering to the Covenant undertake to realize these rights only "progressively" and "to the maximum of available resources," the document uses language of right, undertaking, and commitment by governments, not merely of hope, aspiration, and goal (International Covenant on Economic, Social, and Cultural Rights, art. 2(1)).

The division between civil-political and economic-social rights is not sharp; a few of the rights in the International Covenant on Economic, Social, and Cultural Rights are rights under the U.S. Constitution as well--e.g., the right to choose one's work or to join a trade union. If the government decides to make available economic-social benefits, they must be administered in accordance with law and the due process of law, and invidious discrimination in providing them would be a denial of the equal protection of the laws. But, in the main, the rights in the International Covenant on Economic, Social, and Cultural Rights are not constitutional rights in the United States. There is no constitutional right to "freedom from want," one of the Four Freedoms that Franklin Roosevelt proclaimed to the world. In constitutional principle, Congress could, probably, abolish the welfare system at will, and the states could probably end public education. Surely, the level of subsistence and the quality of education which they provide are limited by policy choices and political forces.

But let there be no doubt: the United States has been, is, and will remain a welfare state. If many of the international economic and social rights are not constitutional rights in the United States, they are rights nonetheless. If we are not a welfare state by constitutional compulsion but by grace of Congress and state legislatures, we are a welfare state nonetheless. The right to public education has been largely guaranteed since early in the nineteenth century. Commitment to minimum levels of individual welfare, social services, and social security has been deeply and ineradicably imbedded in our national life for half a century. The United States is essentially in compliance with the economic and social provisions of the Universal Declaration; it could readily ratify and comply with the International Covenant on Economic, Social, and Cultural Rights.

There is another, different, happier lacuna in the U.S. Constitution that Americans looking around the world today might note with pleasure and pride. Under the International Covenant on Civil and Political Rights, a state may derogate from its obligations to respect many (though not all) rights, to the extent strictly required, in time of a declared public emergency that threatens the nation's life--a condition which, alas, is frequently declared in many countries. The U.S. Constitution cannot be suspended; there is no provision for government by decree, for emergency rule, or for any special arrangement that deviates from government by the people's representatives. There is no provision for suspending any rights; only the privilege of the writ of _habeas corpus_ may be suspended and only by the people's representatives in Congress, only in cases of rebellion or invasion, and only if the public safety requires it.

International Human Rights in United States Law

The differences between rights in the United States and international human rights are not large, and the United States could readily and regularly comply with international standards. The international covenants depend primarily on national institutions for their implementation, and they could be readily implemented in the United States by the political branches and the courts. But the United States has not adhered to these or most other human rights conventions, and there is no sign that the executive branch is eager to ratify them or that the Senate will soon consent to such ratification. For the United States, human rights have been a kind of "white man's burden," and international human rights have been "for export only." An abiding isolationism (or unilateralism), strongly espoused in the Senate (and sometimes in the executive branch), continues to appeal to many Americans, even some who readily judge others and are eager to intervene on behalf of democracy and human rights in other countries. There is some reluctance to accept, and have our courts apply, standards perceived to have been created by others, even if they were borrowed from us and reflect our own values. There is some reluctance to have the United States subject to scrutiny by others, even though Americans pride themselves on an open society.

I believe that most Americans do not share that reluctance, however. They are proud of their society and do not fear scrutiny of their institutions. They would favor active U.S. participation in international human rights; they think that the United States should engage in, not abandon, the ideological competition. They would wish the United States to exert its influence against torture, lawless detention, arbitrary killing or disappearances, fake trials, and for due process of law, freedom of conscience and movement, and freedom from fear. Lawyers generally have been convinced that U.S. adherence to the international covenants would be proper and desirable. The American Bar Association has supported their ratification.

Although the United States has not adhered to any of the principal human rights covenants, international human rights have, to some extent, made their way into U.S. law. The U.N. Charter is a treaty of the United States and in articles 55 and 56, the United States pledged itself to take joint and separate action in cooperation with the United Nations to promote universal respect for, and observance of, human rights. Although a California court held those provisions to be non-self-executing soon after the charter's adoption, it subsequently has been argued that the Universal Declaration defined the obligations of all U.N. members, including the United States, under the Charter, and that at least some provisions of the Universal Declaration have thus become law of the United States. The United States is also a party to the Protocol on the Status of Refugees, and its obligations, not least of which is the obligation not to return a refugee to the country of repression, are law in the United States and have been implemented by congressional legislation.

Others have argued that at least some of the provisions of the Universal Declaration have become customary international law and thereby law of the United States. Even under a conservative view it is now accepted that it is a violation of customary international law if a state, as a matter of state policy, practices, encourages, or condones genocide, arbitrary killing, torture, prolongs arbitrary detention, or systematic racial discrimination. Already a U.S. court has held it to be a violation of international law, and therefore of U.S. law, to keep inadmissible aliens in detention indefinitely. The U.S. Court of Appeals for the Second Circuit has held that torture by a foreign official is a violation of international law, and that Congress gave the federal courts jurisdiction (in 28 U.S.C. §1350) to provide a tort remedy to alien victims of such a violation. It is accepted that a case arising under international law arises under U.S. law for purposes of federal jurisdiction (28 U.S.C. §1331) and other violations of international human rights law may yet make their way into U.S. courts by that route.

International human rights have also entered U.S. law in more subtle ways. Contemporary international human rights values provide the backdrop for examination of the constitutional concepts of liberty, property, and due process of law; they inform inquiry into whether governmental action--e.g., search and seizure--is reasonable, or whether punishment is cruel or unusual; and they color the determination of which of two rights shall prevail in case of conflict, or whether individual rights may be limited in given circumstances for particular reasons of national security or public order. The influence of these human rights values on U.S. law can be seen in the growing number of references in U.S. cases to the Universal Declaration and to international standards and guidelines such as the U.N. Standard Minimum Rules for the Treatment of Prisoners.

Human Rights in U.S. Foreign Policy

Human rights have figured prominently in U.S. foreign policy since the United States helped launch the human rights movement during and after the Second World War. From the beginning of that movement, it has been official U.S. policy to promote human rights and induce compliance with international human rights standards through various organs and programs of international organizations, notably the United Nations, but also the ILO and UNESCO. It must be said, however, that the United States has not always provided leadership in human rights activities or pursued them consistently and energetically. Indeed, the United States has been increasingly unhappy with the politicization of human rights in the United Nations and their subordination to the Third World political agenda, with "selective targeting" of a few countries, such as Israel.

Perhaps because U.N. human rights programs seemed ineffective or distorted, and perhaps too from a conviction that the executive branch was less than dedicated and vigorous, and surely less than effective, in addressing gross human rights violations, the U.S. Congress in the early 1970s embarked on a program to help promote respect for human rights around the world and to dissociate the United States from gross violations and gross violators of human rights. Beginning in 1971, Congress enacted numerous statutes restricting or limiting economic or military assistance, denying credits or favorable trade terms, and restricting imports or exports, to named countries guilty of human rights violations. Congress also adopted a comprehensive program of general legislation denying economic aid, arms sales and other security assistance, and sales of agricultural commodities, to countries guilty of "consistent patterns of gross violations of internationally recognized human rights." United States representatives in international financial institutions were also directed to oppose aid and loans to such countries. Exceptions were permitted under the different programs when assistance was necessary to meet the basic needs of the people, or when the President certified an overriding U.S. interest or that there had been "significant improvement" in the condition of human rights. Congress also established a human rights bureaucracy in the Department of State and in U.S. embassies abroad. It directed the Department of State to publish annually a report on the condition of human rights in every country in the world.

The congressional human rights program, it should be stressed, was not designed to promote parliamentary democracy or to dissociate the United States from authoritarian states generally. (In the main, too, it was not directed at Communist states, which generally do not receive foreign aid or security assistance from the United States.) It was directed at governments, whatever their ideology, that were guilty of consistent and gross violations of specified fundamental human rights--e.g., killing, causing persons to disappear, torture, or arbitrary detention.

This program was adopted by Congress. It was not the result of a presidential initiative, and except during the administration of President Carter it has not had strong presidential support. Sometimes, indeed, presidents have resisted it, and sometimes there have been charges of presidential failure "to take Care that the Laws be faithfully executed" (U.S. Const. art. II, §3). President Carter decided to make concern for human rights an important element in his foreign policy, although at the time his administration, too, was charged with inconsistent and spotty implementation of the congressional program. President Reagan clearly has tended to subordinate the congressional human rights program to other policy concerns. The Reagan administration has seen resistance to the Soviet Union as the principal plank of its foreign policy. Therefore, while it has been vociferous in its condemnation of Communist violations of human rights, as in Poland, it has continued to woo Communist China without regard to its human rights record. For the Reagan administration, non-Communist states are to be encouraged and defended against Communist subversion or influence; U.S. relations with them should not be roiled by criticism of their human rights records nor should they be denied assistance on account of it. The administration believes that human rights considerations should not bar foreign aid or military assistance to regimes--e.g., in Central America--facing insurrection by Communist or leftist elements, sometimes supported by the Soviet Union or Cuba. Congress, however, has maintained its program and has continued to inject human rights concerns and restrictions into particular aid appropriations (including those to Central American governments), although it has not always been able or willing to mobilize itself to insist on presidential respect for the spirit, or even the letter, of its laws.

The congressional program has not been unanimously acclaimed either in the United States or abroad. In the United States, some critics have argued that the program disturbed U.S. relations and hurt other U.S. interests, and did nothing for human rights. Abroad, some governments--particularly those that have been declared by U.S. spokesmen to be gross violators of human rights--charged the United States with interfering in the domestic affairs of other countries.

Some of this criticism is clearly unfounded, and all of it, I believe, is mistaken. The condition of human rights in any country has long ceased to be a matter of its domestic jurisdiction; it is of profound international concern. It is not unlawful intervention or otherwise improper interference for a government to criticize violations of human rights by another government, to deny that government foreign aid or arms (unless required to do so by treaty), or even to disrupt friendly relations with that government. In the United States, the congressional human rights program accurately reflects, I believe, the desire of the American people not to support, or be otherwise associated with, governments guilty of gross violations of human rights. When forthrightly and consistently applied, the program has in fact also evoked wide and positive response around the world and has helped, rather than hurt, the international interests of the United States. And, I am persuaded, it has served the cause of human rights, helping to terminate some violations and to deter many more.

Human rights are deep in the spirit of our times. They reflect the aspirations of human beings everywhere today, permeate international relations and are established in international law. For Americans, the idea of rights, and in particular rights universally and internationally recognized, is wholly congenial. In the United States, with its rich constitutional jurisprudence, concerned Bar, and alert judiciary, international human rights will doubtless remain ancillary to constitutional rights, but international human rights will increasingly supplement and enrich constitutional safeguards. Attention to the condition of international human rights reflects U.S. concern for human beings everywhere, a concern that is its principal appeal and principal weapon in the ideological competition with tyranny.

WESTERN EUROPE AND INTERNATIONAL HUMAN RIGHTS

London Sessions
ABA Annual Meeting 1985
Ballroom, Park Lane Hotel
London, England

Friday, July 19, 1985
10:00 A.M. - 12:00 Noon

Anthony Lester, Q.C.
2 Hare Court
Temple, London EC4Y 7BH

and

Stephen Grosz
Bindman & Partners
1 Euston Road
King's Cross, London NW1 25A

On June 26, 1945, the United Nations (U.N.) Charter was signed at San Francisco. A persistent lobby at San Francisco, led by the United States agencies, had induced the framers of the U.N. Charter to insert repeated references to basic rights and to create a commission to act on them. In February 1946, at its first meeting, the Economic and Social Council set up the Commission on Human Rights to submit proposals on an International Bill of Rights. The Commission was chaired by Eleanor Roosevelt.

Sadly, the Cold War was soon to have its chillng effect. On March 5, 1946, Winston Churchill spoke at Fulton, Missouri, of the Iron Curtain that had descended across Europe. By October 1946, when the International Military Tribunal delivered its judgment at Nuremberg, such enthusiasm as there might have been at the government level about the development of international human rights law under U.N. auspices was waning. In the aftermath of the horror, death, and devastation of the Second World War, there was still sufficient political will to enable the adoption of the Universal Declaration of Human Rights by the General Assembly of the United Nations on December 10, 1948. But behind the scenes, work on the proposed International Bill of Rights was being hindered because of Western fears that the project would be exploited by the Soviet bloc and by the movements for decolonisation and self-determination in Asia and Africa.

On April 12, 1951, the Foreign Secretary, Herbert Morrison, candidly told the British Cabinet that he had always been sceptical about the proposed Covenant on Human Rights but

> As the United Kingdom has played a leading part in promoting them, it would be difficult to draw back at this stage. In these circumstances the prudent course might be to prolong the international discussions, to raise legal and practical difficulties, and to delay the conclusion of the Covenant for as long as possible.

The Cabinet agreed that the Foreign Secretary should instruct his representative in the discussions in the United Nations "to exploit to the full any opportunity for delaying the conclusion of the Covenant."

Similarly negative views were presumably being expressed, and instructions given, in Washington, D.C. and elsewhere. Henceforth, the work was to be done with all deliberate delay. Indeed, what were to become the two U.N. Covenants on Human Rights were not ready for signature until December 1966, 20 years after the original proposal; and they did not come into force for another 10 years. Even now, when the U.N. Covenants have been ratified by more than half the world, they have still not been ratified by the United States, which inspired their creation. The proposal that President Carter submitted to the Senate in 1978 contained reservations providing that ratification of the Covenants would require no modification of U.S. law and that a declaration accompanying ratification would deny to the Covenants self-executing effect, so that they would not in and of themselves become effective as domestic law. The Department of Justice expressed the view that there were no constitutional or other legal objections to ratification. And, at their Michigan meeting in 1979, the American Bar Association recommended ratification on this basis. However, even this modest proposal apparently remains unacceptable in imposing international obligations upon the United States.

As for Western Europe, most of the 21 Member States of the Council of Europe have ratified the U.N. Covenants (and the other major international human rights conventions); but very few have accepted the jurisdiction of the U.N. Human Rights Committee to consider claims of breaches of the Covenants. What has happened instead is that Western Europe has developed its own regional machinery for the protection and enforcement of international human rights.

A second terrible war in half a century and the Nazi holocaust convinced the leaders and statesmen of Western Europe of the need to forge a new Europe built on a greater degree of unity and understanding. By doing so they sought to guard against the rise of new dictatorships and reduce the risk of relapse into disastrous war. This goal inspired the foundation, in May 1949, of the Council of Europe as the first European institution. One of the Council's main tasks was to work for the "maintenance and further realisation of human rights and fundamental freedoms."

Drawing on the Universal Declaration of Human Rights, the Council of Europe drafted a convention that was less extensive in the rights it sought to protect but which was much stronger in the matter of enforcement. For the first time, effective regional enforcement machinery was set up to protect human rights; and Member States undertook not only to accept duties on the inter-state level but also to recognise that individuals have enforceable rights under international law.

The work on the European Convention (in contrast with the work on the U.N. Covenants) was speedily completed. The Convention was signed on November 4, 1950, and came into force on September 3, 1953. It has been ratified by all 21 Member States of the Council of Europe. Seventeen of them (Austria, Belgium, Denmark, France, Federal Republic of Germany, Iceland, Ireland, Italy, Liechtenstein, Luxembourg, Netherlands, Norway, Portugal, Spain, Sweden, Switzerland, and the United Kingdom) have accepted the right of individuals and nongovernmental organisations within their jurisdiction to bring complaints against them alleging that their fundamental human rights or freedoms have been breached by the state concerned. The four Member States that still do not accept the right of individual application are Cyprus, Greece, Malta, and Turkey. Nineteen of the 21 Member States have also agreed to accept compulsory jurisdiction of the European Court of Human Rights.

Most of the rights and freedoms protected by the Convention are of a civil and political nature. They include:

- The right to life;
- The right to liberty and security of persons;
- The right to fair administration of justice (including access to the ordinary courts);
- The prohibition of torture and of inhuman or degrading treatment or punishment;
- The prohibition of slavery, servitude, and forced labour;
- The prohibition of retroactive criminal laws;
- The right to freedom of expression (including imparting and receiving ideas and information regardless of frontiers);
- The right to freedom of thought, conscience, and religion;
- The right to respect for family life, home, and correspondence;
- The right of peaceful assembly and association (including the right to form and join trade unions); and
- The right to marry and to found a family.

Twenty Member States have also ratified Protocol No. 1 to the Convention which guarantees:

- The right to property;
- The right to education (including the right of parents to ensure that education and teaching are in accordance with their own religious and philosophical convictions); and
- The right to free elections in the choice of the legislature.

Thirteen Member States have ratified Protocol No. 4 which guarantees:

- Liberty of movement and freedom to choose where to live;
- The right to leave a country, including one's own;
- The right of a Member State's nationals not to be expelled or denied entry; and
- The prohibition of collective expulsion of aliens.

The enjoyment of these rights and freedoms must be secured by the Member States without discrimination on any grounds such as sex, colour, language, religion, political or other opinion, national or social origin, association with a national minority, property, birth, or other status.

The Convention recognises that most of these rights cannot be absolute and unrestricted in a modern democratic society. Restrictions may therefore be necessary on grounds of public safety, national security, the economic well-being of a country, public health and morals, the prevention of disorder and crime, and the protection of the rights and freedoms of others. However, the European Court and Commission of Human Rights have not permitted these exceptions to impair the substance of the rights and freedoms guaranteed by the Convention. The exceptions are construed strictly by the test of necessity. The burden is upon the Member State to show not only that it has a legitimate aim in interfering with a particular right or freedom but also that the means used are "proportionate" or reasonably related to the aim pursued.

The Convention also permits Member States to suspend their obligations in time of war or public emergency threatening the life of the nation. However, whether in time of war or public emergency, no Member State can avoid its obligation to respect the right to life, or to prevent torture and inhuman or degrading treatment or punishment, or slavery, or retroactive criminal laws. Furthermore, although it falls in the first place to each government, with its responsibility for "the life of the nation," to determine whether that life is threatened by a public emergency, the emergency measures must be no more than is strictly required by the exigencies of the situation, and there is European supervision of the government's justification of emergency measures by the Commission and the Court.

The abolition of the death penalty in Member States has also recently been incorporated into the Convention by Protocol No. 6. In order to become a party to the Protocol, a Member State will have to abolish the death penalty in peacetime. The Protocol has not yet come into force, but the death penalty has already been abolished in the overwhelming majority of Member States (the main exception in practice being Turkey). Efforts are currently being made to widen the Convention further to include rights guaranteed by the U.N. Covenants which are not in the Convention.

Member States are obliged to ensure that their own legislation and administrative practices comply with the Convention, secure Convention rights to the individuals within their jurisdiction, and provide effective remedies before independent authorities to people who claim that their rights have been violated. In addition, the Convention has established organs (which sit in Strasbourg) to ensure that Member States comply with their obligations under the Convention: the European Commission of Human Rights, which receives all applications initially; the European Court of Human Rights, which hears cases referred to it by the Commission or a Member State; and the Committee of Ministers of the Council of Europe, which has an autonomous decision making power if a case has been sent to it by the Commission and has not been brought before the Court. The Committee of Ministers also has the authority to supervise the execution of the Court's judgments against Member States.

There are two types of proceedings that may be brought under the Convention. In an inter-State case, a Member State refers to the Commission what it regards as the failure on the part of another Member State to comply with the Convention, thus participating in what has been called the maintenance of the public order of Europe. Since the coming into force of the Convention there have been five inter-state cases, including the Greek Case (breaches of the Convention by the dictatorship in Greece under the Colonels); the Northern Ireland Case (inhuman and degrading treatment in the interrogation of suspected terrorists in Northern Ireland); the Turkish Cases (Turkey's part in events that took place in Cyprus after the invasion in 1974, and the situation in Turkey thereafter).

The Commission also has jurisdiction to hear individual applications from any person claiming to be the victim of a violation of the Convention by one of the 17 Member States that have accepted this procedure. An individual must exhaust any domestic remedy available to him before applying to the Commission. The Commission may grant free legal aid to an applicant of limited means when there is enough in the case to call for an exchange of arguments between the Member State concerned and the petitioner. Between July 1954, when the Commission was set up, and January 1, 1984, the Commission received 10,709 individual applications of which only 326 were declared admissible (i.e., which satisfied the procedural requirements and disclosed an arguable case).

The procedure is the same in inter-state and individual cases. If an application is declared admissible, the Commission examines it in depth to establish the facts. The Convention requires the Commission to act as a conciliator by placing itself at the disposal of the parties with a view to securing a friendly settlement of the matter. Such a settlement must be based on respect for human rights as defined in the Convention, and the Commission is concerned not only with the individual interests of the applicant but with the general interest. In many cases, such settlements may simply amount to the payment of damages and costs to the applicant or victim, but much of the Commission's most effective work involves changing laws and practices by means of well-negotiated settlements.

If a friendly settlement is reached, its terms are set out in a brief report, which is published. Where no friendly settlement is reached, the Commission draws up a report containing factual findings and a legal opinion as to whether the Convention has been breached by the state concerned. This report is sent to the Committee of Ministers and to the Government, but not to the applicant. It remains confidential unless either the case is brought before the Court or the Committee of Ministers decides to publish it, and the Commission's opinion does not bind the Member State concerned in any event. Proceedings before the Commission are held in private and are confidential.

The case may be referred to the Court by the Commission or by the government for a decision as to whether there has been a breach of the Convention. The individual cannot refer a case to the Court. Once the case is before the Court, the proceedings become judicial in character and are held in public, either before a Chamber of seven judges or before the full Court of 21 judges. The individual applicant may be legally represented to argue against the government before the Court. The Commission assists the Court as defender of the public interest. Under a recent innovation, third parties may also make written comments on relevant issues provided that the Court gives leave for them to do so in the interests of justice.

The Court's judgments are binding on the State concerned and often have important consequences for the laws or practices of other states. The Court may award compensation and legal costs to the victim of a breach of the Convention. Between its creation in 1959, and September 1984, the Court received 78 cases. By September 1984, the Court had found one or more breaches in 43 cases and no breach in 17 cases. The number of cases referred to the Court by the Commission has greatly increased in the past decade and most of the Court's judgments have been given within that period. They have included a wide range of controversial and far-reaching issues, such as:

- Restrictions on prisoners' rights of correspondence and rights of access to the courts;
- Use of the birch as judicial corporal punishment;
- Detention of vagrants without the opportunity to challenge their detention before a court;
- Delays in bringing those on remand to trial;
- Delays in judicial and administrative proceedings;
- Punishments for breaches of military discipline;
- Requiring defendants in criminal cases to pay the costs of interpreters' fees;
- A court ban on publication of a newspaper article about thalidomide children pending the trial of negligence actions;
- Denial of access to a civil court because of the absence of legal aid;
- Trade union rights to bargain collectively;
- Seizure and forfeiture of an obscene book;
- Compulsory sex education in schools;
- Controls of telephone tapping;
- Rights of transsexuals to change their status;
- Criminal sanctions for homosexual conduct by adult males;
- The dismissal of employees for refusing to join trade unions;
- Corporal punishment in schools;
- Rights of mentally abnormal offenders to have their detention reviewed;
- Disciplinary proceedings against doctors; and
- The "blighting" of private property through the operation of planning controls.

Among the cases which the Court will decide in 1985, one case concerns alleged sex and race discrimination in excluding foreign husbands (but not wives) from living in their spouses' country; a second case involves a veterinarian's right to express critical views and to advertise his services contrary to the rules of his professional association; a third case concerns a claim that companies were nationalised without the payment of fair compensation to the former owners.

The Court has held not only the actions of public officials, but also national legislation and judicial decisions, to have breached the Convention. Parliaments and Supreme Courts have been found wanting and the Member States concerned have been compelled to amend their laws to change their practices. The extent of the encroachment upon traditional notions of national sovereignty in favour of individual rights is real and substantial.

The 10 Member States of the Council of Europe, who also belong to the European Economic Community, have made adherence to the Convention a virtual condition of membership of the Community. And the European Court of Justice (in Luxembourg) has regard to the Convention when interpreting Community law.

At the national level, the legal status of the Convention in domestic law varies. In most of the Member States, it forms part of domestic law, sometimes ranking equally with, or even above, the national constitution. In a minority of Member States (of which the United Kingdom is the only major country), the Convention does not form part of domestic law because it has not been incorporated by legislation. British judges are therefore denied the power and the responsibility of safeguarding the fundamental rights and freedoms of the Convention. The House of Lords, and the Court of Appeal when Lord Denning was Master of the Rolls, have sometimes had regard to the Convention to resolve ambiguities in statutory provisions. But, in the absence of parliamentary action to incorporate the Convention, the European Court of Human Rights has increasingly become a substitute for a supreme constitutional court in the United Kingdom.

To be sure, much remains to be done to improve the Convention's system. The scope of the Convention is narrow. The six-month time limit for making complaints is absolute, allowing no discretion for hard cases. The Commission is underfunded and understaffed. Proceedings before the Commission and the Court take far too long. The legal aid scheme is grossly inadequate. Few lawyers have the necessary expertise or commitment to represent applicants effectively and usually with little or no remuneration. The Commission is overburdened by its caseload, especially since its members work only part time, and its permanent secretariat has only about 25 legal experts who have to cope not only with the different laws and practices, but also with the different languages, of the 21 Member States. Moreover, too often the absence of effective national remedies for breaches of the Convention means that the Commission and the Court become tribunals of first recourse, whereas the founders of the Convention intended them to be tribunals of ultimate recourse. Not surprisingly, the Commission rejects more than nine out of 10 applications at the preliminary stage.

Despite these defects in the European Convention system, the record is impressive. One measure of its success is that almost all of the Member States have now accepted the right of individual application against them even though acceptance is optional and not mandatory under the Convention, and even though the Commission and the Court have interpreted the Convention liberally so as to translate its object and purpose into practical reality. France first accepted the right of individual application only in 1981, and from time to time governments hint that they might not renew their acceptance of individual applications if the Commission and the Court continue to interfere so extensively with matters traditionally regarded as falling within their governments' domestic jurisdiction. But in practice, the right of individual application seems unlikely to be withdrawn.

Before accepting the right of individual application, governments used to argue implausibly that it was unnecessary to do so because their laws and practices fully complied with the requirements of the Convention, and their existing legal systems provided effective and sufficient remedies. Apart from the United Kingdom, all of the Member States have written constitutions and enforceable Bills of Rights. Countries such as France and West Germany take justifiable pride in their home-grown systems for the judicial review of legislation and administrative action. It is therefore all the more remarkable that they have been willing to accept the jurisdiction of an international tribunal to decide where state power ends and individual freedom begins within their countries.

The influence of the Convention has not been confined to Europe. Its provisions have been incorporated into the independence constitutions of 26 new Commonwealth countries. It provided the model for the Inter-American Convention on Human Rights. Its case law is increasingly referred to by Canadian courts as a source of interpretation of the new Charter of Rights.

The case law of the U.S. Supreme Court has been a significant influence in Europe and the British Commonwealth. It is strongly arguable that the activism of the Warren Court encouraged the Commission in the late 1960s and the Court in the 1970s to become bolder in their approach. American constitutional law has been especially influential on Convention case law in relation to freedom of expression, equality without discrimination, and due process of law. Federal cases are treated as persuasive authority both by national courts in the Commonwealth and also by the Strasbourg Court and the Luxembourg Court.

Given the role of the United States as the main creator and continuing source of international human rights law, it is regrettable that the precious commodity continues to be regarded as only for export from the United States, with no free trade. In some areas, international human rights law has recently become more liberal than law and practice in the United States. In other areas, it is potentially relevant to the evolving interpretation of the American Bill of Rights and federal legislation (notably the Equal Pay and Civil Rights Acts). But the U.S. judiciary, legal profession, and Law Schools continue (with rare exceptions) to remain as isolated from international human rights law as the legislative and executive branches of the United States.

COST OF LITIGATION IN THE UNITED STATES: CONCERN AND FERMENT

London Sessions
ABA Annual Meeting 1985
Westminster Room, Inter-Continental Hotel
London, England

Friday, July 19, 1985
10:00 A.M. - 12:00 Noon

Prof. A. Leo Levin
Federal Judicial Center
1520 H Street, N.W.
Washington, D.C. 20005

Introduction

The high cost of civil litigation in the United States has become a subject of intense and widespread concern. That concern is reflected in a series of wide-ranging amendments and proposed amendments to the Federal Rules of Civil Procedure, in a proliferation of statutes providing for fee shifting, and in judicial decisions designed to control lawyers' activities in rather basic ways. At stake, in the minds of many, is nothing less than access to justice for many litigants--the availability, not merely in theory but in the reality of the market place, of judicial processes to adjudicate the vast number of disputes that inevitably arise in a complex, heterogeneous society.

The total percentage of the gross national product that is consumed by legal expenses has been rising significantly and, in one form or another, the cost is borne by society. The attorneys'fees awarded in a single case can be staggering, in excess of $45 million to cite one example, and of course this figure does not include the attorneys' fees incurred by the losing litigant. Do such awards, even if justified, reflect a system of dispute resolution as efficient and effective as our society can devise? Finally, there is an element of serious concern with the ethical implications of fees--contingent fees, for example, so large as to appear unconscionable.

It is not necessary to argue that the dimensions of the problem are already of crisis proportions, nor that the sheer number of "horror stories" demonstrate that radical action is urgent if the public is to retain a measure of confidence in law and lawyers. The situation, however, has been recognized as sufficiently serious to have warranted a variety of initiatives in the effort to cope, ameliorate, and to improve. These initiatives in turn present challenges of their own; they raise troublesome issues deserving of analysis.

Control of Litigation Practices: Discovery Abuse

The most dramatic illustrations of how high litigation costs have soared are provided by complex and protracted cases. These cases offer examples of attorney fee awards in the millions of dollars, of literally hundreds of thousands pages of depositions, of countless discovery requests, and of a seemingly endless parade of motions over interrogatories and requests for admission, not to mention depositions. The evidence is clear, however, that these cases are atypical;* they do not reflect the problems involved in what has been termed the mid-range of litigation. The cases in each of these categories are important, but they are different. The problems they present are different and so are the solutions to these problems. The ABA Action Commission to Reduce Court Costs and Delay, which has only recently completed a five-year effort to implement practical programs in furtherance of its mission, chose to focus on civil controversies in the "mid-range . . . involving from $1,000 to $25,000--cases too big for the informal procedures of small claims courts but not big enough to involve the special problems of the megacases." Some of the Commission's report plows familiar ground: vigorous case management by the judge results in speedier dispositions and, there is reason to believe, in less expensive litigation; expedited appeals offer promise, and, where the motivation exists, appropriate programs can be implemented. Less familiar, but quite simple and perhaps obvious, is the use of teleconferencing as a substitute for in-court appearances, a practice that has proved entirely satisfactory to the participants and quite cost effective. The argument of a discovery motion provides a good example. One need think only of the time spent by attorneys coming to court, waiting their turn on the list, and returning to their offices. At current hourly rates, even where all the participants are in the same city, the money involved can easily run into substantial sums, a fortiori, where counsel are from another city, albeit in the same general region, the potential savings are significant. Yet there are serious questions as to who is actually benefited. Are such savings passed on to the clients?

Where billing is by hourly rates, there is evidence that the savings are passed on, although a lawyer may, and some lawyers apparently have, changed their billing practices to charging by the event, at least for some events. Thus, there may be a substantial charge for the argument of a motion, although it took only twenty minutes on the phone, rather than for the three hours the same event would have required formerly. In the case of contingent fees, however, there is substantial doubt that the savings are being passed on. The lawyer benefits, not the client. Perhaps as such savings become more predictable and pervasive, these economies will be reflected in fee adjustments or in lower percentages; perhaps not.

---

*In a study of over 3,000 terminated civil cases in six United States district courts, the Federal Judicial Center found that more than half had no recorded discovery requests and fewer than five percent had more than ten requests. Connolly, Holleman and Kuhlman, Judicial Controls and the Civil Litigative Process: Discovery (FJC 1978).

It is the protracted case, frequently complex and almost always involving large stakes, that presents more dramatic opportunities for effecting efficiencies and more troublesome problems as well. Discovery can go on literally for years. Depositions are seemingly numberless and computerized information systems are developed to cope with massive accumulations of documents. The evidence indicates that strong management on the part of the judge, or in some cases by magistrates who represent them, combined with rigorous adherence to reasonable deadlines, serves not only to avoid delay but to reduce or eliminate repetitive discovery and unnecessary, if not harassing, litigation procedures. The Federal Rules of Civil Procedure have been amended to "encourage pretrial management that meets the needs of modern litigation."

Beyond that there has been a three-pronged approach designed to cope with cost and delay in the big case. The Federal Rules of Civil Procedure have been amended to require more of the lawyer who signs pleadings, seeks discovery, or interposes objections at the pretrial state; there must be more than the absence of bad faith or willful intention to delay. There is an affirmative obligation of reasonable inquiry not only with respect to the filing of a pleading, but with respect to each and every discovery request or objection. (See F.R.Civ.P. 11, 26(g).) Second, sanctions are made mandatory in the effort to assure that the new standards make a difference in the practice. Finally, and perhaps of greatest significance in the true megacase, is the role of the judge in limiting drastically those lawyers' activities for which attorneys' fees will be awarded. Both these judicial initiatives and the developments in the law of sanctions will be discussed more fully below.

Alternative Dispute Resolution

Alternative dispute resolution is a burgeoning industry in the United States. Litigation is too slow, too expensive, and often too traumatic as well. Arbitration has long been an available alternative; so has mediation. Some of the familiar methods have been made available for new and different types of disputes; some new mechanisms have been developed. A number of organizations, designed as profit-making ventures, offer less costly alternatives to formal adjudication. The 1983 amendment to Federal Rule of Civil Procedure 16(c)(7) specifically invites parties to consider "the use of extra judicial procedures to resolve the dispute."

The term alternative dispute resolution has come to embrace a wide spectrum of procedures. Some can be invoked only after a law suit has been filed. For example, in Pennsylvania state courts and in the eastern District of Pennsylvania, court-annexed arbitration is provided for by statute or by rule and is mandatory. All cases of a particular class, and in some courts cases with up to $40,000 as the amount in controversy, are referred to a panel of three lawyer-arbitrators. The award, however, is not binding and trial de novo in court is available to dissatisfied parties, but the evidence is strong that a very substantial number of actual trials are avoided as a result of these programs. Moreover, cases move to termination with dispatch and litigant satisfaction is high. (See Levin, "Court-Annexed Arbitration, 16 Mich. J. L. Reform 537 (1983) reporting, inter alia on Federal Judicial Center studies.) Similarly, a program in the Eastern District of Michigan provides for mediation of cases, utilizing the services of an existing agency established for processing of state cases. Referral to the agency is mandatory, but it is open to the parties to accept or reject the "findings" of the panel. Rejection, however, carries the risk of a substantial monetary penalty in the event that the objecting party does not significantly improve his or her own position.

Other programs, such as summary jury trial, are run under the auspices of a judge, but are intended simply as a means of facilitating settlement. A six-person jury is empanelled and an attorney for each side makes a relatively brief oral presentation of what that party's evidence could be expected to show. The resultant verdict, which need not be unanimous, is made available for the consideration of both parties. The practice originated in the Northern District of Ohio, but it has been used in a fair number of other courts as a result of favorable reports of its utility as a means of promoting settlement of what had been predicted to be long and difficult cases.

The programs described above come into play only after a law suit is already pending and, typically, after substantial activity in the pretrial phase. There are other programs, however, sometimes described as mini-trials, that may allow litigants to avoid the judicial process entirely. Panels of former judges or retired judges are available to preside at informal, confidential hearings, often in the presence of senior corporate personnel. Settlements frequently follow, although the specifics of the agreement between the parties can be shaped to suit the individual case.

Analysis of the cost of litigation rarely takes into account the value of the time and energy of senior executives taken up as a result of the tortuous pace of litigation. Knowledgeable observers have asserted that executive time, properly cost accounted, is the single largest element of litigation expense, even when considering corporate counsel as a lawyer rather than an executive. This is a powerful motivation to fashion out-of-court procedures that expedite resolutions. In short, our society appears to be turning more and more to nonjudicial alternatives as judges seek to divert cases in the effort to cope with caseloads that seem to be burgeoning in exponential proportions and as litigants seek to avoid being caught in the lengthy, expensive, and often traumatic procedures of our judicial system.

Fee Shifting

In contrasting civil litigation in the United States and in England, the most familiar and dramatic difference concerns the award of attorneys' fees to the prevailing party. In the words of Justice White, speaking for the United States Supreme Court, "In the United States, the prevailing litigant is ordinarily not entitled to collect a reasonable attorney's fee from the loser," while in England the practice for centuries has been to award costs, including attorney fees. We still refer to the "American Rule," although by now there are 150 state and federal statutes that provide for fee shifting. Moreover, the trend toward fee shifting continues with the result that attorneys' fees are today awarded to an extent unknown twenty to thirty years ago. No single theory accounts for a decision, legislative or judicial, to shift fees and, indeed, the technicalities of the governing provisions vary substantially from case to case. It is useful to identify at least four separate bases for the award of attorneys' fees and to explore, at least briefly, the implications of each.

First, attorneys' fees may be awarded to an aggrieved party as a sanction for improper conduct by his adversary. Thus, 28 U.S.C. § 1927 provides that an attorney "who so multiplies the proceedings in any case unreasonably and vexatiously may be required by the court to satisfy personally the excess costs, expenses, and attorneys' fees" that result. The sanction is imposed, under this provision, not on the litigant, but on the attorney personally. Moreover, the outcome of the lawsuit is irrelevant to a finding of sanctionable conduct and the imposition of a penalty; the sanction may be imposed upon the attorney for the party who ultimately prevails. Section 1927, however, has hardly been used and its amendment in 1980 to broaden its scope and increase the severity of the penalty has had little impact. Generally speaking, courts have been reluctant to impose sanctions for dilatory tactics or for other abuses of civil process that increase the cost of litigation. The Federal Rules of Civil Procedure, for example, have long provided for the imposition of attorneys' fees in connection with abuse of discovery, but the number of sanctions actually requested by opposing counsel, let alone those imposed, may almost be characterized as de minimis.

In the face of this record and the desire to reduce the burdens of litigation, the federal rules were amended in 1983 to make sanctions mandatory. (See, e.g., F.R.Civ.P. 11 and 26(g).) True, the sanction imposed was left to the discretion of the judge, and while it might include "a reasonable attorney's fee," it might be no more than a token amount, or even an admonition. It is clear, however, that the draftsmen were looking to encourage resort to sanctions, whether or not requested by an opposing party. The Advisory Committee comments state:

> The detection and punishment of a violation of the signing requirement, encouraged by the amended rule, is part of the court's responsibility for securing the system's effective operation.

Formal amendment and hortatory words in Advisory Committee notes do not in themselves suffice to change well-established behavior on the part of bench and bar. Nevertheless, there is a growing amount of evidence, anecdotal to be sure but persuasive nonetheless, that judges are more willing than heretofore to shift attorneys' fees for the purpose of sanctioning unacceptable lawyer conduct that today is a contributing factor to the high cost of litigation.

A significant number of statutes reward the prevailing party with attorneys' fees in order to encourage litigation. These statutes reflect a legislative judgment that it is both efficient and effective to enlist aggrieved parties in the enforcement of legislation, typically in such areas as civil rights; in the familiar idiom, such plaintiffs serve as private attorneys general. Professor Thomas D. Rowe, Jr. has put the matter succinctly:

> Litigation sometimes produces benefits beyond those reaped by the successful party. Such litigation furthers the public interest, or at least a private interest broader than that represented by the actual parties. Yet if the American rule applies in its full rigor, the cost to any private party of conducting the litigation may well exceed any gains he can expect, even though the total gain to all beneficiaries may greatly exceed the costs. As a result, the potential plaintiffs may well refrain from bringing socially beneficial suits because the gains would not sufficiently further their private interests. 1982 DUKE L. J. 651 at 662.

It is precisely this underlying theory with its emphasis on encouraging litigation that has resulted in judicial differentiation between the right of a prevailing attorney to recover reasonable attorneys' fees and the far different standard imposed where the defendant is successful. To quote again from Professor Rowe:

> The rule for much civil rights litigation, for example, is that a prevailing plaintiff "'should ordinarily recover an attorney's fee unless special circumstances would render such an award unjust.'" A prevailing defendant, by contrast, may recover only "upon a finding that the plaintiff's action was frivolous, unreasonable, or without foundation, even though not brought in subjective bad faith." 1982 DUKE L. J. at 678 (footnotes omitted).

The Relationship of Government and its Citizens

A third category concerns the Equal Access to Justice Act which was enacted because, in the view of Congress, citizens were being "deterred from seeking review of, or defending against, unreasonable governmental action because of the expense involved in securing the vindication of their rights in civil actions and in administrative proceedings." In one sense the shifting of attorneys' fees in such cases is but an extension of the theory of the private attorney general: the individual citizen is encouraged to assert his or her legal rights in the furtherance of a public policy of potential significance to large numbers of other citizens. Of course, there are differences. The citizen is encouraged not only to institute litigation, but to defend against governmental action which he or she views as improper. As the title of the act suggests, an important factor is assuring access to justice, particularly when government is the offender. There are, however, limits, and there are statutory provisions that even a litigant who prevails may not recover attorneys' fees where "the court finds that the position of the United States was substantially justified or that special circumstances make an award unjust." Thus, the right of a prevailing citizen to recover attorneys' fees against the government is determined not merely by the ultimate result of the litigation, but also by a judicial judgment that the government action in question was one deserving of particular condemnation.

A Final Basis for Fee Shifting: Simple Equity

A litigant who sues and recovers all that is owed to him, but who is required to bear the expenses of the litigation, is not made whole. This simple fact lies behind one of the strongest arguments for fee shifting. Where a judgment includes pain and suffering, or compensation for permanent deformity, an American Rule plaintiff can, in effect, recoup the cost of litigation from whatever has been awarded for these indeterminate components of the final award.

The argument in favor of making a litigant whole, however powerful, has of course not prevailed in the United States. Concern for assuring access to justice, to avoid a chilling effect on plaintiffs who consider their claims meritorious has carried the day. Yet, the underlying dynamic, the recognition that making a litigant whole does reflect ideas of simple equity, is not altogether lost. It operates with particular force when combined with some other factor arguing for fee shifting. Provisions under which fee shifting would follow rejection of an offer of judgment presents such a situation. Suppose a defendant has, during the course of pretrial preparations, determined to make an offer to the plaintiff of a sum of money, the offer is rejected, and ultimately the party rejecting the offer does not succeed in improving his or her position. Several factors would argue for the shifting of whatever attorneys' fees are incurred after the rejection. Indemnifying a litigant who offers to terminate the litigation on terms that ultimately prove as favorable to the adversary as the final judgment is one factor. Then, too, there is the desire to provide disincentives for continuing fruitless and expensive litigation. We have, in a sense, a form of sanction. The Federal Rules of Civil Procedure have always included a rule providing for some measure of fee shifting following the rejection of a defendant's offer of judgment (Rule 68). The rule stands as an outstanding example of law on the books that has been ignored in practice. The Advisory Committee on Civil Rules recently fashioned a wide-reaching alternative to Rule 68, but it met with significant opposition and has been withdrawn. An alternative amendment has been developed and is soon to be submitted to the profession for review and comment. The details need not concern us at this juncture. It is, however, noteworthy that the Advisory Committee is looking to fee shifting in the effort to strike an appropriate balance between the need to assure access to justice and the equally compelling need not to penalize a litigant who offers "justice" in full measure, sooner and at less expense.

Control of Fee Practices

The Contingent Fee

There are few subjects on which the attitudes of the profession in England and in the United States differ as radically as the subject of contingent fees. While there has been criticism of the contingent fee in this country, and certainly many lawyers have become wealthy as a result of it, there is no serious movement to declare it unethical or otherwise to abolish it. Indeed, perhaps what is most noteworthy in this regard is that Lord Denning argued in favor of allowing contingent fees in England as a rather limited exception to the ordinary rule in the case of minority shareholders' action. As must be immediately evident, a percentage of the recovery that may be modest where a judgment is for $10,000, might be completely unconscionable where judgment is for several million dollars. As a result, a number of states have introduced limitations on the size of the fee an attorney may charge based on a sliding scale. In New York, for example, an attorney may receive one-half of the first $1,000 but only 25 percent of sums above $25,000. New Jersey allows a fee of one-third of the first $250,000 recovered, but limits the attorneys' fees to 20 percent of everything above $500,000.

The strongest argument in favor of the contingent fee is that it does allow for access to the courts by impecunious plaintiffs, particularly in cases of personal injury, employment discrimination, and the violation of other civil rights and civil liberties. It is not only that the plaintiff does not risk being obligated to pay the attorneys' fees of the prevailing defendant in the event he loses, but there is no risk of becoming indebted to one's own attorney for the representation.

Judicial Control Over the Award of Attorneys' Fees

In large numbers of cases, particularly class actions in which recovery may be quite large, the amount of attorneys' fees to be awarded to the prevailing party must be fixed by the court. The judge thus retains a powerful weapon to prevent unconscionable recoveries. In the Fine Paper Antitrust Case, the court reduced a fee request in excess of twenty million dollars to $4,343,103 aside from expenses. Moreover, the trial judge in that case wrote a 400 page opinion articulating clearly the factors he considered and the reasoning that impelled his decision. In such cases, the very process of vising fees may be expected to have a substantial impact on the conduct of counsel in future cases.

The impact on counsel can be far more direct. In In Re Continental Illinois Securities Litigation, United States District Judge John F. Grady entered an order early in the case in which he laid down specific guidelines that would govern his award of attorneys' fees and expenses once the litigation had been concluded. For example, the order specifically provided that "no more than one lawyer should appear for the plaintiffs at the deposition of a witness," or for the argument of a motion. The rates of compensation were to be appropriate to the nature of the work done. Thus, "senior partner rates will be paid only for work that warrants the attention of a senior partner. If a senior partner spends his time reviewing documents or doing research a beginning associate could do, he will be paid at the rate of a beginning associate." Moreover procedural requisites, such as the preparation of contemporaneous time records, are becoming more common as judges continue their efforts to contain costs.

House Counsel

Knowledgeable litigants need not wait for formal rules or for judicial decisions to control practices by attorneys that lead to excessive fees and expenses. Particularly in the case of corporations large enough to have a general counsel, there is evident today an awareness that it is desirable to effectuate economies by specific and often detailed arrangements with retained counsel. In addition, it is also open to such litigants to do a greater percentage of litigation work more economically "in house." Thus, there has been a substantial growth in the size of in-house legal staffs in the corporate world.

* * *

There are no panaceas. There is, however, a widespread awareness that fair, efficient, and reasonable resolution of disputes is indispensable to the well-being of any democratic society. Reform is likely to be incremental. Dramatic breakthroughs are not on the horizon. But the shared heritage of our Anglo-American common law system is to recognize the value of whatever progress the day can bring so long as the journey continues.

THE COSTS OF LITIGATION IN ENGLAND AND WALES AS COMPARED WITH THE UNITED STATES

London Sessions
ABA Annual Meeting 1985
Westminster Room, Inter-Continental Hotel
London, England

Friday, July 19, 1985
10:00 A.M. - 12:00 Noon

The Hon. Mr. Justice Leggatt
Royal Courts of Justice
Strand, London WC2A 2LL

and

John Wickerson
Messrs. Ormerod Morris & Dumont
10 High Street
Croydon CR9 2B8

Cost and delay, which are often concomitant, are two of the oldest matters for which lawyers are criticised. Because a lawyer sets his charges according to what the market will stand, or what convention has ordained, or what statute allows, he does not think of them as excessive. It is to the layman that they may have that appearance. Lack of knowledge of the legal processes, lack of understanding of their purposes, and lack of belief that recourse to law should have been necessary in the first place, colour this outlook. For unlike the doctor, the lawyer does not deal in life and death; his acts can seldom heal; and such financial success as he may win for a client often does not truly compensate for the wrong intended to be requited by it.

Contrasts in Litigation Costs

Assuming that the lawyer is able to justify the cost of what he does, he has to keep his procedures under review. Some procedures, in particular discovery, represent the compromises adopted in practice between the acceptable and the unacceptable in pursuit of justice. The more thorough and painstaking a procedure is, the more expensive and therefore the more unacceptable it becomes. In search of simpler procedures which are yet acceptable, it is natural to turn for inspiration to other common law jurisdictions to see which of their procedures are adaptable to one's own.

At this point, three important truths must be appreciated. First, in an examination and comparison of procedures there is very little room for jurisprudence, for dogma or for doctrine: procedure is merely method, the world of nuts and bolts in which the practitioner operates, making the best of whatever rules he is from time to time required to abide by. Secondly, it is very difficult indeed to borrow individual procedures from another jurisdiction, because each system is found to consist of checks and balances that cannot lightly be interfered with. Thirdly, because delays often are caused and costs incurred not by litigants, but by lawyers, it is desirable that the court should be able to watch over its processes and not merely leave it to the lawyers to operate them as they see fit.

Discovery Practice in the United States

Two discovery procedures in the United States, though potentially valuable, are to English eyes often abused or wasteful: oral depositions and document requests.

The potential advantage of the deposition process have to be tested for expense and usefulness. Clearly it is time-consuming and costly in terms of both lawyers' and witnesses' time. Moreover, because each party ordinarily bears its own costs, there is little incentive to keep depositions short; and the costs rule falls particularly heavily on third parties. The usefulness of the process tends to vary inversely with the sophistication of the witness and the obstructiveness of his attorney. An experienced and prepared witness will give little or nothing away in course of a whole day's testimony. Vociferous and vexatious objection to questions is often undeservedly effective because it costs time and money to apply for an order compelling the witness to answer questions and also because the transcript seldom captures adequately the real vexatiousness of the defending attorney.

Extensive document requests are encouraged in the United States by the fact that each party pays its own costs of discovery. Not only is there little to be lost in seeking the broadest discovery possible, but the heavy costs inflicted on the other side by a huge search (generally exacerbated by disputes over the relevance of various items and the right to claim privilege for particular documents) form part of the war of attrition by which a party may be pressured into settlement. An aspect of the costs rule that seems particularly unfair is its application to third parties. Third-party discovery is very widely available under the Federal Rules and takes the same form as discovery directed to the other side; but the third party is ordinarily obliged to bear its own costs incurred in producing responsive documents.

Although we believe that our system avoids excessive use of document requests, it may well be that it would profit by a procedure of oral depositions for discovery stripped of extravagance. This might entail, as in some of the Provinces of Canada, deposing only the other party or (in the case of a corporation) its representatives. In this way it might be possible to avoid trial by ambush whilst avoiding also some of the excesses which the present system in the United States appears to allow.

Specialised Functions of Barristers and Solicitors

There are many cases in County and Magistrates Courts in which barristers are not involved at all. In cases in which they are in those Courts or the High Court, the division of the profession makes possible the interchangeability of barristers. This is an important advantage. Because in the United States a client deals with only one lawyer throughout, he is unlikely to tolerate a different lawyer conducting his trial from the only one with whom he has previously dealt. So delays accrue because trials have to await the availability of particular trial lawyers. In the English system, flexibility is preserved, sometimes at the cost of the client not having the advocate of his choice.

There is obvious benefit to the client in being able, through his own solicitor, to instruct the advocate most suitable for the case he has in hand. One solicitor can retain a different barrister according to whether his client is concerned with a case of careless driving, the winding up of a company, a dispute about the sale of goods, a divorce, a factory accident, a planning appeal, or an armed robbery. No firm could include trial lawyers capable of undertaking all these matters with equal or sufficient competence. Especially since a barrister's overheads are low as compared with a solicitor's firm, it is unlikely that there would be any material difference between the cost of retaining a solicitors' firm together with a barrister and that of retaining a firm of specialist lawyers. Such duplication as there is in a case of any serious consequence is amply compensated for by the benefit of separate consideration of the problem by two lawyers, one close to the client and his worries, the other with the same concern but more opportunity for detachment.

Juries in Civil Cases

The question whether in civil cases juries are worth the cost seems to presuppose that it is desirable to have them if they are not too expensive. In civil cases in England, however, juries have almost been abolished. In practice, they are to be found here now only in defamation actions in the High Court, of which there are probably no more than 20 or 30 a year. This has not come about because they are too expensive, but rather because they are not found to be necessary. The inconvenience of jury service should obviously be avoided if it can be.

The principal reason why juries are retained in civil cases in the United States presumably is that the Seventh Amendment to the Constitution preserves the right to jury trials for "suits at common law." But apart from the right given by the U.S. Constitution, repeated in most state constitutions, lawyers seem to like trial by jury, whatever the public's attitude may be. Since the system breeds larger awards of damages, it is obvious why plaintiff's lawyers prefer it. It is less easy to see why defendants' lawyers support it, or at any rate do not oppose it. No doubt the use of juries may be justified as an exercise in democracy, resulting in the imposition of community standards. But to non-American eyes this is a high price to pay for the inability to understand complex issues and the irrationality, as well as undue susceptibility to advocacy and propensity to compromise, of which juries are customarily accused. Even with reduction in size of juries and without questioning at *voir dire*, we would in England prefer to have our civil cases tried by judges rather than by juries, before ever having to consider the question whether juries are worth the cost.

Alternatives to Litigation

The only serious alternative to High Court litigation is arbitration. To serve London's commercial community, and in particular the shipping and commodity trades, an arbitration service has grown up over the years. Although domestic in origin, this service has become international in effect. Many commercial contracts, even where both parties are foreigners, provide for disputes to be resolved by arbitration in London. Time is saved in two ways. First, arbitration rules in many trades provide for short litigation periods, so if a dispute is to be prosecuted it has to be commenced within a relatively short time after it has arisen, if it is not to be time-barred. Secondly, there is no time wasted in waiting for a date for hearing in Court. Arbitrators can be appointed who are able to conduct the hearing without delay.

Although in building and insurance disputes arbitration is usually no cheaper, in some commodity arbitrations, which are conducted without the intervention of lawyers, money is saved on that account. Otherwise it may be saved either because the arbitration agreement itself precludes recourse to the Court or because the party not content with the results of arbitration cannot bring himself within the requirements for appealing to the High Court. In England, such an appeal lies on a point of law with the consent of the parties or by leave of the Court. As a matter of practice, the Court does not give leave unless in a "one-off" case the decision of the arbitrator was obviously wrong, or unless it probably was wrong in a case of more general importance. The effect in the ordinary run of arbitrations is to confine parties to the arbitration award and so to save potential appeal costs.

Fee Practices

Before embarking on a comparison of practices that may be assumed to be relevant to the expense of civil litigation, it is instructive to consider the actual expense of a typical action in England. The total costs of one party in a personal injury, action worth £35,000 would be in the region of $3,500, of which solicitors' profit costs would be £2,300, counsel's fees £500, and the balance would be other disbursements including medical and expert fees. The fee charged by both solicitors and counsel are unaffected by success or failure. Against this background, then, let us look at fee practices in our respective jurisdictions.

Contingent Fees

Contingent fees are regarded in North America as fulfilling a social need but in England and Wales as subversive of justice. If a defendant, confronted by an unmeritorious claim, knows that he will not only have to incur costs of defence but will also be unable to recover them at trial, he is liable to pay the nuisance value of the claim.

Contingent fees are regarded in England and Wales as against the public interest. The Legal Aid scheme provides access to the Courts for most of those who might otherwise be denied. We believe that contingent fees encourage lawyers to concentrate only on strong cases or those where the amount involved makes the unmeritorious case worth pursuing. The client loses a proportion, often substantial, of his damages, and the attorney is under pressure to settle the case at an early stage for less than its true value in order more quickly to receive his "commission." Another criticism made of the attorney is that he becomes a partner instead of a counsellor and so loses his objectivity because he has an interest in the outcome. Although some would say that this makes him try harder, it may also lead to undesirable practices, including the construction of evidence and the improper coaching of witnesses, and may lead the advocate into conflict with his duty to the Court in the fair presentation of his client's case.

It is the conflict of interest between the lawyer and his client that underlies the English objection to contingent fees. The rule of law upon which the Court has always insisted that a lawyer cannot make an arrangement of any kind with his client so as to give the lawyer any advantage in respect of the result of the litigation has been laid down expressly in order to preserve the honour and honesty of the profession.

It is difficult for lawyers in a jurisdiction that does not allow contingent fees to make comments to lawyers in one that does that are likely to be acceptable, because such criticisms inevitably look like an attempt to impugn their integrity. But perhaps it is worth considering whether it would be appropriate to order attorneys who institute unmeritorious claims when engaged on a contingent fee to pay or contribute personally to the costs of successful defendants.

Fee Shifting

In England, the Court must normally order the costs to follow the event; that is, award the successful party its costs, unless the unsuccessful party can show some ground for the Court to exercise its jurisdiction to refuse such an order. The English theory is that where contingent fees are not allowed and indigent litigants are entitled to legal aid, it is fairer that the costs of litigating contentious issues should be borne by the loser. Otherwise, by merely bringing a claim, a plaintiff can subject a defendant to a liability to pay his own lawyer's costs, whatever the merits of his defence. This no doubt accounts for the high proportion of personal injury cases in the United States in which the plaintiff recovers some sum by settlement.

It may be doubtful whether adoption in the United States of the system of costs following the event would have much effect, assuming that the contingent-fee arrangement was retained. It would not bulk large at the settlement stage; and an unsuccessful litigant who retains his lawyer on a contingent fee has no costs of his own. A contingent-fee system is plainly more necessary where there is no developed system of legal aid. Given the American predilection for contingent fees, in order to save access to the Courts by those of moderate means, the case for loser-pays-all is diminished.

Supported as it is by a procedure for payment into Court, the English system may make for certainty, but it does not always produce the most just result. Thus it may be preferable to award the winner of a closely contested case a small proportion of his costs and, on the other hand, to oblige a person who has only taken a case to trial through perversity or other wrongful motive to pay indemnity costs.

Legal Aid

In this country, there has been a legal aid and advice scheme since 1949. The present scheme pays lawyers fees in civil litigation in all Courts and some tribunals. It is available to litigants (other than corporations) who can show that they have a prima facie claim or defence, that it is reasonable that they should receive legal aid, and that they fall within the financial limits. These last are measured by a test of disposable capital and income after allowing certain deductions for dependants and expenses. The maximum disposable capital and income at 1st August, 1984 are respectvely £4500 and £4925. Damages recovered by an assisted person are liable to be used for payment of costs if they are not recovered from the other side.

The assisted person enjoys a bargaining advantage over the nonassisted party and nuisance value payments are not uncommon. A successful nonassisted defendant can, in cases of hardship, recover costs against the legal aid fund. It is rare that an order for costs is made against the assisted person.

The most important exclusions from the present scheme are first those people whose income is more than £85 a week, which is modest; secondly, representation before most Tribunals; and thirdly, companies, however small. To bridge the gap it is for consideration whether there should not be introduced a standardised and comprehensive legal costs insurance, effected with insurance companies in the usual way, but supervised by the Government and promoted by the legal profession.

Fee Relationship

Solicitors are remunerated for professional work done for their clients, whether the work is contentious or noncontentious, by costs which are mainly governed by statute or statutory rules and orders. In relation to contentious business, a solicitor is entitled to make a written agreement with his client for work done or to be done. No action may be brought to recover costs due to a solicitor unless specified in a bill of costs delivered to the client in accordance with statutory requirements. The bill must include professional disbursements such as counsel's fees.

Counsel is separately instructed and remunerated for each piece of work done. It follows that he must have a separate brief for each case in which he appears. Once agreed, the brief fee is normally unalterable. The fee in ordinary cases must be marked on the brief before the commencement of the case to which it relates. Because counsel is engaged by a solicitor, it is the solicitor, and not the client who has responsibility for payment of counsel's fees. But a solicitor's general retainer authorises him not only to instruct counsel but also to pay his fees. Because such fees are not recoverable at law they do not constitute a legally binding debt from a client until they have been paid by the solicitor.

The solicitor instructs suitable counsel for the case in hand and fixes the brief fee by arrangement with counsel's clerk. An adjunct of the brief fee is a refresher fee representing the rate of remuneration for each day that the case lasts after the first. Thus the amount of the fees charged is determined by market forces. If counsel's expectations are too high the solicitor will go to another who is less expensive. There is no concept of fee sharing by counsel and solicitor.

Conclusions

To stimulate discussion, let us express our conclusions provocatively:

- The costs of discovery practice in the United States are now out of all proportion to such advantages as might be expected to flow from it;
- In England and Wales, the public interest is better served by a divided profession than a referral system;
- Juries are only worth the cost if the judges cannot be trusted;
- Arbitration, when appropriate, saves time and sometimes money, as well as affording privacy;
- Contingent fees promote unmeritorious litigation;
- Where the plaintiff's lawyer is remunerated by contingent fees, he should if he loses, pay the fees of the defendant's lawyer;
- Even a less-than-satisfactory legal aid system is preferable to contingent fees; and
- Barristers and solicitors do not regard themselves as sharing fees.

AMERICAN REGULATION OF ENERGY PROJECTS: THE CASE OF THE TRANS-ALASKA PIPELINE

London Sessions
ABA Annual Meeting 1985
Ballroom, Inn-on-the-Park
London, England

Friday, July 19, 1985
10:00 A.M. - 12:00 Noon

Kenneth P. Fountain
Exxon Pipeline Company
Post Office Box 2180
Houston, Texas 77001

Introduction

The story of the discovery and development of oilfields on Alaska's North Slope is one of superlatives. It tells of the harsh climate, of the isolation and beauty of America's greatest wilderness, of the frustrating years of early exploration efforts, and of the eventual discovery of the Prudhoe Bay Field, by far the largest oil find ever on the North American continent. It tells also of a trans-Alaska pipeline, 800 miles long, crossing three mountain ranges in its journey south, the first pipeline north of the Arctic Circle, and the largest privately financed and executed project in history.

This is, unfortunately, not that story. This is the story of the other superlatives surrounding North Slope oil: why a pipeline projected to cost one billion dollars required nearly nine billion dollars; why nine years elapsed from the discovery of oil to its delivery to market; and why to this day the rates charged for oil transportation from Prudhoe Bay to the south coast port of Valdez have yet to be finally approved. This, then, is the tale of one of the most regulated--indeed, overregulated--energy projects in history. Because it encountered virtually every form of governmental regulation extant, the Trans-Alaska Pipeline System, or TAPS, is perhaps the paradigmatic case of American regulation of an energy project. It was a crucible for a new era of American regulation, one which placed new emphasis on environmental protection and energy development planning.

TAPS exemplifies the problems of carrying forward a major energy project in the United States, where the legal system is "adversary," where the tripartite federal government is based on a system of checks and balances, where each state has its own sovereign powers, and where special interests can and do make their voices heard in a variety of forums. The Byzantine regulation of TAPS involved state and federal legislatures, courts and the executive branch, as well as numerous regulatory agencies. It has directly or indirectly employed literally hundreds of attorneys, experts, consultants, and witnesses, at a cost of tens of millions of dollars over a period of 15 years. The TAPS project is admittedly an extreme case. But while the nature and degree of regulation may have been unprecedented, the multifarious and often conflicting interests, each well financed and vocal, probably made such regulation inevitable. Furthermore, the political climate of the late 1960s, fueled by the environmental movement, may have made it mandatory.

This paper will examine the TAPS project as a case study of the functioning and malfunctioning of regulation of energy projects in the United States. The paper first outlines the sources of the regulatory authority which so affected the project and the goals that authority is designed to achieve. It next examines the TAPS project itself and the problems it faced: lawsuits, injunctions, special legislation, restrictive conditions for construction and operations, and even more restrictive agency interpretations and oversight. It then concludes with a comment on why the shortest route from Prudhoe Bay to Valdez has involved a slow, arduous detour through Washington, D.C.

The Source of Federal Regulatory Authority

The Constitution vests complete authority in the Congress in all matters relating to federal lands, and permits Congress to exercise the power both of proprietor and of legislator over the public domain. In addition to this plenary authority over federal lands, the Constitution gives Congress the power: "To regulate Commerce with foreign Nations, and among the several States, and with the Indian Tribes . . ." These powers give Congress extremely broad discretion in regulating the public domain.

Pursuant to these constitutional provisions, Congress has passed an almost endless series of laws regulating the public domain and has delegated substantial authority to various commissions and departments of the executive branch. Indeed, as will be seen below, Congress expended considerable effort specifically on the regulation of the TAPS.

The Goals of Regulation in the U.S.A.--An Overview

The American economic system is fundamentally a free enterprise system. Ideally, governmental regulation is imposed only where free markets do not function properly. The primary goal of governmental regulation is to remedy distortions caused by any inadequacies of the free market system.

One distortion of the market system which regulation seeks to rectify is the situation where not all costs are borne by producers or consumers of a particular good or service. The problem of externalities, as such costs are called, reflects a failure of the system to create organized private markets for such goods as clean air and wilderness areas. Regulation can "internalize" an externality by identifying the external costs and requiring the producers or consumers of the related goods or services to bear these costs. Recognition of externalities in the free market is the principal basis for the spate of environmental regulation in the last two decades. The prominent example of such regulation is the National Environmental Policy Act of 1969 which required thorough agency consideration of potential environmental impact before a federal agency could undertake any major action.

A second goal of regulation is to control monopolistic behavior. Historically, regulation has been imposed upon industries such as railroads and oil pipelines which were believed to exhibit the ability to exercise monopoly or market power. One goal of such regulation has been to prevent price discrimination, exclusion of shippers, and the imposition of unjust or unreasonable rates. It was in response to perceived abuses by railroads that Congress passed the Interstate Commerce Act in 1887 making undue discrimination unlawful and guaranteeing just and reasonable rates to all shippers. In like manner, oil pipelines operating in interstate commerce were brought within the purview of the Interstate Commerce Commission in 1906. This statute, now almost a century old, governs the operation of the TAPS.

Another important goal of regulation in the energy arena is the maximization of oil and gas recovery through economic conservation measures. Notable cases of this form of regulation are the establishment by various states of a maximum efficient recovery rate, or MER, for a producing structure, and policies on unitization to prevent damage to and increase lifetime production from a field.

One final goal of regulation applies to energy projects on public lands where the respective governments act as trustees for their constituents. The State of Alaska and the United States are fiduciaries with respect to the development of Alaskan oil and the management of the state and federal public lands. They are responsible for ensuring that the public is properly remunerated for the extraction of its resources and that oil development is carried out in a manner consistent with other uses of the public lands, including water, recreation, fish and wildlife, and wilderness and timber resources.

These goals are some of the most significant objectives of regulatory control over the oil industry in the United States, and each had a role in the evolution of the TAPS.

Regulation of the TAPS Project

The influence of governmental regulation on the TAPS project was largely a result of the political and economic environment of the late 1960s. The Prudhoe Bay discovery in February 1968 came at a time when many Americans were beginning to realize that the days of unlimited cheap energy were near an end. At the same time, many Americans were also concluding that the environment was being irreparably damaged at an alarming rate. To these groups Alaska stood out as the last great wilderness and also a great untapped resource for satisfying America's need for oil.

Alaska in 1969

The situation in Alaska was complicated by the fact that title to Alaska's land and resources had not been settled at the time of the Prudhoe Bay discovery. Alaska had only relatively recently become a state. Under the federal act admitting it into the Union, Alaska was permitted to select approximately 103 million acres of land from the unreserved federal public domain. However, when the State selected lands, title was often contested by Native groups claiming ancestral rights to the same land.

The plight of the Alaskan Native groups was this: with but few exceptions, their rights to tribal lands had been in limbo from the time of the purchase of Alaska from Russia. By April 1966, Native groups had filed claims for lands totalling 296 million acres, or approximately 80 percent of the State. Recognizing that no effective disposition of State selections and Native claims could be made until the claims had been verified, the Secretary of the Interior imposed a "land freeze," indefinitely suspending the patenting of Alaskan lands pending a determination by Congress as to the manner in which the Native claims could be resolved. The Alaska Native Claims Settlement Act of 1971 established guidelines and procedures for such a resolution. In addition to establishing Native corporations, and entitling them to make certain land selections, the Act provided for payment to the Native corporations of $942 million over half of which would come as a two percent royalty on oil and gas production, Prudhoe Bay and other known or producing fields excepted. Significantly, this aspect of the Claims Settlement Act gave the Native corporations an ongoing pecuniary interest in the development of Alaska's petroleum resources.

In addition to the State, the Native groups, the oil industry, and environmental groups, the government of the United States was deeply involved as the proprietor of a major portion of the North Slope's potential oil and gas areas and the majority of the land necessary for the TAPS right of way.

A collision of these various interests was inevitable, but the impact and the aftermath of that collision were beyond anyone's expectations.

The Early Stages of TAPS

The chronology of the TAPS project begins with the first major discovery on the North Slope. Soon after the Prudhoe Bay find, study began of various alternatives for transporting Alaska North Slope oil to the lower forty-eight states. These potential systems included a trans-Alaska pipeline, a trans-Canada pipeline to Chicago, and transportation by icebreaker tankers through the Northwest Passage to the East Coast. The participating oil companies, based on preliminary studies, concluded that the oil should move by pipeline south to the ice-free port of Valdez, thence by tanker to refinery destinations.

The TAPS participants announced their plan for such a pipeline in February 1969. The Department of the Interior thereupon established an interdisciplinary task force to study the problems of developing and transporting North Slope crude. On June 6, 1969, the TAPS participants filed an application with Interior's Bureau of Land Management for the requisite pipeline right-of-way permits pursuant to the Mineral Lands Leasing Act of 1920. This Act gave Interior authority to grant pipeline rights of way across federal lands with the requirement that any pipeline so constructed be operated as a common carrier. However, the width of any such grant was limited to a maximum of 25 feet on each side of the pipeline. Given the 48-inch diameter of the TAPS pipe and the terrain that the system would cross, the pipeline and adjacent workpad needed to be a minimum of 200 feet wide in many places. The TAPS owner companies and the Department of the Interior attempted to finesse the width limitation through a number of special land use permits parallel and adjacent to a 54-foot permanent pipeline right of way.

The following December Congress enacted the National Environmental Policy Act or "NEPA." As mentioned earlier, this legislation requires agencies of the federal government, before taking any major action which might have an impact upon the environment, to prepare a detailed statement on, inter alia, the environmental impact of the proposed action, any unavoidable adverse environmental effects, and alternatives to the proposed action. Shortly thereafter, in March 1970, three private conservation organizations filed suit in the U.S. District Court for the District of Columbia to restrain the Secretary of the Interior from the granting of permits. The court enjoined the issuance of the pipeline permits until all requirements of NEPA and the Mineral Leasing Act had been met.

The Secretary of the Interior subsequently released a preliminary draft of the environmental impact statement in January 1971. Public hearings held in Washington, D.C. and Anchorage, Alaska in February produced some thirty volumes of testimony and exhibits. After conducting intensive studies of the proposal and its alternatives, Interior issued the final draft of the environmental impact statement in March 1972 and announced its intention to issue the permits.

The following August, the District Court ruled that the environmental impact statement reasonably met all requirements of NEPA and lifted the injunction prohibiting the issuance of the pipeline permits. The environmental groups appealed, and in February 1973 the Court of Appeals for the District of Columbia Circuit reversed the District Court and ordered that court to reinstate the injunction. The Court of Appeals rejected the argument that the Department of Interior's long-standing practice of granting special land use permits in connection with rights of way was a valid administrative interpretation of its powers under the Mineral Leasing Act and did not violate that Act's width limitation.

The court, over a strong dissent by three of the seven judges hearing the case, chose not to rule on the issue of Interior's compliance with NEPA and the adequacy of the environmental statement, even though the court recognized that its failure to do so could result in future litigation and additional delay. The Department of the Interior appealed the decision to the Supreme Court. When the Supreme Court refused to review the case, Congress was called upon to act.

Congress held extensive hearings on the subject of legislation which would permit the issuance of an adequate right of way for the TAPS. The decision to authorize Interior to issue a right of way in excess of 50 feet was not the focus of attention. Of primary concern was Interior's compliance with NEPA, particularly with respect to the alternative of developing a pipeline corridor through Canada which could handle lines for both North Slope oil and natural gas and which would avoid the more seismically active areas on the southern end of the TAPS route. Such an overland corridor would also obviate the need for marine transportation, tankers being a major threat to the environment in the eyes of the environmental groups.

After much discussion and debate, Congress enacted the Trans-Alaska Pipeline Authorization Act on November 16, 1973. The major features of the Act were to direct Interior "to issue and take all necessary action to administer and enforce rights of way, permits, leases and other authorizations that are necessary for or related to the construction, operation and maintenance of the trans-Alaska oil pipeline system," and that such actions were to be taken "without further action under the National Environmental Policy Act of 1969" and were "not [to] be subject to judicial review under any law...." The new law also amended the Mineral Leasing Act to permit the Secretary of Interior to issue rights of way in excess of 50 feet if he "finds, and records the reasons for his finding, that in his judgment a wider right of way is necessary." The TAPS right of way was to be issued pursuant to this provision.

The new Mineral Leasing Act sections also gave Interior substantial authority to impose additional requirements on the permittee, authority that was exercised expansively in the negotiation of the final right of way agreement and stipulations.

The TAPS Right of Way Stipulations

Before embarking on a discussion of the regulatory restrictions placed upon the TAPS right-of-way grant, it is important to understand that, until 1968, construction of oil pipelines was virtually unregulated. In fact, it was an industry request to Congress in 1965 for federal regulation to avoid conflicting local regulations which led to the adoption in October 1969 of regulations administered by the Department of Transportation and governing the design, construction, operation, maintenance, and testing of oil pipelines.

The evolution of the right-of-way stipulations highlights the gulf between pipeline regulation prior to 1969 and regulation of the TAPS project. The original June 6, 1969 right-of-way application consisted of a four-page document. Attachments to the application included the applicants' consent to the then customary stipulations, four rudimentary schematics depicting alternative pipeline modes, and a check for ten dollars. The applicants requested that the permits be issued by July 1969. The first 1969 stipulation provided that the applicants would operate the pipeline as a common carrier and that they would file appropriate tariffs. The second, but by no means final, set of stipulations incorporated 13 safeguards imposed by the Department of the Interior on all pipelines constructed in 1969.

No private construction project had ever been asked to accept such strong constraints or such continuing direct control by the federal government. These stipulations, which Interior called "a landmark in the development of environmental management" in the United States, were proposed shortly before the National Environmental Policy Act was passed in late 1969. The litigation which ensued has already been described. The result was continuing reassessment of the stipulations and detailed review of the proposed design of the pipeline.

The end product of these reviews and negotiations was the Agreement and Grant of Right of Way for Trans Alaska Pipeline signed on January 23, 1974, by the United States and the then seven TAPS participants, six years after the initial Prudhoe Bay discovery. Further negotiations with the State of Alaska resulted in a very similar document which was signed in May 1974. These federal and state permits and incorporated stipulations represented a quantum leap in the level of government involvement in projects of this type. An example using regulations designed to protect fish and wildlife will serve to highlight the impact of this government involvement.

Fish and Wildlife Protection in the TAPS Project

Of the many regulations which were designed to protect fish and wildlife, none had a greater impact upon the pipeline than Stipulation 2.5.3--Zones of Restricted Activity. This Stipulation allowed the regulatory agency to proscribe work on the pipeline in certain "key" fish and wildlife areas during breeding, nesting, spawning, lambing, and calving and during major migrations. The periods when construction activities were prohibited left limited periods called fish and wildlife "windows" during which construction could go forward. Specific windows for fish were contained in a list prepared by the Joint State/Federal Fish and Wildlife Advisory Team which described some 310 fish critical streams and indicated that construction across these streams should be prohibited an average of seven months per year. Construction had to be scheduled during the remaining five-month window, which was typically during the winter. The fish and wildlife lists, beginning with the official "fish list" in January 1975, also included designated time periods when raptors, waterfowl, Dall sheep, caribou, and bison were most sensitive to construction activity.

The wildlife windows demonstrate one way in which regulation was used to protect fish and wildlife. Other instances include a stoppage of work when it was discovered that bank swallows had nested in a ditch dug by a contractor and the relocation of Pump Station 2 in order to avoid disturbance to potential peregrine falcon nesting sites located over a mile away. On another occasion, construction crews interrupted their normal progress to avoid disturbing a bear hibernating on the workpad. While these examples are in no way typical, they show the concern for protection of fish and wildlife that attended the construction of the pipeline.

Such regulation of the design, permitting, and construction phases of TAPS unquestionably exceeded the regulation of any remotely similar project. This strict oversight by regulatory agencies continued throughout the project. However, the pervasive regulation of TAPS did not end with the commencement of operation in July 1977. While the environmental regulatory agencies were winding down, the economic regulators were just gearing up.

The TAPS Rate Proceedings

The TAPS rate proceedings have unquestionably matched, if not exceeded, the regulatory indecision and prolongation of the project's design and construction phase. The following discussion will show how elusive the answer has been to the seemingly simple question, "what is the trans-Alaska pipeline worth?"

One of the principal right-of-way requirements under the Mineral Leasing Act was that any pipeline constructed pursuant to a right-of-way grant across federal lands be operated as a common carrier. Since with TAPS the pipeline transportation is part of a longer movement of crude oil from the North Slope to ports on the West and Gulf Coasts of the United States, the pipeline carriers are subject to regulation by the Federal Energy Regulatory Commission under the Interstate Commerce Act. In addition, regulation of TAPS is complicated by the fact that, although physically it is only one pipeline, it is owned by eight distinct pipeline companies, each of which operates its share of the pipeline capacity, filing its own interstate and intrastate tariffs with FERC and the Alaska Public Utilities Commission, respectively. After over seven years of pipeline operation, the tariffs have yet to be approved by either agency.

The United States, the State of Alaska, the Arctic Slope Regional Corporation, MAPCO (an independent shipper with a refinery near Fairbanks), and the staffs of the FERC and APUC have all taken the position that the tariffs are unjustly and unreasonably high in violation of the Interstate Commerce Act. In proceedings which began in 1977 before the Interstate Commerce Commission and the Alaska Pipeline Commission, and which have traveled on separate paths as far as the United States and Alaska Supreme Courts, the tariff wars have continued. The cause of all the furor is not, as it was in 1906 when oil pipelines were first made subject to ICC control, a desire to afford regulatory protection to producers; rather, the controversy results from the fact that the price used to establish royalties, severance taxes, and windfall profits tax is the so-called wellhead price. This price is fixed by reference to the destination price of a barrel of oil less the marine and pipeline transportation costs. High pipeline tariffs reduce the wellhead price and, consequently, reduce the royalty and tax receipts by the Arctic Slope Regional Corporation, the State of Alaska, and the federal government.

It would be simplistic, however, to view the TAPS rate proceedings as nothing more than a squabble over how to divide up the value of the Alaskan crude oil pie. Also at stake is the orderly development of other North Slope fields as well as other frontier areas in Alaska and the outer continental shelf. On the one hand, if tariffs are too high, explorers and producers who do not have an ownership share in the pipeline will be placed at a competitive disadvantage vis-a-vis those producers whose pipeline subsidiaries are TAPS owners. On the other hand, if tariffs are set too low, the incentives necessary to attract the enormous amounts of venture capital for essential pipeline construction will not exist.

A paralysis similar to that which struck the Department of the Interior in its attempts to comply with NEPA and simultaneously to satisfy Alaskans, industry and environmentalists appears to have the FERC in its grip. Never has there been so much at stake in a single rate proceeding. The potential refunds to shippers could amount to billions of dollars. Nor has a single decision had the potential to affect so many different interests on such a scale. The methodology selected could either promote or discourage investment in needed frontier pipelines or expansions of TAPS. It could also have a dramatic effect on the royalty and tax revenues of the United States, Alaska, and the Arctic Slope Regional Corporation.

Just as the TAPS project was a test case for new environmental regulations, the TAPS rate proceedings commenced at a time when the rate methodology used by oil pipeline companies for nearly four decades was being re-examined, but no new methodology was adopted to take its place. The cost of selecting the methodology has been years of hearings and tens of millions of dollars. Though the subject matter differs from Interior's environmental regulation, FERC's attempts at economic regulation shared with Interior the element of dealing with an adversary legal system, and a pluralistic society where each interest avails itself of its right to a hearing.

The administrative proceedings before various administrative law judges have been every bit as contested as a major antitrust case, with jurisdictional and procedural battles being waged all the way to the Supreme Court. Nor is this state of affairs confined to the federal government. The Alaska Pipeline Commission's decision on a tariff methodology was appealed to the State Superior Court which, after three years, issued an opinion reversing the Commission's decision and remanding the entire matter to the APUC for further proceedings. The Alaska Supreme Court has granted the pipeline carriers' petition for review of the case, where the matter presently rests.

The rate proceedings are almost a caricature of American regulation. The goals are simple and laudable--to ensure just and reasonable oil pipeline tariffs and prevent discrimination among shippers. The method of achieving the goals is also well conceived--to vest regulatory jurisdiction in an expert agency. The result has been eight years of uninterrupted litigation and a cloud on the functioning of the oil pipeline industry and the development of Alaskan oil.

The Future of Regulation

One cannot live through a project like TAPS without wishing it could have been done better, and one hopes that some lessons have been learned. It seems fairly clear now, 15 years after the passage of NEPA, that governmental agencies, environmentalists, and industry have a better grasp of what exactly the American environmental policy is and how to implement it. Procedures for assessing environmental impacts have been established and tested. Understanding of the negative impacts of resource development and ways to mitigate or eliminate them are unquestionably improved.

There are also ongoing efforts to decrease or eliminate unnecessary or unwholesome regulation in many aspects of energy-related industries. Oil pipeline deregulation is presently the subject of Congressional subcommittee hearings. The general mood in the United States is that the federal government should regulate less, rather than more. This is particularly apparent in the changed policies of the Justice Department's Antitrust Division and the Federal Trade Commission and their decisions not to challenge a number of mergers of large oil companies. These deregulation or decreased regulation trends are primarily designed to allow the market system to function better domestically and to enable U.S. companies to become more competitive internationally. However, there has been no discernible abatement in the public's desire for environmental protection or health and safety regulation. On the contrary, regulation in these areas has been more the subject of improved implementation rather than elimination.

Viewed in the light of these developments, the unprecedented regulation of the TAPS project comes as no surprise. Indeed, it was probably inevitable that TAPS would be one of the most regulated projects in the history of oil and gas development. The forces which affected the project, the environmental movement, the claims of Alaska's Native groups, the State's social and financial interests, and the federal government's interest in Prudhoe Bay from a fiscal and national security standpoint, were all bound to clash with the plans of the oil companies to develop Prudhoe Bay. Government intervention and time-consuming litigation were the logical result.

Inevitable does not mean, however, that it was foreseeable. In fact such pervasive regulation was largely unforeseen. What could have been anticipated was that a project on the scale of TAPS cannot be insulated from the prevailing social, political, and economic environment. It must necessarily be illuminated by and reflect back the level of enlightenment of its day--be it midnight sun or darkness at noon. Environmental protection, recognition of Alaskan Native claims, and construction of arctic pipelines were relative novelties even in the late 1960s. It is thus small wonder that the agencies charged with the regulation of TAPS could not strike an immediate balance among all the legitimate interests.

It may have been unfortunate that the TAPS project, which faced so many inherent challenges, was also a test case for a new era of government regulation. However, though the individual project may have suffered, on balance the present goals of government regulation of energy projects reflect a positive step over those of the past, with more and better care being taken to consider all the ramifications of a project. Americans of all perspectives still wince when they see how long and circuitous the decision making process has become, but it is now fairly well accepted that energy project planning must include the assessment and mitigation of adverse environmental and social impact, as well as efficient development of energy resources.

Implementation continues to be problematic, but it is much improved over 1970.

REGULATION OF ENERGY PROJECTS ON THE UNITED KINGDOM CONTINENTAL SHELF

London Sessions
ABA Annual Meeting 1985
Ballroom, Inn-on-the Park
London, England

Friday, July 19, 1985
10:00 A.M. - 12:00 Noon

Prof. R. W. Bentham
Centre for Petroleum and
Mineral Law Studies
University of Dundee
Dundee, Scotland DD1 4HN

In this brief paper I wish to take an actual example of an operational project--the Forties Field--and then describe the application to it of the regulatory regime in the United Kingdom.

The Forties oilfield lies 110 miles off the east coast of Scotland, east-north-east of Aberdeen. The water depth in the area varies from 340 to 420 feet. The field is oval shaped, 10 miles long by 5 miles wide, with the oil 7,000 feet below sea level. Originally, it was estimated that the field held about 4 billion barrels of oil, of which something over 50 percent will be recoverable. Peak production from the field has run at about 550,000 barrels per day--30 million tons per year--although this figure is now falling as the field ages.

The field was discovered by BP Petroleum Development Limited in the autumn of 1970, the first major oilfield to be discovered on the U.K. continental shelf. In order to develop the field and maintain the desired rate of production, a complex development programme has been implemented. Four steel platforms, each capable of drilling and producing oil from a pattern of 27 wells, were erected, each containing more steel than the Forth Bridge, each measuring some 690 feet. A 107-mile, 32-inch pipeline was laid from the platforms to the Scottish coast and another 130-mile, 36-inch pipeline laid overland to BP's refinery near Edinburgh. A tanker terminal for tankers of up to 250,000 tons has been constructed in the Firth of Forth, including a tank farm and another 12-mile pipeline. The offshore work had to be carried out under, and be capable of withstanding, some of the world's worst weather. In the "Roaring Forties" 43 days each year are described by the Meteorological Service as "fair" or "good"--the remainder are "marginal" or "bad." The platforms are designed to withstand 94-foot waves and winds of 130 miles per hour, the "hundred-year storm" of maritime lawyers. In 1972 BP borrowed £360,000,000 towards its expenditure to finance the development programme, which eventually cost £1,000,000,000. The lenders were a consortium of 67 banks from 12 countries.

Such are the facts of Forties. It remains to examine how BP acquired the right to explore for and produce the field, and how the conduct of the company's operations has been regulated.

While the first petroleum legislation in the United Kingdom was passed in the period 1917-18, the principal legislation presently in force consists of the Petroleum (Production) Act (1934), the Continental Shelf Act (1964), and Rules and Regulations made under those Acts--currently the Petroleum (Production) Regulations of 1982 as subsequently amended.

The effect of this legislation is, inter alia, to vest in the Crown "any rights exerciseable by the United Kingdom outside territorial waters with respect to the seabed and subsoil and their natural resources," except rights in respect of coal. (Section 1(1) of the 1964 Act). At the same time, the Secretary of State for Energy is empowered to grant "to such persons as [he] thinks fit, licences to search and bore for and get petroleum" (Petroleum Production Act 1934 section 2(1) as extended to the Continental Shelf). He is also empowered under the legislation to make regulations regarding applications for licences, licence fees, the size and shape of licenced areas, and "model" clauses to be incorporated in the licences. (Section 6 of the 1934 Act). Hence the granting of licences and their terms is a matter for ministerial discretion.

For licensing purposes, the U.K. continental shelf is divided into "blocks" of about 250 square kilometres, and offshore license applications have been invited by government from applicants in a series of licensing "rounds." The first round was held in 1964; the ninth round began in 1984. The criteria upon which allocation of licences will be made to applicants have varied from round to round and are published at the opening of each round. Applications are sometimes invited for applicants to make lump sum bids for specified blocks, but, more commonly, general criteria have been used in the selection process; e.g., technical competence and financial capability, the past performance of applicants who already hold U.K. continental shelf licences, their contribution to the U.K. economy, and so on. Consequently, at the selection stage, the Department of Energy is in a position to grant licences only to those applicants it considers can, and will, perform, their obligations (including work obligations) under the licence. This selection process, and the conditions imposed in its course, may properly be viewed as the first--and in some ways the most important single step--in governmental control of offshore petroleum projects.

The minister, in the exercise of his discretion, awarded Production License P057 to BP durng the second offshore licensing round in 1965, that licence subsequently being replaced in respect of the discovered Forties Field by Production Licence P246 in 1972, to permit the financing operation needed for field development. Licence P246 takes the form of a deed, executed on behalf of the minister and of the company, as do all Production Licences. It incorporates by reference the majority of the "model" clauses under the regulations then in force (S.I. No. 8987 of 1966 and S.I. No. 814 of 1971). It grants the (usual) "exclusive right to search and bore for and get" petroleum within the field area in Block 21/10, the term of the licence being 40 years.

The obligations imposed upon the company by the licence in 1972, leaving aside financial commitments, included the obligation to keep proper accounts; to provide half-yearly statements of the value of petroleum saved; to obtain ministerial consent to the abandonment of wells; to employ "good oilfield practice" in operations and avoid pollution; not to interfere unjustifiably with fishing and navigation; to care for the safety, health and welfare of employees; to comply with ministerial directives as to unitisation; to deliver petroleum onshore in the United Kingdom unless the minister agreed otherwise; to keep records and samples and furnish them to government (including access for government inspectors); to indemnify the minister against third-party claims; to make no statement that in the government's view any part of the area was likely to yield petroleum; and not to assign the licence without consent. (See Model Clauses 10 and 11, 13 to 27, and 30 to 32 as they stood in 1972).

Under the licence the minister obtained powers of distress and attachment in the case of nonpayment of the licence considerations (fees, rents, royalties, etc.) and the power to revoke the licence in the event of nonpayment or of a breach of any of the other terms of the licence (Model Clause 33).

In general, those were the terms of the licence when development was begun on Forties in 1972. Before its completion, however, substantial new duties were imposed upon existing licensees, including BP, under the Petroleum and Submarine Pipelines Act of 1975--a measure severely criticised at the time, and since. Under the Act, gas was not to be flared without ministerial consent, exploration work programmes could be imposed by ministerial direction, and development work programmes and production/depletion rates could be controlled if they were "contrary to good oilfield practice" or, in the minister's opinion, "not in the national interest." (See now the 1982 Regulations : Model Clauses 21(3), 13, 14, and 15).

The 1975 Act took effect in 1976, and since then BP has obtained periodic consents from the ministry for the flaring of gas and for development plans and production rates. The latter consents are given by reference to a detailed development and production programme, and are frequently given on the basis that production shall be at a stated rate, e.g., not greater than 455,000 barrels per day.

Apart from the terms of the licensing regime itself, other special legal rulês also regulate offshore petroleum projects. These include the Mineral Workings (Offshore Installations) Act 1971 and Regulations made thereunder, which deal with the certification, inspection, and operation of offshore installations, the keeping of log books, registration of deaths occurring offshore, and so on. A recent unofficial listing of statutes and regulations, in fact, indicates that no less than 140 regulations may be of relevance to offshore operations, but space does not permit a consideration of them, nor of the problems connected with onshore planning law.

One can but conclude that U.K. petroleum projects are strictly regulated, but close co-operation between the oil companies and government has contributed to successful development.

ENERGY REGULATIONS IN THE UNITED KINGDOM: A LEGAL VIEW FROM WITHIN THE COAL INDUSTRY

London Sessions
ABA Annual Meeting 1985
Ballroom, Inn-on-the-Park
London, England

Friday, July 19, 1985
10:00 A.M. - 12:00 Noon

Ronald V. Cowles
National Coal Board
Hobart House
Grosvenor Place
London SW1X 7AE

Introduction

Past fluctuations in the market share of different primary energy sources, and uncertainties as to their future role, make the task of energy planning very difficult. Nevertheless the decisions must be made, as most energy projects have very long lead time and operating lives. A modern nuclear power station may take ten years or more to come on stream and may then be expected to operate for a further 40 years. The working life of an underground coal mine will be considerably longer than this.

In the United Kingdom, most of the energy industry, including almost all of the electricity, gas, coal, and nuclear industries, is nationalised. The oil industry, which remains largely in the private sector, is an exception, although the government exercises close control over petroleum production.

Despite the considerable state involvement in the energy industry, however, the nationalised corporations are independent bodies and not mere arms of the government. In theory, it is for each corporation to make its own decisions. There are no specific agencies regulating energy development. However, energy developments must comply with essentially the same authorisation requirements as other industrial development. The purpose of this paper is to examine the impact of these controls on the coal industry, with particular reference to one project, the Belvoir Project.

Development Control

In the United Kingdom, since 1948, a framework of control over all development has been provided by the planning control system. The current statute in England and Wales is the Town and Country Planning Act 1971 (TCPA). Under Section 23, TCPA planning permission is needed for the development of land. "Development" means the carrying out of engineering, mining, or other operations in, on, over, or under land, or any material change of use of any buildings or other land. All mining operations, including prospecting and the working of waste tips, constitute development for this purpose.

Applications for planning permission are made to the local planning authority, which for most purposes is the District Council. However, an application for mineral development will be decided by the County Council as "mineral planning authority." Applications are considered in the light of statutory land use plans for the area. If an application for planning permission is refused or granted subject to conditions, an appeal may be made to a minister (in England, the Secretary of State for the Environment) whose decision is final, though recourse may be had to the courts on a point of law. The Secretary of State also has a power to "call-in" applications for his own decision, if he considers important national or regional issues to be involved.

In the case both of appeals and of a "call-in," the Secretary of State may, and if the applicant or the local planning authority require it, must, cause a public inquiry to be held as a preliminary to his decision.

The need for planning permission can subject development projects to a detailed scrutiny as to environmental, economic, and social impacts. Whether a project can then go ahead depends on the exercise of an administrative discretion. For the National Coal Board, who have a virtual monopoly of the ownership of coal, and extensive rights to work it, planning control is the principal constraint, other than financial, on their operations.

The Belvoir Project

The Project

The Belvoir Project, called after the Vale of Belvoir (pronounced "Beaver"), had as its purpose the exploitation of a coalfield which extends 250 square kilometres in the North East of Leicestershire (which contains the Vale), and adjacent parts of Lincolnshire and Nottinghamshire, and comprises some 510 million tons of recoverable reserves. Exploration of this coalfield was carried out between 1973 and 1975.

The coalfield offered profitable capacity to meet the high forecasts for future coal demand then current. However, the area was mainly rural, with little industry. Consequently, environmental factors would be important in planning mining activity. Furthermore there would be considerable local opposition.

Preliminary Assessments

Three main sites, Saltby, Asfordby, and Hose, were selected after a series of assessments in which underground mining, operational, and finally environmental considerations were successively taken into account. A full environmental impact analysis (not at present a statutory requirement) was produced, and extensive consultations were held with local and other government authorities, public utilities, local interest groups, and the public at large. In retrospect, this may have facilitated the organisation of opposition to the project. However the Board's detailed forward planning enabled prior agreements on infrastructure and landscaping, conditional on the project going ahead, to be made with the local authorities concerned, despite the fact that most of the authorities were opposed to the Project.

Applications and "Call-in"

Applications for planning permission to win and work coal in the coalfield were submitted to the District Councils concerned on 24th August 1978. On 23rd January 1979, the Secretary of State for the Environment called the applications in for determination by himself after a public inquiry.

The Public Inquiry

The inquiry was opened at Stoke Rochford Hall, a local teacher training college, on 13th October 1979, and sat for 84 days, closing on 2nd May 1980.

At the inquiry, the National Coal Board founded their case for the project heavily on government energy policy as determining the need for coal. They relied on the legal principle that it was not within the purposes of the inquiry to examine the merits of this policy: it should confine itself to site-specific issues. The Board argued that the project, which would provide nearly 4,000 jobs in the area, was necessary to supply new and efficient capacity for the expanding coal industry envisaged by government policy, and that nothing in the environmental cases against the project outweighed this need.

The project was opposed by Leicestershire County Council who challenged the assumptions behind the government figures for future coal demand and argued that any shortfall in coal production could be met by economically priced imports.

Additional opposition came from the "Alliance," an organisation comprising the 4,380 strong Vale of Belvoir Protection Group, 30 local parish councils, and the National Farmers Union. They also challenged the Board's "need" case and argued that valuable farmland would be damaged and the recreational and tourist value of a tranquil area of rural England diminished.

The Inspector's Report and the Secretary of State's Decision

The Inspector published his report on 26th November 1980. He recommended that planning permission should be granted for the mines, but not for two of the tips envisaged. This was on the basis that he accepted, with some slight hesitation, the Coal Board's "need" case, and also accepted that the project was necessary to meet the need. He further concluded that the environmental impacts of the mines would be acceptable in view of the need to meet demand, but that the impact of the two tips would not be.

After 16 months consideration, the Secretary of State decided to reject the Inspector's advice and refuse planning permission. He took the view that the visual impact of the mine at Hose would be unacceptable, even without its tip. As he was advised that he could not grant the applications in part only they must be refused. However, he said that fresh applications in respect of Asfordby and Saltby would be favourably considered.

Sequel

A new application was made just over three months later for a single mine at Asfordby. This was not called in, and planning permission was granted on 17th May 1983. However, the scheme could not go ahead without governmental financial backing. The scheme was assessed by a private firm of consultants, and financial approval was finally given on 1st January 1984.

Governmental Energy Policy After the Vale of Belvoir Decision and Public Inquiries for Energy Projects

In 1981, a government appointed commission (the Flowers Commission), appointed to advise on the "interaction between energy policy and the environment," reported critically on the cost and delay occasioned by long public inquiries such as the Belvoir Inquiry. They thought much of this was due to inquiries considering issues of national energy policy rather than site-specific issues.

In their response to the Flowers Report, however, the government took the position that inquiries should consider all relevant issues of national policy. The new government saw themselves as having no role as energy planners. Energy supply and demand should, in their view, be determined by market forces and particular investments planned and justified by the industries themselves against economic, and other, including environmental, criteria.

It is doubtful whether this view is entirely realistic, as major energy projects have lead times and projected life spans far in excess of those in which the market deals. Moreover, the government has financial control over such projects and also the last word in the planning system. The ultimate decision power cannot, therefore, be abdicated in favour of a big inquiry. The disadvantages of appearing to do so can be seen in the current inquiry into the Sizewell B PWR project. Discussion of the need issue alone in this inquiry has taken almost a whole year. It would seem at least arguable that if such issues were rigorously excluded from consideration at public inquiries and reserved for debate in Parliament, not only would the inquiries be less wasteful of time and money, but national debate on energy policy would be more constructive, since it would be free from entanglement with local issues raised by particular projects.

IMPROVING PUBLIC PROCUREMENT PRACTICES

London Sessions
ABA Annual Meeting 1985
Audley Suite, Grosvenor House Hotel
London, England

Friday, July 19, 1985
10:00 A.M. - 12:00 Noon

Thomas J. Madden
Suite 1150, 1575 I Street, N.W.
Washington, D.C. 20006

Public procurement by state and local governments of supplies, services, and construction is governed in the United States by a myriad of special laws which vary from jurisdiction to jurisdiction. In an effort to help establish more uniform public procurement procedures and practices throughout the United States, the American Bar Association drafted the Model Procurement Code for State and Local Governments (the "Model Code" or "Code"). Three key parts of the Model Code will be discussed in this paper.

The Model Code was completed in 1979 after over five years of intensive study and drafting by literally hundreds of individuals involved in public procurement at the federal, state, and local level. The development of the Model Code was part of a broader effort in the 1970s to reform procurement at the federal, state, and local level. At this time, 11 states and several units of local government have adopted legislation based on the Model Code.

The purposes and policies of the Model Code are set forth in Article I of the Code and include the following:

- Simplification, clarification, and modernization of state and local laws governing procurement;
- Consistency in procurement laws among various jurisdictions within a state and between states;
- Increased public confidence in the procedures followed in public procurement;
- Fair and equitable treatment of all persons and organizations who deal with the procurement systems of state and local government;
- Increased economy in public procurement; and
- Provision of legal and administrative remedies to provide due process protections for those who contract or seek to contract with government and to help insure the integrity of public purchasing practices.[1]

Goals and Features of the Code

Early in the Model Code's development, it was decided to develop a model rather than a uniform code to allow adaptation of the Model Code's provisions to local needs. As a model, it is equally beneficial to a jurisdiction needing selected improvements and to a jurisdiction desiring a total overhaul of its procurement system. The Model Code's structure also contemplates the issuance of implementing regulations to carry out the fundamental policy guidelines and principles established in the Code.[2]

One of the principal benefits of the Code is that it provides a uniform set of procedures for the entire public procurement cycle, including the solicitation, award, administration, and performance of government contracts. Adoption of the Model Code can limit the possibilities for ad hoc decisions and inconsistent treatment of procurement problems and needs within a given jurisdiction. At the same time, the Code is sufficiently flexible to allow governmental units to deal with special problems such as an emergency need or the procurement of unique services or supplies.

This paper briefly addresses three articles of the Model Code that embody its basic principles and policies. These articles are: Article 3-Source Selection and Contract Formation; Article 9-Legal and Contractual Remedies; and Article 12-Ethics in Public Contracting.

Article 3 - Source Selection and Contract Formation

The Model Code recognizes that fair and open competition for contracts must be a basic tenet of public procurement. Such competition reduces the opportunity for favoritism and fosters public confidence in public procurement. Because the marketplace is different for various supplies, services, or construction, a variety of methods for securing competition are set forth in the Model Code. The two principal means of ensuring competition are competitive sealed bidding and competitive sealed proposals.

Competitive Sealed Bidding

Competitive sealed bidding is the procurement method by which all potential contractors are notified of a contracting opportunity and requested to submit bids setting forth firm prices to provide services or supplies or to undertake construction.[3] This is the preferred method of source selection under the Model Code because it is designed to assure open and honest contract awards.[4]

The essential features of the competitive sealed bidding process are:

- An invitation for bids (IFB), which is publicly advertised and sets forth a fixed period for submitting bids;
- A description in the IFB of the needed supplies, services, or construction and the criteria upon which a contract would be awarded;
- Submission of bids in sealed envelopes;
- Public opening of bids;

- Contract award to the contractor who submits the lowest responsive bid to the IFB and who has the capacity to perform the contract; and

- The award of a fixed-price contract.[5]

The essential legal issues in any controversy involving competitive sealed bidding are whether the contractor submits a responsive bid and whether or not the contractor is a responsible contractor.[6] The requirements for responsiveness and responsibility are common features of all public procurement methods in the United States.

Under the Code, a bidder who has submitted a bid that conforms in all material respects to the IFB is a responsive bidder.[7] If a bid is nonresponsive, it must be rejected. The purpose of this requirement is to give all bidders an equal opportunity to compete for contracts, to assure that the contract price is fair, and to prevent fraud.[8]

When it has been established that a bidder has the technical capability, financial capacity, technical resources, and manpower required to perform, and a record of having met schedules, that bidder is considered responsible.[9] The bidder must also have a record of integrity and must agree to comply with appropriate public policy, e.g., compliance with pertinent environmental or equal opportunity regulations.

Under particular circumstances or for certain type purchases, such as for maintenance or construction, a contractor to be considered responsible must have the necessary organization, experience, operational controls, and technical skills, or the ability to obtain them, as well as the necessary construction, maintenance, and technical equipment and facilities, or the ability to obtain them.

The protest procedures described below in the discussion of Article 9 allow disappointed bidders to challenge decisions of procuring officials with respect to responsiveness and responsibility. Such protests can be filed by a bidder whose bid has been deemed nonresponsive or who has been found not to be a responsible contractor, or by a disappointed bidder who claims that the government agency has acted improperly in deciding that the bidder selected to receive a contract is a responsible bidder or has submitted a responsive bid.

Competitive Sealed Proposals

Competitive sealed proposals is the procurement method in which potential contractors are requested to submit proposals describing the supplies, services, or construction that they propose to provide.[10] This method of source selection is preferred whenever there is insufficient information or time to prepare a detailed set of specifications describing the government needs or whenever such issues as the quality of the needed supplies, services, or construction are more important than price.[11]

The essential elements of the competitive sealed proposal process are:

- o The issuance of a request for proposals (RFP), which is publicly announced and calls for submissions of proposals within a specified time;
- o A general description in the RFP of the needed supplies, services, or construction and the criteria upon which proposals will be evaluated;
- o Submission by potential contractors of their sealed proposals, which include technical, management, and cost sections;
- o Opening of proposals, not in public, but rather in the presence of designated government officials;
- o Contract award, as a general matter, after discussions or negotiations with prospective contractors. Award is made to the party whose proposal is found to be most advantageous to the government based on price, technical ability, and the relative merits of the proposals. An evaluation is also made of the potential contractor's capacity to perform the contract; and
- o Award of either a cost-reimbursement contract or a fixed-price contract.[12]

Many items and services needed by a jurisdiction cannot be defined because of variables that defy definition, much less standardization. For example, research and development requirements present problems in that the end product, as originally described in the procurement proposal, is no more than a functional need, a theory, an assumption, or a concept. The competitive sealed proposal method of source selection allows procurement officials to meet and cope with these situations.

This flexibility is available because of a very important distinction that relates to the type of evaluations permitted after offers are received. In situations where evaluation of the relative abilities of offerors to perform, including degrees of technical or professional experience or expertise, is required, use of competitive sealed proposals is the appropriate procurement method because it provides the necessary flexibility. Similarly, the competitive sealed proposals method is the better source-selection technique where the type of public need to be satisfied involves weighing artistic and aesthetic values to the extent that price is a secondary consideration. Finally, where the types of supplies, services or construction being procured require the use of comparative, judgmental criteria to evaluate adequately, use of competitive sealed proposals is likely to be the better method.

The key legal issues in the competitive sealed proposal process are whether the prospective contractor has adequately described the services, supplies, or construction it proposes to provide and the extent to which all proposals are evaluated on an equal basis and all prospective contractors receive equal treatment. The protest procedures set forth in Article 9 allow disappointed bidders to challenge decisions relating to these and other contract award decisions.

The competitive sealed proposal process vests procuring officials with substantial discretion to select contractors. The Model Code recognizes this fact and sets out provisions to structure the exercise of this discretion to assure that the successful contractor has provided the proposal which is in fact most advantageous to the government.[13]

Article 9 - Legal and Contractual Remedies

The Model Code includes extensive legal and contractual remedies for the resolution of disputes arising out of the award and performance of contracts, as well as the debarment or suspension of actual and prospective contractors. In addition, the Model Code provides procedures for voiding contracts awarded in violation of the law.

The remedy-granting provisions of the Model Code break new ground. At the time the Code was adopted, only the federal government provided the full range of remedies set forth in the Model Code. Because many state and local governments have existing laws which prevent the use of the Model Code's remedies, and the Code's provisions for award of contracts or even contract performance, the Model Code includes special provisions waiving the sovereign immunity of state and local governments for legal actions seeking the remedies provided in the Model Code.[14] This is particularly important because in the United States, state governments are generally immune to being sued unless they have adopted constitutional provisions or laws allowing suits against them in state courts.

Pre-award and Award Controversies

Legal issues arising out of the solicitation of bids or proposals and the award of contracts can be resolved through a special "protest" procedure established in the Model Code.[15] The Code authorizes administrative officials to settle or resolve protests filed by an aggrieved bidder, offeror, or actual or prospective contractor, concerning the solicitation or award of the contract.[16] Any party who seeks to participate or who participates in public procurement can file such a protest. The administrative official responsible for the procurement must issue a decision on the protest which sets forth the reasons for the action taken and informs the protestor of the right to judicial or administrative review if the protestor is not satisfied with the decision. The Code contemplates that contract award or performance would be stayed during the pendency of the protest unless a determination is made that the award or performance of the contract is necessary to protect substantial interest of the state or local government.

A party whose protest is denied by a chief procuring officer or who is adversely affected by the protest decision could bring an appropriate legal action in a state court or could bring an action before a special administrative body, the Procurement Appeals Board, established pursuant to the Code, with authority to resolve issues relating to award and performance of contracts.[17-18]

The Code expressly provides that if, prior to award, it is determined that a solicitation or proposed award of a contract is in violation of the law, the solicitation or proposed award must be cancelled or revised to comply with the law.[19] If, after contract award is made, it is determined that the award is in violation of the law, the contract may be ratified or affirmed provided it is in the best interest of the government.[20] In the alternative, the contract may be terminated and the person awarded the contract shall be compensated for actual expense reasonably incurred and a reasonable profit, unless the person awarded the contract received the contract through fraudulent or improper conduct.[21]

Breach of Contract and Contract-Performance Controversies

The Model Code establishes special procedures for resolving breach of contract or contract-performance controversies, including controversies based on mistake, misrepresentation, or contract modification or recision.[22] Breach of contract or contract-performance controversies are to be resolved first by the chief procurement officer or the head of the procuring agency. This initial decision can be reviewed by a state court or by the Procurement Appeals Board.[23]

Debarment or Suspension of Actual or Prospective Contractors

The Code also establishes a formal procedure with appropriate due process protections for debarring or suspending contractors after reasonable notice and opportunity for a hearing.[24] Under this authority, the head of the purchasing agency would have authority to debar a person for cause from consideration for award of contracts for up to three years. The same officer would have the authority to suspend a person from consideration for award of contracts pending the resolution of a debarment proceeding if there is probable cause for debarment. The suspension would be for a limited period, generally not exceeding three months. Cause for debarment or suspension includes conviction for commission of offenses indicating a lack of business integrity or honesty that "seriously" and "directly" affects a contractor's responsibility, or a recent record of failure to perform public contracts in accordance with the terms of the contracts.[25] The Code provides for review of debarment and suspension decisions by a state court or by the Procurement Appeals Board.[26]

Article 12 - Ethics in Public Contracting

Preservation of the integrity of the procurement process and fostering public confidence in it are core goals of the Model Code. In furtherance of these goals, the Code sets forth standards of conduct for government procurement officials as well as government contractors.[27] The Model Code makes illegal the payment of gratuities to government officials who award and administer contracts and prohibits the payment of kickbacks by actual or potential contractors.[28] It requires procurement officials to disclose their financial interests in companies and organizations when they receive government contracts.[29] The Code also contains numerous restrictions on the activities of present and former government officials if those activities would undermine the integrity of the procurement process or give an actual or prospective contractor an unfair advantage.[30]

Civil and administrative remedies are provided under the Code for violation of the ethical standards. The sanctions against employees range from oral or written reprimands to termination of employment.[31] Contractors can be suspended or debarred from receiving further contracts for violating the standards set forth in the Code or for employing individuals who violate the standards.[32] Provisions in the Code allow recovery of kickbacks and gratuities by the state and for terminating contracts awarded in violation of the Model Code.

In an effort to assure effective implementation of ethical standards, the Code provides for the establishment by jurisdictions of an Ethics Commission.[33] This Commission would have authority to promulgate regulations to carry out the provisions of the Code and to issue advisory opinions. The Ethics Commission would also have responsibility for imposing the various civil and administrative sanctions. Decisions of the Ethics Commission on matters other than issuance of advisory opinions would be reviewable in the state courts in accordance with state law.[34]

Conclusions

Billions of dollars are spent each year by state and local governments to procure a broad range of services, supplies, and construction, and the Model Code was drafted as an effort by the American Bar Association to provide the best possible standards for such procurements. The basic principles set forth in the Code, the legal and contractual remedies, and the ethical standards, all were written to provide or to help assure that government procurements are carried out fairly and that government tax revenues are used in the most cost-effective manner. In the coming years, it is expected that more and more jurisdictions within the United States will evaluate the Model Code and tailor it to meet their special needs.

FOOTNOTES

1. Model Procurement Code for State and Local Governments §1-101 (1979).

2. The ABA Coordinating Committee on Model Procurement Code developed a set of "recommended regulations" as a model for state and local governments. These regulations were approved by the ABA Council of the Section of Public Contract Law and the Council of the Section of Urban, State and Local Government Law on August 2, 1980.

3. Model Code §3-202.

4. Model Code §3-201.

5. Model Code §3-202.

6. _Id_.

7. Model Code §3-101(7).

8. _Prestex Inc. v. United States_, 320 F.2d 367 (Ct. Cl. 1963).

9. Model Code §3-101(6).

10. Model Code §3-203.

11. Model Code §3-203 Commentary.

12. Model Code §3-203.

13. Model Code §3-203(6). This section and its accompanying commentary require procuring officials to make every effort to assure that all offerors receive "fair and equal treatment" in the evaluation and discussion of their proposals.

14. Model Code §9-401.

15. Model Code §9-101(2).

16. _Id._

17. Model Code §9-401.

18. Model Code §9-505.

19. Model Code §9-202.

20. Model Code §9-203.

21. _Id._

22. Model Code §9-103.

23. Model Code §9-103(5).

24. Model Code §9-102.

25. _Id._

26. _Id._

27. Model Code Article 12, Part B, Standards of Conduct.

28. Model Code §12-206.

29. Model Code §12-205.

30. Model Code §12-208.

31. Model Code §12-301.

32. Model Code §12-302.

33. Model Code §12-401.

34. Model Code §12-402.

INFLUENCE OF SUBSTANTIVE LAW ON PROCUREMENT PRACTICES OF U.K. PUBLIC AUTHORITIES

London Sessions
ABA Annual Meeting 1985
Audley Suite, Grosvenor House Hotel
London, England

Friday, July 19, 1985
10:00 A.M. - 12:00 Noon

C. T. Peach
National Coal Board
23 Regent Square
Doncaster, South Yorkshire DN1 2DU

No counterpart to the A.B.A. Model Procurement Code has been incorporated or is available for incorporation into U.K. legislation.[1] English common law has developed no general principles of special application to public authorities. Although most authorities are likely to have their own manual of practice and procedure, these remain matters essentially of internal administration conferring no rights on, and regarded as no concern of, outsiders.

With some exceptions, modern legislation of relevance has been aimed not so much at affecting public authorities on account of their "public" nature, but more on account of their tendency to represent monopoly or dominant influences on particular markets and with the aim of improving competition.

General Background

Central Government Departments

The main source of Government Departmental practices is the Treasury, the department which is primarily responsible for controlling public expenditure. The main contracting departments sit on the Treasury's Procurement Policy Committee. In addition, the Treasury initiate rules of general application, and directions are issued within each department. These principles and instructions are of internal effect only and (in the absence of special circumstances or agreement) unenforceable by any third party.

Local Government

Local Government authorities are subject to public, general, or local legislation and to their own standing orders. By virtue of S.135 Local Government Act 1972, standing orders must provide for the securing of competition and regulate the manner in which tenders are invited subject to permissible exemptions for contracts of a low value or where special circumstances apply.[2] While noncompliance with standing orders will not invalidate a contract, the duty to observe the standing orders is enforceable in the courts.[3-4] A plaintiff must have a sufficient interest to initiate such proceedings.[5]

Public Corporations

These bodies occupy a hybrid position--on the "public" side of a line drawn between Departments of State and private business. Central Government retains an overriding control over them through funding, appointment of members of their boards, and through the statutory authority of ministers to issue general directions. Their functions are mainly of an industrial or commercial nature (e.g., the production and sale of electricity, gas, coal, or steel etc.) or of a social nature (e.g., the administration of hospitals). Each has its own internal procedures which will be "codified" to a varying extent and which may vary widely.

European Economic Community Law

EEC Law and Procurement Contracts

An additional source of law was incorporated into the U.K. legal system by the accession of the U.K. to the European Communities. Many of the provisions of the Treaties establishing the European Economic Community (EEC) and the European Coal and Steel Community (ECSC), and secondary legislation made under them, operate directly as part of U.K. law.

The EEC Treaty states among the objectives "....(c) the abolition, as between Member States, of obstacles to freedom of movement for persons, services and capital; ....(f) the institution of a system ensuring that competition in the common market is not distorted...."[6]

Secondary Legislation

Article 189 EEC Treaty provides that "In order to carry out their task the Council and the Commission shall in accordance with the provisions of this Treaty, make regulations, issue directives, take decisions, make recommendations, or deliver opinions."[7] Directives affecting public purchasing are of special concern in this context.

Public Works Contracts

Two such directives are Directive 71/304, concerning the abolition of restrictions on freedom to provide services in respect of public works contracts (and on the award of public works contracts to contractors acting through agencies or branches), and Directive 71/305, dealing with the coordination of procedures for the award of public works contracts.

Directive 71/304. This directive provides for the removal by Member States of discrimination between nationals of the State concerned and other community nationals in the award of public contracts relating to construction and associated civil engineering work (Article 1). This, given the overwhelming importance in the construction business of contracts awarded at the discretion of public authorities, was considered essential, if discrimination in favour of national operators was to be removed. The directive does not apply to all works (e.g., those in the mining industry).

Article 3(1) of the directive refers in particular to the abolition by a member State of those restrictions preventing the provision of services under the same conditions and with the same rights as nationals of that Member State; those existing by reason of administrative practices; and those existing which, although applicable irrespective of nationality, hinder the activities of nationals of other Member States--in particular discriminatory technical specifications.[8] Article 3(2) provides that Member States shall ensure that beneficiaries may obtain under the same conditions as nationals the various forms of credit, aid and subsidy provided for the purpose by the public authorities and that they shall have access to the supply of facilities, controlled by the State, needed for the performance of their contract.[9]

Directive 71/305. The aim of this directive is to facilitate the effective exercise of the freedom of establishment and supply of services. This is attained by providing "harmonised" rules for the contents of specifications, advertising, and the use of objective economic criteria for the award of contracts. It deals with the methods by which Directive 71/304 is to be implemented.[10] The following are its main provisions.

"Public works contracts are contracts for pecuniary consideration between a contractor and an authority awarding contracts" which have as their object one of the activities referred to in Article 2 of Directive 71/304 (para 11 supra). "Authorities awarding contracts" are defined as the State, Regional, or Local Authorities and the legal persons governed by public law or, in Member States where this concept is unknown, equivalent bodies specified in the directive including U.K. local authorities (Article 1).[11] Authorities are to apply their national procedures adapted to the provisions of the directive (Article 2).

National procedures are divided into:

- "open procedures" whereby any interested contractor may tender;

- "restricted procedures" whereby contractors may tender only by invitation; and

- a number of exemptions, e.g., for reason of national security.[12]

Common rules are laid down in the technical field, on advertising, and on participation. These rules apply to public works contracts, the estimated value of which net of VAT is not less than 1,000,000 European Units of account (Article 7).[13] (For the purposes of the directive 1 EUa = £0.59.)[14]

Directive 77/62. This directive is an application to goods of the principles of Directives 71/304 and 71/305. It aims to enable suppliers of products throughout the Community to compete for public supply contracts on equal terms.

Treaty Provisions

ECSC Treaty. U.K. restrictive trade practices law excludes from its ambit coal and steel, which is reserved to the ECSC. "Measures or practices which discriminate between producers, between purchasers or between consumers, especially in prices and delivery terms or transport rates and conditions" are amongst those measures which are prohibited within the common market for coal and steel.

Decision 4/53 lays down the rules relating to the publication of price lists and conditions of sale for coal. Decision 30/53 is concerned with the general duty imposed on coal and steel producers under the Treaty not to discriminate between their customers. Purchases of coal and steel (whether by public authorities or by private persons) are therefore regulated by the ECSC Treaty to a certain extent both as to prices and to conditions of sale.

EEC Treaty. Two of the most important articles of the EEC Treaty which can affect public purchasing (and other) contracts are Articles 85 and 86. Article 85 concerns restrictive agreements or practices involving some degree of collusion between undertakings that are economically independent of each other. Article 86 concerns the problem where one undertaking or a group of undertakings has reached a position of such strength in a given market that the normal constraints of competition no longer apply to its activities. In this event, the undertaking is considered under community law to hold a "dominant position" and it is the "abuse" of such a dominant position which is controlled.[15]

Article 85(1) provides that "all agreements between undertakings, decisions by associations of undertakings and concerted practices which may affect trade between Member States and which have as their object or effect the prevention, restriction or distortion of competition within the common market" shall be prohibited as incompatible with the common market. Article 85(2) provides that such agreements and decisions are automatically void. Article 85(3) provides for an exemption for arrangements which while harming competition may have beneficial attributes which outweigh the harm to competition.

In carrying out its purchasing policy, an authority must have regard to EEC Article 85. Consider, for example, the case of an organisation which hitherto has purchased items from two or more sources for reasons of security of supply, but now, considering supply to be assured, wishes to purchase from only one source. An agreement to do so might have "the object or effect" of preventing restricting or distorting competition within the common market and be liable to be attacked as being void under Article 85(2).

Article 86 prohibits "any abuse by one or more undertakings of a dominant position within the common market or in a substantial part of it.... as incompatible with the common market in so far as it may affect trade between Member States." The concept of dominance is not defined in the Treaty but has been defined by the Court of Justice as "relating to a position of economic strength enjoyed by an undertaking which enables it to prevent effective competition being maintained on the relevant market by giving it the power to behave to an appreciable extent independently of its competitors, customers and ultimately of its consumers." Although dominant positions most often relate to the supply of goods or services, they may also exist where there is a dominant purchaser. In the case of Eurofima, a purchaser of railway rolling stock was regarded as occupying a dominant position on the common market and exception was taken by the Commission to some of the terms of the tender, which appeared to be too severe.[16]

Judicial Remedies in the EEC

The cumbersome and possibly inconclusive enforcement procedures contained in GATT agreement on Government Procurement (Article VII) may be contrasted with the more direct remedies available under EEC law. The Court of Justice was asked at an early stage to consider whether certain Treaty provisions had modified the legal position of individuals vis-a-vis Member States. Subsequently the Court acknowledged that some provisions of the EEC Treaty are capable of modifying the rights of individuals inter se. In particular, Articles 85(1) and 86 "tend by their very nature to produce direct effects in relations between individuals" and "create direct rights in respect of the individuals concerned which the national courts must safeguard."[17] Public authorities actions can therefore be subject to direct action in the courts at the suit of contractors, where Treaty provisions are infringed. This is, however, a developing area of the law and one which can present a national court with difficulties when it seeks to apply Article 85.

It is not at present beyond doubt that the obligations imposed on Member States (e.g., to harmonise national rules) can give rise to rights in individuals as against other individuals. However it appears that this may be so. The directives discussed above may also therefore be capable of conferring rights and obligations not only on Member States but on public authorities and on individuals whom the legislation is intended to benefit.

Particular Topics

Contractual Restrictions

There is no general regulation having legal force in the United Kingdom as to the manner in which tenders are invited, who is invited to tender, collusion by tenderers, awarding contracts, and contract terms.

The Method of Inviting Tenders

Within Central Government Departments, the general principle applies that whenever possible, contracts should be placed by competitive tender, but it is left to the Departments to decide in a particular case whether this is appropriate.

Local Authority standing orders commonly require contracts to be placed by competitive tender. The Model Standing Orders published by the Department of Environment provide for criteria to be established for the use of selective and open tendering.[18] The Notes of the Model Standing Orders discourage the use of the latter, perceiving it to be a waste of resources.

Under EEC Directive 71/305, a Local Authority's intention to award a public works contract has to be made known by means of a notice in the Official Journal of the European Communities. Minimum time limits both for open and restricted procedures are laid down for receipt of tenders, replies to requests for further information, and site inspections (Articles 13 and 14). Article 15 provides for time limits in case of urgency. Articles 16, 17, and 18 lay down the minimum information required to be included in notices under open and restricted procedures and in invitations for tender under restricted procedures.

Directive 71/305 also lays down rules in the technical field (e.g., technical specifications) and a description of testing, checking, acceptance and calculation methods is to be concluded in the contractual documents. Indications of trade marks, patents, types, etc. are prohibited. However if such indication is accompanied by the words "or equivalent" it is authorised, if the specification would not otherwise be sufficiently precise.

Who is Invited to Tender

EEC law provides some rules in this field. Directive 71/305 lays down criteria of economic and financial standing and of technical knowledge or ability. Contractors may be excluded from participation if, for example, they are insolvent or have been convicted of offences concerning their professional conduct. Financial and economic standing may, as a general rule, be proved inter alia by reference from bankers. Technical knowledge or ability may be proved by appropriate statements as to qualification of managerial and technical staff.

Collusion by Tenderers

Collusive tendering may amount to the tort of conspiracy, although the evidential burden on a public authority seeking to mount an action on that basis would be heavy. Given the appropriate market conditions, tendering agreements are likely to be anticompetitive practices under the Competition Act 1980.

The tenderers may all belong to a trade association. If they do so, and the association makes recommendations regarding the prices or other terms upon which they will contract, that agreement is registrable under the Restrictive Trade Practices Act 1976. Parties can be required to remove the relevant restrictions unless these are justified as being in the public interest. If tenderers were to agree together about their terms, this might in some cases also constitute a breach of Article 85 of the EEC Treaty and even of Article 86.

Awarding Contracts

In some jurisdictions the selected contractor is automatically the lowest bidder. English law knows of no such automatic selection. Those who invite tenders are not legally obliged to accept any tender, not even the lowest.

As regards Local Authorities, Model Standing Orders provide that a tender other than the lowest should not be accepted except as authorised by the Council or a committee empowered to do so. Under EEC Directive 71/305, the criteria for awarding contracts are to be either on the basis of lowest price only or, when the award is made, to the most economically advantageous tender, according to the criteria stated in the contract notice. If the documents relating to the contract provide for its award at the lowest price tendered, the authority must justify to the Advisory Committee set up by the Council the rejection of tenders which it considers to be too low.

Contract Terms

A public authority cannot by contract limit the subsequent exercise of its statutory powers.[19] A public contract is implied to be subject to the exercise of those powers, and action taken in pursuance of them does not constitute a breach of contract even if it impedes the contractor's performance of his obligations, unless the action was taken to frustrate the commercial purpose of the contract.[20] As regards Central Government, the contractor is at a disadvantage (as compared to his remedies against a private body or other public organisation) since the remedies of specific performance and injunction are not usually available, although damages may be awarded.

The main common law principle which may impinge upon the freedom of public bodies to negotiate any terms into their procurement contracts is the doctrine of restraint of trade. It is possible that this doctrine would be used to prevent a public authority or corporation from using its power to restrict unduly a supplier's or contractor's power to make agreements with others. However, the legal authorities on this doctrine have concerned particular types of contract (e.g., employment and solus) and there is authority for the proposition that it does not apply to ordinary commercial contracts for the regulation and promotion of trade during the existence of the contract.[21]

Among the restrictions upon freedom of contract the Competition Act 1980 could be invoked against any public body operating a course of conduct intended or likely to distort competition or, in the case of a public corporation such as a nationalised industry, which constituted an abuse of a monopoly position.

The effect of the Restrictive Trade Practices Act 1976 is to prevent certain restrictions being imposed or accepted by two or more parties unless they can be shown to operate in the public interest. The Act applies equally to public as to private organisations, but only to those which are persons carrying on business within the United Kingdom. This excludes Local Authorities and Government Departments, for example, but not public corporations running nationalised industries.

Central and Local Government are more likely to be called to account for their conduct with regard to the ethics of their contractual procedures through constitutional means than through the courts. The emphasis of these remedies is generally upon the overall protection of the public interest rather than vindicating the rights of a particular contractor or supplier. Such constitutional checks apply also, but to a lesser extent, to public corporations. Examples of the way in which such matters may be investigated are as follows.

A complaint of maladministration by Local Authorities and similar bodies, such as Water Authorities, may be investigated by Local Commissioners. There is authority that "maladministration" includes bias, neglect, inattention, delay, incompetence, ineptitude, perversity, turpitude, and arbitrariness.[22]

A person aggrieved by Central Government may petition either House of Parliament.[23] If introduced into the House of Commons by a member, and calling for urgent redress, the matter may be debated straight away (H of C Standing Orders (1971) (Public Business) no. 101). Other public petitions are referred to a committee on Public Petitions (H of C Standing Orders (1971) (Public Business) no. 102). As regards public corporations administering nationalised industries, the responsible minister may be questioned in Parliament on matters which fall within his statutory responsibility. Questions regarding such industries may also be raised in debates on the annual reports and accounts (which are required to be laid before Parliament) and on discussion of legislation relating to the industries. The working of these industries is scrutinised by the Select Committee on Nationalised Industries, their accounts are examined by the Public Accounts Committee of the House of Commons and their spending may be examined by the Expenditure Committee of the House.

Conclusion

The existing remedies within the United Kingdom with regard to public procurement contracts are aimed at the general public interest in having free competition and in unbiased decision-making by Central and Local Government. Generally speaking, the law is not specifically addressed to the grievances of contractors over their treatment at the hands of public bodies but the introduction of ECC law is a new influence the effects of which are yet to be fully worked out.

FOOTNOTES

1. There is unlikely to be unanimity as to which bodies properly fall to be classified as "public authorities" under English law.

2. See also Local Government Planning and Land Act 1980 Part III.

3. Section 135(4) of the 1972 Act, and R. v. Hereford Corporation ex parte Harrower (1970) 3 All ER 460.

4. R. (McKee) v. Belfast Corporation (1954) NI 122.

5. R. v. Hereford Corporation ex parte Harrower. A person had such interest as ratepayer but not as prospective contractor. A disappointed tenderer may have a remedy in the English courts if the failure to comply with standard orders is a breach of the ECC Directives (see para 25 post).

6. Article 3.

7. For a general discussion of the Community and its administration see Mathijsen "A Guide to European Community Law."

8. Discrimination in favour of English nationals in the commercial field has recently been held unlawful in the field of licensing: R. v. Trinity House London Pilotage Committee ex parte Jensen and others (Financial Times 6th August 1984).

9. It remains a matter of some doubt whether these directives are themselves enforceable as part of U.K. law against Local Authorities. See Whyatt and Dashwood "Substantive Law of the EEC" (1980) pp. 40-42.

10. For the text of the directive see J.O. 1971, L185/1; OJ 1971, 678.

11. (Article 1). Bodies described in this paper as "public corporations" are not governed by the directive.

12. Compare this with similar terminology in the GATT agreement, Article 5.

13. Value Added Tax.

14. At October 1984 rounded to nearest penny.

15. Article 86 was invoked, for example, in an attempt to secure an interlocutory injunction against the Government-funded Milk Marketing Board which withdrew supplies of butter for resale from one Company. The House of Lords held that, if an infringement of Article 86 were found, the Plaintiffs could be compensated in damages: Garden Cottage Foods Ltd. v. Milk Marketing Board (1983) 3 WLR 143.

16. (1973) C.M.L.R. D. 217.

17. Belgische Radio En Televisie v. Sabam (1974) ECR 51 at p.62, (1974) 2 CMLR 231 at p.271.

18. H.M.S.O. June 1983.

19. William Cory & Sons Ltd. v. City of London Corporation (1951) 2 KB 476 CA.

20. Commissioners of Crown Lands v. Page (1960) 2 QB 274 CA.

21. Esso Petroleum Co. Ltd. v. Harper's Garage (Stourport) Ltd. (1968) AC 269, 297.

22. R. v. Local Commissioner for North Area of England ex parte Bradford City Metropolitan Council (1978) JPL 767 at 768.

23. Or theoretically may petition the Queen.

PUBLIC EMPLOYEE WORK STOPPAGES AND ALTERNATIVES: A BRIEF REVIEW OF THE UNITED STATES EXPERIENCE

London Sessions
ABA Annual Meeting 1985
Westminster Room, Inter-Continental Hotel
London, England

Friday, July 19, 1985
2:00 P.M. - 4:00 P.M.

James Baird
55 East Monroe Street
Chicago, Illinois 60603

This paper will briefly discuss the history in the United States of public employee strike rights and remedies.[1] It will then explore America's experience with binding arbitration and other alternatives to the right to strike in public employment.[2] Finally, personal conclusions concerning strike rights and alternatives will be offered in hopes of provoking additional thought and discussion.

History of Common Law Strike Rights in the Public Sector

Originally, all union activity in the United States, whether in the public or private sector, was outlawed as a criminal conspiracy.[3] In the latter part of the 19th century, the legal treatment of collective action against an employer shifted from criminal conspiracy to the tort of intentional infliction of unjustifiable harm.[4]

At the time of this shift, most strikes--whether public or private--were considered to be unlawful; however, union activity among private sector employees "instituted for mutual help and lawfully carrying out [the union's] legitimate objects" soon became permissible.[5] In 1935, the Wagner Act was passed by the U.S. Congress. This Act--the cornerstone of U. S. labor legislation--granted collective bargaining and strike rights to private sector employees, rights they still enjoy to this day.

In the public sector there is no similar federal legislation granting uniform collective bargaining and/or strike rights to employees. In the absence of uniform federal legislation, the 50 individual states and the federal government have been left to create their own rules and regulations relative to bargaining and strikes by public employees. So far, approximately 39 states have enacted some sort of legislation regulating these matters, as has Congress for federal employees.

Because each state's treatment of bargaining impasses differs, the states are considered "laboratories" in which various impasse resolution techniques are being tested. So far, the results of these tests are less than conclusive.

Most governmental employees have not yet been granted the lawful right to strike their employer, with the sovereign role of government often cited as the reason. For example, one state supreme court stated:

> In the American system, sovereignty is inherent in the people. They can delegate it to a government which they create and operate by law. They can give to that government the power and authority to perform certain duties and furnish certain services. The government so created and empowered must employ people to carry on its task. Those people are agents of the government. They exercise some part of the sovereignty entrusted to it.

They occupy a status entirely different from those who carry on a private enterprise. They serve the public welfare and not a private purpose. To say that they can strike is the equivalent of saying that they can deny the authority of government and contravene the public welfare.

Currently, strikes by state employees are illegal in most jurisdictions, either by statute or at common law,[6] and strikes by employees of the U.S. government are proscribed by statute.[7] Strike prohibitions have been, and still are, enforced by injunction coupled with the contempt power and by criminal penalty, including fine and imprisonment.

Prohibitions against public employee strikes have been based on two theories. They are: (1) strikes by public employees constitute a rejection of the sovereignty of government and, as such, represent an illegal threat to the public welfare; and/or (2) granting public employees the right to strike provides them a disproportionate amount of power because the nonpublic employee can only influence government with his/her vote while the public employee becomes part of a constituent group with both vote <u>and</u> strike power. This latter theory was summarized by Wellington and Winter when they stated:

> [I]f [public employee] unions are able to withhold labor--to strike--as well as to employ the usual methods of political pressure they may possess a disproportionate share of effective powers in the process of a decision. Collective bargaining would then be so effective a pressure as to skew the results of the "normal" American political process.[8]

In 1958, there were approximately 15 public sector strikes involving about 7,510 governmental employees. Since that time the number of such strikes has increased dramatically, especially among teachers.[9]

Legislative Erosion of Common Law Prohibitions on the Right to Strike by Public Employees

Strike prohibition laws alone could not stop the wave of public sector strikes that occurred in the 1960s and 1970s, and which have carried over into the 1980s. During these past 20 years, many union officers and employees have been sent to jail for defying court injunctions; they have continued to negotiate from behind jailhouse doors. Union leaders contend, with some justification, that the jails are not large enough to hold all potential strikers. Whatever the case, public sector strikes in the United States have continued.

In certain cases, enforcement of the strike prohibitions through the imposition of criminal penalties has simply aggravated the strike situation by inducing greater solidarity on the part of striking workers and by inducing sympathy strikes on the part of other previously nonstriking public employee groups. The threat of strike penalties, including suspension or termination from employment, loss of wages, or elimination of union dues checkoff and/or union representation privileges, has also resulted in several "amnesty strikes" in which employees refuse to resume work until all strikers are granted amnesty for striking.

Public unions in the United States have been quite creative in their attempts to pressure management while not violating state no-strike laws. Several quasi-strike tactics, such as "sickouts," "slowdowns," refusals to train, or coordinated "work to the rule" job actions have been utilized on many occasions. The inability of public management to maintain order, provide services, or enforce the law in the face of obvious job actions has at times fostered disrespect for law and for government.

Can There be Meaningful Collective Bargaining Without the Right to Strike?

The need for the strike right often depends upon one's perspective. Thus, many (but not all) management representatives believe that meaningful public sector bargaining is possible without employees possessing the lawful right to strike. In support, approximately 99 percent of all public sector contracts are negotiated without use of the strike and under conditions where the strike is not lawful. If something works 99 percent of the time, so the argument goes, it cannot be so bad.

The pressure on public management to make concessions in bargaining where there are no strike rights is said to be twofold. First, normal political pressure requires that elected officials be responsive to the needs of employees who are usually constituents and often campaign contributors. This need is reinforced through union political action efforts, which in many jurisdictions are said to be unequalled by other special-interest groups.

Secondly, the pressure of existing impasse procedures is said to force management to adopt reasonable bargaining positions at the negotiating table. For example, where a fact-finder's or advisory arbitrator's adverse recommendations will soon be released to the public, this pressure will lead the employer to modify and improve its bargaining offers.

The union position on the strike right is rather easy to summarize. First, most union leaders, and many academicians, vigorously maintain there can be no meaningful collective bargaining without the absolute right of employees to strike. Indeed, it is contended that the strike right lies at the heart of our country's successful private sector bargaining system. This right must be present, it is maintained, if public employees are to have equality of bargaining rights and to be able to make meaningful bargaining gains in negotiations with their employers.

It is the threat of the strike, as much as its actual exercise, that makes bargaining "work" and which accounts for the many public sector contracts which have emerged over the past 30 years, according to several union proponents. Finally, it is contended that without the threat of a strike, management will simply "not move" off of its unreasonable bargaining positions and the bargaining process will break down.

Insofar as existing impasse procedures are concerned, most are considered by strike-right proponents as laborious, cumbersome, expensive, and/or simply ineffective. The obvious exception, of course, is binding arbitration, which more and more labor leaders are beginning to embrace.

Some argue that while private employees, such as those working in hospitals, coal mines, or for utility companies, properly possess the lawful right to strike, such right nonetheless should be denied to their public sector counterparts. Other practitioners and some jurists consider this position ludicrous.[10]

Are There Alternatives to the Absolute Right to Strike in Public Employment?

Proposed Alternatives: The Limited Right to Strike and Mandatory Impasse Resolution Procedures

Two general, alternative solutions to the problem of public employee strikes have recently been utilized, both of which address the alleged failure of the no-strike laws to prevent strikes and the unique need to prevent strikes in the public sector. These two general solutions, which are quite complementary, consist of (1) the grant of a limited right to strike to certain nonessential employees; and (2) mandated impasse resolution procedures--usually compulsory binding arbitration--where it is believed that strikes by essential employees will endanger the public health, safety, or welfare.[11]

These alternative solutions are based on the theories that (1) aggrieved employees voluntarily refrain from striking only if they have an equally fruitful, alternative means to be heard; and (2) where nonessential public employees can strike without harming the public welfare, bargaining will be enhanced (and the incidence of strikes reduced) by granting to those employees the power to strike and to their employer the power to take a strike.[12] The prevalent concept in the United States of differential treatment between essential and nonessential public employees is embodied in the recognition that the harm caused by the strike is directly related to the type of service provided--police or fire protection, for example--and not the character of the employer, whether government or nongovernment.

Several states, including Alaska, Hawaii, Illinois, Minnesota, Montana, Ohio, Oregon, Pennsylvania, Vermont, and Wisconsin, have employed this dual solution, granting nonessential public employees a limited right to strike by statute which can be exercised after the exhaustion of prescribed impasse resolution procedures. With the exception of Montana, however, an otherwise legal strike is subject to injunction upon a finding that it will threaten certain elements of the public health, safety, and/or welfare.[13] Experimentation with the strike right in these states is continuing, and no consensus has yet emerged. It does appear, however, that legalizing the right to strike may increase--not decrease--the actual number of public sector work stoppages.

<u>Binding-Interest Arbitration as an Alternative to the Right to Strike in Public Employment</u>

More than 20 states have enacted legislation providing for compulsory, binding arbitration of certain public sector negotiation impasses. Generally, these statutes have been applicable to police, fire, and security personnel.[14]

With conventional binding-interest arbitration, the parties--once impasse has been reached and mediation has failed--either voluntarily or by law cede their power to an arbitrator to write their contract for them. The arbitrator, usually after a public hearing, considers the proposals and arguments of the parties and then formulates the terms of a contract consistent with pre-established statutory criteria. The arbitrator may accept one or the other party's proposals or may make an award somewhere in between on each issue in dispute.

A variation on the theme of conventional binding-interest arbitration is "last best offer" or "final offer" arbitration. With "last best" or "final offer" arbitration the parties each submit a final offer which the arbitrator evaluates generally in accordance with the same criteria used in conventional arbitration. The arbitrator then selects the overall best offer for use in the contract. Such offers can be made on an issue-by-issue basis or in the form of a total package.

The issue-by-issue arbitration approach has the initial appeal of allowing each negotiating party a greater opportunity to have at least some of its proposals included in the contract, but it can result in a total package that is unreasonable to one of the parties. In total package arbitration, the arbitrator simply selects one party's final offer as the most reasonable--that offer in its entirety then becomes the contract between the parties for its term.

"Mediation-arbitration" (med-arb) has recently emerged as a hybrid alternative to binding-interest arbitration. With med-arb, the neutral third party joins the negotiations as a mediator and attempts to bring the negotiating positions closer together. If an impasse develops, the mediator then shifts his role to that of arbitrator with the power to formulate binding contract terms.

In most jurisdictions, public employers cannot submit unresolved collective bargaining disputes to interest arbitration in the absence of an authorizing statute. Where an arbirator's award is made pursuant to statute, it will generally be sustained by the courts: (1) if the award is supported by substantial, credible evidence in the record; (2) if the arbitrator gave due weight to all relevant factors arising from case law or statutes; and (3) if the award was "reasonable."[15]

Arguments for and Against Binding Arbitration as an Alternative to the Right to Strike in Public Employment

Supporters of binding-interest arbitration argue that the process may be the only effective way to ensure the strike-free resolution of negotiations impasses in the public sector. Moreover, it is argued that binding arbitration promotes good faith negotiating by imposing a definite deadline on the parties and that it provides finality to the bargaining process. Finally, supporters of the process contend that binding arbitration is fair to employers, employees, and the public and that it fosters respect for law and order.

There are numerous criticisms of binding arbitration, and its critics would either completely bar its use or, at a minimum, limit its use to situations where strikes involve only the most essential of personnel.[16] Indeed, many public employers experienced with binding arbitration have indicated that they would prefer to accept the consequences of a strike by any group of public employees rather than be faced with the consequences of a binding arbitration award.

The critics of binding arbitration note the chilling effect that the process tends to have on negotiations and its built-in tendency toward overuse. They also note the loss of management's ability to determine its own agreement; the fact that the arbitrator becomes a de facto regulator of the disputed issues; and the fact that the parties are forced to accept a contract not of their own design.

There is concern over whether or not arbitrators give adequate consideration and weight to other legislative enactments that affect their sphere, such as financial "cap" or "lid" laws. There is also concern about an arbitrator's level of familiarity with the intricacies of any particular negotiations or financial structure and about the legitimacy of some of the analytical methods used by arbitrators. For example, critics dispute the legitimacy of basing wage rates on the prevailing wage in the private sector for "similar" work where the similarities between the public and private sector work may be distant. Finally, binding arbitration allegedly relieves elected officials of their responsibility to control the public purse and to make essentially political decisions between competing public priorities.

Other Forms of Impasse Resolution in Public Employment and Their Feasibility as Strike Alternatives

Other forms of impasse resolution are used in the public sector. "Mediation," previously discussed as a component of mediation-arbitration, informally involves a neutral third party in the dispute, thereby improving communication and lessening any imbalance of power. Many states and the federal government have provided for mediation of negotiation disputes. However, mediation only serves to diminish the threat of a strike by helping negotiations succeed; it cannot, in and of itself, terminate an impasse.

"Fact-finding" involves the settlement of factual disputes by a neutral third party. The findings of fact are not binding on the parties, but the neutrality of the fact-finder gives them force. Publication of such findings often influences public opinion, which lies at the core of the public sector employer's bargaining power. Fact-finding is often helpful in resolving public sector disputes, but it is a relatively slow process.

The "legislative hearing" is also employed as an impasse resolution procedure. Some states allow the legislative body to act as the ultimate authority for establishing the terms and conditions of a public employee contract. Of course, the legislative body also holds the purse strings and is responsible for establishing the public entity's fiscal priorities.

A logical extension of the legislative hearing concept involves vesting review authority in the public by means of a referendum. This "public referendum" form of impasse resolution, utilized by some Colorado jurisdictions, allows the public to vote directly on disputed provisions of a proposed contract.[17]

Conclusion: Trends for the Future

As more public employees experience collective bargaining with their employers in the 1980s, there are several somewhat contradictory trends that are likely to emerge in the United States.

First, there will be an increase--not a decrease--in the number of public employee strikes. Many of these strikes will result from the passage of state legislation legalizing such strike activity; this new strike "right" will be utilized by public employees.

Second, public employers--following the Reagan administration's example in the PATCO strike and that of several other municipal, educational, and private sector employers--will take a more professional stance when employee work stoppages occur. Even where the strike is legal, public employers will no longer lose such strikes; rather, they will be better prepared to hold their own through the use of traditional private sector self-help tactics.

Third, as public employers learn they can survive a strike (through use of subcontracting, hiring of replacements, cross-training of managerial employees, and increased public pressure to reduce, not increase, governmental costs), the push by unions for enactment of binding arbitration laws will increase. It is quite possible that public sector unions which have heretofore sought the right to strike, such as the National Education Association (for teachers) and the American Federation of State, County, and Municipal Employees (for state and local workers), will soon join the police and fire unions in an all-out effort to ban the strike and substitute in its place some form of compulsory, binding arbitration of interest disputes.

Management's representatives, for their part, will likely oppose such enactments--sometimes advancing the argument that binding arbitration destroys good-faith bargaining while the right to strike enhances such bargaining. At this point, the circle will have almost become complete.

Another anticipated trend will involve a push for uniform national legislation to regulate public sector bargaining and related bargaining disputes. Such a push, energized by organized labor, will trigger a debate within America on several important issues. These issues will likely include:

- o Should a uniform, federal law regulating state and local governmental labor relations and collective bargaining be enacted by Congress?
- o Should America's public employees (or at least her state and local governmental employees) be granted some rights to strike their employer?
- o Should compulsory, binding arbitration become the mandatory terminal step in resolving public sector bargaining impasses?

There is one final trend to anticipate. That is, in ten years both employer and union counsel will respond to the three issues raised above with considerably different answers than they would give today. After all, the one certainty that experience teaches public sector management advocates and labor advocates alike is that the positions of our clients on these important issues will continue to change over time.

FOOTNOTES

1. For a review of public sector strike rights, see generally, Hanslowe & Acierno, The Law and Theory of Strikes by Government Employees, 67 Cornell L. Rev. 1055 (1982); Burton & Krider, The Role and Consequences of Strikes by Public Employees, 79 Yale L. J. 418 (1970).

2. For a review of alternatives to the strike right in public employment, see generally, Bernstein, Alternatives to the Strike in Public Labor Relations, 85 Harv. L. Rev. 459 (1971); Anderson, Strikes and Impasse Resolution in Public Employment, 67 Mich. L. Rev. 943 (1969).

3. Commonwealth v. Pullis (Philadelphia Mayor's Court, 1806).

4. See, Commonwealth v. Hunt, 45 Mass. 111 (1871).

5. American Steel Foundries v. Tri-City Cent. Trades Council, 257 U.S. 184, 209 (1920).

6. K. Hanslowe and J. Acierno, The Law and Theory of Strikes by Government Employees, 67 Cornell L. Rev. 1055 (1982), at 1059, 1060.

7. 5 U.S.C. § 7311 (1976).

8. Wellington and Winter, The Limits of Collective Bargaining in Public Employment, 78 Yale L. J. 1107, 1123 (1969).

9. The Handbook of Labor Statistics, U.S. Dept. of Labor, Bureau of Labor Statistics, Bulletin 2175 (December, 1983) reveals the following incidence of public sector strike activity:

Year	Number of Public Employee Strikes	Number of Workers Involved (In Thousands)	Worker Days Idle (In Thousands)
1969	411	160	745
1970	412	333	2,043
1971	329	152	901
1972	375	142	1,257
1973	387	195	2,299
1974	384	160	1,404
1975	478	318	2,204
1976	378	180	1,690
1977	413	170	1,765
1978	481	193	1,706
1979	593	254	2,982
1980	536	223	2,347

The incidence of public sector strike activity has varied depending upon the occupation involved in the dispute. In 1980, the latest year of available statistics, U.S. governmental strike activity (as reported in Work Stoppages in Government, 1980, 71 Gov't Empl. Rel. Rep. (BNA) 1017 (11-23-81)) was as follows (workers and days idle in thousands):

Occupation	Stoppages	Workers Involved	Days Idle
TOTAL	536	223.6	2,347.8
Professional and Technical	257	113.2	1,351.7
Teachers	232	107.7	1,290.1
Nurses	8	3.1	24.3
Other	17	2.4	37.3
Clerical	10	.9	12.6
Production and Maintenance	138	47.1	458.2
Sanitation	9	1.3	5.8
Crafts	5	1.5	25.3
Other	124	44.3	427.1
Protective	60	13.3	97.9
Police	37	3.7	11.5
Fire	9	5.8	72.6
Police & Fire	6	2.3	5.3
Other	8	1.5	8.5
Other	71	48.9	427.4

10. Anderson Federation of Teachers v. School City of Anderson, 252 Ind. 558, 569, 251 N.E.2d 15, 21 (1969) (dissenting opinion of Chief Justice DeBruler).

11. See, R. Theodore Clark, Jr., Public Sector Strikes: The Need for a Comprehensive Approach, 221, 231 (1979).

12. Comment, supra at 773; Report and Recommendation of June 1968, Governor's Commission to Revise the Public Employee Laws of Pennsylvania, reprinted in, 251 Gov't Empl. Rel. Rep. (BNA) E-1, E-3 (1968).

13. Coughlin & Raider, Right to Strike and Compulsory Arbitration: Panacea or Placebo, 58 Marq. L. Rev. 205, 216 (1973).

14. For a review of interest arbitration, see Feuille, Final-Offer Arbitration and Negotiating Incentives, 32 Arbitration J. 203 (1977); Berkowitz, Arbitration of Public Sector Interest Disputes: Economics, Politics and Equity, 29 Proc. National Academy of Arbitrators 151 (1976).

15. Minami, Interest Arbitration: Can the Public Sector Afford It? Developing Limitations on the Process, 34th Annual Meeting of the National Academy of Arbitrators, Maui, Hawaii, May 8, 1981, at 243.

16. E.g., R. Theodore Clark, Jr., Public Sector Impasse Procedures Revisited; IRRA Spring Meeting, Milwaukee (April 29, 1982).

17. See generally, Helburn & Matthews, The Referendum as an Alternative to Bargaining, 9 J. of Collective Negotiations in the Public Sector 93 (1980); Katz, Public Referendums and Public Employee Collective Bargaining: Are They Compatible? 8 J. of Collective Negotiations in the Public Sector 183 (1979).

PUBLIC EMPLOYEE WORK STOPPAGES AND ALTERNATIVES: A BRITISH PERSPECTIVE

London Sessions
ABA Annual Meeting 1985
Westminster Room, Inter-Continental Hotel
London, England

Friday, July 19, 1985
2:00 P.M. - 4:00 P.M.

David Cockburn
Pattinson & Brewer
30 Great James Street
London, WC1N 3HA

and

Christopher Carr, Q.C.
1 Essex Court
Temple, London EC4Y 9AR

The Industrial Relations Background to Public Sector Employment in Britain

In order to derive any benefit from a study of comparative labour law, it is first necessary to appreciate the different industrial relations contexts in which the laws of the respective countries operate. Needless to say, this has been the subject of numerous books[1] but for present purposes it is sufficient to refer briefly to the following aspects.

The Scope of Public Employment

The public sector in Britain comprises a large, complex, and diversified set of industries and services which broadly fall into three categories. First, there is Central Government, consisting of both the blue and white collar (industrial and nonindustrial) civil service and the other organisations which are responsible to Government Departments and are funded through taxation, e.g., the National Health Service. Secondly, there are the Local Authorities, which are responsible for a range of services including education, housing, social services, police and fire services and are financed mainly through a combination of Government grants and local taxation (rates). Thirdly, there are the public corporations, mainly the nationalised industries, such as the National Coal Board, the Central Electricity Generating Board, the British Steel Corporation, British Shipbuilders, British Railways, and British Gas. There are also those privatised public corporations in which the Government retains a majority interest, such as British Telecom and the British National Oil Corporation. These are all trading corporations which have significant but varying degrees of financial independence from the Government.

The scale of public employment so defined is immense, employing roughly one-third of the nation's labour force and with staff costs representing about 32 percent of total public spending.

Trade Union Activity and Collective Bargaining

It has long been a cornerstone of industrial relations thinking in Britain that collective bargaining is the best means of regulating employment relationships. It is therefore consistent with this view of their social responsibilities that public sector employers should encourage not only collective bargaining but also Trade Union membership. Indeed, in the case of certain public corporations, such as British Steel and Central Electricity Generating Board, there is a statutory obligation on the employers to recognise, consult, and negotiate with the appropriate Unions. As a consequence, Trade Union density as a percentage of the total workforce is particularly high in the public sector. A study published in 1983 put the total public sector union density (excluding the British Steel Corporation) at 82.4 percent.[2] The same study reported that in 1979, Union density in certain groups of the public sector were as follows: (1) National Government, 91.3 percent; (2) Local Government and Education, 77.5 percent; (3) Health Services, 73.7 percent; (4) Post and Telecommunications, 99.9 percent; (5) Coal Mining, 97.1 percent; (6) Gas, 90.3 percent; (7) Electricity, 99.1 percent; and (8) Water, 92.7 percent.

Within such a huge public sector there are, of course, widely varying types of collective bargaining machinery but the predominant model is still centralised and rather bureaucratic nature. This machinery has evolved principally from the reports of the Whitley Committee in 1917-18, which resulted in a system of national negotiating machinery and local consultative committees. Until recently, this broad model has been flexible enough to accommodate the changes that have occurred in public sector bargaining over the years.

Industrial Action in the Public Sector

The overall pattern of strikes is difficult to assess since the published figures on the distribution of strikes by industry do not allow the public and private sectors to be clearly separated. It is, however, generally accepted that the public sector (excluding coal and steel) has had a lower strike record than the private sector. One study shows, for example, that in the period 1970-75 local authorities had an average of 5.2 strikes per 100,000 workers as against an average of 22.9 strikes in manufacturing and 12.4 in all other industries.[3]

It would, however, appear that this traditional pattern may be changing. In a series of incomes policies since 1961, the public sector Unions see the Government as using them as the group of workers whose income can be most easily controlled. This has led to well-established comparisons with the private sector being disturbed and a growing sense of disenchantment amongst public sector Unions. This in turn has strengthened Shop Steward organisation and local Union activity as well as causing the Union leaders to reconsider their political perspectives. Since 1976, Governments have attempted to control increases in public sector incomes by means of cash limits, developing this in later years to incorporate a percentage wage increase assumption in the funds made available. At the same time, there have been considerable efforts to make the public sector more cost effective, both by internal re-organisation and by subcontracting to the private sector. Central Government has taken a firm stand in disputes, even where the cost to them of the strike has proved to be far more than the cost of settlement.[4]

A system of assessing comparisons with the public sector using a Pay Research Unit, which had been in existence since 1956, was unilaterally abandoned by the Government in 1981, on the Government's belief that its recommendations were having an inflationary effect. A Committee was then set up to inquire into how a new remuneration system might be established but the resulting "Megaw Report" is still the subject of negotiations. In the meantime, pay negotiations continue to take place but without the benefit of any systematic comparison with similar negotiations in the private sector. It would seem that the Government is sufficiently confident of its bargaining strength to lapse back into power bargaining.

This pragmatic approach by Government is capable of great flexibility should the need arise. After a prolonged strike by firemen, and the mere threat of industrial action by policemen in 1979, both groups of workers achieved large pay increases and an indexation formula to sustain their more favourable pay relativities in the future. The political support given to the nurses has secured for them a separate review body.

The picture is therefore one of a public sector with diminished job security, pay increases usually falling below the level of inflation, and growing union militancy both at local and national level. Faced with this situation, it would appear that the Government has concluded that it will generally be less inflationary to rely on power bargaining techniques rather than the more traditional techniques of comparability and arbitration.

The Extent of the Debate in Britain

It is a matter of fact that far less consideration has been given to the alternatives to work stoppages in the public sector in Britain than in the United States. This is true for a number of reasons. First, the public sector in Britain is so vast and complex that it would not be sensible to apply totally different standards to it than are applied in the private sector. Secondly, there is no general prohibition on public sector workers taking industrial action which distinguishes them as requiring separate treatment. Thirdly, the established pattern of collective bargaining has, until recently, operated with enough success that alternative models were not actively sought. Fourthly, the ability to take industrial action is guarded so jealously by the trade union movement that whilst the established machinery was working acceptably, it would have been regarded as inflammatory even to suggest any restrictions. Fifthly, it must always be remembered that neither Unions nor employers use lawyers to negotiate or draft their collective agreements; neither do they use lawyers in normal industrial arbitration. The distrust of the legal profession in industrial relations is such that lawyers generally are kept at arms' length from all industrial relations issues.

Such debate as is presently taking place is concerned not so much with the public sector but with the attempts by the Union involved in the electronics industry to gain sole recognition agreements with new high technology companies by offering binding procedure agreements ending in compulsory, normally last offer, arbitration. These agreements have provoked an outcry from most other Unions, which see any restriction on the ability to strike, whether self-imposed or not, as an anathema.

The growth of militancy within the public sector since the mid-1970s has caused the Government to reconsider its position but it has never been suggested that special provisions should be applied to public sector employees as such. Rather, it is being suggested that special consideration might be given to those involved in essential services, be they in the public or private sector.

Should the Criteria for Regulation be Public Employment or Essential Services

From the British perspective, the justifications usually given for according special treatment to the public sector workforce appear less than convincing.

The argument that the taking of industrial action by any public sector employee is incompatible with the sovereignty of Government is viewed with particular suspicion. Indeed, the concept of such employees owing a duty to democracy over that of private sector employees appears in this country to be as realistic as the theory in Socialist countries that strikes are impermissible because there is no conflict between the interests of the workers and the State. Even if the validity of this argument were to be accepted for certain high-level Government officials, its relevance for the vast majority of the public sector workforce is highly dubious. The job seeker is hardly likely to be more influenced by the identity of the employer than by the nature of the job and its terms and conditions. Similarly, it is doubtful if a dispute about terms and conditions of employment would be viewed by the employee as a challenge to the authority of Government. From the point of view of the public sector employers, it is of course often impossible for them to provide the model terms and conditions of employment that they might wish to provide because of the many financial and political constraints upon them. It is, therefore, not surprising that the employees wish to have some direct influence on the decision-making process through effective collective bargaining.

The rationale for according special treatment to public sector employees is further eroded when considering how fortuitous it often is that certain workgroups are classified as being in the public and private sectors. In Britain, the sector to which any group of workers might belong is often a matter of political and economic policy, as can be seen by contrasting the position of many public sector workers in this country with their private sector counterparts in the United States. Furthermore, the boundaries of the public sector in this country are constantly shifting as new industries are nationalised or privatised by successive Governments and services are either being taken over by public authorities or being subcontracted to the private sector.

Insofar as the justification of special treatment is an attempt to protect the community from irreparable harm or injury, then the argument is of course unassailable. However, the British perspective would then question whether all public sector disputes put the community at such risks and whether a more selective approach, regulating only the essential services, might be more appropriate.

The Legal Framework of Industrial Action in Britain

The General Background

There is no legal right to strike in Britain, unlike in certain other European countries where such a right is constitutionally guaranteed. In fact, practically all industrial action in Britain would be subject to civil and criminal sanctions were it not for protective legislation that has been enacted from time to time. The classic pattern in which labour law in Britain has developed has been for the Courts, applying the common law, to establish principles upon which to find industrial action unlawful and for Parliament then to enact legislation to restore the status quo. This pattern has become known as "Judge-made liabilities and statutory immunities." The profound distrust of the law and lawyers amongst many Trade Unionists in Britain is due, in part, to this type of judicial involvement in industrial relations.

For over 60 years, the impact of the law on industrial action was largely regulated by the Trade Dispute Act of 1906. This period was characterised by judicial abstention from industrial relations. In 1971, however, the Conservative Government enacted the Industrial Relations Act, the drafting of which owed much to the Taft Hartley Act. This met with considerable resistance and was repealed by the Labour Government in 1974. The present Government has not attempted a similar root and branch reform but has, since 1980, enacted three statutes in a so called step-by-step approach with the stated intention of reducing the power of the Unions.

One reform that is causing particular concern to the public sector Unions is the redefinition of a Trade Dispute. This is because the cornerstone of the statutory immunities given to participants in industrial action is the requirement that the industrial action must be "In Contemplation or Furtherance of a Trade Dispute" (the so called "golden formula"). The purpose of this particular reform is to exclude strikes over predominantly political issues. However, it is often difficult to distinguish political from industrial issues in the public sector. Quite often, the influence of cash limits and Government policy means that the employer with whom the negotiations are being conducted is not the person who needs to be most influenced, and any industrial action aimed ultimately at changing Government policy could be at risk of losing its statutory immunity.

Laws Regulating Particular Groups of Workers

Specific statures have prohibited industrial action by the armed forces since 1797 and the police since 1919. In 1976-77, the Police pressed for the restoration of the right to strike but this was willingly dropped following the establishement of a favourable pay review structure. Merchant Seamen can only take industrial action if they give 24 hours notice and their vessel is securely moored in a safe berth. The position of postal and telecommunication workers is unclear as provisions intended to deter individual acts of industrial misconduct may now have the effect of making any industrial action unlawful.[5] The Government considers that such workers are free to strike but not to take discriminatory action against individual customers.[6] Between 1875 and 1971, workers in the Gas, Water, and Electricity supply industries were also subject to specific regulations, but these regulations were repealed on the grounds that action likely to endanger life would still be unlawful under the more general provisions.

The Regulation of Essential Services

Since 1875, it has been an offence "wilfully and maliciously" to breach "a contract of service knowing or having reasonable cause to believe that the probable consequence of.... so doing, either alone or in contribution with others would be to endanger human life or cause serious bodily injury or to expose valuable property to destruction or serious injury."[7] The penalty is a maximum of three months imprisonment or a £20 fine. There is no record of this provision ever being used, despite ample opportunity. In 1968, the Donovan Commission recommended leaving it undisturbed on grounds that its repeal might be seen as condoning that which had previously been prohibited.

In practice, British laws have been directed at securing the continuation of services rather than forstalling disruption by such measures as cooling off periods.[8] The Emergency Powers Act of 1920 enables the Crown to declare a state of emergency if "at any time it appears to Her Majesty that there have occurred or are about to occur events of such a nature as to be calculated, by interfering with the supply and distribution of food, water, fuel or light or with the means of locomotion to deprive the community, or any substantial part of it, of the essentials of life." The executive may then make regulations for securing these essentials. States of emergency under these Regulations have only been proclaimed on 12 occasions.[9] The Emergency Powers Act of 1964 enables troops to be used for urgent work of national importance. The Energy Act of 1976 gives the Government extensive powers when energy supplies are threatened.

In addition to these statutory measures, Trade Unions are continually emphasising their desire to safeguard public health and safety when taking industrial action. In 1979, this policy was given formal expression in "The TUC Guide to Affiliated Unions on the conduct of Industrial Disputes." A more specific code of practice has been subsequently agreed upon in the National Health Service in 1981.

Although there are no mandatory procedures public sector Unions must follow before taking industrial action, there are well-established institutions for voluntary conciliation, mediation, arbitration, and fact-finding.[10] All of these functions can be carried out by a Government-funded but independently constituted body known as the Advisory, Conciliation, and Arbitration Service (ACAS). This body will only intervene at the request or with the consent of the parties. It may conciliate at any stage of the dispute and maintains a list of arbitrators upon whom it can call.

The process of fact-finding has in the past been relatively successful when an impasse is reached in a major national stoppage but has fallen somewhat into disuse, again probably because of its perceived inflationary effect.[11]

Future Trends

The major determining factors in industrial relations in Britain are economic not legal. An unemployment rate of near 13 percent has proved to be a far greater deterrent to industrial action and inflationary wage claims than the previous 20 years of incomes policy. It is, however, argued that the Government is at the same time operating a covert incomes policy on the public sector through the mechanism of cash limits. The result is a largely compliant workforce with a sense of grievance. The question remains, however, whether that sense of grievance can be contained indefinitely or whether we are merely storing up trouble for a later date.

That part of the public sector which is principally blue-collar and is involved in commercial activities has a long tradition of collective bargaining strength and is unlikely to be seeking alternative straightforward power bargaining in the forseeable future.

On the other hand, the white-collar civil servants and municipal employees with a less militant tradition can see advantages in procedures aimed at avoiding industrial action. It is generally accepted that the first stage of such a procedure would be a comparability study. The Megaw Committee recommended that an independent Pay Board should carry out an annual examination of the trend of percentage movements in pay being awarded to groups of workers undertaking jobs of comparable weight in the private sector. In every fourth year, a further review of total remuneration would also be completed. Negotiators would have to reach pay settlements within the inter quartile range (25%-75%) of percentage movements. Where exactly it would fall would depend on bargaining. In the event of an impasse, they recommend arbitration only if both sides consented and then subject to the overriding veto of Parliament. The public sector Unions are prepared, it would seem, to accept some sort of arbitration but are sceptical about whether this type of arbitration would be fair. They want unilateral access to arbitration and a commitment that the Government will not use its majority in Parliament simply to override any arbitration award it dislikes.

The present trend would therefore seem to be for the Government to be sceptical of giving over the settlement of disputes to third parties. Instead, they prefer to rely upon their bargaining strength, only turning to arbitration if it becomes expedient to do so in the circumstances of the particular case.

FOOTNOTES

1. See the bibliography in "Industrial Conflict; The Role of Government and the Law in the U.S. and U.K." Socio-legal Studies No. 2., Social Science Research Council 1983.

2. Price and Bain. "Union Growth in Britain; Retrospect and Prospect." British Journal of Industrial Relations, March 1983.

3. Smith et al. 1978. "Strikes in Britain. A Research Study of Industrial Stoppages in the U.K." Department of Employment Manpower Papers 15 London HMSO.

4. The 1981 Civil Service Strike cost the Government about 1 billion pounds when the sum being sought was only about £400,000. The 1984 Strike of computer staff at the Department of Health and Social Security in Newcastle again cost the Government far more to win by resisting the strike than it would have cost by conceding.

5. See K.W. Wedderburn "The Worker and the Law" 1971. Chapter 8 "The Right to Strike." Penguin.

6. Gouriet v. UPOW (1978) ACT 435.

7. Kenneth Baker, Minister for Industry and Information Technology H.C. Debate, Vol. 2, col. 313. (1st April 1981).

8. Conspiracy & Protection of Property Act 1975; Section 5.

9. The Industrial Relations Act 1971 contained a cooling-off period for emergency disputes. This provision was used only once in a national railway dispute before the Act was repealed. The ballot of workers was strongly in favour of the dispute, and it is argued that the ballot strengthened the Union's resolve.

10. Mainly coal miners and dockers but also railwaymen, electricity supply workers, seamen, and London busmen.

11. The present system has its origins in the Conciliation Act 1896 and the Industrial Courts Act 1919.

CONDUCTING DISCOVERY ABROAD:
DISCOVERY ABROAD UNDER FRCP, HAGUE CONVENTION AND UNDER HISPANIC AND FRENCH CODES

London Sessions
ABA Annual Meeting 1985
Audley Suite, Grosvenor House Hotel
London, England

Friday, July 19, 1985
2:00 P.M. - 4:00 P.M.

David Epstein
U.S. Department of Justice
10th & Constitution Ave., N.W.
Washington, D.C. 20530

Nuria Rahola Beltran
4837 Loughboro Road
Washington, D.C. 20016

Paul L. Friedman
Suite 500
1747 Pennsylvania Ave., N.W.
Washington, D.C. 20006

Bruno A. Ristau
1218 16th Street, N.W.
Washington, D.C. 20036

Commercial litigation has become increasingly transnational, creating a frequent need for U.S. litigators to seek discovery of documents and testimony of witnesses located abroad. The conduct of extraterritorial discovery has been an area of considerable controversy.[1] Foreign officials have often objected when U.S. discovery procedures are extended to their territory or citizens. These objections stem from traditional notions of sovereignty, which hold that a State has exclusive jurisdiction over its territory and its citizens. Efforts by one State to apply its laws within the territory or to the citizens of another State may be considered an infringement of the other State's sovereignty.[2]

The modern concept of sovereignty is somewhat more flexible, so that the extraterritorial application of a State's laws is considered appropriate when applied to the conduct of its nationals located abroad, to the conduct of foreign nationals occurring within its territory, and to certain activities occurring outside of its territory which cause effects within its territory. United States courts today generally consider the conduct of discovery abroad to be a valid exercise of this extraterritorial power, so long as it does not violate the laws of the foreign state.

The procedures for taking evidence and the scope of permissible discovery vary from country to country.[3] The procedures in the United States are among the most liberal, particularly with regard to discovery, which is controlled almost entirely by counsel and results in virtually boundless access to witnesses, documents, or other tangible things. This liberal attitude is completely alien to most other States where the institution of "discovery" is unknown in civil law jurisdictions, and the taking of evidence during the trial is conducted by the judge, with some limited assistance of counsel. Other common law countries have discovery, but it generally is limited (<u>see</u> English paper).[4] The perception by many foreign States of intrusive and unsupervised U.S. discovery procedures has led to the enactment of foreign blocking legislation designed to limit the extent of U.S. discovery in other countries.[5]

This restrictive approach is balanced by a countertrend toward increased international judicial cooperation. The Hague Convention on the Taking of Evidence Abroad in Civil or Commercial Matters (the "Convention") is a recent example of this more liberal trend.[6] It has helped make foreign officials and lawyers more familiar with U.S. discovery procedures and has created an awareness on the part of U.S. courts and attorneys that they must tailor their discovery procedures in view of foreign law.[7]

Whether proceeding under an international agreement such as the Convention or otherwise, several factors will influence the choice of procedures used in obtaining evidence abroad. Among those to consider are:

- Is the evidence for use in a civil or criminal case?

- Can the information be obtained without the formal intervention of foreign authorities?

- Are the witnesses willing to testify or produce documents?
- Is the evidence to be used at trial, or is it for purposes of grand jury proceedings or civil discovery?
- Does the foreign State in which the evidence is sought operate under a common law, civil, or other legal system?
- Has the foreign State imposed any specific restrictions or prohibitions on the giving of evidence for use in judicial proceedings in the United States, by legislation or otherwise?[8]

Conducting Discovery Abroad Under the Federal Rules of Civil Procedure

In the absence of treaty or multilateral agreement such as the Convention, discovery abroad will be governed by Rule 28(b) of the Federal Rules of Civil Procedure (FRCP) and the applicable municipal law in the country where the evidence is sought. Rule 28(b) provides three methods for obtaining foreign evidence for use in civil litigation in the United States: depositions on notice, commission, and letters rogatory.

The first method provides for depositions to be taken on notice to the other parties, before an officer authorized by U.S or municipal law to administer oaths in the place in which the examination is to be held. United States foreign service officers are authorized to "administer and to take from any person any oath, affirmation, affidavit or deposition and to perform any other notarial act."[9] Thus, U.S. consular officers may take depositions under the notice procedure unless prohibited by local law.[10] In some countries, this authority may be limited to taking depositions of U.S. citizens and third-country nationals.[11] Such depositions may proceed by oral examination or by written interrogatories pursuant to Rules 30 and 31 FRCP. The notice procedure does not require any court intervention, and therefore is the simplest and most expeditious method of conducting discovery abroad.[12]

By contrast, the second method of obtaining evidence under Rule 28(b) involves application to the U.S. district court in which the case is pending for the commission of a designated individual to take the deposition.[13] The commission carries with it the power to administer the necessary oath. Again, the authority to take evidence by commission may be limited by the law of the State in which the deposition is to take place.

These two methods of obtaining evidence abroad are possible only if the deponent agrees to appear voluntarily. A U.S. consular officer has no authority to compel attendance of a witness at his office for the purpose of taking testimony. Few, if any, foreign States would permit a U.S. court to compel a person within their territory to attend a deposition or answer requests for documents, unless that State is involved in or oversees the proceeding.[14] In the case of an unwilling witness, or simply to ensure that a voluntary witness appears at the designated time and place, it is necessary for the U.S. court to make a formal request for the issuance of a letter rogatory to the appropriate judicial authority in the foreign State.[15]

A letter rogatory is a formal request from a U.S. court to a foreign court having jurisdiction that the foreign court invoke its usual process to compel production of the documents or the witness' testimony.[16] The letter may be transmitted to the foreign court through diplomatic channels or presented by local counsel.[17] In executing letters rogatory, the foreign court follows its own procedural rules. It is prudent, therefore, to consult local counsel regarding local procedural requirements before requesting the issuance of the letter.[18] Although the foreign court may apply sanctions in order to compel the production of evidence, in the absence of a treaty, letters rogatory are honored solely on the basis of comity.[19] Access to the desired information therefore cannot be guaranteed even when using a letter rogatory.

Because the U.S. concept of liberal discovery is alien to most foreign countries, it is necessary to frame the letter rogatory in terms the foreign court will approve. At the very least the letter should specify that the request is for evidence to be used at trial, and not just for discovery. With regard to production of documents, the request should be as specific as possible. The documents sought should be individually identified. Broad requests for "any and all documents referring to, relating to or consisting of" should be avoided.

Requests for oral depositions should also be as specific as possible. In most civil law jurisdictions a U..S attorney will not be permitted to participate in such a proceeding.[20] Rather, the foreign judge will conduct the examination, and will ask the witness questions set forth in the letter rogatory. The U.S. lawyer may request in the letter that he be permitted to question the witness directly, but such permission is rarely granted. In some instances the foreign court may allow the U.S. lawyer to suggest follow-up questions, which the judge will then ask of the witness being deposed.

Other procedural differences may bear upon the admissibility in the U.S. court of the evidence obtained in the foreign proceeding. For instance, many foreign jurisdictions do not use court reporters or provide a verbatim transcript. Rather, the presiding judge typically will dictate a summary of the witness' testimony, which the witness may be asked to approve. In many states it is not customary to administer an oath prior to obtaining testimony from a witness. Rarely is there an opportunity for cross-examining the witness, and the judicial officer conducting the examination may fail to obtain the relevant information. Finally, there is concern with accuracy since the witness often will be testifying in a foreign language.[21]

Rule 28(b), FRCP, allows for some flexibility when the evidence obtained abroad does not meet the usual U.S. standards of admissibility. It provides that evidence obtained in response to a letter rogatory need not be excluded merely because of departures from the usual requirements for depositions taken within the United States. The rule, however, makes admissibility of the evidence discretionary with the judge.

Conducting Discovery Abroad Under The Hague Convention

The Convention entered into force in the United States in 1972. Where the evidence sought is located in another State party to the Convention, the standardized procedures that it prescribes must be followed.[22] To facilitate judicial cooperation, the Convention endeavors to bridge the differences in procedures for obtaining evidence in common law systems, where the parties are responsible for obtaining and presenting the evidence, and in civil law systems, where the courts carry out these functions.[23] Because the Convention imposes certain international obligations on the contracting States, attorneys no longer need to rely on comity to secure foreign judicial assistance in obtaining evidence abroad.

The Convention parallels the three methods of obtaining evidence under Federal Rule 28(b). Chapter I, which is mandatory, provides for the obtaining of evidence by means of letters of request. Chapter II, which is optional with each contracting State, provides for the notice and commission methods of obtaining evidence abroad.

Letters of request--the only method for the taking of evidence abroad known to the civil law--are the principal vehicles for obtaining evidence under the Convention. The Convention procedures both expedite and simplify the process for execution of such letters. This is achieved primarily through the Article 2 requirement that each State designate a central authority to receive the letters from the requesting State and to transmit them to the appropriate court. In some instances, however, it is still possible to transmit a letter of request directly from the U.S. court to the foreign court when the proper tribunal is known in advance.[24]

The scope of the Convention is limited to civil matters; it does not apply to criminal or administrative proceedings, or to arbitrations.[25] Under Article 5 of the Convention, a contracting State is obligated to execute a letter of request unless the request is outside the scope of, or does not comply with, the formal requirements of the Convention. Article 3 of the Convention prescribes the contents of a letter of request. A contracting State may also refuse to execute a letter of request if its execution is not within the function of the judiciary of that State, or if its execution would prejudice the sovereignty or national security of that State.[26] But execution may not be refused solely on the ground that the executing State claims exclusive jurisdiction over the subject matter of the action, or because its municipal law does not recognize a similar right of action.[27] These limitations greatly enhance the reliability of foreign judicial assistance in obtaining evidence located within States that are parties to the Convention.

Article 9 of the Convention provides that the judicial authority which executes a letter of request shall apply its own law as to the methods and procedures to be followed. While this provision is similar to the traditional procedure for letters rogatory, the Convention contains several important qualifications. For instance, under Article 7, representatives of the requesting party have a right to be present at the execution of the letter of request. Although there is no right to U.S.-style direct and cross-examination of the witness by an attorney, Article 9 of the Convention provides that the executing authority "will comply with such a request of the issuing court that a special method or procedure be followed."[28] Thus one may ask that a representative of the court making the request be permitted to participate in the foreign proceeding, or that the witness be sworn, or that his responses be furnished in writing under oath, or that a verbatim transcript be made of the proceedings. Article 9, however, does not require the foreign court to comply with such a request if the requested procedure "is incompatible with the internal law of the state of execution, or is impossible of performance by reason of its internal practice and procedure or by reason of practical difficulties."

By providing for increased flexibility in executing a letter of request, the Convention avoids many of the evidentiary difficulties associated with letters rogatory. There are, however, restrictions on the nature of the evidence that can be obtained through letters of request. Under Article 1 of the Convention, such letters can be issued only to obtain evidence "for use in judicial proceedings, commenced or contemplated. In addition, Article 23 of the Convention permits a contracting State to declare that it will not execute a letter of request for purposes "of obtaining pre-trial discovery of documents." Most contracting States have made such a reservation. For these reasons a request should avoid completely the term "pre-trial discovery," and should stress that the evidence sought is to be used directly at trial.[29]

It also should be noted that the standard of relevancy under Rule 26(b), FRCP, is not accepted abroad. Rather, courts in most signator States are likely to impose their own standard of relevancy. Foreign courts therefore may refuse to execute a letter of request that does not designate with specificity the evidence or documents sought; overly broad and ill-defined requests for production are likely to be perceived as "fishing expeditions," and will not be honored. Requests for testimony also must be specific. Article 3(f) of the Convention requires either a listing of questions to be asked or "a statement of the subject matter about which ... [the persons] are to be examined."

Article 10 of the Convention requires a State party to compel a recalcitrant witness to appear and answer a particular question or to furnish particular documents. Unlike the traditional letters rogatory procedure, the application of compulsory measures under Article 10 is not discretionary with the foreign court. But compulsion is limited to what would be available under similar circumstances in a domestic proceeding in the foreign State.[30] This obligation to compel testimony may also be limited by the Article 12 "infringement of sovereignty" or "national security" grounds for refusal to execute a letter of request.

The Convention provides certain additional limitations on obtaining evidence. Article 11 allows a witness to invoke any testimonial privilege available to him under the law of either the requesting State or the State of execution. Further, under Article 11, a contracting State may declare that it will respect privileges existing under the law of States other than the requesting State or the State of execution.

Chapter II of The Hague Convention deals with the taking of evidence by consular officers on notice to the parties, and by the appointment of commissioners. Article 33 of the Convention permits, and most states have made, reservations excluding or limiting the deposition procedures in Chapter II. To the extent that a State party has acceded to Chapter II, the notice and commission methods authorized by the FRCP, generally may be followed under the Convention.[31]

Article 15 allows a consular officer or a commissioner to take voluntarily furnished testimony from nationals of their home State within the State in which they are then located. No compulsion is permitted. A State party, however, may declare that the officer must apply to the designated authority for prior permission in each case. Officers may also take testimony from nationals of the State of execution, or of other States, but only with the consent of the State of execution, unless it has declared otherwise, either by general declaration or on an individual basis.[32]

Article 21 provides that a foreign officer may take evidence under the procedures of the court of origin, unless such procedures are prohibited by the law of the State where the evidence is to be taken. A contracting State may file a declaration permitting consular officers to apply to the foreign authority for the use of coercive measures in obtaining evidence from a recalcitrant witness. Granting of an application is discretionary. Finally, Article 22 allows for alternate methods of requesting discovery, so that if one procedure fails another may be utilized.

The Convention establishes minimum standards for international judicial assistance. While the Convention is not as liberal as the FRCP for U.S. discovery, it represents a movement toward greater liberality and provides a flexible framework for the continued growth of international cooperation in the taking of evidence.

Discovery Under the Hispanic Civil Code

In a civil law country such as Spain, which is not a party to the Convention, the procedures for conducting discovery are governed by the concept of "judicial sovereignty." Under this concept, the act of taking evidence is a judicial function which only authorized persons may perform. Any unauthorized taking of evidence may be regarded as a violation of Spanish judicial sovereignty.[33] There is, however, no express prohibition in the Spanish civil code against the taking of testimony by a U.S. consular officer or a Spanish or U.S. attorney.[34] Nor is there a prohibition against the voluntary production of tangible evidence or documents for use in proceedings outside Spain, provided production does not threaten the security interests of Spain or violate any of its other laws.[35] Thus both the notice and commission methods of taking evidence under Rule 28(b), FRCP, may be employed.

Judicial assistance in obtaining evidence in Spain will be given only if requested by letters rogatory, which must be transmitted through diplomatic channels. Letters rogatory will be executed regardless of nationality unless the proceeding would contravene the public policy of Spain, or execution would interfere with Spanish sovereignty or national security.[36] Evidence is taken in accordance with the Spanish procedural law.

Spain is typical of civil law countries in that it utilizes an "inquisitorial" rather than an "adversarial" system of justice. The attorneys initiate the proceedings by filing pleadings which contain all the relevant facts and the legal arguments supporting the case, and supply whatever proof they might have. The court conducts its own inquiry as to the facts so that the judge, not the parties, is responsible for gathering evidence by requesting documents and questioning the witnesses.[37]

Witnesses give their testimony under oath, and may be penalized for false testimony. Their answers are recorded verbatim, and the transcript must be subscribed by the witness, the judge, the clerk, and any parties present.[38]

Discovery, especially as it is known in the United States, is an alien concept in Spain as in most other civil law jurisdictions. The trial is not considered a separate part of the proceedings, thus pre-trial procedures are viewed as part of the judicial function.[39] Document demands are strictly confined so that individual documents must be identified, and broad requests will not be tolerated. The U.S. standard of relevance is not recognized; rather the evidence sought must be relevant to the case itself.[40]

Discovery Under the French Civil Code

The Convention entered into force in France in 1974. Under the implementing legislation of the Convention, procedures are available in France which enable U.S. attorneys to obtain deposition evidence for use in U.S. litigation in a manner more comparable to that of common law countries.[41]

In order to accommodate letters of request under the Convention, the French Code of Civil Procedure was amended so that questions and answers may be transcribed or recorded in full if specifically requested, and the parties and their counsel, upon authorization by the judge, may ask questions, in French only, of the witnesses.[42] In addition, witnesses generally must testify under oath.[43] Although these new procedures are subject to the consent of the French court, international comity and judicial courtesy usually compel such consent.[44]

Some impediments to conducting common-law-style discovery still remain. For instance, a French court may refuse to execute a letter of request it considers beyond its jurisdiction or threat to the sovereignty or national security of France.[45] More importantly, France has made a declaration under Article 23 of the Convention whereby it will refuse to execute letters of request issued for the purpose of obtaining "pre-trial discovery of documents as known in common law countries."

If proceeding before a diplomatic or consular officer under Chapter II of the Convention, evidence may be obtained in France by using depositions, written interrogatories, or document production. The specific procedure to be followed depends upon whether a U.S., French, or third-country national is involved.[46] United States diplomatic officers in France may take voluntary evidence from U.S. nationals without prior approval by the French authorities, but with regard to French or third-country nationals, prior consent from the central authority must be obtained in each case.[47]

The most direct method of obtaining evidence in France is by appointment of an official commissioner to take voluntary evidence pursuant to Article 17 of the Convention. France requires prior consent from its central authority for the appointment of a commissioner in all cases, without regard to the nationality of the person from whom the evidence is sought.[48]

The selection of the method used to take evidence often will depend upon whether the witness will appear voluntarily. Article 10 of the Convention provides that in executing a letter of request, the foreign tribunal should apply the same means of compulsion as would be appropriate under municipal law. Under the French Code of Civil Procedure, compulsory measures include a judicial order to a party or a nonparty to produce any written documents, with a daily fine for noncompliance. A judge may also order the personal appearance of the party, but no legal sanction may be applied if the party refuses to appear. Moreover, the judge may, in appropriate situations, draw an adverse inference from failure to produce evidence which a party would normally be presumed to possess.[49]

There are no compulsory measures available in proceedings before diplomatic or consular officers and official commissioners in France, as France has not made a declaration, pursuant to Article 18 of The Hague Convention, which provides for the imposition of such measures on application. Thus the reliability of such proceedings in France continues to depend entirely on the cooperation of the individuals from whom the evidence is sought.[50]

Conclusion

The conduct of U.S. discovery abroad reflects two countertrends in international law. In general, the attitude among foreign countries with respect to extraterritorial discovery is one of accommodation and increased judicial assistance in expanding the available procedures for taking evidence in different countries. The Convention is both an indication of, and an impetus to, this liberalizing trend.

Conversely, the enactment of foreign blocking legislation designed to limit the reach of U.S. discovery in certain circumstances indicates an attitude of suspicion and resentment among foreign States when U.S. laws are applied within their territory. Traditional notions of sovereignty coupled with the perception of intrusive and unsupervised U.S. discovery procedures have contributed to this countertrend.

While it is difficult to predict the future course of either of these trends, the tendency by U.S. courts to ignore the concept of international comity in enforcing discovery orders despite foreign blocking legislation, may lead foreign States to ignore the precepts of comity so often essential in carrying out U.S. requests for discovery abroad.

FOOTNOTES

1. *See* Note, "Extraterritorial Discovery: An Analysis Based on Good Faith," 83 *Colum. L. Rev.* 1320 (1983).

2. Carter, "Obtaining Foreign Discovery and Evidence for Use in Litigation in the United States--Existing Rules and Procedures," 13 *Int'l Law.* 5 (1979).

3. Generally, these procedures may be grouped into broad categories depending upon whether the country operates under a common law, civil, socialist, communist, or Islamic legal system. Seidel, "Introduction and Overview: Extraterritorial Discovery in International Litigation," 248 *P.L.I. Litig. Course Handbook Ser.* 22 (1984).

4. Additional complications arise when substantive law and policy differences between the States come into play. For example, most foreign States resent the application of U.S. antitrust or securities laws to their nationals and therefore are reluctant to assist in obtaining evidence relating to the enforcement of such laws. Seidel, *supra* n.3 at 13-14.

5. Examples of such blocking legislation include Canada's 1976 "Uranium Information Securities Regulations," which were enacted to limit the sweep of U.S. discovery regarding uranium marketing activities in connection with an antitrust investigation [Batista, "Confronting Foreign 'Blocking' Legislation: A Guide to Securing Disclosure from Non-Resident Parties to American Litigation," 17 *Int'l. Law.* 61, 70-71 (1983)]; France's 1980 "Law Relating to the Communication of Economic, Commercial, Industrial, Financial or Technical Documents or Information to Foreign Natural or Legal Persons," which prohibits any person residing in French territory from disclosing certain documents or information intended for use as evidence "in connection with pending or prospective foreign judicial or administrative

proceedings"; and the U.K.'s Protection of Trading Interests Act of 1980, which authorizes the Secretary of State to prohibit compliance with extraterritorial orders for evidence in a variety of circumstances.

6. 23 U.S.T. 2555, T.I.A.S. No. 7444, 8 I.L.M. 37 (1969).

7. Carter, _supra_ n.2 at 7.

8. Augustine, "Obtaining International Judicial Assistance Under the Federal Rules and The Hague Convention," 10 _Ga. J. Int'l & Comp. L._ 101, 108 (1980).

9. 22 U.S.C. §§ 1195, 1203 (1979).

10. 22 C.F.R. §92.55(c) (1983). U.S. officials are required to refuse requests which contravene the laws of the country in which they are stationed. _Id._

11. Countries in which consular depositions are prohibited regardless of the witness' nationality include Austria, Angola, Bulgaria, Cuba, Denmark, Iran, Libya, Liechtenstein, Malawi, Mali, Sierra Leone, Swaziland, Switzerland, and Venezuela. Romania and the U.S.S.R. only permit the taking of depositions of U.S. citizens and third-country nationals. Countries which permit consular depositions of U.S. nationals alone include Bolivia, Central African Republic, Colombia, Greece, Honduras, Hungary, and Turkey.

12. _See_ Note, "Taking Evidence Outside of the United States," 55 _B.U.L. Rev._ 368, 369 (1975).

13. _See_ J. Underwood, _A Guide to Federal Discovery Rules_ 90 (1979).

14. _See_ Stein, "Depositions in Foreign Jurisdictions: 'Innocence Abroad,'" 7 _Litig._ 14, 15 (1981). It should be noted, however, that 28 U.S.C. § 1783 provides a jurisdictional basis for the issuance of a subpoena to compel appearance of an American national located abroad. Carter, _supra_ n.2, at 8 n.6. Fed. R. Civ. P. 45(e)(2) expressly authorizes this procedure. _See_ Augustine, _supra_ n.8, at 112-113.

15. This is also necessary where the foreign country prohibits the use of consular or commissioner depositions with respect to that class of witness.

16. _See_ J. Underwood, _supra_ n.13 at 90, citing _The Signe_, 37 F. Supp. 819, 820, (E.D. La. 1941).

17. 28 U.S.C. § 1781 (1970).

18. Information concerning local procedural requirements may be obtained from the Office of Special Consular Services in the State Department or the U.S. embassy or legation in the foreign capital. *See* 22 C.F.R. § 92.66(b) (1983).

19. Therefore, the last sentence of a letter rogatory usually promises reciprocity. Note, *supra* n.12 at 372 n.26.

20. In common law jurisdictions, the courts appoint a special examiner or master before whom the attorneys take evidence as usual. Note, *supra* n.12 at 373 n.34.

21. *See* Seidel, "United States Trial Considerations When Obtaining Evidence Abroad," 248 *P.L.I. Litig. Course Handbook Ser.* 429, 441-43 (1984).

22. The following countries have ratified the Convention: Barbados, Czechoslovakia, Denmark, Finland, France, Federal Republic of Germany, Israel, Italy, Luxembourg, The Netherlands, Norway, Portugal, Singapore, Sweden, United Kingdom, and United States. 28 U.S.C. § 1781 (Supp. 1984).

23. See Augustine, *supra* n.8 at 128 n.146, citing "Report of the United States Delegation to the Eleventh Session of The Hague Conference in Private International Law," 8 *I.L.M.* at 23 (1969).

24. Article 27 permits a state to declare that letters of request may be transmitted to its judicial authorities by channels other than the designated central authority, and Article 24 allows the designation of additional authorities for receipt of letters of request.

25. *See, e.g., Rio Tinto Zinc Corp. v. Westinghouse Electric Corp.*, [1978] A.C. 547, 628 (House of Lords, Speech of Viscount Dilhorne), in which the Lords voiced their concern that the U.S. letter of request sought information from a neutral witness which would be used against that witness in parallel criminal proceedings.

26. Article 12, The Hague Convention, *supra* n.6.

27. *Id.*

28. Augustine, *supra* n.8 at 128.

29. *See* Stein, *supra* n.14, at 16.

30. Augustine, *supra* n.8 at 129.

31. Note, *supra* n.12, at 384.

32. Article 16, The Hague Convention, *supra* n.6.

33. Augustine, *supra* n.8 at 121 n.106.

34. Article 320 of the Spanish Criminal Code provides that a person "without title or legitimate reason" who "performs acts proper to any authority or public functionary" will be punished with a prison term. Washburn, et al., "International Cooperation in Litigation: Spain", *International Cooperation in Litigation: Europe* 316, 329 (1965).

35. *Id.* at 330.

36. Spanish Code of Civil Procedure, art. 601(2); Washburn, *supra* n.34 at 326. Article 300 of the Spanish Code of Civil Procedure specifies that "the principle of reciprocity will be observed."

37. G. Glos, *Comparative Law* 578 (1979). See also Washburn, *supra* n.34, at 327-8.

38. Washburn, *supra* n.34 at 328.

39. Augustine, *supra* n.8 at 109 n.21.

40. Stein, "The Conduct of Discovery Proceedings Abroad," 248 *P.L.I. Litig. Course Handbook Ser.* 151, 173 (1984).

41. Borel and Boyd, "Opportunities for and Obstacles to Obtaining Evidence in France for Use in Litigation in the United States," 13 *Int'l. Law* 35, 37 (1979).

42. C. Pr. Civ. Arts. 739-40 (Fr.), adopted pursuant to Decree No. 75-1123 of December 5, 1975.

43. Borel and Boyd, *supra* n.41 at 40.

44. *Id.* at 39.

45. C. Pr. Civ., *supra* n.42, art. 743.

46. Borel and Boyd, *supra* n.41, at 41.

47. Declaration of the French Government pursuant to Article 16, The Hague Convention, *supra* n.6.

48. Declaration of the French Government pursuant to Article 17, The Hague Convention, *supra* n.6.

49. Borel and Boyd, *supra* n.41 at 40.

50. *Id.* at 43.

CONDUCTING DISCOVERY ABROAD: DISCOVERY PERMITTED UNDER ENGLISH LAW

London Sessions
ABA Annual Meeting 1985
Audley Suite, Grosvenor House Hotel
London, England

Friday, July 19, 1985
2:00 P.M. - 4:00 P.M.

David Donaldson, Q.C.
2 Hare Court
Temple, London EC4Y 7BH

and

Graeme R. Brister
Linklaters & Paines
Barrington House
59-67 Gresham Street
London EC2V 7JA

A U.S. lawyer with only limited knowledge of the English legal system could properly be forgiven for the belief that England would be a familiar and fruitful environment in which to conduct overseas discovery pursuant to letters rogatory. There is the same common law tradition; a similar, if not always identical, legal language; and the freedom given to the U.S. attorney to carry out the examination of the witness himself without the frustrating interposition of a foreign lawyer or judge to ask the questions. Though genuine advantages, these mask considerable restrictions which can give rise to irritating difficulties for the U.S. lawyer who has not given advance thought to the matter.

The fundamental willingness of the English courts to respond to requests for judicial assistance from a foreign court in the taking of evidence is not in doubt and is of long standing. It goes back at least to 1856, the date of the Foreign Tribunals Evidence Act, which--with various amendments and supplements--governed the position until 1976. In that year, the United Kingdom ratified the Hague Convention on the Taking of Evidence Abroad in Civil or Commercial Matters and brought into force the Evidence (Proceedings in Other Jurisdictions) Act, 1975 ("the Act"). There is a substantial body of case law on the previous legislation (much of it still relevant); and many of the problems arising under the 1975 Act have been the subject of discussion and decision in the House of Lords in the case of Rio Tinto Zinc Corporation v. Westinghouse Electric Corporation, [1977].[1]

Most of the case law, and the RTZ case in particular, is directed to letters of request issued by U.S. courts, and the greater part of the problems arise from the U.S. concept of pre-trial discovery. This may appear odd at first blush, given the common legal heritage of the United States and England. In matters of procedure, however, the two legal systems have since 1776 diverged at least as much as in substantive law. A reader of the Federal Rules of Procedure would be hard put to identify much similarity with the English Supreme Court Practice. He would certainly be struck by the differences in the attitude toward discovery. English lawyers tend to look upon U.S. discovery procedures with reserve often bordering on hostility. They regard these procedures as "fishing," find them oppressive in their width and impact, and suspect that they are abused in battles of forensic attrition.[2] The U.S. lawyer in turn will no doubt find English procedures disappointingly timorous and overprotective of litigants and witnesses. He must, however, accommodate himself to English rules and attitudes in order to obtain proper benefit from a letter of request addressed to an English court, for an essential restriction on the powers of the English court in enforcing any such letter of request is that:

> An order...shall not require any particular steps to be taken unless they are steps which can be required to be taken by way of obtaining evidence for the purpose of civil proceedings in the [English] court...[3]

In other words, the evidence is limited (at least) to that which could have been obtained in an English case (though not necessarily of the same description as the U.S. action).[4] The U.S. lawyer must, therefore, be ready to view his case through English procedural eyes. In practice, he would be ill-advised to attempt this operation himself, and should consult an English practitioner acquainted with these problems. Such advice from a local lawyer should be sought before, not after, the letter of request has been issued by the U.S. court. Failure to do so can be fatal or at least highly prejudicial to the full acceptance and enforcement of the letter of request by the English court. At the lowest, an ill-considered letter of request may provide considerable scope for challenge in the English court. Even if such challenge is ultimately fended off, the contest can cause serious expense and delay. By contrast, most problems can be avoided by proper drafting of the letter of request. Time and again letters rogatory sent to English lawyers for presentation to the English Court are in a wholly unacceptable form. If English procedure and rules are taken into account from the first, it is in general a comparatively simple process to obtain the evidence required.

Under the 1975 Act, an order for evidence can be obtained for the purpose of civil proceedings (i.e., civil and commercial proceedings), which includes proceedings contemplated but not yet instituted.[5-6] The evidence sought must be for the purpose of those proceedings.[7] The type of judicial assistance available covers orders for:

- o Examination of witnesses, orally or in writing;
- o Production of documents;
- o Inspection, photographing, preservation, custody, or detention of any property;
- o Taking of samples of any property and the carrying out of any experiments on or with any property;
- o Medical examination of any person; and
- o Taking and testing of samples of blood from any person.[8]

Due to space constraints we shall confine our remarks to oral and documentary evidence.

We have already drawn attention to the provision (Section 2(3)) of the 1975 Act which restricts what can be ordered to that which could have been ordered in English civil proceedings. The main effect, and indeed purpose, of this provision is to oust U.S.-style pre-trial discovery. Against a person not party to the action, an English court can make no order for oral testimony or the production of documentary material which is not admissible as evidence at trial. English procedural law would not contemplate an order for the examination of or the production of documents by a nonparty for the purpose of seeking information which, though not in itself admissible, is reasonably calculated to lead to the obtaining of admissible evidence.[9]

So far as oral testimony is concerned, this must be restricted to matters on which the deposition could be put in evidence at trial. In other words, the purpose of taking the deposition cannot be to ascertain lines of further enquiry: it must rather be the expectation that the witness will not attend the trial of the U.S. action to give evidence *viva voce*, e.g., because he is ill or otherwise unable or unwilling to travel to the United States, or because the nature of the evidence does not appear to justify the expense or inconvenience of producing the witness at trial in the United States. Similarly, with regard to documentary testimony, the documents requested must be such as to be admissible as evidence at the U.S. trial.

Sometimes, the "fishing" or discovery purpose of the application will be strongly suggested by the form of the request itself, especially where documents are concerned. Sometimes, it will require little, and simple, analysis of the U.S. pleadings to divine that the requested examination of a witness or production of documents has no direct or proximate connection with the issues in the action and that its function is therefore almost certainly that of inquisitive discovery. Where, however, it appears that the U.S. court has given thought to the distinction between trial evidence and pre-trial discovery and made clear that its request is concerned with the former (either by so stating in its request or by judicial statement at the time of ordering or approving the issue of the letter rogatory), an English court will be slow to go behind this. As was said in the *RTZ* case:

> In the face of a statement in letters rogatory that a certain person is a necessary witness for the applicant, I am of the opinion that the court of request should not be astute to examine the issues in the action and the circumstances of the case with excessive particularity for the purpose of determining in advance whether the evidence of that person will be relevant and admissible. That is essentially a matter for the requesting court.[10]

However, when there is a reason to believe that the purpose of the request may be of a discovery nature, the court will investigate and, where appropriate, refuse to enforce the request.

There are a number of simple pointers for the U.S. lawyer:

- Letters of request should be drafted in terms which state explicitly that the evidence is required for trial purposes;

- Letters of request should not include anything which an opponent could reasonably contend is required for pre-trial purposes. Though it may be excised by the English court by use of the "blue pencil," leaving untouched the permissible parts of the request, there is a serious danger that the valid parts may be tainted by the invalid--by casting doubt on the basic contention that the evidence is required for trial purposes. The U.S. lawyer must therefore forget all the discovery requests he has ever drafted before. He must drop from his legal vocabulary such words as "all" or "any," as in such phrases as "all letters between..." or "any telexes between..." and he must resist the temptation to insert general sweep-up requests such as "any other documents relating to...". Words and phrases like these will be seen by the English court as "tell-tale" signs of an intention to "fish" or engage in discovery; and

- Letters of request should include a brief description, on affidavit of the relevant issues in the U.S. action and how the evidence requested relates to these issues. This may prove of considerable assistance in countering any challenge based on the allegation that the evidence is required for "fishing" or discovery purposes. It may also help at the deposition itself in dealing with arguments that particular questions are not relevant or admissible (even though the examiner cannot himself effectively rule thereon).

As regards documents, the rule prohibiting orders for pre-trial discovery is fortified by two further important provisions of the 1975 Act:

- An order cannot be made requiring a person "to state what documents relevant to the proceedings...are or have been in his possession, custody or power."[11] Accordingly, it is necessary to be able to specify in advance the documents required; and

- An order must specify precisely the documents desired. The order may not extend beyond the production of "any documents other than particular documents specified in the order as being documents appearing to the court making the order to be, or likely to be, in his possession, custody or power."[12] For example, requests made in the RTZ case for "any memoranda, correspondence, or other documents referred to therein" did not satisfy this test of specificity, which was interpreted as requiring the order to be in respect of "individual documents separately described."[13]

A witness can invoke privileges available both under English and U.S. law.[14] Apart from legal privilege, one is most likely to be concerned with the privilege against self-incrimination. So far as English law is concerned, this is now enshrined in Section 14 of the Civil Evidence Act, 1968, which provides that no person can be compelled to answer any questions which would tend to expose him to proceedings for an offence or the recovery of a penalty.[15] The test is not a rigorous one: a mere tendency to expose is enough. And it is sufficient that the answer to the question or the production of documents would reinforce existing evidence in the hands of a potential prosecutor or could otherwise move him to a prosecution from which he might have abstained. For example, in the

RTZ case--where the apprehended "penalty" was a fine by the EEC Commission--it was pointed out that the Commission was well aware of the uranium cartel of which RTZ apparently formed part and had abstained from taking any action under Article 85 of the ECC Treaty. This did not affect the result, even though the EEC Commission had itself power to compel the production of the documents sought by the U.S. letters rogatory. As Lord Diplock put it in his speech:

> I do not think your Lordships are entitled to dismiss as fanciful the risk that if the documents relating to the cartel were produced at the trial in the Virginia proceedings and came, as they then would, into the public domain, the resulting publicity in this sensitive political field might result in pressure on the commission to take against the RTZ companies speedier and severer action than they might otherwise have done and that such action might well include the imposition of penalties under Article 15 of the EEC Council Regulation 17/62.[16]

So far as privilege under U.S. law is concerned, the 1975 Act requires this to be ignored in the taking of a deposition (or the production of documents) unless the right to claim privilege is set out in the letter of request or conceded by the applicant to the order. Otherwise, the evidence must be given by the witness, but will not be transmitted to the requesting court if that court, on the matter being referred to it, upholds the claim to privilege.[17]

In addition, a witness will be excused from giving any evidence (or producing any document) pursuant to letters rogatory where that would be prejudicial to the security of the United Kingdom; and a certificate by the Secretary of State to that effect is conclusive.[18] Indeed, under Section 4 of the Protection of Trading Interests Act, 1980, the court may not make an order giving effect to a letter of request

> if it is shown that the request infringes the jurisdiction of the United Kingdom or is otherwise prejudicial to the sovereignty of the United Kingdom and a certificate signed by or on behalf of the Secretary of State to the effect that it infringes that jurisdiction or is so prejudicial shall be conclusive evidence of that fact.

This section is directly aimed at what the United Kingdom has consistently regarded as excessive assertion of jurisdiction by U.S. courts and authorities over non-U.S. matters, notably in anti-trust cases (by reliance on the "effects doctrine") or, more recently, in matters arising under the U.S. Export Administration Act 1979.

We also draw brief attention to the emergence of recent attempts in the United States effectively to circumvent the letters rogatory procedure. This involves the use of subpoenas issued by, or though, a U.S. court requiring the production of documents or the provision of information located outside the United States, for example in

London. Plainly, such a subpoena cannot be enforced in England. However, in the case of a multinational organisation or an international bank, for example, it is often possible to serve the subpoena on that part of the organisation which is present in the United States, notwithstanding that what is sought is compliance with the English arm of the organisation. Problems arise where the provision of the evidence is prohibited by English law. In the case of a bank, it will normally involve a breach of its obligation of confidentiality under English law to divulge the information.[19] It seems clear that an English court will have little sympathy with this indirect attempt to by-pass the procedures and restrictions of the 1975 Act and is prepared to reinforce the obligation of confidentiality by granting an injunction against disclosure of the English-based material sought by the U.S. subpoena.[20] A similar impasse can arise where the Secretary of State makes use of powers under Section 2 of the Protection of Trading Interests Act, 1980, to forbid compliance with the subpoena in respect of any commercial documents not within the territorial jurisdiction of the U.S. court or any commercial information (unrestricted by reference to any geographical location).[21] For this purpose, the Secretary of State must be satisfied that: (1) the subpoena infringes the jurisdiction of the United Kingdom or is otherwise prejudicial to the sovereignty of the United Kingdom; (2) compliance with the subpoena would be prejudical to the security of the United Kingdom or to the relations of the Government of the United Kingdom with the Government of any other country; or (3) the subpoena requires a person to state what documents relevant to such proceedings are or have been in his possession, custody, or power or to produce for the purposes of any such proceedings any documents other than particular documents specified in this subpoena.[22]

Finally, it will be clear that our discussion has been limited to discovery in England for U.S. proceedings by compulsory methods. There is no prohibition against taking depositions on a voluntary basis by whatever means are acceptable to the parties, the deponent (if a nonparty), and the U.S. court. Depositions before the U.S. Consul in London are a common occurrence, and we can envisage no objection to the implementation in any other form of the notice of commission procedures of, for example, Rule 28(b) of the Federal Rules of Procedure.

FOOTNOTES

1. 1978 A.C. 547. Under the earlier legislation see in particular Radio Corporation of America v. Rauland [1956] 1 Q.B. 618.

2. See, for example, the comments of Lord Diplock in British Airways Board v. Laker Airways Limited, [1984] A.C. ______ at ______; and also the various references in the RTZ case, loc. cit.

3. Evidence (Proceedings in Other Jurisdictions) Act, 1975, Section 2(3).

4. 1975 Act, Section 2(3).

5. 1975 Act, Section 9(1).

6. 1975 Act, Section 1(b). Evidence can also be ordered for the purpose of pending criminal proceedings.

7. 1975 Act, Section 1(b).

8. 1975 Act, Section 2(2).

9. See the RTZ case, [1978] A.C. 547. (We have not sought here to explore the complications which may arise from the principle laid down in Norwich Pharmacal Co. v. Commissioners of Customs and Excise, [1974] A.C. 133, which permits an action for discovery for limited purposes against a person who is more than a "mere witness" in that he has been innocently involved in the facilitation of tortious acts of others). The position is somewhat different under English law, when one is concerned with a party. Documentary discovery is then not restricted to material directly relevant to the matters in dispute but extends to any document which might suggest a line of enquiry leading to such evidence (see e.g., per Lord Esher M.R. in Compagnie Financiere du Pacifique v. Peruvian Guano Co. [1882] 11 Q.B.D. 55 at 62f), though this rule may well in practice be administered on a less generous basis than Rule 26 of the Federal Rules of Procedure. Oral deposition of an opposing party is not available, but interrogatories can, with leave of the court, be administered--i.e., written questions to an opposing party to be answered on oath. The purpose of such interrogatories is to obtain evidence for trial or to secure an admission which will limit the scope of the trial or enable the parties to prepare better for trial. They are not intended to fulfill the general exploratory function of U.S. discovery provisions. We have not sought to consider the application of the 1975 Act to a U.S. letter of request for the testimony of a party (or the production of documents by him). Though a theoretical possibility, such a request is unlikely to occur often in practice: the U.S. Court can itself order the examination of, or production of documents by, a party to the U.S. proceedings and impose its own sanctions for noncompliance, e.g., by dismissal of the action or striking out the defence.

10. [1978] A.C. 547 at 654 per Lord Keith; applied by Drake J., in Securities and Exchange Commission v. Purchasers of Stock and Call Options of Sante Fe International Corporation 23.2.1984 cf per Lord Diplock in the RTZ case, [1978] A.C. 547 at 634.

11. 1975 Act, Section 2(4)(a).

12. 1975 Act, Section 2(4)(b).

13. 1978 A.C. 647 at 635 per Lord Diplock.

14. 1975 Act, Section 3(1).

15. The privilege is dispensed with by statute in certain limited cases in return for immunity from criminal prosecution. Most notably, Section 72(3) of the Supreme Court Act, 1981, removes the privilege in cases concerning infringement of intellectual property rights or passing off. For a discussion on the impact of this sub-section on Section 3(1) of the 1975 Act see the judgment of French J. in Overseas Programming Co. Ltd. v. Cinematographische Commerzabstalt, The Times 16.5.84.

16. [1978] A.C. 547 at 637. Section 14 of the Civil Evidence Act, 1968, restricts the privilege against self-incrimination to apprehended charges or penalties under United Kingdom law; but a penalty under EEC law was considered part of English law for this purpose.

17. 1975 Act, Section 3(2). For details of the procedure, see Rules of the Supreme Court Order 70 Rule 6.

18. 1975 Act, Section 3(3). It is to be noted that the absence of such a certificate leaves the question at large for decision by the court, and there is no provision for a certificate that the giving of the evidence would not be prejudicial to the security of the United Kingdom.

19. The bank cannot invoke the defence of compulsion of law based on the subpoena in relation to information or documents located in England; see XAG v. A Bank [1983] 2 All E.R. 464.

20. XAG v. A Bank, loc. cit.

21. The recipient of the subpoena is placed in the unenviable Catch-22 position of having to disobey the orders of either the English or the U.S. Court with the risk of attendant penalties for contempt of one or other court.

22. For an example of the use of these powers reference is made to Laker Airways litigation, where the direction of the Secretary of State provided that:

> Except with the consent of the Secretary of State no person or persons in the United Kingdom shall comply or cause or permit compliance, whether by themselves, their officers, servants or agents, with any requirement to produce or furnish to the United States

> Department of Justice, the Grand Jury or the District Court any document in the United Kingdom or any commercial information which relates to the said Department of Justice investigation or the Grand Jury or District Court proceedings.

(quoted in British Airways Board v. Laker Airways Limited [1984] A.C. ________________ at _____________).

AUTHOR INDEX

TITLE INDEX